SUPPORTING CHILDREN WHEN PARENTS SEPARATE

Embedding a crisis intervention approach within family justice, education and mental health policy

Mervyn Murch

D1610782

P

First published in Great Britain in 2018 by

Policy Press
University of Bristol
1-9 Old Park Hill
Bristol
BS2 8BB
UK
t: +44 (0)117 954 5940
pp-info@bristol.ac.uk
www.policypress.co.uk

North America office:
Policy Press
c/o The University of Chicago Press
1427 East 60th Street
Chicago, IL 60637, USA
t: +1 773 702 7700
f: +1 773-702-9756
sales@press.uchicago.edu
www.press.uchicago.edu

British Library Cataloguing in Publication Data
A catalogue record for this book is available from the British Library

Library of Congress Cataloging-in-Publication Data
A catalog record for this book has been requested

ISBN 978-1-4473-4596-1 paperback
ISBN 978-1-4473-4594-7 hardcover
ISBN 978-1-4473-4597-8 ePub
ISBN 978-1-4473-4598-5 Mobi
ISBN 978-1-4473-4595-4 epdf

Cover design by Hayes Design
Front cover image: Nigel Downing
Printed and bound in Great Britain by CMP, Poole
Policy Press uses environmentally responsible print partners

I dedicate this book to the memory of two dear
friends who encouraged it's inception but who
died tragically before it's completion:
Emeritus Professor Douglas Hooper,
clinical and social psychologist, and
Sir Nicholas Wall, former President of the
Family Division of the High Court of Justice.

Contents

Acknowledgements   vii
Preface   ix

Part I   Illuminating the field of policy   1
Introduction to Part I:
          Some key background data

one   Setting out the stall   3
two   Numbers, scale and trends   11
three   Summarised research reviews upon which to   21
           promote social and emotional wellbeing in
           children of separated parents
four   Hearing the voice of the child: messages from   45
           research that expose gaps between theory,
           principle and reality

Part II   Primary prevention   63
Introduction to Part II:
          Children dealing with the crisis of parental separation:
          towards new supportive practice and policy

five   Children in crisis speak out   69
six   The crisis model of preventive mental health and   89
           its potential application for support services for
           children coping with parental separation
seven   The pros and cons of the preventive mental   113
           health approach
eight   Providing short-term primary preventive crisis   125
           intervention for children in schools

Part III   Secondary prevention   **149**

Introduction to Part III:
            Family justice policy under the Coalition government
            (2010–15): how will a new regime meet the needs of
            children with separating and divorcing parents?

nine   The repeal of Section 41 of the Matrimonial   155
            Causes Act 1973 and related reforms: is the state
            turning a blind eye to the needs of children in
            divorce proceedings?

ten   Demolition and reconstruction in the family   179
            justice regime: what can be salvaged for children
            whose parents separate and divorce?

eleven   Changing the culture of family justice: barriers to   241
            be overcome

Part IV   Embedding the crisis intervention approach   **275**

Introduction to Part IV:
            The future policy and practice challenge

twelve   Barriers obstructing a preventive mental health   281
            approach

thirteen   Policy and practice proposals to support children   299
            and young people coping with interparental
            conflict and separation

fourteen   Scanning the horizon   343

Index   375

Acknowledgements

My first thanks are due to the children and families who participated in the socio-legal research to which I refer in this book, and who for obvious reasons cannot be named. My fellow interdisciplinary researchers and co-authors are cited in the text. I thank them for the exceptional skill and knowledge which they brought to these studies. I owe a special debt of gratitude for the constant support, advice and encouragement I have received from my colleagues at Cardiff University's School of Law and Politics: Clare Pike, Julie Doughty, Gillian Douglas, Joan Hunt, Nigel Lowe and Lucy Series.

Gordon Harold, now at Sussex University, introduced me to policy related family conflict research from the field of cognitive developmental psychology. Oliver Russell, a psychiatrist who studied with Gerald Caplan at Harvard, reminded me of the early days of the social psychiatry movement and Verna Beckford shared her recent experience of community mental health. I have learnt much from my fellow members at the Centre for Social Policy at Dartington, particularly Christopher Clulow, Bill Jordan, Arran Poyser, Ludwig Salgo and the eductionalists James Wetz and Kathleen Weare. Natalie Taylor, a school administrator, kept me informed about the impact of austerity cuts in schools committed to enhancing their pupils' emotional resilience and well-being.

My thanks too to my daughter and literary agent, Lorna Downing, her artist husband Nigel Downing and my grandchildren Camsell and Fenton Downing and their cousin Shola McDonald who all made valuable contributions to my understanding.

I am particularly grateful for the diligent preparatory work of the editorial team at Bristol University's Policy Press: Helen Davis, Jessica Miles, Ruth Wallace and Kathleen Steeden.

For many years while my ideas for this book were germinating my wife, Iris, has shown loving forbearance particularly when I have been preoccupied with the many knotty problems encountered in trying to keep up to date with a fast moving uncoordinated interdisciplinary government policy. By safeguarding my well-being she should take great credit for helping me complete the book. Finally my thanks to Murphy, my Irish feline companion, who always reminded me when it was time to take a tea break!

Preface

This book is about supporting children and young people through critical life-changing events associated with serious conflicts between their parents leading to parental separation and divorce. It is worth remembering that every year about 200,000 children will have experienced their parents' separation and divorce. Almost a third of all British children will have experienced this by the time they reach the school leaving age of 16.[1] So we are considering the needs of a very large number of children indeed.

I was prompted to write this book because I became increasingly dismayed by a number of cost-cutting measures introduced during David Cameron's governments (2010–16) in response to the economic crisis of 2007–08 and its aftermath. These damaged such limited services that previously existed to support children and their families in these circumstances. Of particular concern were major cuts to civil legal aid, which inadvertently reduced the fragile network of family mediation services. Also, cuts to the budgets of already overstretched child and adolescent mental health services have produced serious delays and further restricted eligibility of those children who develop long-term mental disorders and behavioural problems in reaction to the difficulties between their parents. Moreover, recent cuts in educational budgets led to reductions in some school counselling support services.

Even so, Theresa May, the Prime Minister, in a speech to the Charity Commission on 9 January 2017, pledged to help schools and companies in England deal with 'the hidden injustice' of mental illness. In this speech she announced several measures which chime with the subjects covered in this book: namely, that every school will be offered 'mental health first aid training'; attempts to strengthen links between schools and NHS specialist staff, including a review of child and adolescent services across the country to be led by the Care Quality Commission. This produced its phase one report from its ongoing review of children and young people's mental health services in October 2017 when this book was going to press (see further Chapter Thirteen)[2] with greater focus on community care. In her first major speech on health, Mrs May sought to raise the profile of children and young people's mental

---

[1]   See Chapters Two (p12) and Three for discussion of the limitations of available statistics.

[2]   Care Quality Commission (October 2017) *Review of Children and Young People's Mental Health Services* www.cqc.org.uk

health, and reaffirmed the government's drive to give the issue "parity of esteem" with physical health. This speech followed an announcement in which she expressed a wish to create "a shared society", with the state taking a greater role in ending "unfairness". Subsequently, on 8 February 2017, in answer to a parliamentary question, she announced that later that year there would be a Green Paper on child and adolescent mental health services to be issued jointly by the Department for Education and the Department of Health. She further said that she would look into the extent and location of delays in getting children seen by child and adolescent mental health services. After the General Election of June 2017, no longer with an overall parliamentary majority, Mrs May stuck to her pledge to help schools tackle the issue of children's mental health. Thus in the debate on the Queen's Speech, in answer to a question from James Morris MP, she stated:

> 'I want to ensure that every school – every primary and secondary – has a member of staff who is trained to identify mental health problems and knows how to deal with these issues.'

Further, she reported that after a visit to the charity Young Minds she was impressed by the need to raise awareness of mental health problems, observing that:

> 'The earlier we can address these issues the better we can deal with them.'

Moreover, as a separate line of social policy development under Mrs May's premiership, it emerged that the Department for Work and Pensions (DWP) was undertaking investigations into families with multiple problems.[3] These included a study into the extent to which poverty and other stresses contribute to parental conflict and its impact on children. On 4 April 2017 Damian Green MP, the then Work and Pensions Minister, announced that a further £215 million would be committed to the much criticised Troubled Families Programme.[4] This was originally launched in April 2012 with a £448 million grant from the Department for Communities and Local Government in liaison

---

3   See A Asthana (4 April 2017) 'Children's chances hit by parental rows' *The Guardian*.
4   L Day, C Bryson, C White, S Purdon, H Bewley, L Kirchner Sala and J Portes (October 2016) *National Evaluation of the Troubled Families Programme: Final Synthesis Report* Department of Communities and Local Government.

with the DWP and local authorities 'to encourage greater employability, less criminality, better school attendance and improved child welfare so as to "turn around" 120,000 English families with multiple problems'. Included in the extra money committed to Troubled Families in April 2017 was £30 million for a new programme to enable independent providers to help resolve parental conflict.

So it is to be hoped that the combined effect of these anticipated policy developments will eventually improve the lives and wellbeing of thousands of children affected by parental conflict and separation. It all depends on whether Prime Minister May's aspirational rhetoric can be translated into realistic policies and practices with an emphasis on early preventive intervention developed in a coordinated way across departmental and professional boundaries.

This was the purpose of the Green Paper *Transforming Children and Young People's Mental Health Provision* issued for consultation by the Departments of Health and Education in December 2017[5] at the time of writing. It proposed that every primary and secondary school should have a senior designated mental health lead person to improve early preventive work, and new mental health support teams linked to schools and colleges: 'To provide specific early intervention and ongoing help supervised by NHS Children and Young People's mental health staff whose work will be jointly managed by schools and the NHS.'[6]

I welcome these structural proposals and the general direction of thinking underlying them. Even so, the approach to preventive work which I develop in Part II of this book is not mentioned. But, as I shall explain in certain specific respects, it complements the Green Paper's proposals and should be seen therefore as additional to them. Thus I hope this book will help in the endeavour to develop a coordinated network of support services able to forestall the onset of more serious problems with children reacting to destabilising family change. I shall argue that, from a social policy perspective, this will involve tackling fundamental structural and mindset problems. These arise because most services, including government departments, are organised in strong vertical 'silos', while horizontal links between them

---

[5] Department of Health and Department for Education (December 2017) *Transforming Children and Young People's Mental Health Provision: a Green Paper* CM 9523 p18.

[6] Department of Health and Department for Education (December 2017) *Transforming Children and Young People's Mental Health Provision: a Green Paper* CM 9523 p18.

are weak and need strengthening. (This is, of course, a general problem which also applies to the care of the frail and elderly.)

Like many others and the latest Green Paper, I argue for early intervention in order to shift the emphasis of policy and practice away from conventional last-minute fire-fighting when things have gone badly wrong – which is often expensive and sometimes ineffective – towards policies and practices which enable first responder services in everyday contact with children (particularly schools but also primary healthcare teams) to offer them more immediate support. I also argue that the constitutionally independent family court and its support services should be viewed not just in orthodox jurisprudential terms, but from the perspective of preventive mental health.

The interdisciplinary text is divided into four parts. Each contains chapters with a particular focus and which can thus be read as freestanding essays. For readers who first want to get an empathetic appreciation of how children and young people experience intense parental conflict, separation and divorce, I suggest they should start by reading Chapter Five. Even so, the whole book is better viewed as being greater than the sum of its parts in order to set these experiences in a wider policy and practice context informed by behavioural and socio-legal research. I hope that it will encourage students of family law, social policy, education and mental health to look outside their professional silos so as to develop a broader interdisciplinary understanding.

Part I is intended primarily for policy makers and officials who are often too busy to undertake extensive in-depth inquiry into complex policy issues, particularly those which cross a number of specialist subject areas and departmental boundaries. To help them produce evidence-based policy, they will find in Chapters Two, Three and Four demographic information and findings from educational, social and behavioural science research.

Part II (Chapters Five, Six, Seven and Eight) focuses on preventive community mental health issues. Being more practice-orientated, it is aimed especially at those who come into direct contact with children and young people and those who have responsibility for training practitioners. Even so, it is still relevant to policy makers and law reformers seeking to find more effective and economical ways of helping children in these circumstances. To illustrate the way that parental separation and divorce impacts on children and young people Chapter Five draws on qualitative research evidence gathered from children themselves. This shows how they reacted to the growing tensions and eventual breakdown of their parents' relationships.

This chapter prepares the ground for an exposition of a conceptual framework known as the crisis model of mental health, and a method of short-term early intervention to support children and help them adapt successfully to the stressful changes occurring within their family. In this respect, my aim is to revive interest in an approach which was originally developed in the United States in the 1960s but for reasons which I will explain never caught on in family support services in the United Kingdom. Nevertheless, I see it as having real advantages in this field. First, it tunes in with current thinking about the need for early intervention. Second, it is relatively easy to understand since it is based on observations of normal human reactions to temporarily overwhelming stress and the normally helpful community support this invokes from those close by. However, as will be explained, there are a number of reasons why this is often not available to children facing family breakdown, who often feel confused, lonely and marginalised – hence their need for special support from more formal social agencies. Third, the proposed approach is not unduly specialised and can therefore be applied by practitioners across a range of services, using a 'common language'. This in itself should facilitate interagency collaboration. Part II is largely concerned with primary prevention as applied in schools.

In Part III (Chapters Nine, Ten and Eleven) I address a number of contentious child-related policy and law reform issues concerning the interdisciplinary family justice system which occurred during the Conservative-led coalition government (2010–15). These include the repeal of the so-called welfare check in undefended divorce proceedings, major cuts to civil legal aid which have impacted adversely on family courts and mediation services, and the question of whether children who wish to do so should have a voice in the new Mediation Information and Assessment Meetings (MIAMs), attendance at which is now compulsory for parents instituting child-related proceedings. I consider these issues in the light of the Child Arrangements Programme (CAP) introduced in 2014 by the President of the Family Division in response to the findings of the Family Justice Review (the Norgrove Review), which reported in 2011. I focus particularly on the secondary backup preventive role of family courts and their associated welfare support service – the Children and Family Court Advisory and Support Service.

Part IV (Chapters Twelve, Thirteen and Fourteen) looks into the future. It offers a number of policy and practice proposals based on the preventive mental health approach. It thus challenges a number of conventional assumptions, such as, for example, that family justice matters should still be thought about primarily in orthodox jurisprudential terms, or that schools should concentrate solely on academic learning rather than trying to promote the wellbeing of the whole child. I suggest a number of proposals that might flow from giving greater prominence to the preventive mental health approach: for example, that *family* legal aid should be distinct from other forms of civil legal aid and should be paid for in part out of the health and education budgets.

Longer term (Chapter Fourteen), in scanning the horizon, I raise questions about the likely impact of rapid advances in information technology. This is altering children's lives and their capacity to seek information and support on their own initiative. It is also radically changing, and will probably reduce, the way professionals provide services to children and their parents. I also point to the growing movement to open up social institutions and professional organisations so as to avoid the so-called 'silo effect' caused by excessive specialisation. In this respect, I invite policy makers, practitioners and academics who read this book to worry less about what goes on within their own single disciplinary and organisational boundaries and to pay more attention to what goes on beyond them – particularly to look at the world through the eyes of children and their parents who are on the receiving end of existing fragmented policies and practices.

Some readers may wonder why a retired law professor and socio-legal researcher should venture beyond his main interest in family justice processes into contiguous social policy areas of education, social psychology, and child and adolescent mental health. The reasons lie partly in my temperament and partly in my varied professional background. As far as temperament is concerned, like many social researchers I have always considered myself as something of an outsider, closely observing from the boundary the workings of the social institutions with which I have been involved at various stages in my long professional life.[7]

---

[7] Initially this was as a generically trained social worker in the probation service following an Oxford degree in jurisprudence and a two-year spell as a national service army teacher. I also worked for several years as a probation officer in the 1960s, during which time I was introduced to divorce court welfare work and taught law part-time at a University in the South West. Then for 11 years I was a university lecturer in social administration (now termed social policy) and taught social work to postgraduate social work students. During this time I also worked as a part-time social worker at Bristol University's Mental Health Department, then led by Professor Derek Russell Davis. He was a radically different psychiatrist from most of his generation, in that he perceived the origins of most short-term

It is always difficult to summarise one's career without appearing immodest. Often others do a better job. Christopher Clulow, a Senior Fellow at the Tavistock Centre for Couple Relationships in London, a former probation officer and Vice-Chair of the British Society of Couple Psychotherapists and Counsellors, has written:

> Mervyn Murch ... drawing on more than forty years experience of working in the family justice system – a term he was instrumental in coining (Murch and Hooper 1992)[8] – has a unique perspective on the slowly changing ways in which separation and divorce have been managed in this country. Poacher turned game-keeper (he started his professional life as a social worker and is now an emeritus professor of law), he has been at the forefront of interweaving an understanding of the psychodynamics of family life with a keen knowledge of legal process, to signal directions of change that might enhance community well-being. In particular, he has identified the importance of interdisciplinary working if families undergoing stressful change are to be empowered to behave responsibly.[9]

This pretty well sums up my general approach in this book.

---

psychological disturbance, such as the sudden onset of clinical depression and anxiety states, to be reactions to critical stressful life-changing events best treated by short-term psychotherapy. It was in his department that I met Douglas Hooper, a clinical and counselling psychologist involved in practice and research concerning couple and family relationship breakdown. I was to collaborate with him over many years as a socio-legal family researcher – see M Murch, D Hooper (2005) *The Family Justice System* Jordan's Family Law, Bristol.

8   M Murch, D Hooper (1992) *The Family Justice System* Jordan's Family Law, Bristol.

9   C Clulow (2012) 'Commentary' in A Balfour, M Morgan and C Vincent (eds) *How Couple Relationships Shape Our World: Clinical Practice, Research and Policy Perspectives* Karnac Books, London at p129.

Part I
Illuminating the field of policy

Introduction to Part I:
Some key background data

The basic proposal in this book is the need to provide children and young people with support as they cope with critical family change resulting from serious parental conflict and separation. The overall aim is to encourage policy makers, politicians and law reformers to develop coordinated preventive early intervention, policies and practice in the fields of education, family justice and mental health. These should seek to reduce adverse impact on children's educational performance and reduce the risks that some youngsters will develop long-term more deep-rooted behavioural and mental health problems. The purpose, therefore, of this first part is to convey some idea of the numbers of those potentially at risk and to review educational and behavioural science research which highlights the adverse effects of acrimonious interparental conflict and separation on children's educational and psychological development and wellbeing. This helps to prepare the background for certain policy and practice proposals which I set out in my conclusions (Chapter Thirteen) concerning short-term crisis intervention programmes in schools and, as a backup, in the context of the interdisciplinary family justice regime now operating the new Child Arrangements Programme in family courts.

ONE

Setting out the stall

Introduction

As mentioned in the Preface, every year at least 200,000 children and young people experience parental separation, often preceded and accompanied by intense, frequent interparental conflict and domestic violence. It goes without saying that for the children this is usually stressful, even traumatic. Not only does it impact on their wellbeing within the family, it often affects, at least temporarily, their school performance.

While in the long term most children and young people adjust to parental breakup without serious behavioural and mental health complications, even in the short term (ie over a period of months rather than years) most will experience the separation of their parents as a crisis, akin to a grief reaction, which temporarily overwhelms their normal coping mechanism, that is, initial shock and disbelief, a slump in morale and self-esteem, and a preoccupation with what has happened, before some sort of adjustment to the changed family circumstance takes place. Sadly, they are often left to face these family disturbances alone, especially if their parents too are in a state of emotional turmoil.

As a socio-legal researcher I have had a longstanding concern for this large group of children and young people. In comparison to the subject of child abuse and neglect, the general needs of children whose parents split up receive relatively little attention from public services unless they are considered 'at risk', which of course some are.

I was prompted to write this book because I became increasingly dismayed professionally by measures introduced by David Cameron's coalition government (2010–15) which seemed to be damaging the family justice system, particularly the service it offered families and children caught up in the all too common process of parental separation and family reconstruction. With colleagues, I had spent the greater part of my professional academic career attempting to harness empirical socio-legal research, including feedback from children as well as their parents, to the processes of social policy and law reform. The aim had been to assist through prior evidence-based research the evolution of a more coherent, compassionate and efficient system. Likewise, scores of

3

family justice practitioners (mediators, court social workers, solicitors, barristers and judges), who over the years have worked towards that objective, became alarmed by the way the coalition government set about cutting legal aid and reforming the system – notwithstanding welcome endorsement of the value of mediation and the introduction of a long-overdue unified system of local family courts.

Initially, for understandable reasons, cuts to civil legal aid and other services were the result of economic policies designed to cut Britain's deficit following the recession of 2007/08, with a view to eliminating it by 2015. But, because that target had not been achieved, a further round of major deficit reduction measures seemed likely to continue at least until 2019.[10] That indeed proved to be the case following the incoming Conservative administration's first budget in June 2015. Nevertheless, it soon became apparent that, at least as far as family justice was concerned, these were not just driven by economic necessity but tuned in with a political philosophy that in principle sought to reduce the size of public services and to transfer many of their functions to the private sector where competitive market forces rule. This dogma might have blinded some to the likely consequences for families and their children.

As the *Economist* newspaper – hardly a left-wing radical publication – reported in November 2014:

> Where cuts have been made they are being felt. The problems are particularly acute in family law. The government hoped that people would turn to mediation for which money is still available. But the numbers are down 40% compared with last year. Without legal aid many people are not getting advice from lawyers who might in the past have suggested mediation.
>
> Instead more and more Britons are representing themselves (as 'litigants in person'), often poorly. The proportion of family law cases in which neither party was represented grew from 17% to 29% between March 2011 and December 2013. Cases without lawyers take longer, pushing up costs, and the quality of justice suffers.

---

[10] See *Financial Times* (10 November 2014) leader: 'Osborne faces doubling austerity cuts to £48bn a year to hit targets'. In this article it was reported that 'if the next government continues to ring-fence health, schools and overseas aid, the non-protected departments face real cuts of 33% against the 21% they faced between 2009–10 and 2014–15'.

Litigants in person struggle to make their cases properly. One barrister likened watching them to 'the frustration a surgeon would feel watching someone trying to take out their own liver with a spoon'. Women are cross-examined by abusive former partners. People cannot afford expert fees or services, so critical evidence, such as paternity tests, may be missing.[11]

Moreover, in a report from the National Audit Office in November 2014 the number of family court cases involving contact with children in which neither parent was represented had nearly doubled since civil legal aid was cut.[12] There were 17,268 such cases, an increase of 80% on the previous year.

Cuts to legal aid undermine the principles of equality before the law and access to justice upon which the foundations of our legal system are built. Even so, the state has always been ambivalent about viewing the legal system as a public service. Recent cuts seem likely to return us to the days when, as Sir James Matthew, an Irish judge at the turn of 20th century, quipped: "In England, justice is open to all, like the Ritz Hotel."

Capitalising on a populist mood that distrusts the legal profession, cuts to civil legal aid may not be the last of the austerity measures emanating from the Ministry of Justice. According to *The Times* newspaper, it is now giving thought as to how the courts might be privatised.[13] Were that to happen, it might call into question the constitutional independence of the family justice system and the courts' support services upon which they depend.[14]

Access to courts with an independent judiciary is a vital safeguard to the welfare of children in all cases where their future care and education are at stake. Thus, s1(1) of the Children Act 1989 lays down the cardinal principle that:

---

[11] See the *Economist* (1 November 2014) 'Justice in a cold climate: austerity and the law' p29.

[12] National Audit Office (20 November 2014) *Report by the Comptroller and Auditor General Ministry of Justice and Legal Aid Agency: Implementing Reforms to Civil Legal Aid* HC 784 Session 2014–15.

[13] See article by Frances Gibb and Richard Ford in *The Times* (23 May 2013) 'Courts to be privatised in radical justice shake-up'.

[14] J Doughty and M Murch (2012) 'Judicial independence and restructuring of family courts and their support services' 3 *Child and Family Law Quarterly* pp333–354.

When a court determines any question with respect to:
  (a) the upbringing of a child or
  (b) the administration of a child's property or the
      application of any income arising from it,
the child's welfare shall be the court's paramount consideration.

This principle – which can be traced back to the Middle Ages, to the sovereign's protective role as parens patriae and to wardship – applies not only to public law proceedings brought by the state where there are allegations of child neglect and abuse, but also to so-called 'private' child-related cases involving disputes between parents. In this book I argue that this distinction has unfortunately, in both practice and policy, led to resources being concentrated on the former, to the detriment of measures to protect and support children and young people in cases of parental dispute. This is particularly regrettable when children wish to have their voices acknowledged and taken into account when decisions about their future are being made – a requirement under the act's welfare checklist, which in the past was more honoured in the breach (see Chapters Nine, Ten and Eleven).

Until recently the media debate about children and the family justice system has focused on shocking recurrent public law cases of serious neglect and abuse in which the State's protective services have failed. This was highlighted in 2014 by widespread evidence that children and young people, many in care, were being groomed for sexual exploitation. The social histories of many of these youngsters reveal unstable family backgrounds blighted by poverty, parental conflict and separation. Yet only in November 2014 did *The Times* newspaper carry a headline, obviously intended to surprise the public, proclaiming 'Revealed: shocking cost of divorce for children: young lives devastated by family breakdown, national survey finds'. This front page item reported a survey of 500 children and young people, aged 14–22, commissioned by Resolution, the Association of Family Lawyers in England and Wales. *The Times* reported that this children's survey showed:

> Divorce has a devastating impact on the children of divided couples, leading to poor examination results, driving them to abuse alcohol or drugs. Two thirds said the breakup affected their GCSEs. One in eight said they had turned to drugs to ease the stress. Divorce also appears to trigger eating disorders, with almost one in three saying they ate

more or less after the family breakup ... The survey also showed the pressure that parents put on children during the divorce process. Nearly one in three said one parent had tried to turn them against the other and a quarter said their parents tried to involve them in their dispute. Almost a fifth said they never saw grandparents again. The survey also found almost a quarter struggled to complete homework, essays or assignments. 12% confessed to skipping lessons and 11% found themselves getting into more trouble in school, college or university.[15]

What the Resolution survey showed was that family breakup (so often loosely referred to as 'divorce', but of course, increasingly affecting separated, unmarried parental partnerships) and its impact on children has to be thought about in interdisciplinary terms since it concerns children's health and education, often long before issues reach the lawyers and the courts.

The Times 'revelation' came as absolutely no surprise to family justice practitioners and academics. For years, as I will show, there has been growing evidence from around the developed world concerning the problems that children and young people face in these circumstances. What has been alarming and difficult to explain is the way it has been largely ignored by UK politicians, and until recently, the media. This may be because it is now so commonplace as to be regarded as a sad but acceptable part of everyday family life. Yet if we are to put the wellbeing of children first, this is an assumption that needs to be challenged; as is the related assumption that when public services grapple with cuts that are forced on them by the government's austerity measures, there is little that can be done other than turn a blind eye to the needs of children unless they are found to be at serious risk of abuse or neglect.

Moreover, as far as the family justice system is concerned, if the parents' relationship breaks down and parents are effectively denied access to supportive legal advice and representation in the family courts, will their disputes about the children and their family's future become more inflamed? Will more parents be left with a sense of injustice, further corroding their capacity to work together as parents for the benefit and wellbeing of their children? Will the consequent tasks of mediators and family court judges become that much more difficult, as current evidence suggests is the case? Or can the government take remedial steps to repair some of the serious damage to the system

---

[15]   F Gibbs (24 November 2014) 'Shocking cost of divorce to children', *The Times*.

that has already occurred? This seems to have been the government's intention when in 2014 it established a Mediation Task Force chaired by David Norgrove, former Chair of the Family Justice Review, under the guidance of Simon Hughes MP, then Minister of Justice (see Chapter Ten below).

While the services of the interdisciplinary family justice system, including mediation, may appear to be the main focus of contemporary law reform and policy (and indeed are the focus of Part III) and take up a large part of this book, should we not be thinking more broadly in preventive terms? Insofar as attention falls on the role of educational and child and adolescent mental health services, like the family justice system, each tends to be addressed as a completely separate area of policy. Where there is little joined-up thinking, organisational boundaries become barriers to effective collaboration between services, while parents and children are faced with an obstacle course when they seek help. Therefore, should we not develop measures that will pick up and respond earlier to children's and young people's worries about their troubled home lives when they first present them to alert-minded school teachers, early years childcare professionals, general medical practitioners and others in the health service? I suggest some answers to these questions in Part IV (Chapters Twelve, Thirteen and Fourteen).

So the basic questions which this book seeks to address are these: Against the harsher economic and political climate, how will the interests of children be protected when their parent's relationship runs into difficulties leading to separation and divorce? Above all, will more and more children feel sidelined? Will they find that their needs for support and information are ignored when having to cope with stressful problems at home? These are important questions, particularly as there is mounting evidence of the potentially adverse consequences for their education, social wellbeing and mental health – to say nothing of the likelihood that some will be at risk of serious abuse and/or exploitation.

As I have worked on this book I have become increasingly aware that however hard one might try to mobilise support for a new approach to provide more effective early intervention and support for children grappling with the problems arising from the breakdown of their parents' relationship, there are still fundamental questions of political and economic philosophy to be confronted. Given the current trend towards the privatisation of public services, one must ask how the needs of children in these circumstances will be met, since most will come from families facing difficult economic circumstances, and the children and young people themselves have little purchasing power? Who would be the providers of preventive support services targeted specifically at them and how would those services be paid for? Can the state be persuaded to guarantee a network of services, as proposed in this book, that are free at the point of use? Will it seek to engage private providers from the voluntary sector or on a commercial basis where the profit motive applies? Clearly this is a vital and complex area of social policy. Is it one where we have reached the moral limits of markets? Again, I address these questions in Part IV.

These and many other questions need to be considered by readers of this book. If it prompts creative positive thinking it will have served its purpose.

TWO

Numbers, scale and trends

Introduction

In this chapter I summarise some key social and demographic statistics from England and Wales which illustrate the scale of the challenge which faces any governments should they wish to develop strategic preventative social and legal policies to better support children and young people caught up in the critical family transitions following the breakdown of their parents' relationship (see further below in Part II).[16]

Aggregated statistics by themselves do not of course convey any idea of the real impact of individual experience. So I have attempted to compensate for this in Chapter Five, which illustrates children's own individual experiences of living through their parents' separation and divorce. Even so, policy makers and law reformers do need to have an idea of the scale of the issues that they are dealing with and the direction of social trends. In this particular chapter I wish to make several preliminary observations which may not be immediately apparent from the bold figures.

First, in the past, considerable attention has been paid to divorce statistics, particularly by social commentators who believe that marriage breakdown and divorce are indicators of moral decline. However that may be, the evidence suggests, as we shall see, that divorce is related to marriage rates. These have declined over the years because marriage nowadays normally occurs after couples have cohabited for some time. Unsurprisingly, it is early marriage and early cohabitation which tend to carry the greater risk of separation.

Second, as far as the welfare of children is concerned, which has come to be the paramount concern of the state, it has become increasingly clear that it is the social institution of parenthood rather than marriage that is of greater social importance. Yet this is not always reflected in the way social statistics are collected and compiled, nor in the way

---

[16] I here distinguish between the English Whitehall Government and the Welsh Government because the Welsh government has separate responsibility for health and education in Wales, as well as a separate organisation for the Children and Family Court Advisory and Support Service (Cafcass Cymru).

politicians, religious leaders and establishment figures in general usually refer to these matters.

Third, attempts to quantify the numbers of children affected by serious conflicts, separation and divorce are hampered by the way they are compiled. Thus it is very difficult to get an overall picture. This is largely because such official statistics as are collected are gathered by individual government departments and particular services reflecting their particular policy areas of responsibility. Moreover, it should be borne in mind that there is always a 'dark figure' about data which could be collected but which is not, possibly because it would open up for hard-pressed officials inconvenient policy reviews. Thus it should be noted that while the Office for National Statistics (ONS) has modernised the content and format of its outputs concerning marriage, divorce and adoption,[17] for our purposes in seeking to obtain a reliable picture of the overall number of children whose parents have separated, it is more difficult to obtain data concerning the number of children where cohabiting non-married parents separate than it is in the case of divorcing parents. Nor do ONS statistics take into account married couples who separate but do not divorce.[18] There are also differences in data published by ONS and the Ministry of Justice.[19] In July 2017 the Children's Commissioner for England, Anne Longfield, issued a paper designed to draw attention to the need for better statistics on the number of vulnerable children in England and Wales. By 'vulnerability' the paper means the additional needs or barriers children face that prevent them living 'healthy, happy, safe lives' or which mean they are 'less likely to have successful transitions to adulthood'. The paper points out that there are many areas where much-needed statistical information is poor or non-existent. These include children who are exposed to domestic violence, those where there is serious interparental conflict, and those whose parents use substances problematically and who are not in contact with treatment services. The commissioner refers to these gaps in statistical data as 'invisible' children.[20]

Fourth, as with so much in this field of critical family change, there is a tendency for the published figures to concentrate on the adult parents rather than the children. Furthermore, such data are largely

---

[17] For a whole range of revised tables for various topics, see www.statistics.gov.uk – particularly Series FM2.

[18] ONS (8 December 2011) *Statistical Bulletin: Divorces in England and Wales* 2010 www.ons.gov.uk – background note 4.

[19] Ibid – background note 2.

[20] Children's Commissioner for England (July 2017) *On Measuring the Number of Vulnerable Children in England* www.childrencommissioner.gov.uk at pp17–18.

of the simple snapshot variety, meaning that it is difficult to get a clear view of the moving picture of changing lives over time, as families transition through the process of breakdown to reconstruction. But that, of course, is the kind of information most needed when considering the provision of child and parental relationship support services, and the development and evaluation of early intervention policies.

Fluctuating divorce rates and the increase in cohabitation[21]

The changing marriage and divorce statistics

In most Western developed countries, children and adults are living through a period of rapid social, economic and demographic change in which different kinds of family structures exist. The growing diversity of arrangements in family life associated with many changes in modern life – such as the growing participation of women in the labour market, new technologies, new patterns of employment and unemployment, geographical and social mobility, widening disparities in family income between the rich and the poor, and a diverse (sometimes) conflicting range of social values – all bring stresses as well as rewards. In the UK over the last 40 years, there has been a significant decline in the proportion of two-parent families living in first marriages. In common with most Northern European and North American countries, the period between 1960 and 1990 saw a substantial rise in divorce rates in England and Wales, expressed as a proportion of the number of married couples in the population as a whole.

According to the ONS *Statistical Bulletin*, the first notable increase in divorce in the late 1940s, following the Second World War, was 'attributable to women's increase in the labour force, which meant couples were no longer as financially dependent on each other'.[22] The next big jump in the figures from 58,239 in 1970 to 74,439 in 1971 and 119,025 in 1972 was associated with the Divorce Reform Act 1969, which came into effect on 1 January 1971. Thereafter, while the annual number of marriages fell steadily from over 400,000 in the early 1970s to less than 250,000 by 2010,[23] the number of divorces fluctuated during

---

[21] For a broader overview of this subject, see G Douglas and N Lowe (eds) (2009) *The Continuing Evolution of Family Law* Jordan's Family Law, Bristol at pp3–8.

[22] ONS (8 December 2011) *Statistical Bulletin: Divorces in England and Wales 2010* www.ons.gov.uk

[23] Ibid – see Chart and Commentary at p12.

the 1980s and 1990s from 148,301 in 1980 to its peak at 165,018 in 1993, and remained relatively stable up until 2010.[24] Thereafter, it dropped to 118,014 in 2012; by a further 2.9% to 114,720[25] in 2013; and compared to 2014 it fell an additional 9% to 101,505 in 2015 – altogether a decline of 34% since a peak of 153,065 in 2003.[26] But it has to be remembered that the fall in the number of couples getting divorced reflects a major decrease earlier in the numbers getting married, and to the increased proportion of cohabiting relationships, many preceding marriage (considered further below). Even so, for those married in 1972, 22% of marriages had ended in divorce by their 15th wedding anniversary, whereas for those married in 1997, almost a third had ended by this time.[27]

A further point to note is that the probability of divorce rises rapidly over the first five years of marriage, reaching a peak between the fourth and eighth wedding anniversaries, when the probability of divorce by the next anniversary is over 3%. Thereafter it decreases steadily.[28] These data have a bearing on the political discussion about the relative stability of marriage compared to those cohabiting (see further below). We know that cohabitations, which often precede marriage, are less stable than marriages overall. But from these data we can also see that the early years of marriage are relatively unstable too. Taken overall, both these kinds of couples are the ones that are most likely to have young children. So while politicians such as former Prime Minister Cameron 'stand up' for marriage and wish to see it recognised in the tax system, it might be more appropriate to concentrate tax advantages on the institution of parenthood rather than marriage. Indeed, Cameron, to give him his due, in the same speech recognised that "more parents split up in the first years after a child's birth than at any other time".[29]

[24] ONS (6 February 2014) *Statistical Bulletin: Divorces in England and Wales* at p12.
[25] Ibid at p8.
[26] ONS (2015) 'Divorces in England and Wales: 2015', Office for National Statistics, www.ons.gov.uk/peoplepopulationandcommunity/birthsdeathsandmarriages/divorce/bulletins/divorcesinenglandandwales/2015
[27] Ibid at p12.
[28] ONS (6 February 2014) *Statistical Bulletin: Divorces in England and Wales* at p11.
[29] 'David Cameron on Families' (18 August 2014) Prime Minister's speech to the Relationships Alliance Summit www.gov.uk/government/speeches/david-cameron-on-families

Numbers of children with divorcing parents

The rise and fall in the numbers of divorces is of course reflected in fluctuations in the corresponding number of children involved. Back in 1971 when the Divorce Reform Act 1969 came into force, out of the 74,432 couples divorcing, 42,039 had dependent children under the age of 16, totalling 82,304, with a further 34,422 aged 16 or over in full-time education. In 1993, when the number of divorces peaked at 165,018, the corresponding figures for children under 16 was 175,961, with a further 70,204 aged 16 years or more. In 2013, the latest figures available, the total number of divorces was 114,720, for which children under 16 totalled 94,864. The ONS reports that 'over a fifth (21%) in 2013 were under five and that 65% were under 11. In 2012 there was an average of 1.75 children aged under 16 per divorcing couple. This compares to 1.84 in 2002. These proportions may reflect the increasing proportion of children born to cohabiting rather than married couples'[30] (see further below). Nevertheless, as I will explain later, these large numbers, underestimated by the reference solely to divorcing parents, may well have deterred successive governments, because of high costs, from designing and developing policies to identify and support those children most likely to be adversely affected by their parents' separation and divorce.

Increased cohabitation

Coinciding with the fall in the numbers getting married and divorced has been a major increase in cohabitation (ie non-married heterosexual partnerships). Beaujouan and Bhrolcháin, using data from the General Household Survey 1979–2007, present the most reliable overview of British trends in cohabitation and marriage and the relationship between them.[31] They deal with such matters as the frequency of premarital cohabitations, the average time spent in different types of partnership and the breakdown rate in both. Although their review does

---

[30] ONS (6 February 2014) *Statistical Bulletin: Divorces in England and Wales* at p8. Also note that 'the number of divorces as indicated by ONS and MoJ statistics, while similar, do not match exactly, since after 2007 divorce figures published by the MoJ have included dissolutions of civil partnerships, which are not included in the ONS figures. There are also other minor differences in the way the two government departments collect and collate data.

[31] E Beaujouan and M Bhrolcháin (2011) *Cohabitation and Marriage in Britain since the 1970s* Population Trends nr 145 ONS.

not consider the issue of children, a number of key points concerning the stability or otherwise of marriage and cohabitations emerge. First:

> although marriage rates have been in decline for decades, this is from one perspective statistically understandable since marriage rates in the 1960s and early 1970s were at an all time high.

Second, couples are now getting married later than at any time in the last century. Third, 'there has been a countervailing trend in the rise of cohabitation'. Living with a partner before a first marriage has become a majority practice since the early 1990s. Around eight in 10 of those marrying for the first time in 2004–07 lived together beforehand, up from three in 10 in 1980–84. Fourth, 'there has been no flight from partnerships per se ... around 89–91 percent of men and 94–96 percent of women reaching 40 in the last 20 years have been in at least one partnership, whether cohabitation or marriage.'

In 1993 Kiernan and Estaugh showed that cohabiting couples constituted three quite different groups: young childless couples who had never married; couples who had been previously married; and never married couples with children, the majority of whom lived in economically disadvantaged circumstances.[32] More recent statistics from the ONS showed that 'the proportion of non-married women aged 18–45 who were cohabiting increased from one in ten (11% in 1979) to one third (34% in 2011)'.[33] With respect to the relative stability of cohabitations and marriage, Beaujouan and Bhrolcháin indicate that while cohabitations have a shorter duration than marriages and have become more unstable over time, this instability of cohabitations is not reflected to the same extent in modern marriages. This may be because of the trend to later marriage following a period of cohabitation. As the authors state: 'relationships may be subject to greater testing before marriage than in the recent past, with cohabitations screening out weaker partnerships.'[34] In that sense, the growth of 'cohabitation' may be a cause of the recent stabilisation of marriage and the incipient decline in rates of marital disruption.

---

[32] K E Kiernan and V Estaugh (1993) *Cohabitation and Extra-marital Childbearing and Social Policy* Family Policy Studies Centre, London. See also, S McRae (1993) *Cohabiting Mothers: Changing Marriage and Motherhood* Policy Studies Institute, London.

[33] ONS (7 March 2013) *General Lifestyle Survey Overview* at p4.

[34] E Beaujouan and M Bhrolcháin (2011) *Cohabitation and Marriage in Britain since the 1970s* Population Trends nr 145 ONS.

Diversity and critical transition in the family life course

Survey data also shows that children live in an increasing variety of family structures during their lives. As *Social Trends* for 2007 observed: 'typically if their parents separate they will start to live in a lone parent family or as a step family ... formed when an adult with a child lives in partnership with someone who is not the parent of that child (or children).'[35] According to the ONS in 2011, 51% of lone parents had dependent children, an increase from 42% in 2001. It is stated that 'one contributory factor to this is the increase in cohabiting couples whose relationships are known to be less stable than married couples'.[36]

Comment

The relative decline in marriage and related divorce statistics, accompanied by the rise in cohabiting parental partnerships which appear less stable, clearly has considerable significance when estimating the number of children affected by the breakup of their parents' relationship. It is one factor which it can be argued added weight to the case for the repeal of s41 of the Matrimonial Causes Act 1973, the so-called welfare check, linked as it was to only undefended divorce petitions. After all, why should children of divorcing parents be singled out for welfare checks when those with cohabiting parents who separate are not? (See further below in Chapter Nine.)

As I will argue in the conclusions of this book (Chapters Thirteen and Fourteen), concerning children of separating, divorcing and cohabiting parents, these trends, taken together with what we know about the increased risk to education and wellbeing (see Chapter Four), strengthen the case for a more strategic preventative set of social, educational and family justice policies. These policies should be aimed at identifying *all* those children most at risk, and offering them support so as to boost their resilience as their families pass through critical and potentially stressful transitions.

---

[35] ONS (2008) *Social Trends 38* Chapter 2 'Household and Families' at p17.
[36] ONS (19 January 2012) *Lone parents with dependent children* www.ons.gov.uk

Statistical problems concerning the number of children involved in private law litigation involving contact and residence orders

Even before the provisions of the Children and Families Act 2014 become operative, when the government intended to substantially reduce the number of cases coming to court (see further in Chapters Nine and Ten), it is not as easy as it might seem to identify the number of Child Arrangement Orders (as they are now collectively termed) made by the family court. This is because of the way in which applications are counted, some of which apply twice to the same child (ie for both contact and residence). Moreover, where a case involves more than one child, each child is counted separately. According to the interim report of the Norgrove Family Justice Review in 2011, s8 Residence Order applications increased by 11% on the previous year to about 45,000 children, while Contact Order applications increased by 23% to about 53,000. Moreover, the number of children involved in all private law applications had increased every year since 2006.[37]

Nevertheless, the Ministry of Justice figures for 2010 indicated a slight fall, showing that there were 40,420 children involved in applications for residence and 46,350 involved in contact applications.[38] Unsurprisingly, it was reported that 'contact cases tended to be protracted when there was a high degree of hostility between the parents'.[39] Moreover, qualitative research studies indicate that both kinds of child-related dispute 'are often fuelled by other issues to do with financial and housing matters and the quality of poor relationships'.[40]

Since 2005, the Children and Family Court Advisory and Support Service (Cafcass) in England has been encouraged by government to reduce the time devoted to preparing welfare reports in disputed contact and residence cases under s7 of the Children Act 1989.[41]

---

[37] Family Justice Review (March 2011) *Interim Report* Ministry of Justice, Department for Education and Welsh Assembly Government at para 5.8.

[38] E Giovannini (2011) *Research Summary 6/11: Outcomes of Family Justice Children's Proceedings – a review of the evidence* Ministry of Justice at p8.

[39] Ibid at p9.

[40] Ibid at p9. See also C Smart, V May, A Wade and C Furniss (2003) *Residence and Contact Disputes in Court* Vol 1 DCA Research Series No 6/2003 (now MoJ). See also C Smart et al (2005) *Residence and Contact Disputes in Court* Vol 2 DCA Research Series No 4/2005 (now MoJ); and L Trinder, J Connolly, J Kellet, C Notley and C Swift (2006) *Making Contact Happen or Making Contact Work? The Process and Outcomes of In-court Conciliation* DCA Research Series No 3/2006.

[41] Cafcass (12 July 2012) *Annual Report and Accounts 2011–12* HC310 The Stationery Office, London.

Instead, it has sought to concentrate more on developing conciliation and other diversionary services such as Separated Parents Information Programmes (SPIPs). Even so, in the year 2011–12 it received 41,778 requests for court welfare reports, a drop of four% from the 43,712 cases the previous year. However, between April 2013 and March 2014, it received a total of 46,626 new private law cases, a 2% increase from the 45,605 cases the previous year.[42] But this was followed by a large decrease of 26.3% to 34,357 in the year 2014–15. Even so, the number of cases has remained high meaning that it makes up a substantial proportion of the service's work. This is especially so when it is remembered that, under the President of the Family Division's Private Law Programme, Cafcass has to undertake a risk assessment in all private law cases. These involve checks with the police and local authority as well as interviews with each parent before filing a Schedule 2 letter with the court before the hearing date.[43]

Although in July 2013 it was too early to assess the full impact of the withdrawal in April 2013 of legal aid in private family law proceedings, monthly returns for Cafcass England showed a record-breaking increase in private law cases in April and May to 9,392 – a jump of 25% from 7,388 for the corresponding previous year, possibly due to attempts to beat the impact of cuts in legal aid.[44] Overall, the number of children involved in private law orders increased steadily between 2007 and 2011, although this trend slowed in 2012, when approximately 192,000 orders were made – 36% in contact applications, 31% in residence applications, 16% in applications for prohibited step orders and 17% in specific issues orders.[45] Nevertheless, as was expected from a peak in the summer of 2013, the number of private law cases involving both the courts and Cafcass fell substantially throughout 2014, so that the number of such cases started in the family courts from January to March 2015 was reported as being 10,569, down 12% from the equivalent quarter of 2014.[46]

---

[42] Cafcass (12 November 2014) Cafcass Press Release www.cafcass.gov.uk – slightly amended by figures in Cafcass *Annual Report and Accounts 2014–15*.

[43] Ibid.

[44] See www.cafcass.gov.uk/news/2013/record-breaking-month

[45] MoJ (May 2013) *Quarterly Court Statistics Oct–Dec 2012* https://www.gov.uk/government/collections/court-statistics-quarterly at p18.

[46] MoJ (June 2015) *Family Court Statistics Quarterly January to March 2015* at p10. This document also has a chart showing the number of private law cases received as recorded by Cafcass and the MoJ from January – March 2011 to January – March 2015. Both sets of data reveal the drop in numbers from a peak of around 30,000 per quarter in 2013 to about 10,000 in 2014 (see Figure 1 in the document).

However, it should also be noted that despite the apparent overall fall in the number of private law child-related cases referred to Cafcass, there was an increase of 6.6% in cases involving r16.4 application for the appointment of a guardian, enabling a child to be separately represented where a family court judge deemed the case to be 'exceptional and of special difficulty' (see further below in Chapters Nine and Ten). These increased from 1,571 in 2013–14 to 1,674 in 2014–15, an increase of 6.6%.[47]

---

[47] Cafcass (2015) *Annual Report and Accounts* 2014–15 www.cafcass.gov.uk

THREE

Summarised research reviews upon which to promote social and emotional wellbeing in children of separated parents

Introduction

The Joint Department of Health and Department for Education Green Paper, published in December 2017, cites various recent studies which give a general indication of the prevalence of mental health issues experienced by one in ten children and young people. It suggests that: 'This equates to around 850,000 children with a diagnosable mental health disorder in the UK today.'[48]

Disorders referred to include high anxiety, depression, conduct disorders, eating disorders and autism spectrum disorder. The Green Paper refers to recent research which suggests that self harm may be increasing particularly amongst girls aged 13–16.[49] Worrying though these data are with respect to this book, two points need to be noted. First, there is a problematic issue about the definition of particular disorders (see below). Secondly, the general picture does not focus specifically on the relationship between parental conflict, separation and divorce and the potential impact on children's social and emotional wellbeing. So in this chapter I summarise the principal research findings of social and behavioural science which highlight factors concerning risk and resilience in children when parental conflict results in the breakup of their families. It is not meant to be a fully comprehensive review. For that I refer readers to authorities cited below. My purpose here is simply to indicate the growing background knowledge base for the practice and policy proposals for preventive support services for

---

[48] Department of Health and Department for Education (December 2017) *Transforming Children and Young People's Mental Health Provision: a Green Paper* CM 9523 Ch1 pp6–10.
[49] Based on 2016 ONS *Population Estimates* for ages 5–16. ONS *Overview of the Population* February 2016.

children which I advance in Part II – Chapters Six and Seven – and the book's conclusions.

An initial point to note: with the exception of a Rowntree programme referred to in the next chapter, much of this research is linked to separate policy areas such as education, the family justice system and child and adolescent mental health services. Consequently, as far as children are concerned, it is not easy to view the relevant knowledge base as a whole, particularly when each area of policy often develops within its own idiosyncratic 'silo' and does not always use the same terms. Yet in practice, concepts and definitions often overlap or mean much the same thing.

I consider two main streams of research. The first focuses on the social and emotional wellbeing of children in *schools*. As the Green Paper explains, these institutions have a primary preventive role, as indeed do primary healthcare teams (which I only touch on in this book). The other, drawn largely from the field of developmental psychology, focuses more on *intra-familial* behavioural issues. This is a rapidly growing area of knowledge which is being recognised and applied more particularly to the field of parental conflict resolution and in the context of the interdisciplinary family justice system, the recent policy developments under the coalition government aspects for which I examine in Part III (Chapters Nine, Ten and Eleven).

Further initial points to note are that the first area of research concerning the wellbeing of children in schools does not focus specifically on parental conflict and separation, regarding it as just one of a number of factors seen as posing a threat to children's wellbeing and behaviour in schools; while the second stream, although focusing on parental conflict and its potential impact on children, tends to address primarily the dyadic parental relationship. This is so particularly when it comes to application of remedial intervention.

Consequently, many of these studies do not focus directly on the support needs of the children, which is my main concern. Furthermore, two distinct streams of research have clear policy implications since they tend both to reflect and to point to reform of existing service and agency practices – a matter considered further in the conclusions to this book – rather than indicating and enabling the development of new cross-departmental, joined-up, child-friendly approaches to preventive support services, where the voice of the individual child is centre stage and can be appropriately ascertained and responded to. The exception to this last general point is recent socio-legal research associated with the family justice system, which is opening up the field, as I will explain in Part III.

Useful research reviews

Educational research

Since the early 1990s there has been a growing recognition of the need to promote positive social and emotional wellbeing in schools for the benefit both of the pupils' academic attainment and teachers' morale and effectiveness.

In the next Chapter I refer more fully to a programme of research funded projects by the Joseph Rowntree Foundation, a review of which was published in 2003.[50] The third largest of these projects concerned school-based support for children of separated parents.[51] Then, in 2007, the National Institute for Health and Clinical Excellence (NICE) and the University of Warwick Medical School and Centre for Public Health published an important review of national and international studies examining the effectiveness of various kinds of intervention to promote wellbeing in schools.[52] In 2015, Professor Kathleen Weare, one of the UK's leading educational authorities in this field, published a very useful background paper targeted at school teachers.[53] This covered a wide range of national and international research relevant to the preparation and design of school-based programmes to promote social wellbeing in pupils and teachers, using what she termed 'a whole school approach'. I recommend all three reviews to anyone who might

---

[50] J Hawthorne, J Jessop, J Pryor and M Richards (March 2003) *Supporting Children Through Family Change: A Review of Interventions and Services for Children of Divorcing and Separating Parents* Joseph Rowntree Foundation, York.

[51] A Wilson, J Edwards with S Allen and C Dasgupta (April 2003) *Schools and Family Change: School-based Support for Children Experiencing Divorce and Separation* Joseph Rowntree Foundation – summarised in *Findings: School-based Support Work for Children Whose Parents Have Separated* www.jrf.org.uk

[52] Y Adi, A Killoran, K Janmohamed, and S Stewart-Brown (2007) *Systematic Review of the Effectiveness of Interventions to Promote Mental Wellbeing in Children in Primary Education. Report 1: Universal Approaches: Non-violence Related Outcomes* Warwick University Medical School and Centre for Public Health and NICE www.nice. org.uk/guidance/ph12/evidence/universal-approaches-which-do-not-focus-on-violence-or-bullying-warwick-university-review-1-pdf-369936685. See also Y Adi, A Schrader McMillan, A Killoran, S Stewart-Brown (2007) *Systematic Review of the Effectiveness of Interventions to Promote Mental Wellbeing in Primary Schools Report 3: Universal Approaches with Focus on Prevention of Violence and Bullying* Warwick University Medical School and Centre for Public Health and NICE www.nice. org.uk/guidance/ph12/evidence/universal-approaches-with-focus-on-prevention-of-violence-and-bullying-warwick-university-review-3-pdf-369937981.

[53] K Weare (2015) *What Works in Promoting Social and Emotional Well-being and Responding to Mental Health Problems in Schools?* National Children's Bureau, London.

wish to follow up the extensive number of research papers which they cover. The Warwick Review, in particular, classifies these studies according to a 'quality grading'.[54] This is based on such factors as the representativeness of sample size, whether there was a comparative randomised control sample, the outcome measures used, the length and duration of the study and whether there was any longer-term follow-up to assess effectiveness.

In a factsheet published in 2008 by the Department of Health for head teachers, community paediatric teams, children's services, child and adolescent mental health services and other professionals working with children and young people, it was observed that:

> the UK comes bottom of the rank for children's wellbeing in a recent UNICEF study in comparison with North American and 18 European Countries.[55]

The Department of Health factsheet further reported that:

- One in ten children and young people aged 5–16 had a clinically diagnosed mental disorder (anxiety and depression); six percent had a conduct disorder and two percent had a hyperkinetic disorder.
- Boys (ten percent) were more likely than girls (five percent) in the 5–10 age group to have behaviour problems. In the older age group (11–16) the proportions were higher – 13 percent for boys and ten percent for girls.
- When analysed by family type, the prevalence of mental disorder was greater in lone parent families (16 percent) compared with two parent families (eight percent).[56]

---

[54]   Y Adi, A Killoran, K Janmohamed, and S Stewart-Brown (2007) *Systematic Review of the Effectiveness of Interventions to Promote Mental Wellbeing in Children in Primary Education. Report 1: Universal Approaches: Non-violence Related Outcomes* Warwick University Medical School and Centre for Public Health and NICE. See also Y Adi, A Schrader McMillan, A Killoran, S Stewart-Brown (2007) *Systematic Review of the Effectiveness of Interventions to Promote Mental Wellbeing in Primary Schools Report 3: Universal Approaches with Focus on Prevention of Violence and Bullying* University of Warwick and NICE.

[55]   Department of Health (June 2008) *Children and Young People: Promoting Emotional Health and Wellbeing* at p3. For the UNICEF study see UNICEF (2007) *Child Poverty in Perspective: An Overview of Child Wellbeing in Rich Countries* Innocenti Research Centre – report Cmd 7 at https://www.unicef-irc.org/publications/pdf/rc7_eng.pdf

[56]   Department of Health, Ibid at n129 – see pp6–8 for data presented in chart form.

All these research reviews contributed to a flurry of educational policy papers.[57] These were aimed at raising pupils' academic attainment levels, but also at raising a whole school awareness not only of the 10% of young people aged 5–16 known to have a clinically diagnosed mental disorder, but of the further 'approximately 15%' with problems that are less severe but which put them at increased risk of developing mental health problems in the future.[58]

As far as this book is concerned, four points need to be made with respect to the general research reviews targeted at educationalists. First, the authors are generally careful not to infer causes in the range of factors which are associated with pupil mental health and behavioural problems, even though the associations may appear suggestive of a likely cause or connection. Second, while the association of parental discord and pupils' behavioural and mental health problems emerges regularly, as we shall see, it is just one of a number of factors which the educational research reviewers and policy makers draw attention to. Third, all the reviews emphasise the importance of identifying mental health and behavioural problems early so as to ensure that, as Kathleen Weare puts it:

> Problems can be resolved with the least fuss and disruption
> ... early intervention prevents initially more minor health
> problems becoming of clinical significance and significantly
> reduces the need for more expensive investments or
> sanctions at a later stage.[59]

---

[57]　See Public Health England (November 2014) *The Link Between Pupil Health and Wellbeing and Attainment: A Briefing for Head Teachers, Governors and Staff in Educational Settings*; and Department for Education (March 2016) *Mental Health and Behaviour in Schools: Departmental advice for school staff* www.gov.uk.

[58]　But note that Steve Hilton, a former policy adviser to Prime Minister Cameron, in his challenging book *More Human: Designing a World Where People Come First* warns against policy makers' obsession with raising educational attainment levels, achieved by a culture of testing which neglects 'unquantifiable skills that are actually – and increasingly – more important'. Moreover, he argues that 'many existing schools have no incentive to think about social and emotional learning, character, or twenty-first century skills unless they serve the very instrumental function of improving test scores'.

[59]　K Weare (2015) *What Works in Promoting Social and Emotional Well-being and Responding to Mental Health Problems in Schools?* National Children's Bureau, London at p6.

Fourth, the emphasis is largely on behavioural and mental health problems as they occur in the school setting, so the link between the child's home experience and school is not always drawn out even though, of course, the two interact and may, from the child's viewpoint, be inseparable. School bullying, for example, may adversely impact on a child's home life and add to a child's insecurities unsettled by discord between the parents.

Intra-familial behavioural studies

I turn now to the other stream of research drawn largely from the field of developmental psychology. This specifically highlights the link between parental discord and the risk to children's wellbeing. In this area, three important research reviews are first and foremost the British Academy report *Social Science and Family Policies,* prepared by Sir Michael Rutter, the leading British authority.[60] Chapter Two of that report is particularly valuable, pointing out, among other things, that it is not the single event of parental separation or divorce that is the major risk factor for children, but the existence of serious parental discord before, during and after divorce, coupled with what is termed 'poor parenting'. Therefore, how the process of family breakup and reconstitution is managed is crucial in considering the wellbeing of children. Second, for an international perspective, the review by Jan Pryor and Brian Rogers, although published in 2001, still contains much useful demographic and psychological information.[61] Third, a more recent updated research review, aimed at adult-focused remedial services, published by the organisation One Plus One, is recommended.[62] I summarise key points from these developmental psychology studies later in this chapter. But first I need to deal with a point about the use of terms and definitions.

The use of terms and definitions

At this point it is necessary to make an important caveat. The use of the term 'mental disorder' has become widespread, not only in

---

[60] British Academy Working Group report chaired by Sir Michael Rutter (2010) *Social Science and Family Policies* British Academy and Policy Centre.

[61] J Pryor and B Rodgers (2001) *Children in Changing Families: Life after Parental Separation* Blackwell Publishers, Oxford.

[62] J Reynolds, C Houlston, L Coleman, G Harold (2014) *Parental Conflict: Outcomes and Interventions for Children and Families* Policy Press and One Plus One.

psychiatry but more generally among the social work and medical health professions. Over the years, the number and range of mental disorders and syndromes has expanded considerably, largely due to the acceptance by the psychiatric profession of a growing number of classifications which appear in the American Psychiatric Association's *Diagnostic and Statistical Manual of Mental Disorders* (DSM-5).[63] This covers a range of behaviours which years ago would have been simply viewed as troublesome within a particular social context. But, through the influence of this manual, accepted by the mainstream psychiatric profession, they have now acquired medicalised labels and may be treated by drugs, some of which can become addictive, even though many such disorders have no clear physiological cause. Indeed, there is now a small group of concerned British psychiatrists who have established the Council for Evidence-based Psychiatry. Among other things, the council challenges the origins of many of the classifications used in the DSM. This concern was prompted by the view that people (including children) were being diagnosed and treated medically, quite often unnecessarily, when they were experiencing entirely normal if uncomfortable experiences such as mild anxiety or depression, or expressing challenging behaviour in reaction to stressful life experiences.[64]

As we shall see, some of these behaviours are reactions to stressful events. Moreover, depressive disorders, for example, encompass a large array of psychological experiences, ranging from short-term mildly depressed moods, irritability, disturbance of sleep and general lack of energy, classified by some as 'depressive syndrome', to more severe and persistent states and psychological impairment, classified as depressive disorder.[65] However, Hewison, Clulow and Drake, in their very illuminating book on *Couple Therapy for Depression*, point out that:

> Defining depression by describing its symptoms is fraught with difficulty. To say that a list of symptoms constitutes depression and that depression comprises a list of symptoms is at worst tautological; at best it simply renames clusters of symptoms as syndromes ... whether or not a person is judged

---

[63] American Psychiatric Association (2013) *Diagnostic and Statistical Manual of Mental Disorders: DSM-5* (5th edition) APA, Washington, DC.

[64] J Davies (2013) *Cracked: Why Psychiatry Is Doing More Harm than Good* Icon Books, London.

[65] E Fombonne (1997) 'Depressive disorders: time trends and possible explanatory mechanisms' in M Rutter and D Smith (eds) *Psychosocial Disorders in Young People: Time Trends and their Causes* Wiley, Chichester at p545.

to have depressive symptoms mostly depends on self-report rather than clinical investigations ... yet questionnaires and structured assessment interviews focus only on answers that subjects provide to the questions that are asked. Questions may not be understood or they may not address the kernel of discomfort that someone is experiencing ... Even if answers accurately reflect experience, who is to decide what is normal and what is not? The threshold between normality and abnormality may be arbitrarily changing and subjectively defined.[66]

A further caveat to consider when using terms and definitions of mental disorders and behavioural difficulties is the issue of stigma. It is all too easy to label a child's challenging or unusually problematic behaviour as something inherent rather than just a reaction to a stressful and confusing home life undergoing critical change. As interactionist sociologists such as Erving Goffman and Howard Becker have shown, ascriptive labels conferred upon actors (ie children) in certain social situations can stick.[67] In this respect, schools, medical and social services, and courts are all social mechanisms by which negative labels can be applied or more positively, on occasion, removed. For example, a family court judge dealing with a family dispute, in delivering a carefully thought-out judgment, may praise the way parents and children have coped with difficult circumstances. This can be experienced as a powerful boost to their morale. Likewise, school teachers and school counsellors supporting children dealing with the crisis of parent conflict and separation can, by praise, strengthen a child's confidence and wellbeing. As we shall see in Part II, the prevention of negative labels is one important aspect of crisis intervention and support. Of course, it should not be forgotten that parents, particularly those who are angry or upset, can apply negative labels to children which can seriously damage their self-image, while the converse is also true.

---

[66] D Hewison, C Clulow and H Drake (2014) *Couple Therapy for Depression: A Clinician's Guide to Integrative Practice*, Oxford University Press at p6.

[67] E Goffman (1969) *Stigma: Notes on the Management of Spoiled Identity* Prentice Hall; and (1959) *Presentation of Self in Everyday Life*, Penguin. H S Becker (1966) *Outsiders: Studies in the Sociology of Deviants*, Free Press. Becker writes: 'social groups create division by making the rules whose infraction constitutes deviants and by applying these rules to particular people are labelling them as outsiders ... the deviant is one to whom the label has been successfully applied; deviant behaviour is behaviour that people so label.'

Moreover, the new digital culture of social media and smartphones, which is increasingly a powerful influence on the world of modern childhood, provides scope for negative labelling by children themselves through cyberbullying. This can be very damaging to the self-image of children feeling vulnerable because of the pressure of tensions between their parents and the breakup of their family life. Teenage girls may be particularly vulnerable, a factor which might explain reports of rising instances of depression and self-harm.

According to an NHS survey, conducted every seven years, self-harm in young women in the 16–24 age group increased from 6% in 2007 to 20% in 2014.[68] This is twice the rate reported for young men. Overall, 26% of young women reported common mental disorders (CMO) such as self-harm, acute anxiety and depression, compared to 9% for men. It is suggested that while social media can help people feel less isolated, it carries risks for those feeling emotionally vulnerable because:

> Its instantaneous and anonymous nature means that it is easy for people to make hasty and sometimes ill-advised comments which can negatively affect other people's mental health.

The relevance to young people feeling vulnerable because of family conflict and parental separation is obvious.

In what follows in this chapter, these are vital issues that need to be borne in mind when considering any list of so-called disorders or syndromes. They are particularly relevant to children who may present distressing and problematic reactions to the experience of their parents' conflicts and family breakdown, matters I deal with particularly in Part II, Chapters Five and Six.

So having made these cautionary points, I turn again to the way the main research reviews deal with the current use of terms. As pointed out, different authorities use slightly different definitions and classifications, but in broad terms a fundamental distinction is made between, on the one hand, social, emotional and mental wellbeing,

---

[68] See NHS Digital National Study of Health and Wellbeing (29 September 2016), also known as the Adult Psychiatric Morbidity Survey. See also article in *Guardian* (29 September 2016) by Denis Campbell and Haroon Siddique, www.theguardian. com/lifeandstyle/2016/sep/29/self-harm-ptsd-and-mental-illness-soaring-among-young-women-in-england-survey. This refers to an NHS inquiry into the state of mental health in England which 'blames social media pressures for a dramatic increase in the number of young women self-harming and having post-traumatic stress disorders or a chronic mental illness'.

and on the other, mental problems and disorder. This sometimes boils down to a distinction between positive mental health and mental illness, but as the Warwick Review points out, this needs qualification and unpacking.[69] Kathleen Weare offers a useful basic distinction between social/emotional wellbeing and mental health problems, although clearly the dividing line between the two can be difficult to draw.

Thus she descriptively explains that social and emotional wellbeing:

> refers to a state of positive mental health. It involves a sense of optimism, confidence, happiness, clarity, vitality, self-worth, achievement, having meaning and purpose, engagement, supportive and satisfying relationships with others and understanding oneself and responding effectively to one's own emotions.[70]

The Warwick Review nevertheless observes that this kind of description of wellbeing adopts what could be called 'a hedonistic perspective focusing on the subjective experience of happiness and life satisfaction'.[71] It further points out that the construct of wellbeing is independent of the construct of mental illness and that people with a diagnosis of mental illness may have variable levels of mental wellbeing, while sizable proportions of the general population who do not have mental illness may lack mental wellbeing.[72]

Kathleen Weare uses the term 'mental health problems' to apply, in the educational context, to both pupils and school staff. She refers to 'a wide range of social challenges, difficulties and illnesses that can beset

[69] Y Adi, A Killoran, K Janmohamed, and S Stewart-Brown (2007) *Systematic Review of the Effectiveness of Interventions to Promote Mental Wellbeing in Children in Primary Education. Report 1: Universal Approaches: Non-violence Related Outcomes* Warwick University Medical School and Centre for Public Health and NICE at pp20-26.

[70] K Weare (2015) *What Works in Promoting Social and Emotional Well-being and Responding to Mental Health Problems in Schools?* National Children's Bureau, London at p5.

[71] Y Adi, A Killoran, K Janmohamed, and S Stewart-Brown (2007) *Systematic Review of the Effectiveness of Interventions to Promote Mental Wellbeing in Children in Primary Education. Report 1: Universal Approaches: Non-violence Related Outcomes* Warwick University Medical School and Centre for Public Health and NICE at p20; after E Diener and R J Larson (1993) 'The experience of emotional wellbeing' in M Lewis and J M Haviland (eds) *Handbook of Emotions* Guildford, New York at pp405–415.

[72] Y Adi, A Killoran, K Janmohamed, and S Stewart-Brown (2007) *Systematic Review of the Effectiveness of Interventions to Promote Mental Wellbeing in Children in Primary Education. Report 1: Universal Approaches: Non-violence Related Outcomes* Warwick University Medical School and Centre for Public Health and NICE at pp20–21.

pupils, including stress (and for staff "burnout"), anxiety, depression, attachment difficulties and behavioural problems'.[73]

The Warwick Review elaborates this range of problems with respect to children by commenting that:

> the diagnosis of mental health problems in children is made on the basis of a constellation of symptoms which occur from time to time in most children but which are distinguished by their persistence and severity. Amongst the commonest mental disorders is conduct disorder, a syndrome which covers aggressive, anti-social behaviour and defiance, and attention deficit disorder which covers the constellation of behaviours suggested by the name.[74]

The Warwick Review describes both of these kinds of disorder collectively as 'externalising disorders'. By contrast, 'internalising disorders' include anxiety, phobias (such as school phobia), depression (regarded as rare in primary school-aged children), self-harming behaviours and eating disorders, which become more common in adolescence.

The Warwick Review further reports that studies of mental disorder in childhood (in contrast to NHS surveys in the 16–24 age group as cited above) 'show prevalence to be higher in boys than girls, affecting 10.4% of 5–11 year olds (5.8% in girls of this age group). The commonest mental disorder in this 5–11 age group is conduct disorder (6.5% boys and 2.7% girls) followed by emotional disorder (3.3% in both sexes). Behavioural problems which fall short of the diagnosis of conduct disorder may affect 10% of the population.'[75] Citing research by Meltzer,[76] the Warwick Review observes that most children with mental health problems do *not* find their way to child and adolescent mental health services, and in the majority of instances

---

[73] K Weare (2015) *What Works in Promoting Social and Emotional Well-being and Responding to Mental Health Problems in Schools?* National Children's Bureau, London at p5.

[74] Y Adi, A Killoran, K Janmohamed, and S Stewart-Brown (2007) *Systematic Review of the Effectiveness of Interventions to Promote Mental Wellbeing in Children in Primary Education. Report 1: Universal Approaches: Non-violence Related Outcomes* Warwick University Medical School and Centre for Public Health and NICE at p22.

[75] Ibid at p23.

[76] H Meltzer (2000) (ed) *The Mental Health of Children and Adolescents in Great Britain* Office of National Statistics.

the problem is not recognised by the parents.[77] These two points have serious implications for children who react negatively to their parents discord, pointing to the need for better identification and preventive intervention by first responder services such as schools and primary healthcare.

The Warwick Review makes three further cautionary points that should be kept in mind when considering the use of terms such as mental wellbeing and mental disorder:

- First 'that suitable measures that capture changes in mental wellbeing attributable to interventions are few and far between. Most programme evaluations depend on measures that focus on mental health problems.'[78]
- Second, there is a methodological problem in estimating changes over time, since these 'depend on stable definitions of disease problems and on robust survey data'. The best available in 2007 were merely impressionistic, but suggest that 'the incidence of mental health problems in childhood rose between 1974 and 1999.'[79]
- Third, 'The determinants of mental wellbeing and mental illness are complex and these operate at different levels (individual, family, community). The idea of risk and protective factors is an important focus for exploring the relationship between the determinants of mental health and interventions and outcomes. Policies, programmes and interventions may be viewed in terms of the extent to which they remove/decrease risk factors or foster protective factors.'

This is an important point for anyone wishing to design research to evaluate the proposals for a scheme of joined-up preventive child support measures (allowing for appropriate changes over time). It would be vital for any such research initiative to be properly monitored and evaluated, ideally with a randomised control comparator built into it.

With respect to risk and protective factors (which bolster a child's resilience), the Warwick Review observes that:

[77] Y Adi, A Killoran, K Janmohamed, and S Stewart-Brown (2007) *Systematic Review of the Effectiveness of Interventions to Promote Mental Wellbeing in Children in Primary Education. Report 1: Universal Approaches: Non-violence Related Outcomes* Warwick University Medical School and Centre for Public Health and NICE

[78] Ibid at p24.

[79] S Collishaw, B Maughan, B R Goodman and A Pickles (2004) 'Time trends in adolescent mental health' *Journal of Child Psychology and Psychiatry* 45(8) at pp1350–1367.

evidence suggests that the more risks in a child's life are reduced – for example by improving parents' management and parenting skills, increasing support for children with learning difficulties and effectively treating mental disorders – the less vulnerable that child will be to subsequent health and social problems. Protective factors such as good family relationships, good parenting and academic performance enable the development of resilience in coping skills which help to safeguard young people from mental health problems.[80]

Here, in a nutshell, we have the essential rationale for a programme of preventive mental health measures to be applied in schools – perhaps the best site for primary prevention offering independent support for children. And seemingly for more targeted intervention with families to promote parenting skills and to resolve interparental conflict through mediation and other remedial measures particularly the work of an enlightened and properly resourced family justice system dealing with parental separation and divorce. Here the support needs and voices of children are increasingly recognised.

Risk factors

The 2008 Department of Health factsheet referred to above also presented an analysis of risk factors associated with developing an 'emotional disorder' (which appears to be the same definition as 'mental disorder' outlined above). The factsheet lists a large number of such factors (after adjusting for socioeconomic factors), which include:

> increasing age, physical illness and a number of stressful life events; whilst independent risk factors for developing conduct disorders include: being male, having special educational needs, step-children in the family and poor maternal mental health [ie depressive illness and acute anxiety] and whether the child was frequently shouted at.[81]

---

[80] Y Adi, A Killoran, K Janmohamed, and S Stewart-Brown (2007) *Systematic Review of the Effectiveness of Interventions to Promote Mental Wellbeing in Children in Primary Education. Report 1: Universal Approaches: Non-violence Related Outcomes* Warwick University Medical School and Centre for Public Health and NICE at p25 para 2.5.

[81] The Department of Health (2008) *Children and Young People: Promoting Emotional Health and Wellbeing*, here refer to a 2003 study: H Meltzer, R Gatward, T Corbin,

The Department of Health factsheet also included the following points concerning the risk of children and young people becoming violent or abusive. I quote:

- 'adverse childhood experiences of one or either: emotional, physical or sexual abuse; household substance abuse; mental illness; incarceration; parental domestic violence, separation or divorce; increased the lifetime risk of attempted suicide by 2–5 fold compared to no adverse childhood experiences. The more adverse experiences the greater the risks.'[82]
- 'A history of child abuse (emotional, physical or sexual) increases the risk of lifetime prevalence of depression by 1.8–2.7 times for women and 1.6–2.6 times for men compared with no history of child abuse.'[83]
- 'Children who have been abused or witnessed family violence are more likely to show aggressive anti-social behaviour, have low self-esteem and do less well at school.'[84]

Readers should note that the references above to 'emotional abuse' can include being ignored or being subjected to 'poor parenting', for example, being on the receiving end of inconsistent behaviour. Reynolds et al, in their 2014 research review, point out:

- Children can develop difficulties when conflict between parents is handled destructively.
- Destructive conflict includes behaving in a way which is physically and verbally aggressive; or the 'silent treatment'; getting caught up in highly intense or heated arguments; and withdrawing or walking away from an argument.

R Goodman and T Ford (2003) *Persistence, Onset, Risk Factors and Outcomes of Childhood Mental Disorders* ONS www.statistics.gov.uk

[82] S R Dube, R F Anda, V J Felitti, D P Chapman, D F Williamson and W H Giles (2001) 'Childhood abuse, household disfunction and the risk of attempted suicide throughout the lifespan' *JAMA* 286(24) pp3089–3096.

[83] D P Chapman, C G Whitfield, V J Felitti, S R Dube, V S Edwards, R F Anda (2004) 'Adverse childhood experiences and the risk of depressive disorders in adulthood' *Journal of Affective Disorders* 82 pp217–225.

[84] M Dixon, H Reed, B Rogers and L Stone (2006) *Crime Share: The Unequal Impact of Crime* Institute of Public Policy, London.

- Children are particularly upset when they, or issues relevant to them, are the subject of an argument.[85]

Protective factors

Reynolds and co-authors raise a crucial question: why are some children affected by parental conflict more than others?[86] Their review shows that as well as there being a number of risk factors predisposing children towards problematic behaviours, there can also be a number of protective factors, such as the individual child's positive temperament (defined as low in negative emotionality!), and the coping strategies adopted by the children in the face of their parents' discord. These 'may play a mediating and moderating role in linking interparental conflict to children's adjustment,' by helping children to distance themselves from the parent's conflict.[87]

I consider what can be done to help children bolster their capacity to withstand parental discord in Parts II and IV of this book, where I outline a scheme for early prevention focused specifically on the children rather than their parents.

The impact of interparental conflict on children's academic attainment

As we have seen, there are a growing number of studies and policy papers which highlight a link between parental conflict, separation and divorce, and the risk to children of psychosocial disorder. But the impact on children's educational attainment, so important for their future life chances, was relatively unexplored until the 1990s.[88] Except for an important paper by Rutter,[89] and another by Elliot and

---

85   J Reynolds, C Houlston, L Coleman, G Harold (2014) *Parental Conflict: Outcomes and Interventions for Children and Families* Policy Press and One Plus One at p21.

86   J Reynolds, C Houlston, L Coleman, G Harold (2014) *Parental Conflict: Outcomes and Interventions for Children and Families* Policy Press and One Plus One Chapter 5 at pp51–75, which explores this issue more fully than I can here.

87   K Shelton and G Harold (2008) 'Cognitive appraisals and coping strategies psychological adjustment: bridging links through children's pathways between interparental conflict and adolescent psychological adjustment' *Journal of Early Adolescence* 28(14) pp555–582.

88   J N Melby and R D Conger (1996) 'Parental behaviours and adolescent academic performance' *Journal of Research and Adolescence* 6 pp113–137.

89   M Rutter (1985) 'Family and school influences on behavioural development' *Journal of Child Psychology and Psychiatry* 26 pp349–368.

Richards,[90] until quite recently the impact of parental conflict on children's academic attainment has been a largely neglected subject. Certainly, this is often overlooked by family justice practitioners (ie judges, Cafcass staff and mediators). In the 1990s Kiernan, in a study of family disruptions caused by death or divorce followed by remarriage, found that poor educational attainment was linked to children and young people leaving school and home earlier.[91] Economic pressures caused by drops in family income that commonly accompany parental separation, as well as often aggravating interparental conflict, can serve to cut short a young person's educational career and school attainment. Clearly this too may impact on the young person's self-esteem.

In 2003 the Joseph Rowntree Foundation published a study titled *School based support work for children whose parents have separated.*[92] This local intervention project (based on interviews and group work with children), run by two counsellors with follow-up interviews with parents, school teachers and the counsellors themselves, was aimed at enabling children to better adjust to their parents' separation. It was not, therefore, specifically concerned with improving children's educational performance, although this could be a useful spin-off. The study was conducted in seven state schools in a large city in East Anglia, with the consent of the resident parents. It drew a sample of 69 children aged 5–11, all of whom came from single-parent households. Using psychometric scales completed as a baseline and two follow-up stages, it covered the children's mental health, outlook and general level of happiness and wellbeing, as well as the parents' and teachers' assessment of the children's behaviour and classroom competence. In this last respect, after the interventions from counsellors had concluded, it was found that:

---

[90] J Elliot and M Richards (1991) 'Children and divorce: educational performance and behaviour before and after parental separation' *Journal of Law and the Family* 5 pp258–276. Also, J Elliot and M Richards (1991) 'Parental divorce and the life chances of children' *Family Law* vol 21 at pp481–484.

[91] K E Kiernan (1992) 'The impact of family disruption in childhood on transitions made in young adult life' *Population Studies* 46 pp213–234.

[92] Joseph Rowntree Foundation (2003) *School-based support work for children whose parents have separated* Joseph Rowntree Foundation. See also A Wilson, J Edwards with S Allen and C Dasgupta (April 2003) *Schools and Family Change: School-based Support for Children Experiencing Divorce and Separation* Joseph Rowntree Foundation, see Chapter of Conclusions at p37 – summarised in *Findings: School-based Support for Children Whose Parents Have Separated* www.jrf.org.uk.

Both parents and teachers reported improvements in children's attitudes to school. Children were described as being more sure of their school work; able to concentrate for longer; were more positive about attending and generally more settled.

I refer to the possible implications of this study further in the conclusions of this book (Part IV) when considering the school setting as one of the sites for primary prevention.

A major step forward in this area emerged from a three-wave longitudinal psychological study of 387 school children (aged 11–13), their parents and teachers, conducted at Cardiff University between 1999 and 2001.[93] This indicated that what was particularly important was the link in high-conflict families between children who blame themselves for the parental conflict and their low educational performance; in other words, the interplay between interparental conflict and parent/child conflict, child behaviour problems (such as aggression at school) and academic attainment. This study concluded that:

> Simply addressing family effects on children at the level of parenting only substantially misses out on an important mechanism for which children's academic success may be affected: the attributional processes engendered in children who live in households marked by high levels of interparental conflict and hostility. While treating family relationship, effects on children **are** important, treating children's perceptions of family relationships may be even more important when it comes to academic success and wellbeing.[94]

As we shall see in Part III, this finding conveys an important message for mediators, who still largely focus on the relationship between the parents in the mediation process and when conducting compulsory Mediation, Information and Assessment Meetings (MIAMs) for parents applying for child-related private law orders, mostly without ascertaining the wishes and feelings of the child.

---

[93] G T Harold, J Aitken and K H Shelton (2007) 'Inter-parental conflict and children's academic attainment: a longitudinal analysis' *Journal of Child Psychology and Psychiatry* 48(12) pp1223–1232.

[94] Ibid at p1231.

Findings from child and family developmental psychology

At this point I turn specifically to the second stream of research, which deals with *intra-familial* risk and resilience issues. This is largely drawn from the increasingly important field of developmental psychology, the pioneer of which in the UK is Professor Sir Michael Rutter. Two of his papers are particularly relevant to the question of parental conflict, separation and children's resilience to stress.[95] In them he explores the link between children's personalities and their resistance to adverse life events, and has teased out a number of key interacting variables, such as age, temperament, availability of social support, and the significance of prior experiences and patterns of parent/child interaction.[96] He also identifies a number of factors which appear to increase children's resilience in the face of stress:

> showing that they can be strengthened and their self-esteem and problem solving skills enhanced by being offered appropriate support from others when the stress occurs. Moreover, enabling children to cope successfully with stress situations tends to strengthen their longer term capacity to cope with further difficulties – nothing succeeds like success.[97]

This is a particularly important point because it justifies crisis intervention support (a point which I develop in Chapters Five, Six, Seven and Eight). So, I return to the issue of how and when to support children during the crisis of parental separation in Part II of this book.

In 2001, Grych and Fincham published a collection of papers which comprehensively reviewed family conflict psychology research at that time, not only pointing to the complexity of integrating different theoretical perspectives with empirical investigations, many of which were snapshot rather than longitudinal, but outlining the need for

---

[95] M Rutter (1985) 'Resilience in the face of adversity: protective factors and resistance to psychiatric disorder' *British Journal of Psychology* 147 at p598. M Rutter (1987) 'Psycho-social resilience and protective mechanisms' *American Journal of Orthopsychiatry* Vol 57 at pp316–331.

[96] M Rutter (1980) (ed) *Scientific Foundations of Developmental Psychiatry* Heinemann Books, London. Papers by Rutter therein are 'Attachment and development of social relations'; and 'Emotional Development and Psycho-sexual development'. M Rutter (1971) 'Parent-child separation: psychological effects on the children' *Journal of Child Psychology and Psychiatry* 12 pp233–260.

[97] M Rutter (1985) Ibid at p598.

further research on such questions as the differences between boys and girls, and the need to investigate their separate relationships with the gender of the parents.[98] Moreover, they pointed to the need to be more specific about the type, frequency and severity of interparental conflict, and the need for studies to set such conflicts in not only familial but non-familial contexts, including potential stressors such as inadequate housing, financial difficulties, and the presence of alcohol and substance abuse.

These points were followed up, particularly in the UK, by a series of further studies led by Gordon Harold, now Professor of Psychology at the University of Sussex. His studies take up a number of points made by Grych and Fincham. Responding to Rutter's call for more rigorous testing of hypotheses about causal mechanisms, particularly in relation to risk mechanisms which involve a more complex range of happenings (ie serious parental conflict) both before and after parental separation and divorce, Harold and colleagues conducted a longitudinal study. Psychological measurements were taken at 12 and 24 months. Through their research, they were among the first to identify marital conflict as a *causal* agent in the developments of children's emotional and behavioural problems.[99]

A number of key points emerging from Harold's research-based papers translate into several firm propositions relevant to the policy approach which I advance in my conclusions in this book.

First, conflict in the context of interparental relationships must be considered as a natural and normal part of family life. Unsurprisingly, it is 'conflict which is frequent, intense and child-related and poorly resolved' which is particularly upsetting for all children, particularly if accompanied by domestic violence. Conversely, if conflict is expressed without animosity, is unrelated to the child and is successfully resolved through negotiation or even submissive acceptance by one partner, children cope with it more easily and may learn valuable lessons about how to deal with conflict in their own life later. However, if parents are emotionally withdrawn from each other and show no warmth or

---

[98] J H Grych and F D Fincham (2001) *Interparental Conflict and Child Development: Theory, Research and Application* Cambridge University Press at p447.

[99] For a more recent comprehensive review of this line of research, see G T Harold and L D Leve (2012) 'Parents as partners: how parental relationships affect children's psychological development' in A Balfour, M Morgan and C Vincent (eds) *How Couple Relationships Shape Our World: Clinical Practice Research and Policy Perspectives*, Karnac Books, London at pp25–56. See also J Reynolds, C Houlston, L Coleman, G Harold (2014) *Parental Conflict: Outcomes and Interventions for Children and Families* Policy Press and One Plus One at pp13–22.

affection, this too may put children at risk of longer-term emotional and behavioural problems.

Second, it is important not only to focus on the relationship between the parents, as many mediators and marital therapists currently do, but to ascertain and understand the child's wishes – which may differ between children even in the same family.

Modern research goes on unravelling the psychological processes by which parental conflict directly affects children.[100] In this respect, one has to consider the child's feelings of threat and self-blame arising from it. Thus, Grych, Harold and Miles have shown how girls and boys tend to react differently, with girls feelings of threat appearing to aggravate internalising symptoms of depression and anxiety, while boys are more likely to externalise feelings of self-blame and responsibility for conflict in aggressive, hostile and antisocial behaviour.[101] Boys and girls may therefore be differentially at risk in the context of acrimonious inter-personal relationships.[102]

A further important point to emerge from research using a family-wide model of interparental conflict, is that the way in which children perceive their parents' behaviour towards each other (ie the parental conflict) can determine how the children expect their parents to behave towards them. This in turn appears to affect their symptoms of distress.

In the past it was often mistakenly asserted that such behavioural problems that occurred in children of divorcing parents could be attributed to the divorce itself. This view has since been largely discredited. Elliot and Richards, for example, in an analysis of a national sample of British children, confirmed problems found among children *after* divorce actually began long *before* marital separation.[103]

---

[100] J H Grych and F D Fincham (1992) 'Interventions for children: towards greater integration and research in action' *Psychological Bulletin* 111. Also J H Grych, F D Fincham, E N Jouriles and R MacDonald (2000) 'Inter-parental conflict and child adjustment: testing the mediated role of appraisals in the cognitive contextual framework' *Child Development* 71(6) at p1661.

[101] J H Grych, G T Harold and C Miles (2003) 'A prospective investigation of appraisals as mediators of the link between inter-parental conflict and child adjustment' *Child Development* 74(4) at p1193.

[102] G T Harold and L D Leve (2012) 'Parents as partners: how parental relationships affect children's psychological development' in A Balfour, M Morgan and C Vincent (eds) *How Couple Relationships Shape Our World: Clinical Practice Research and Policy Perspectives*, Karnac Books, London at p38.

[103] J Elliot and M Richards (1991) 'Children and divorce: educational performance and behaviour before and after parental separation' *Journal of Law and the Family* 5 pp258–276. Also, J Elliot and M Richards (1991) 'Parental divorce and the life chances of children' *Family Law* vol 21 at pp481–484.

Moreover, in a review of some 200 studies around the world examining the outcomes of children who have experienced parental separation, it was found that the evidence indicates unequivocally that children whose parents separate are at significantly greater risk of a wide range of negative outcomes in social, psychological and physical development than those whose parents remain together.[104] It was also found when examining well-constructed longitudinal studies that:

> levels of behaviour and educational difficulties are higher in children whose parents later separate than in those who do not. In other words poor outcomes are in place before separation, suggesting other or additional causes of long-term disadvantage.

All kinds of stressors, such as poverty, drug and alcohol abuse can contribute to parental conflict. As one would expect, children react to their parents' conflicts as the parental relationship deteriorates and as disagreements become more intense, frequent and unresolved.

Although it is often asserted that the majority of children are resilient and cope with their parents' relationship discord and separation, a significant minority manifest longer–term, more serious behavioural problems. In an evaluated review of the application of a specialist psychometric instrument used in Wales by Family Court Advisers employed by Cafcass Cymru in contested child-related private law cases, it was found that children assessed using the instrument had a significantly higher rate of psychosocial dysfunction (32–7% – more than would be expected for children in the general population, for whom the rate is 10–20%). Moreover, the proportion of children showing emotional and behavioural problems increased by up to a further 10 percentage points in families where there had been physical domestic violence.[105] This confirmed a Ministry of Justice review of outcomes of family justice children's proceedings.[106] This found that in child-related studies using the standard Symptoms and Difficulties Questionnaire (SDQ) (a brief behavioural screening questionnaire for 3–16 year-olds covering emotional symptoms, contact problems, hyperactivity,

---

[104] J Pryor and B Rodgers (2001) *Children in Changing Families: Life after Parental Separation* Blackwell Publishers, Oxford.

[105] G T Harold (2012) *The Cafcass Cymru Child and Adolescent Welfare Assessment Checklist (CC-CAWAC) Development and Implementation Review.* Obtainable from Professor Harold, University of Sussex.

[106] E. Giovannini and Ministry of Justice (2012) *Outcomes of Family Justice Children's Proceedings – A Review of the Evidence,* pp8–10.

peer relationships and social behaviour) there were 'abnormal levels of distress in children during and shortly after separation'. Moreover, children seemed to take longer to recover than their parents who had been subject to the General Health Questionnaire (GHQ), a tool to identify minor psychiatric disorders. This finding confirmed that of an earlier study by Buchanan et al, which also, according to the Ministry of Justice review, suggested 'that the adjustment for children maybe more difficult than for parents'.[107]

Disruption to the policy-making process under the coalition government

Here I only want to observe that despite all the 'Every Child Matters' work emanating from the Department for Education and Skills and the Department of Health in the decade before the global financial crisis of 2007/08, the momentum to improve the nation's child and adolescent mental health services stalled in the face of a tidal wave of cuts introduced by the coalition government as part of its deficit reduction measures. This was so after the previous government had published in 2010 its response to the independent review of CAMHS,[108] and had set up a National Advisory Council for Children's Mental Health and Psychological Wellbeing to 'hold local commissioners to account' on implementing the review's recommendations.[109]

However, following a resolute campaign by *The Times* newspaper in the final months of the coalition government and a courageous positive response by the then Liberal Minister of Health, Norman Lamb MP, there were signs that the momentum for change in policy had picked up again. Thus, as we have seen, Public Health England and the Department for Education renewed a campaign to make head

---

[107] E. Giovannini and Ministry of Justice (2012) *Outcomes of Family Justice Children's Proceedings – A Review of the Evidence*, pp8–10.

[108] Department for Children, Schools and Families and Department of Health (2010) *Keeping Children and Young People in Mind: The Government's Response to the Review of CAMHS*.

[109] NAC (March 2011) *Making Children's Mental Health Everyone's Responsibility – Final Report to Ministers*, para 1.1. Department of Health (2004) *National Framework for Children, Young People and Maternity Services: The Mental Health and Psychological Wellbeing of Children and Young People*. Also Department of Health (2007) *You're Welcome: Quality Criteria in Making Health Services Young People Friendly*. The independent review of the National Advisory Council gives a comprehensive description of what were deemed to be effective services already in existence in 'good local areas' which were intended to 'support children and young people's emotional wellbeing and mental health'.

teachers, school governors and other staff more aware of the link between pupil health, wellbeing and their educational attainment.[110] The general aim was to recognise that poor pupil behaviour in schools, which can be very disruptive, may well reflect mental health problems, the determinants of which might lie in the child's home background. What is noticeable is that emphasis is given to the way schools can assist children experiencing mental health problems, helping them to be resilient and mentally healthy. Moreover, the Department for Education's advice (March 2015) clearly expects schools to ensure that where severe mental health problems occur, schools should enlist the support of specialist child and adolescent mental health services, and should ensure that parents and children participate as fully as possible in decisions, and are provided with information and support. Significantly, the advice states that 'the views, wishes and feelings of the pupil and their parents/carers should always be considered'.[111]

This point was endorsed when, in December 2017, the Department of Health and Department for Education issued their Green Paper.[112] Thus in support of its important structural proposals designed to advance early preventive intervention it stated that: 'In order to make changes that are meaningful to children, young people, parents and carers, we need to ensure that their continued involvement in all key decisions – about their care, about service design and evaluation and about commissioning.'

In this respect it reported that NHS England has commissioned Young Minds to run a 'four year national participation programme'. Nevertheless, I think it fair to say that until now this particular point has received far more consideration by those responsible for policy delivery in the family justice system. I deal with it first in the next chapter (Chapter Four) as well as again in Chapter Ten. I shall return to the broader social policy issues concerning the promotion of better

---

[110] Public Health England (November 2014) *The Link Between Pupil Health and Wellbeing and Attainment: A Briefing for Head Teachers, Governors and Staff in Educational Settings.* Department for Education (June 2014) *Mental Health and Behaviour in Schools.* Also Department for Education (March 2015) *Mental Health and Behaviour in Schools: Departmental Advice for School Staff* www.gov.uk/government/publications

[111] Department for Education (March 2015) *Mental Health and Behaviour in Schools: Departmental Advice for School Staff* www.gov.uk/government/uploads/system/uploads/attachment_data/file/508847/Mental_Health_and_Behaviour_-_advice_for_Schools_160316.pdf at p6.

[112] Department of Health and Department for Education (December 2017) *Transforming Children and Young People's Mental Health Provision: a Green Paper* CM 9523 para 4.1 p18

mental health services and the need for preventive support for children and families in Chapter Twelve, when considering the current barriers obstructing social reform in this field. I explore the issues again in Chapter Thirteen, where I propose ways in which schools as first responders can utilise crisis intervention support for children as part of a coordinated programme of primary prevention.

FOUR

Hearing the voice of the child: messages from research that expose gaps between theory, principle and reality

Introduction

This chapter draws attention to the developing field of policy and practice related research which specifically seeks to take account of the views and experiences of children. Much of that to which I will refer concerns parental breakdown and separation since that is the main focus of this book. It should be read in conjunction with Chapter Five, which contains a number of verbatim extracts taken from a Cardiff University research study. This set out to record the views of children and young people whose parents had divorced, to show the impact of parental separation on their social and emotional wellbeing. By contrast, in this particular chapter I look at largely quantitative research materials.

It should be acknowledged that overall research into a wide range of children's life experiences is developing fast, representing something of a cultural shift since the 1970s. Even before then certain pioneering researchers, such as Royston Lambert and Spencer Millham, in their research in the 1960s for the Public Schools Commission, sought to sample the views of children.[113] This led on to a number of other studies concerned with listening to children in educational and other professional services contexts.[114]

Another initial point to note is that the very concept of childhood and the idea of children's right to be heard is culturally defined. Moreover,

---

[113] R Lambert and S Millham (1967) *The Hothouse Society: An Exploration of Boarding-school Life Through the Boys' and Girls' Own Writing* Weidenfeld and Nicolson, London.

[114] I Butler and H Williamson (1994) *Children Speak: Children, Trauma and Social Work* Longman, London. See also D Glaser (1996) 'The voice of the child in mental health practice' in R Davie, G Upton, V Varma (eds) *The Voice of the Child: A Handbook for Professionals*, Falmer Press pp78–91.

that culture is constantly and rapidly changing. For example, Hilton, citing an OFCOM report,[115] points out that nowadays:

> the average British child receives his or her first mobile phone at the age of twelve; nearly one in ten receives one before the age of five. A third of children aged five to fifteen have a smartphone, and two-thirds of twelve- to fifteen-year-olds do; nearly half of three- to four-year-olds own some kind of device, while a majority of those age eight to fifteen have three or more.

He adds:

> It is normal for young people to be inundated with technology. They are using it to go online without supervision and these trends are accelerating.[116]

We have yet to have available well-constructed socio-legal research to evaluate the effects of this technological revolution on children facing parental conflict and separation. It should be noted, however, that the coalition government appeared keen to promote the use of the internet, having received the Final Report of the Voice of the Child Dispute Resolution Advisory Group.[117] This recommended that high-quality, consistent, accessible and age-appropriate information should be made available via leaflets, booklets, videos, support services and websites to all children and young people experiencing parental separation.[118]

It should be noted that much of the research to which I shall refer in this chapter took place in the 1990s and early 2000s, before the full impact of modern information technology had been felt and prior to the almost ubiquitous availability of smartphones for children. Some recent commentators, such as Steve Hilton – one-time strategic advisor

---

[115] Ofcom (2014) *Children and Parents: Media Use and Attitudes Report* www.ofcom.org.uk

[116] S Hilton (2015) *More Human: Designing a World Where People Come First* WH Allen, London.

[117] Ministry of Justice (March 2015) *Final Report of the Voice of the Child Dispute Resolution Advisory Group* Recommendation 25 at p51.

[118] For a broader picture of international perspectives, see the text by P Parkinson and J Cashmore (2008) *The Voice of the Child in Family Law Disputes* Oxford University Press. For a more detailed and more up-to-date exposition of the legal position concerning the voice of the child, see N Lowe and G Douglas G (2015) *Bromley's Family Law* (11th edition) Oxford University Press Chapter 13.

to Prime Minister David Cameron, in the early days of the coalition government – have since warned of the dangers to children caused by smartphones especially for vulnerable children and the early availability of online pornography. In his view:

> Devices have brought children entertainment and education, but they've also erased the boundaries between the child and adult worlds.[119]

I have received anecdotal evidence that suggests that children going through the crisis of parental separation and family breakdown often nowadays communicate with friends via their smartphones for support. Others turn to more institutionalised neutral information and crisis support services such as Childline, Voices in the Middle and Place2Be. The value of such services could be greatly increased if they were given more resources from central government as part of its Early Intervention Foundation programme.

The voice of the child in family justice

A major feature of modern family justice has been the increasing recognition being given to the voice of the child, particularly in the public law field – less so in practice in private law because of economic constraints. Even so, it may not just be current economic pressures that restrict the opportunities to take account of children's views when their parents divorce or separate. There is a more fundamental point to be considered: namely, that within our culture there is a strong tendency to socially construct the process of family breakdown in purely adult terms. Indeed, one of the features of the psychological drama of serious parental conflict is that it tends to focus the attention of outsiders (whether other relatives and friends or professional interveners) on the conflict between the adults, while the children lurk unseen or unheard, as it were, in the wings.

Until recently the same could be said for children affected by parental alcohol abuse – a point made by Judith Harwin and colleagues in a study of the experimental Family Drug and Alcohol Court in London set up by His Honour Judge Nicholas Crichton.[120] Indeed, a recent

---

[119] S Hilton (2015) *More Human: Designing a World Where People Come First* WH Allen, London at p229.
[120] J Harwin, M Ryan, J Tunnard et al (2011) *The Family Drug and Alchohol Court (FDAC) Evaluation Project Final Report* Brunel University.

comprehensive research review in this field conducted by the former Children's Commissioner for England, Dr Maggie Atkinson, confirms that:

> a significant feature of many children's experience is that parental substance misuse is often highly correlated with family disharmony and/or conflict (including domestic violence and abuse). Furthermore, some research has suggested that children can be more affected by this family disharmony than by the drinking or drug use itself.[121]

The child's right to be heard when administrative and legal decisions are taken: a summary of the law

As pointed out in a previous publication, my co-authors and I took the view that:

> parents and others cannot be considered an entirely reliable source of information on the child's experience of divorce ... in this sense children are not only relevant and competent witnesses to the processes of their parents' divorce, they are also often the only reliable witness of their own experience.[122]

This has implications for the way our society constructs and gives effect to the concept of children's rights within the privacy of the family, as

---

[121] J Adamson and L Templeton (September 2012) *Silent Voices: Supporting Children and Young People Affected by Parental Alcohol Mmisuse: A Report for the Children's Commissioner for England* www.childrenscommissioner.gov.uk at p34. See also J Harwin, B Alrouh, M Ryan and J Tunnard (2014) *Introducing the Main Findings from: Changing Lifestyles, Keeping Children Safe: An Evaluation of the First Drug and Alcohol Court (FDAC) in Care Proceedings* Nuffield Foundation and Brunel University www.nuffieldfoundation.org.uk

[122] I Butler, L Scanlan, M Robinson, G Douglas and M Murch (2003) *Divorcing Children: Children's Experience of Their Parents' Divorce* Jessica Kingsley, London at p12. See also A L James and A James (1999) 'Pump up the volume: listening to children in separation and divorce' *Childhood* 6.2 pp189–206. Also G Douglas, M Murch, C Miles and L Scanlan (2006) *Research Into the Operation of Rule 9.5 of the Family Proceedings Rules 1991: A report to the Department for Constitutional Affairs.* www.dca.gov.uk/family/familyprocedures-research.pdf

Jeremy Roche discusses.[123] I suggest that this should be borne in mind when considering the evolving state of law in this matter.

The principle set out in Article 12 of the United Nations Convention on the Rights of the Child (UNCRC) is to 'assure to the child who is capable of forming his or her view, the right to express those views freely in all matters affecting the child, [such views] being given due weight in accordance with the age and maturity of the child'. Article 12(3) goes on to require states in particular to provide the child with 'the opportunity to be heard in any judicial and administrative proceedings affecting the child either directly or through a representative in a manner consistent with the procedural rules of national law'. Family courts, under s1(3) of the Children Act 1989, have had a clear obligation to ascertain 'the wishes and feelings of the child' and to give due weight to them, 'having regard to their age and understanding'. This applies also in adoption proceedings, care proceedings and contested private law proceedings about a child's care and upbringing brought under s8 of the Children Act 1989. Thus the paramountcy of the welfare principle under the Children Act 1989 is augmented by a checklist in s1(3)(a), which provides a mandatory direction to family courts to take account of the child's wishes and feelings in all such cases. As pointed out in Chapter One, Nigel Lowe and I have suggested that this development marks a shift from the traditional position where children's futures were decided solely on the views of adults, that is, parents and professionals, to one where children are no longer seen as passive victims of family breakdown, but increasingly as participants and actors in the family justice process.[124] As pointed out in the book *Divorcing Children*,[125] this approach to seeing children as participant social actors reflects an increasingly significant strand of socio-legal and sociological thought about modern childhood, 'which sets out to understand children's experience in their own terms and take the child's word as the primary source of knowledge about that experience'.

Herring, Probert and Gilmore in a chapter on debates about children's rights, which curiously gives scant attention to the issue of the voice of the child, nevertheless rightly point out that discussion

---

[123] J Roche (1999) 'Children at divorce: a private affair?' in S Day Scalter and C Piper (eds) *Undercurrents of Divorce* Ashgate Publishing, Aldershot at pp55–76.

[124] N Lowe and M Murch (2001) 'Children's participation in the family justice system: translating principles into practice' *Child and Family Law Quarterly* 13 pp137–158.

[125] I Butler, L Scanlan, M Robinson, G Douglas and M Murch (2003) *Divorcing Children: Children's Experience of Their Parents' Divorce* Jessica Kingsley, London at p185. See also M Murch (2010) 'The voice of the child in private family law proceedings: time to rethink the approach' *Seen and Heard* 20(1) pp36–48.

of children's rights is complicated by the fact that childhood is socially constructed.[126] Although raising a number of criticisms that can be levelled at the paramountcy principle of the child's welfare, Jonathan Herring has acknowledged that it has the virtue of focusing the court's attention on 'the person whose voice may be the quietest both literally and metaphorically'.[127] Moreover, he and his co-authors appear to conclude that despite the criticisms that can be made of the Human Rights Act 1998, the law appears to be 'converging on the view that decision-making in children's cases should be a process in which all the participants' interests are considered, and in which the children's interests are privileged, but not automatically decisive of the outcome'.[128]

In my conclusions I pick up the point that decision-making in family justice is a process over time in which children are invariably active participants one way or another. Indeed, I coined the phrase 'participant family justice' many years ago and outlined a behavioural science theory drawn from small group psychology on which it is based.[129] This was developed in the 1960s at the Tavistock Institute of Human Relations by Bion, Miller, Rice and others.[130] Here suffice to say that in essence this way of thinking starts from the proposition that there is a common objective about which all parties could reach agreement. The aim is that of arriving at a fair and reasonable basis upon which the family can reconstitute itself following separation or divorce, paying due regard to the interests of the children. Once it is accepted that there is such a common, albeit elusive objective, all the actors within the machinery of justice – judges, solicitors, barristers, Cafcass officers and mediators, as well as the family members themselves, including any children who wish to have a voice – can be perceived as being

---

[126] J Herring, R Probert and S Gilmore (2012) *Great Debates: Family Law* Palgrave Macmillan, Basingstoke at pp57–59

[127] Ibid at pp80. See also J Herring 'The welfare principle and the rights of parents' in A Bainham, S Day Sclater, M Richards (1999) *What is a Parent: Socio-legal Analysis* Bloomsbury pp89–106.

[128] Ibid at p83.

[129] M Murch (1980) *Justice and Welfare in Divorce* Sweet and Maxwell, London at pp218–219. See also M Murch (2012) The role of the family court system of England and Wales in child-related disputes: towards a new concept of family justice process' and commentary by C Clulow in A Balfour, M Morgan and C Vincent (eds) *How Couple Relationships Shape Our World: Clinical Practice, Research and Policy Perspectives* Karnac Books, London at pp91–135.

[130] W R Bion (1961) *Experiences in Groups* Tavistock, London. See also E J Miller and A K Rice (1967) *Systems of Organisation* Tavistock, London; and E J Miller (1976) *Task and Organisation* Wiley, London.

bound together in a common pursuit of an agreed aim. I termed this way of viewing the family justice process 'participant justice' because it involves family justice practitioners with various roles all working *with* the family rather than them doing things *to* it (see further in Chapter Thirteen at p324).[131]

Messages from socio-legal research

In the 1980s and 1990s in England and Wales, a number of pioneering studies explored ways and means of sampling children's views and experiences of their parents' divorce, including those of Walczak and Burns, Mitchell, Cockett and Tripp, Lyons et al, Neale and Smart, O'Quigley, and Dunn et al.[132] Three particularly relevant projects funded by the Joseph Rowntree Foundation were published in the spring of 2003.[133] The first, by Dunn and Deater-Deckard was part of a large longitudinal representative survey of 9,000 families.[134] An intensive sample of 192 families was drawn where parents had separated, divorced and/or re-partnered, with a view to considering the perspectives of 467 children aged between five and 16 (including 113 from two-parent 'intact' families). This study has particularly interesting data concerning children's use of support systems, and draws attention to the importance of friends and grandparents – points which I consider further below in Chapter Five. The views of children as young as five, obtained using

---

[131] M Murch (1980) *Justice and Welfare in Divorce* Sweet and Maxwell, London Chapter 14 at pp219–229.

[132] Y Walczak and S Burns (1984) *Divorce: The Child's Point of View* Harper and Row, London. A Mitchell (1985) *Children in the Middle* Tavistock, London. M Cockett and J Tripp (1994) *The Exeter Family Study: Family Breakdown and Its Impact on Children* University of Exeter. C M Lyons, E Surrey and J Timms (1998) *Effective Support Services for Children and Young People When Parental Relationships Break Down* Calouste Gulbenkin Foundation, London. B Neale and C Smart (2001) *Good to Talk: Conversations With Children After Divorce* Young Voice, London. A O'Quigley (2000) *Listening to Children's Views: The Findings and Recommendations of Recent Research* Joseph Rowntree Foundation, York. J Dunn, L C Davies, T G O'Connor and W Sturgess (2001) 'Family lives and friendships: the perspectives of children in step-, single-parent and nonstep families' *Journal of Family Psychology* 15 pp272–287.

[133] A Wilson, J Edwards with S Allen and C Dasgupta (April 2003) *Schools and Family Change: School-based Support for Children Experiencing Divorce and Separation* Joseph Rowntree Foundation – summarised in *Findings: School-based Support for Children Whose Parents Have Separated* www.jrf.org.uk

[134] J Dunn and K Deater-Deckard (2001) *Children's Views of Their Changing Families* Joseph Rowntree Foundation, York.

drawings and family maps, produced findings which were broadly similar to verbal accounts given by older children.

The second Rowntree study, a review of services, was undertaken jointly by Martin Richards and colleagues at the Centre for Family Research at the University of Cambridge and by Jan Pryor from Victoria University, Wellington, New Zealand.[135] It found that in the UK there were a great many organisations, mostly voluntary, which in a variety of ways claimed to be concerned for children facing parental conflict, separation and divorce — some willing to provide direct services for children, while others, the majority, were aimed more at the parents. With regard to research concerning children's views, the authors comment that:

> it is remarkable, looking back at the beginning of the twenty-first century, that decades of research examining outcomes for children whose parents separated and re-partnered, has failed, with very few exceptions, to ask how children experienced these changes.

The most notable exceptions were the early studies in the UK by Walczak and Burns and Mitchell.[136] The Rowntree Review noted that the few available children's studies at the time confirmed that 'children usually report feeling distressed, angry or sad when they find their parents are parting', though some felt indifferent or positive about it because they felt 'released from conflicted family situations brought about by separation'. The available studies also showed 'that children are rarely told what is going on when parents part but find out when one parent leaves home or they themselves leave with a parent'.[137]

I develop these points by reference to children's verbatim accounts in Chapter Five below.

Quoting the study of Judy Dunn and colleagues, drawing on data from the Avon Longitudinal Study of Parents and Children (ALSPAC), the Rowntree Review further reported that only 'five per cent of children whose parents had separated felt they had a full explanation

---

[135] J Hawthorne, J Jessop, J Pryor and M Richards (March 2003) *Supporting Children Through Family Change: A Review of Interventions and Services for Children of Divorcing and Separating Parents* Joseph Rowntree Foundation, York at p9.

[136] Y Walczak and S Burns (1984) *Divorce: The Child's Point of View* Harper and Row, London. A Mitchell (1985) *Children in the Middle* Tavistock, London.

[137] J Hawthorne, J Jessop, J Pryor and M Richards (March 2003) *Supporting Children Through Family Change: A Review of Interventions and Services for Children of Divorcing and Separating Parents* Joseph Rowntree Foundation, York at p9.

of the separation'. Moreover, the research review found that it was 'not often that the children are consulted about the living arrangements that are made for them after separation ... Yet it is clear that children and young people do have opinions about these major changes in their lives'.[138]

Another theme emerging from this review was the distress that many children experience at the loss of day–to-day contact with the parent who leaves – usually the father. For many, this loss becomes permanent, since over time many fathers and their children lose contact altogether. On the other hand, there was evidence from Walczak and Burns that those 'who did retain good relations with both parents felt that they had coped well, in comparison with those who did not'.[139]

The Cardiff Children in Divorce research programme

The Rowntree studies referred to above were preceded by a three-year study carried out by an interdisciplinary team at Cardiff University, funded by the Economic and Social Research Council (ESRC), as part of its Children 5–16 Research Programme directed by Professor Alan Prout. It is from this study that I summarise the principal findings. These have been fully written up elsewhere with carefully chosen representative extracts from children's interviews.[140] I shall quote some of these in Chapter Five, to illustrate the impact of the parents' separation and the need for supportive crisis intervention services as part of the community-based preventive programme which I propose in my conclusions. A related, more specialist, Cardiff study concerning children who were separately represented in contested child-related cases was funded by the then government Department for Constitutional Affairs (now Ministry of Justice).[141] Another important, if less representative, 'feedback' consultation from children and young people was reported by Cafcass in 2010, to which I also refer below when considering their support needs.[142] Even allowing for differences in methodology and sampling size, and of course acknowledging

---

[138] Ibid p10.

[139] Ibid p10.

[140] I Butler, L Scanlan, M Robinson, G Douglas and M Murch (2003) *Divorcing Children: Children's Experience of Their Parents' Divorce* Jessica Kingsley, London.

[141] G Douglas, M Murch, C Miles and L Scanlan (March 2006) *Research Into the Operation of Rule 9.5 of the Family Proceedings Rules 1991* Department for Constitutional Affairs, London.

[142] Cafcass (January 2010) *Private Law Consultation: How It Looks To Me* University of Sheffield Centre for the Study of Childhood and Youth, and Cafcass.

that children of various ages from different social backgrounds differ considerably in their experience of parental separation, sometimes even within the same family, certain clear common feelings and perspectives emerged from children in all the studies concerning their experiences of parental separation. These may be briefly summarised as follows.

Parental separation as a family crisis: its impact on children and young people

First and foremost for most children, parental separation constitutes a major crisis and turning point in their family life. Even though many children will have been aware of strains and tensions in the parents' relationship, sometimes accompanied by violence, the actual separation itself is typically a blow, precipitating what in mental health terms could be described as a kind of bereavement response: that is, a sense of shock, even disbelief, followed by a period of emotional distress in which morale and self-esteem slump. This is invariably accompanied by a preoccupation with what has happened (difficulties in concentration in normal life tasks, tearfulness, anger and/or depression etc), although most children adapt to radically changed family circumstances and recover a sense of emotional equilibrium. Yet, as mentioned in Chapters One and Three, the crisis can impact adversely on their educational performance and general social relationships.[143] I illustrate this point in Chapter Five, using verbatim extracts from children in the Cardiff Children in Divorce project.

Even so, for some children parental separation comes as a relief from the intensity of parental conflict and violence, and leads to a safer home life. For example, the Cafcass consultation study reported that out of 102 respondents, 67 reported that there were fewer arguments and 59 said their parents were happier. Half said that they felt safer and were more able to concentrate.[144] Nevertheless, quite often family finances deteriorated, as did the child's relationship with the non-resident parent. As explained in Chapter Three, when considering findings from cognitive developmental psychological research, boys and girls tend to differ in their responses, with boys typically acting more aggressively and girls depressively. One should also not forget

---

[143] I consider further aspects of what has become known as the 'crisis' model of mental health and related methods of support and intervention in Chapter Six below.

[144] Cafcass (January 2010 *Private Law Consultation: "How It Looks to Me"* University of Sheffield Centre for the Study of Childhood and Youth, and Cafcass, paras 3.6 and 5.7.

that separating parents, too, are likely to experience a crisis response in relation to loss or threat of loss in practical and emotional terms, and with a good deal of anxiety about the future after separation. This may add to their difficulty in responding appropriately to the children, also in crisis.

Despite its relatively small sample, the 2010 Cafcass Consultation Report states in a nutshell the multiple effects that children and young people generally feel their parents' separation has had on their life. Thus the report states:

> the overwhelming majority of young people said that they were unsettled at school, with 87 (77%) out of 113 respondents saying this. Sixty-six (58%) said they were depressed; 73 (65%) were not able to concentrate; 65 (58%) were not sleeping.[145]

Nevertheless, as the Cafcass report also points out, it is difficult to generalise about children's feelings at any one time because parental separation can be met by a mixture of sadness and relief. Many children surveyed worried about the implications of the separation for themselves, both short-term and long-term: would they have to move, change schools, lose friends? Would family income reduce? Would relationships with other relatives (siblings, grandparents etc) change? They also worried about their parents' wellbeing. Relationships with the non-resident parent, and with any new friends and partners found by their parents were generally initially complex and emotionally fraught. Children wondered whether new partners would become step-parents and what their relationship would be with any children the new partner might have. Depending on the nature of their relationship with the parent who had left, many were concerned about contact arrangements and whether rows and differences between their parents would continue.

A number were particularly concerned that their relationship with grandparents would be adversely affected, especially if before their parents' separation they had had regular contact with them. As I explain further below in this chapter, another exploratory study, arising from the Cardiff Law School's Children and Divorce programme, looked specifically at the role of grandparents from the perspectives of parents,

---

[145] Cafcass (January 2010 *Private Law Consultation: "How It Looks to Me"* University of Sheffield Centre for the Study of Childhood and Youth, and Cafcass, para 8.5.

grandparents and children.[146] Although the sample of grandchildren was quite small, it nevertheless confirmed the findings of another study that grandparents can be key confidants for a significant minority of children.[147] Thus Dunn and Deater-Deckard noted that in a sample of 62 children, 14% confided in their grandparents, but almost one in four did not talk to anyone about their parents' separation.

As is well known, some children tend to blame themselves for the family's problems, sometimes quite irrationally.[148] Many experience divided loyalties and feelings which can fluctuate with recurrent family crises. While most children come through the crisis of parental separation relatively unscathed, some experience longer-term, more persistent adverse reactions, such as severe depression and other reactive disorders more akin to post-traumatic stress, especially if they have witnessed domestic violence. But, as I have stressed before, even a short-term crisis response lasting months rather than years can impact adversely on educational performance, for example, at times of key examinations, which may result in longer-term sequilae, a point to which I return in Chapter Thirteen when considering the implications for preventive mental health in the context of schools.

Children's information needs

A further key point to emerge is the importance to children of obtaining reliable information about their parents' separation and divorce, so that

---

[146] N Ferguson with G Douglas, N Lowe, M Murch and M Robinson (2004) *Grandparents in Divorced Families* Policy Press, Bristol at pp21–32.

[147] J Dunn and K Deater-Deckard (2001) *Children's Views of Their Changing Families* Joseph Rowntree Foundation, York at p278.

[148] See, for example, CAADA (February 2014) *In Plain Sight: Effective Help for Children Exposed to Domestic Abuse* Insight Report No 2 www.caada.org.uk This report by CAADA (Coordinated Action Against Domestic Abuse) – a service designed to support a multidisciplinary agency response to domestic violence – conducted a survey of 877 children's cases known to specialist children's workers supplemented by data collected directly from 331 children. This reported that at first contact with the service, 60% of the children felt they were responsible for their parents' difficulties. But it should also be noted that there is social science evidence, reported in a recent review by the British Academy, which shows that the risks to children that arose from parental family discord/conflict associated with family breakup in some instances, 'were mainly brought about by environmental influences; that the effects involved bi-directional effects (i.e. children's effects on parents as well as parent's effects on children)' – M Rutter (2010) *Social Science and Family Policies* British Academy and Policy Centre at p10.

they can have a better understanding of what was happening and what to expect. As the Cardiff research observed:

> those who were well informed appeared better able to buffer the impact of the crisis and to have stronger self-esteem and a capacity to understand and manage their lives. By contrast, lack of information and confusion added to the children's uncertainties and sometimes seemed to have longer-term adverse repercussions, for example, in their relationship with their parents and any new partners.[149]

It might be thought that parents are the obvious source of information and support. Yet, as the earlier Rowntree and the Cardiff researchers found, although almost all the parents interviewed said they had spoken to the children about imminent or actual separation and subsequent divorce, many children recalled this differently Almost a third of the children in the Cardiff study could not remember being told anything by either parent. Moreover, the younger the child, the greater the chances of not being told: only 52% of those under 10 being able to recall anything.[150] Similarly, in the Cafcass consultation feedback study, while two-thirds reported their parents had explained they were separating, the remainder commented they were left completely in the dark.[151]

Being kept informed as the family coped with the changes following parental separation is closely related to the issue of whether the children and young people had a say in the family's future. Butler, Robinson and Scanlan suggested that this may in part be due to the style of parenting and 'the degree to which children are able to exercise their claim to participate in the everyday routines of domestic decision-making'.[152] They concluded that:

> decision-making processes in families are complex, cumulative, subtle and dynamic. They rely on shared

---

[149] I Butler, L Scanlan, M Robinson, G Douglas and M Murch (2003) *Divorcing Children: Children's Experience of Their Parents' Divorce* Jessica Kingsley, London at p186.

[150] Op cit Butler et al 2003 at p187.

[151] Op cit Cafcass 2010 paras 6.12 and 6.17.

[152] I Butler, M Robinson and L Scanlan (2005) *Children and Decision Making* National Children's Bureau and Joseph Rowntree Foundation, London at p24. See also Joseph Rowntree Foundation (July 2005) *Children's Involvement in Family Decision Making* at p2.

intimate knowledge of precedent, mutual trust and a common understanding of the family's unique 'culture'. Such findings may shed light on some of the difficulties faced by step-parents, who initially are seeking to blend divergent family cultures.

When it came to parental separation and divorce, the Cardiff *Divorcing children* study found that one of the problems reported most frequently by both parents and children was that they were unsure what to say or how to say it. As explained elsewhere:

> parents said they did not know what was happening themselves so did not know what to tell the children. Children in their turn felt they did not know how to ask for information that they felt they needed.[153]

Another common problem was that both parents and children wanted to avoid upsetting the other by talking about the 'divorce'. But what parents did not appreciate was that by trying to protect their children, 'they ran the risk of compounding the children's confusion and uncertainty about the future'.[154]

Moreover, it is clear that as family circumstances change during the separation and divorce process, children have continuing information needs if they are to gain a sense of control over their lives and adjust appropriately over time to the new situation: telling children is not, therefore, a one-off event. Parents and those others in a position to support children through the crisis need to be willing to answer questions about what is happening and the changes within the family, and to share uncertainties about the future.

---

[153] M Robinson, I Butler, L Scanlan, G Douglas and M Murch (2003) 'Children's experience of their parents' divorce' in A M Jensen and L McKee (eds) *Children and the Changing Family: Between Transformation and Negotiation* Routledge, Falmer, London at p78.

[154] Ibid.

Other social network support

The role of grandparents

The 2003 Cardiff study,[155] like others in both the UK and elsewhere,[156] revealed that children faced with their parents' separation employ various coping strategies and support mechanisms to help them deal with it. Most demonstrated a remarkable capacity to seek out and use appropriate and available help and support from their own resources. Parents were the obvious providers of emotional support, information and advice but not all children chose to turn to them. Some felt their parents did not understand what they were experiencing or were too upset themselves to help. Surprisingly, few turned to siblings for support.

Both the Cardiff *Divorcing children* study and a Cafcass consultation highlighted the importance of support from grandparents for some children, particularly if they felt that their resident parents were themselves in crisis and too distracted and preoccupied to give them

---

[155] I Butler, L Scanlan, M Robinson, G Douglas and M Murch (2003) *Divorcing Children: Children's Experience of Their Parents' Divorce* Jessica Kingsley, London.

[156] C Smart, B Neale and A Wade (2001) *The Changing Experiences of Childhood: Families and Divorce* Polity Press, Cambridge. M Cockett and J Tripp (1994) *The Exeter Family Study: Family Breakdown and Its Impact on Children* University of Exeter. V May and C Smart (2004) 'Silence in court? Hearing children in residence contact disputes' *Child and Family Law Quarterly* 16 pp305–316. M Gollop, A B Smith and N Taylor (2000) 'Children's involvement in custody and access arrangements after parental separation' *Child and Family Law Quarterly* 12 pp383–399. J Dunn and K Deater-Deckard (2001) *Children's Views of Their Changing Families* Joseph Rowntree Foundation, York. C Smart and B Neale (2000) 'It's my life too: children's experience of post-divorce parenting' *Family Law* 30 pp163–169. Also B Neale and C Smart (2001) *Good to Talk: Conversations With Children After Divorce* Report to the Nuffield Foundation. For a key study from the Irish Republic, see D Hogan, A M Halpenny and S Greene (2002) *Children's Experiences of Parental Separation* Children's Research Centre, Trinity College, Dublin. Also D Hogan, A M Halpenny and S Greene (2003) 'Change and continuity after parental separation: children's experiences of family transitions in Ireland' *Childhood* 10(2) p163. For a Norwegian child-focused study, see K Moxnes (2003) 'Children coping with parental divorce: what helps, what hurts?' in A M Jensen and L McKee (eds) (2003) *Children and the Changing Family: Between Transformation and Negotiation* Routledge, Falmer, London pp90–104. For a comprehensive study which sets Australian experience in a wider international context, see P Parkinson and J Cashmore (2008) *The Voice of the Child in Family Law Disputes* Oxford University Press at pp64–76 and pp160–164.

the attention they needed.[157] For some, grandparents' homes provided 'safe' or 'neutral' territory in which children could take refuge from the emotional turmoil at home. Yet, as the exploratory Cardiff study by Ferguson et al concluded:

> the grandparents who were reluctant to get involved with their grandchildren before the divorce did not become more enthusiastic when the parents separated.[158]

The nature of the grandparent/grandchild relationship before the break-up of the family is, on this evidence, an important predictor of the post-divorce relationship. Ferguson points out that a number of other factors unrelated specifically to the parents' separation, such as the age of the child and teenagers' growing independence from their families, also influence the grandparent/grandchild relationship. This can give rise to an 'asymmetric relationship' in which grandparents' expectations of and affection for the grandchildren are often rather one-sided. [159]

Support from friends

By contrast, close friends, particularly those who had divorced parents themselves, were an extremely important source of comfort and support, being seen as more accessible and understanding. Thus the Cardiff *Divorcing children* study reported that 'more than two thirds said that they talked to their best friend and 86 per cent said that it had helped'.[160]

Other potential supporters

It should be noted that most children were ambivalent about seeking support from professionals like teachers, doctors and social workers. Most saw their parental conflict and separation as a very private matter.

---

[157] I Butler, L Scanlan, M Robinson, G Douglas and M Murch (2003) *Divorcing Children: Children's Experience of Their Parents' Divorce* Jessica Kingsley, London pp144–160. Cafcass (January 2010 *Private Law Consultation: "How It Looks to Me"* University of Sheffield Centre for the Study of Childhood and Youth, and Cafcass.

[158] Op cit Ferguson et al 2004 at para 8.6.

[159] Ibid at p24.

[160] I Butler, L Scanlan, M Robinson, G Douglas and M Murch (2003) *Divorcing Children: Children's Experience of Their Parents' Divorce* Jessica Kingsley, London, at pp60–90 also pp153–154.

They were unsure who they could trust to understand and accept them with their emotional difficulties, apart from close friends. Thus, besides grandparents and close friends, children in the Cardiff study were very uncertain about seeking outside support. More than half said they had no unrelated adult to whom they felt able to talk. Just a few had talked to teachers or counsellors, and a few commented positively on the support they had received when they contacted Childline.[161] Indeed, of the 136 young people taking part in the Cafcass consultation (most subject to a Cafcass Inquiry Report) 49 had approached Childline and 27 had seen a counsellor.[162]

The difficulty in finding an outsider to trust also emerged strongly from a recent study of children affected by their parents' alcohol misuse, which of course often coexists with a range of other problems such as family conflict and domestic violence.[163] That study observed 'that children want a patient, empathetic and sensitive approach based on trust in which someone who is helpful, caring and encouraging and who recognises their circumstances takes time to get to know them.'[164] This is an important point that potential first responder support staff in schools should note.

An important investigation of the perspective of young adults (aged 18–35) who had experienced the breakup of their parents' relationship before they had reached the age of 16 reported that a number had felt extremely 'lonely without anyone to confide in over their distress or their parents' separation'.[165] Many of these young adults, looking back on their experience at the time of the breakup of their parents' relationship and the emotional turmoil and distress which it caused them, told the researchers that because their parents had been so overwhelmed by their own practical and emotional problems, they as children simply 'did not know where to turn for help ... they sometimes recognised that things hidden away and feelings bottled up because

---

[161] I Butler, L Scanlan, M Robinson, G Douglas and M Murch (2003) *Divorcing Children: Children's Experience of Their Parents' Divorce* Jessica Kingsley, London pp144–160.

[162] Cafcass (January 2010 *Private Law Consultation: "How It Looks to Me"* University of Sheffield Centre for the Study of Childhood and Youth, and Cafcass at para 8.6.

[163] J Adamson and L Templeton (September 2012) *Silent Voices: Supporting Children and Young People Affected by Parental Alcohol Mmisuse: A Report for the Children's Commissioner for England* www.childrenscommissioner.gov.uk at p10.

[164] Ibid at p65.

[165] J Fortin, J Hunt and L Scanlan (2012) *Taking a Longer View of Contact: The Perspectives of Young Adults Who Experienced Parental Separation in Their Youth* University of Sussex Law School at p290.

they felt unable to talk about them had contributed to severe emotional difficulties later in life'.[166]

This fairly recent British study therefore confirms the findings of several earlier US studies reviewed by Emery and Foreland,[167] namely, that although 'coping successfully with the many challenges and emotional upsets resulting from their parents' divorce, many children retain lingering and painful thoughts, feelings and memories long into adult life'.[168]

---

[166] Ibid at p336.

[167] R E Emery and R Foreland (1996) 'Parental divorce and children's wellbeing: a focus on resilience' in R J Haggerty, L R Sherrod, N Garmezy and M Rutter (eds) *Stress, Risk and Resilience in Children and Adolescents: Process, Mechanisms and Interventions* Cambridge University Press at pp64–99. Although published almost 20 years ago, I strongly recommend this article for the clarity and vigour of its overview of research which explores both risk factors and those protective influences which help children successfully adapt to their parents' separation and divorce.

[168] Ibid at p77.

Part II
Primary prevention

Introduction to Part II:
Children dealing with the crisis of parental separation: towards new supportive practice and policy

At this point I widen the focus to consider ways and means to establish and strengthen a joined-up network of preventive community support services specifically for children and young people caught up in the process of critical family change resulting from serious parental conflict, separation and divorce. In so doing, I adopt the standard classification of preventive services, generally held to have three tiers: primary,[169] secondary,[170] tertiary.[171]

In the light of the Government's Green paper *Transforming Children and Young People's Mental Health Provision* issued in December 2017

---

[169] M Little and K Mount (1999) *Prevention and Early Intervention With Children in Need* Ashgate, Aldershot. These authorities describe '*Primary prevention* as intervening with an entire population to stop a problem emerging. The promotion of wellbeing as opposed to the prevention of problems is part of the new way of conceptualising preventive work. *Secondary prevention/early intervention* – aimed at stopping those at high risk of developing particular social or psychological problems or those who show the first signs of difficulty or displaying unnecessarily long or serious symptoms. *Tertiary prevention/treatment* – seeks to stabilise or achieve realistic outcomes amongst those who developed the most serious manifestations of social or psychological problems focusing on the particular circumstances of the individual.'

[170] A Buchanan, J Hunt, J Bretherton and V Bream (2001) *Families in Conflict: Perspectives of Children and Parents of the Family Court Welfare Service* Policy Press, Bristol at pp97–100.

[171] E Monroe (May 2011) *Review of Child Protection: Final Report: A Child-centred System* Department for Education CM 8062 at pp79 para 5.30. Note: Professor Monroe refers to selective primary prevention – focusing on groups which research has indicated are at a 'higher than average risk of developing problems'; while 'secondary prevention aims to "respond quickly" when low level problems arise in order to prevent them getting worse'.

two introductory points need to be made with respect to the approach to early preventive mental health which I advocate in this part of the book. First: while the Green Paper deals with general mental health problems presented by children and young people in schools, I focus specifically on the support needs of youngsters whose wellbeing and mental health can be put at risk by serious parental conflict, separation and divorce – an experience which for many is a complex form of bereavement. Secondly, the Green Paper mentions four specific preventive interventions[172] – cognitive behavioural therapy (CBT), mindfulness, family based behavioural change and group based intervention – whereas in this book I aim to examine and revive interest in the application of a particular form of non-stigmatic primary preventive community mental health support. This is based on a conceptual framework developed originally in the United States by the social psychiatry movement (see Chapter Six). Nevertheless I see this as complementary to the interventions mentioned in the Green Paper. For example, all these different forms of preventive supportive intervention should be applied by 'appropriately trained supported staff such as teachers, school nurses, counsellors and teaching assistants'.[173]

As mentioned in the Preface, and like the Green Paper, I argue for a network of preventive services capable of deploying practitioners trained in face-to-face work with young people and able to sensitively apply short-term supportive crisis intervention techniques (see further below). This will involve 'first responder' organisations such as schools and primary healthcare teams, as well as 'secondary' support services linked, for example, to the family justice system (considered in Part III) – all settings where the primary task is to help children navigate critical transitions in their home life so as to adapt socially and psychologically to the difficulties between their parents. The aim is to buffer the negative impact on the young people, to strengthen their resilience to cope with future life challenges and to minimise potential damage to their educational performance.

First, in Chapter Five, I illustrate the way children and young people experience parental separation using verbatim extracts from a multidisciplinary ESRC research study in which I took part with

---

[172] Department of Health and Department for Education (December 2017) *Transforming Children and Young People's Mental Health Provision: a Green Paper* CM 9523 para 23 p21

[173] Ibid Appendix A para 5 also at paras 79–80 at p2

colleagues at Cardiff University.[174] As explained in Chapter Four, that study was just one of a number of other researches around the turn of the century that sought to examine children's experiences of divorce and family reconstruction. These reflected a cultural shift across the Western world that is a reaction against the traditional highly paternalistic view of childhood. The modern emphasis seeks to understand children's varied lives in their own terms. That was indeed the aim of the large ESRC Children 5–16 Research Programme of which the Cardiff study was just one part. That programme was directed by a sociologist, Alan Prout, editor of the resulting *Future of childhood* series, who with colleagues had published two important theoretical studies explaining the changing construction of childhood as a social institution.[175] With respect to the whole field of family litigation and the voice of the child, which I consider in Part III, a most valuable international review, which includes their own empirical Australian work, is that of Patrick Parkinson and Judy Cashmore.[176]

In the UK, the Leeds-based sociologists Carol Smart, Amanda Wade and Bren Neale produced a whole series of studies of family breakdown, which includes the perspective of parents and children themselves.[177] One particular paper by Amanda Wade and Carol Smart is significant in the context of family justice because it highlights concepts of fairness when it comes to issues of contact and spending time between resident and non-resident parents after divorce.[178]

Although the Cardiff *Divorcing children* study was carried out some years ago, I believe that, in substance, the findings are as relevant today as they were then. The approach adopted was to interview children relatively soon after their parents' divorce while their memories were still fresh. Using their own accounts, the resulting publication showed

---

[174] I Butler, L Scanlan, M Robinson, G Douglas and M Murch (2003) *Divorcing Children: Children's Experience of Their Parents' Divorce* Jessica Kingsley, London

[175] A James and A Prout (eds) (1997) *Constructing and Reconstructing Childhood: Contemporary Issues in the Sociological Study of Childhood* (2nd edition) Falmer Press, London. See also A James, C Jenks and A Prout (1998) *Theorising Childhood* Polity Press, Cambridge.

[176] P Parkinson and J Cashmore (2008) *The Voice of the Child in Family Law Disputes* Oxford University Press.

[177] C Smart and B Neale (1999) *Family Fragments* Polity Press, Cambridge. C Smart and B Neale (2000) 'It's my life too: children's experience of post-divorce parenting' *Family Law* 30 pp163–169. C Smart, B Neale and A Wade (2001) *The Changing Experience of Childhood: Families and Divorce* Polity Press, Cambridge.

[178] A Wade and C Smart (2003) 'As fair as it can be? Childhood after divorce' in A M Jensen and L McKee (eds) *Children and the Changing Family: Between Transformation and Negotiation* Routledge, Falmer.

how children were not only witnesses to but also participants and actors in the reconstruction of their family life after 'divorce'. By this they meant the entire experience of their parents' relationship breakdown and the consequences.

Taking children's own accounts as the primary source of information, it became clear to the research team that most children experience the breakup and separation of their parents as a 'crisis', that is to say, a major disruption in their everyday lives: a stressful turning point where the events leading up to their parents' separation and the separation itself at least temporarily upset the children's normal psychological and social equilibrium. It was clear that this crisis challenged them (and their parents) to discover new ways of functioning in the face of radically changed circumstances, for example, whether, and if so, how to deal with contact with the parent who has left home, learning to take on new roles within the family, managing and expressing distress, coping with the uncertainties over the family's future and so on.

In reviewing the children's evidence, the research team thought that a useful way of conceptualising what many children had experienced was to consider the school of thought known as the crisis model of mental health. As I explain in the Preface and Chapter Six below, this was developed in the United States following the Second World War. It was based on a number of empirical studies of people's reactions to stressful life-changing events. Linked to this model was a method of preventive short-term support known as crisis intervention. In the book *Divorcing children* my co-authors and I put forward a number of social policy proposals based on this line of thought. Although at the time the book was published in 2003 it was well received, for reasons which I will consider later our ideas in this respect did not meet with the policy response we had hoped for.

However, since then the socioeconomic climate has changed much, not just in political terms. There appears now to be much greater awareness in educational, family justice and mental health circles of the factors which can hamper the social and emotional wellbeing of children and young people. There is also greater awareness of the need for practice and policies to be joined up and not simply developed within professional and policy 'silos',[179] or 'ghettos' as they are sometimes referred to (see further below in Chapter Fourteen).[180]

---

[179] G Tett (2015) *The Silo Effect: The Peril of Expertise and the Promise of Breaking Down Barriers* Simon and Schuster, New York.

[180] M Murch, D Hooper (1992) *The Family Justice System* Jordan's Family Law, Bristol at pp42–43.

There is also a greater appreciation of the tensions that can arise where practitioners have conflicting conceptions of the needs of children and their families, stemming from different training backgrounds and professional cultures. There is thus a compensating need to develop a 'common language' applicable horizontally across professional boundaries. The crisis model offers a way of doing this, as I will explain in Chapter Six. For all these reasons, when thinking about this book I decided the time had come to try and revive interest in the crisis model and crisis intervention, to see how such ideas might be applied in a modern context to help children and young people facing the all too common experience of parental conflict and separation.

I appreciate that in order to move policies and practice in this direction there will be many barriers to overcome, especially since the finances of so many public and voluntary services are currently severely constrained. But is it possible to turn austerity to advantage to prompt new thinking about ways of preventing or ameliorating the more serious problems that we know, under existing arrangements, a significant number of children will have later? Can we thereby reduce the demand for more specialist and expensive services? I explore these questions in the final two chapters (Thirteen and Fourteen) of this book, but readers might like to keep them in mind before they reach Part IV.

FIVE

Children in crisis speak out

Introduction

In Chapter Three I summarised a number of studies which have highlighted factors concerning risk and resilience in children when parental conflict results in parental separation. Very few of these largely statistical quantitative outcome studies say much about the emotional impact of parental separation on individual children's lives, or about how they learn to live with the consequences. So in what follows I have selected a number of verbatim extracts taken from the book *Divorcing children*.[181] These illustrate the way children cope with the crisis of parental separation and what it *feels* like to be faced not only with warring parents who distrust each other, but with the changes and uncertainties children encounter as a result of their parents' separation.

In this chapter I do not go into the details of the research methodology, which is fully explained in the book *Divorcing children*. Suffice to say this produced a representative sample of 104 children aged 7–15 with recent experience of divorce drawn from six county courts across South West England and South Wales. Taken together, the sample gave a demographic and geographical mix of city, town and country. Great care was taken, with the collaboration of the court authorities, to ensure that participating parents and children understood the nature of the research so that their consent was freely given. We promised confidentiality would be respected and their identities concealed in any publications. Full details of the research methodology are given in an appendix in the original book.[182]

The challenge of communicating effectively with children was central to all aspects of the research design. We wanted the children to talk freely to us in their own way using their own words. In this respect, the research team were greatly helped by the previous childhood research

---

[181] I Butler, L Scanlan, M Robinson, G Douglas and M Murch (2003) *Divorcing Children: Children's Experience of Their Parents' Divorce* Jessica Kingsley, London.

[182] Ibid at pp207–227.

experience of Ian Butler,[183] a social work teacher, and Lesley Scanlan, a psychologist who conducted the interviews. Considerable thought was put into the design of the research procedures and tools, which included an activity book for children to complete. This helped them to feel in control of the interview, which they could stop at any time. This also helped them establish rapport with the researcher. The team put great store on giving children and parents feedback on the progress of the research in the form of a newsletter and a specially designed website, which many of the children visited.[184]

The extracts which I have selected from this study broadly follow the children's reactions to key stages in the deterioration of their parents' relationship before, during and after the divorce. Of course it has to be remembered that while preparing the original publication the research team considered the selected extracts were fairly typical; each child was an individual with a unique story to tell. At any one time in the process of their family's critical change, their views and feelings related to their *own* experiences, perceptions and attributions of what was happening in the family. Thus we recognised that these could change over time and may well, for a host of reasons, have differed from the experiences and feelings of any siblings.

Key stages in the divorce process from a child's viewpoint: finding out

As Harold and Leve have observed, conflict in the context of personal and family relationships is a relatively 'normal' part of life:

> with effects on children being influenced more by the expressed intensity, duration, severity, content and resolution properties employed by parents as compared to the single occurrence of conflict per se.[185]

---

[183] I Butler and H Williamson (1994) *Children Speak: Children, Trauma and Social Work* Longman, London.

[184] I Butler, L Scanlan, M Robinson, G Douglas and M Murch (2003) *Divorcing Children: Children's Experience of Their Parents' Divorce* Jessica Kingsley, London, pp215–217.

[185] G T Harold and L D Leve (2012) 'Parents as partners: how parental relationships affect children's psychological development' in A Balfour, M Morgan and C Vincent (eds) *How Couple Relationships Shape Our World: Clinical Practice, Research and Policy Perspectives* Karnac Publications, London at p7.

Some children described a gradual breakdown of their parents' relationship, witnessing them growing apart or coming to realise that they were just not suited to each other. Thus a 10-year-old girl said:

> 'I think they don't get on as well as other parents do really. They don't really suit. They don't really have the same things in common. When I was quite young I thought they were OK together but then as I got older I could sense that they weren't right together.'[186]

Other children attributed the separation to particular behaviours or incidents which they blamed on a specific parent. Factors cited included the use and abuse of alcohol, domestic violence, financial difficulties and infidelity. Some children blamed themselves. For example, one 13-year-old girl dreamt that her parents would divorce, and when the separation occurred a month later she felt she had caused it. As she told the researchers:

> 'Well, I had a dream about it, so I blamed myself for about half a year. It was about a month before it happened; I dreamt that my mum and dad were getting divorced. I just felt it was my fault 'cos I had the dream. No one else did.'[187]

As children became aware of growing tensions and quarrels between their parents, they often sensed that the family status quo was about to alter radically and that their parents' separation was inevitable. As a 12-year-old girl told us:

> 'I used to hear them arguing. They always used to shout at each other and basically scream their heads off at each other. Me and my brother were at the top of the stairs and we used to hear them shouting in the kitchen. It felt horrible. I felt that I was the only child that's parents were getting divorced. Every morning you could hear them shouting and every evening when we got back from school and it was non-stop arguing.'[188]

---

[186] I Butler, L Scanlan, M Robinson, G Douglas and M Murch (2003) *Divorcing Children: Children's Experience of Their Parents' Divorce* Jessica Kingsley, London, p54.

[187] Ibid at p55.

[188] Ibid at p34.

A 12-year-old boy told us:

> 'I was in bed trying to take my mind off it, trying to watch TV and all that. They were talking so loud I just decided to listen and listen until I heard a massive great big THUMP and that's when I started to cry. I didn't want it to happen any more.'[189]

A number of children witnessed incidents of violence between their parents which were traumatic. A 12-year-old girl told us:

> 'It was so vicious – me and my brother were in the kitchen; we were under the table. Mum and my stepfather walked in to the kitchen arguing and he got so mad he threw plates at Mum and Mum was like crying and screaming and I was so scared. We were sitting there for ages just shaking, crying and screaming and it was just horrible.'[190]

Children's reactions to the parental separation event

Parental separation is of course the major turning point for most children in these circumstances. Their emotional reactions were often powerful and conflicting. Initially most described feeling sad and upset. Many said they had cried on finding out:

> 'I was very upset. I tried to hold it in and I couldn't hold it in so I burst out crying.'[191] (Boy aged eight)

> 'I just sat there feeling really sad. My eyes were watering and I started crying. Then there was just me sat there feeling sad.'[192] (Girl aged 13)

> 'Well, I had a long long cry. Then when he had gone we stood in the hallway for quite a while just hugging each other and sobbing our hearts out. You know it was quite hard.'[193] (Girl aged 12)

---

[189] Ibid at p34.
[190] Ibid at p35.
[191] Ibid at p44.
[192] Ibid at p44.
[193] Ibid at p44.

Even though many parents had told the children in advance, the majority of children found the reality of the separation very hard to accept. As one 10-year-old boy said:

> 'The worst part about it was the night when my mum and dad really broke up. That's the worst part because we were in the front room, me, my brother and sister and we were just really worried and frightened.'[194]

As we reported, characteristically children described feeling shocked, particularly when the parents' separation was unexpected and one left without warning or even when the separation seemed to have been triggered by a single isolated incident such as a parent finding out about an affair.[195] As an eight–year-old girl told us:

> 'I was in bed when he actually left and he just went in the middle of the night. And in the morning my mum and me and everybody in my family were crying. I thought he was going to come back later, in about a month or two months or even a week but nothing happened.'

A common initial reaction was one of anger, usually directed at the parent who the child felt was responsible for the family breakdown:

> 'I was just crying and everything. I was just punching stuff and ripping down stuff. I was getting all my anger out.'[196]

This 12-year-old boy later told the researchers that his anger got him into fights at school and caused further difficulties with his father.
Some children felt angry with both parents:

> 'I was very angry with my mum and dad. I didn't speak to them for a couple of days. I didn't really take my anger out on them. I just felt it inside; that I was annoyed with them because they just got divorced.'[197] (Girl aged 12)

---

[194] Ibid at p44.
[195] Ibid at pp43 and 44.
[196] Ibid at p45.
[197] Ibid at p45.

A number of children said they felt suddenly lonely as well as angry. Thus the 12-year-old girl quoted above told the researchers that she felt:

> 'Very empty and lonely – as though I had no one to talk to. Because you know all my mum's family were like comforting her and my dad's family were comforting him and I thought that me and my brother had no one to go to because, like, there were sides. But there wasn't really – it's just like if you went over to Mum's they were too busy looking after Mum ... I felt that Mum had to be comforted and Dad had to be comforted and I thought there is no one in between for me and my brother.'[198]

By contrast, a few children reported feeling relief when the separation occurred. They had usually realised that their parents' conflict had become intolerable. For example, a 13-year-old girl told the researchers that she was both:

> 'Relieved and upset. I was just really upset at the time but it took a lot of pressure off the whole family.'[199]

Confusion and uncertainty were common once the initial shock of their parents' separation had worn off. A boy of 15 reported that he was:

> 'Very confused. I didn't expect it and everyone else had their mums and dads together. So it was being different ... I wish they were together again.'[200]

A few children found it very hard to accept that their parents had really separated and continued to hope for reconciliation. Some of these children recalled feeling that the whole experience was a dream from which they would wake up and then it would all be over. For example, a 10-year-old boy said:

> 'I first thought I would wake up tomorrow morning and everything would be OK. I keep on thinking the same thing and I still do ... I'd like it to happen that I'd wake

---

[198] Ibid at p45.
[199] Ibid at p45.
[200] Ibid at p45.

up and think "Oh, I've woken up and it was all a dream, a nightmare."[201]

Preparing for separation: whether children were told in advance

When it came to preparing children for actual separation and telling them explicitly about it, children and parents tended to recall the process differently. As was reported:

> Over two thirds (70.9%) of the children indicated that they had been told by one or both parents, with the remaining third (29.1%) reporting that they had not been told. In contrast, every parent (except one) indicated that they had either separately or jointly told the children about the separation.[202]

It was clear to the researchers that 'telling' or 'not telling' was a function of the quality of the exchange, and it should not be thought that either parents or children were deliberately misrepresenting the communication between them. The discrepancies between parents and children could be due to a number of factors, such as differential recall of events and the age of the child, since while all the children over 12 could recall being told, only 66% of those under 10 did so.

Another aspect to emerge was the children's views about *how* they should be told.[203] While 46.6% believed that both parents should have told them, this occurred in only 12.6% of cases. Most girls (81%) were reported as being told about the separation by their mother. This compared with only 67% for the boys. Only 6.7% of the children were told by their fathers, mostly in families where the mother had left or was about to leave. The researchers concluded that most children seemed to have difficulty talking to their fathers about sensitive and emotive issues. Half of the children said that their fathers knew little or nothing about how they as children felt about the divorce.[204] Thus, communication with the parent who left, usually the father, is clearly a difficult area for most children.

---

[201] Ibid at p45.
[202] Ibid at p35.
[203] Ibid at p37.
[204] Ibid at p39.

As we shall see in the next chapter with respect to the application of the crisis model of mental health and the related preventive practice of short-term crisis intervention, being well informed helps buffer the impact of the crisis. Thus, the person faced with an imminent crisis can be helped to anticipate it realistically and prepare themselves psychologically. By contrast, being kept in the dark is generally experienced as disabling, and the impact of the stressful event when it occurs is the more severe.

Keeping children reliably informed throughout the process of family breakdown

We have seen how children stress the importance, where possible, of being told about their parents' imminent separation. A number not only wanted an explanation, but needed to be reassured that the departing parents still cared about them. The experience of being rejected by the parent who had left could be very intense, particularly if there was no explanation.

As reported, children expressed the need to be kept informed throughout the process of family breakdown and reconstitution.[205] Some children recognised that this task was not easy for their parents. For example, one boy aged 14 was asked by the interviewer whether he had spoken to his mother about his parents' separation:

Interviewer:	'Have you talked to your mum about it?'
Participant:	'No, not particularly.'
Interviewer:	'Why is that?'
Participant:	''Cos I know that I'd get upset and I know Mum would get upset as well.'

Some children appreciated their parents' efforts to protect them from additional upset. As a 13-year-old girl told the researcher:

'I think it was alright because what I didn't know didn't really hurt me. If I'd known more about it I would have been more upset about it.'[206]

The research concluded that children's accounts of their parents' separation might remain incomplete for a variety of reasons. Some

---

[205] Ibid at p51.
[206] Ibid at p52.

derived from the parents' inability and reluctance to keep them informed; others derived from reticence or reluctance on the children's part to ask questions or engage in 'difficult' conversations with their parents. Nevertheless, many children expressed the view that they wanted to know what was happening. Not being kept sufficiently informed was often experienced as alienating and affected the pattern of further parent/child relationships. For example, a 14-year-old girl, living with her mother, told us:

> 'I wanted some answers and Mum didn't want to give me any answers. It would have been better if she had told me then maybe we would have had a closer relationship now. ... I think it would've [helped], 'cos if we knew the truth, then we could have cleared the air but that didn't happen. It's still going on now. You never talk about it but it's still there.'[207]

This business of keeping children and young people informed as changes in the family occur is obviously a tricky matter for both children and parents, given the complex emotions that invariably go with parental conflict and separation. Some parents succeed in doing so by resolving their interpersonal differences while keeping separate their mutual responsibilities to maintain an effective parental coalition for the children. Many, however, do not, at least not in the weeks or months when families are caught up in the emotional crisis of separation, with all its attendant uncertainties. As we have seen, this is the hardest time for children to come to terms with what has happened and to work out how they are to manage and adapt to the changed relationship between their parents, particularly in the critical early stages when children seek to regain some equilibrium and sense of normality in their lives.

Although I do not deal with them here because I want to focus on the immediate impact of the crisis of separation, the book *Divorcing children: Children's experience of their parents' divorce* contains important chapters on children's varying perceptions of their changing relationships with their parents, particularly the matter of how contact with the non-resident parent was perceived and managed. As expected, this proved to be the most difficult aspect of the whole process of separation and divorce. As numerous other studies and commentators have shown,

---

[207] Ibid at p55.

disputed issues about contact have been one of the most problematic aspects of family justice, and continue to be so.[208]

As Butler et al wrote in 2003:

> When on the surface family relationships appear to have reached a new equilibrium, contact arrangements retain a destructive potential to reopen old wounds and tensions.[209]

Telling others

As colleagues and I reported in 2003:

> Despite the fact that many children are left with an inadequate sense of what is happening around them, one of the more immediate tasks facing them once the crisis of their parents' divorce has arisen, is deciding what and how to 'tell others'. This is something children are faced with almost immediately, no matter what they have themselves been told.[210]

As we shall see, the issue of whether to tell others outside the family is complex, raising a number of immediate problematic issues for the child: who to tell, how to tell and when to tell.

Of the 104 children (51 girls and 53 boys) aged 7–15 in the Cardiff *Divorcing children* study, when asked who, if anyone, they had told about their parents' separation, a third said no one. Of the majority, most turned to their friends as their primary confidante; of these,

---

[208] Children Act Sub-committee of the Advisory Board of Family Law (2002) *Making Contact Work: A Report to the Lord Chancellor on the Facilitation of Arrangements for Contact Between Children and Their Non-residential Parent and the Enforcement of Court Orders for Contact* Lord Chancellor's Department, London. L Trinder, J Hunt, A Macleod, J Pearce and H Woodward (2013) *Enforcing Contact Orders: Problem-solving or Punishment?* Nuffield Foundation and the University of Exeter. J Hunt and A Macleod (2008) *Outcomes of Application to Court for Contact Orders after Parental Separation and Divorce* Ministry of Justice, London. L Trinder, J Connolly, J Kellet, C Notley and C Swift (2006) *Making Contact Happen or Making Contact Work? The Process and Outcomes of In-court Conciliation* DCA Research Series No 3/2006.

[209] I Butler, L Scanlan, M Robinson, G Douglas and M Murch (2003) *Divorcing Children: Children's Experience of Their Parents' Divorce* Jessica Kingsley, London at p118.

[210] Ibid at p59.

most were careful to tell only their best friend.[211] The researchers then concluded that:

> It was clearly important to children in the immediate aftermath of the crisis that only a few people outside the family should know.[212]

The notion of protecting family privacy is clearly a very important deep-seated and cultural social value – a matter I examine more fully later when considering practice and policy matters, since its impact is often underestimated in the design and provision of services (though this could be an unconscious rationing mechanism). However, with respect to children, as we shall see, it often conflicted with their need to unburden their sense of hurt and emotional distress. So most children were very careful about where they placed their trust. Thus, typically, a 10-year-old girl told the researcher:

> 'I told my best friend and that was about it really. 'Cos I could trust her and I didn't want her to say anything.'[213]

Similarly, a 12-year-old boy said he only told his best friend once he got to know him sufficiently to trust him:

> 'Like Mum and Dad splitting up and getting a divorce, some "secrets" that I knew he could keep.'[214]

Another point to emerge was that children were generally more likely to tell other children who had themselves experienced family breakdown, because they would be more likely to respect privacy. So, for example, a 10-year-old boy told the researcher:

> 'I told my friend because his parents are divorced so he knew what it's going to be like and that. And I told him 'cos I knew him and he promised not to say anything.'

It seemed to the researchers that the main benefit of talking to others who had 'been there' was that it provided children with a context

---

[211] Ibid at p60.
[212] Ibid at p81.
[213] Ibid at p61.
[214] Ibid at p61.

within which to place their own experience so that their unique circumstances, feelings and emotions could appear less extraordinary. This appeared to help them recover a sense of normality, which many so actively sought. At the same time, by being careful in their choice of friend to tell, it allowed them to exercise some actual as well as cognitive control over what was happening.

It should be noted, however, that 30% of the children reported that they told no one about their parent's separation. Indeed, the younger children in the sample (seven-, eight- and nine-year olds) seemed more likely to be among this group. Again, a notion of family privacy seemed to be the main reason for the reluctance to tell others. As a 10-year-old boy in this group said:

> 'I just wanted to keep it to our family. I wanted to keep it to myself; not telling everyone with them spreading it.'[215]

Another reason for not telling anyone was the fear of becoming emotionally upset. A 15-year-old boy whose mother had told his friend's parents about the separation told the interviewer:

> 'They were actually wondering where my dad was. I couldn't actually tell them 'cos I wasn't up to it. I was upset and couldn't talk about it.'[216]

Others felt inhibited because they believed that by telling someone outside the family they would upset their parents, particularly their resident parent – another aspect of the privacy issue.

A small but significant number of children reported being embarrassed or ashamed about what was happening in the family. Others were just too confused or knew very little about what was happening, which added to their difficulties in talking to others. A large number of children told the researchers that they feared being teased or rejected by their friends. This inhibited them from talking freely. As a 10-year-old boy said:

> 'Well I kept it secret 'cos they'll probably tease me and all that. I told one of my friends and he called me "dad-less".'[217]

---

[215] Ibid at p64.
[216] Ibid at p64.
[217] Ibid at p65.

Teenagers commonly expressed the fear that they might be thought of as 'different' or 'weird' if they revealed that their parents had separated.

Reasons for telling outsiders

Despite the reluctance many felt, they simply had to talk to friends whom they felt they could trust and other outsiders about their parents' separation. For example, a 12-year-old girl said:

> 'I just wanted to get it out ... I think the first day I went back to school after it happened.'[218]

And a 13-year-old boy similarly said:

> 'It meant that I had someone to share it with, so you know I wasn't keeping it inside me.'[219]

As a girl aged 10 told us:

> 'My mother said "Don't tell anyone yet," but I had to tell someone. I was just crying so I told my best friend.'[220]

Children generally had very clear ideas of what they wanted to achieve by talking to others. We observed that their capacity to discriminate in their support-seeking, including where and when to do so, was very marked. The timing of telling others was important for many. As was reported, some of the children talked of their need to come to terms with what was happening before they felt able to tell others.[221] For some, the need to talk to others, usually trusted friends, was felt almost immediately after parents separated, yet for a few, weeks or months were to pass before they could do so. It seemed as if, for some, telling others was helpful in recovering a sense of emotional balance; while, for others, they needed first to feel comfortable, that they had 'gotten it together' and 'normalised', before they could do so.[222]

---

[218] Ibid at p67.
[219] Ibid at p67.
[220] Ibid at p68.
[221] Ibid at pp69–71.
[222] Ibid at pp69–71.

Informing the school and talking to teachers

As far as parents were concerned, of those taking part in the Cardiff *Divorcing children* study, the majority reported informing the children's school about the separation; most doing so within a day or so. But not all of these parents told their children they had done so. Only 14% of the parents did not tell the school. So, at least on this evidence, it is clear that schools are in a position to be a 'first responder', offering support to the children if it seems necessary. This is why, as we shall see in Chapters Six and Eight, I take the view that schools should better appreciate that they are best placed to play a key role as a primary preventive service for children, ideally within a joined-up network of community mental health services for children and young people.

As was reported, as far as the children in the Cardiff study were concerned, the majority of parents felt it was important that the school knew what had happened, so that it could be taken into account were their child to show sudden changes in behaviour or performance.[223] As a 14-year-old boy said:

> 'It helped a bit ... 'cos I knew that if I had done something wrong and I was in a mood because of the divorce, they would understand.'[224]

Yet children mostly considered that their teacher needed to be sensitive and aware that children can have ambivalent feelings about when and how to talk to them. For a number, controlling the timing of the teacher's response was important. So typically, the researchers received mixed messages on this subject. Much depended on whether the child liked and trusted the teacher. For example, a 12-year-old girl said:

> 'I liked my teacher. He was really nice. It was good to know he understood and was talking to me about it. It was quite nice to know I wasn't on my own.'[225]

Even so, a number of children were uncomfortable with their teachers trying to help. As was reported:

---

[223] Ibid at pp76–78

[224] Ibid at pp76–78.

[225] Ibid at pp76–78.

Offers of support and understanding from teachers were quite frequently interpreted as unnecessary (and unwelcome) fuss.[226]

As one 13-year-old boy told the researcher:

'Teachers were like, "Oh, are you alright?" Well yes, I'm fine thank you. The teachers were like, "If you need to go out of the classroom, just go." Errgh! I just want to be normal thank you. That was the most annoying thing.'[227]

A number of children took the view that teachers should know about the change in their family circumstances but should not 'interfere'. The researchers concluded that schools have to be careful how they handle the knowledge that a child's parents have separated and in deciding when to offer support and comfort to a child, since many, at least on this research evidence, do not particularly enjoy being made a fuss of or treated differently from other children. Just listening when a child is struggling to say something may be all that is acceptable at the time. As the researchers concluded:

Children, like adults, needed time to adjust and be able to put on and maintain the right public face when it came to discussing their private lives and personal feelings. The pace at which children reached the point where telling others was less of an issue varied considerably.[228]

When parents had explained what was happening it helped children to be able to tell others. Those parents who had prohibited their children from talking to friends and teachers added to the children's burdens, as they struggled through the crisis of parental separation looking to find a new point of balance and some 'normality' in their lives.

Surviving and learning from the breakup

One should not think that the crisis of parental separation, stressful as it undoubtedly is for many children, inevitably has damaging consequences. On the contrary, the children in the Cardiff study mostly

---

[226] Ibid at pp76–78.

[227] Ibid at pp76–78.

[228] Ibid at p81.

told us what they had learnt from it, how they had accommodated the various changes that had occurred, what coping strategies they employed to manage change, how they had adapted to their altered family circumstances, and how in the process they had discovered a new sense of psychological and behavioural balance.[229] As the researchers observed:

> Children were remarkably active and creative in the methods they used to cope with difficult times. Most notably, children demonstrated an impressive capacity for drawing on the resources of others around them for help.[230]

Of course, there was a wide diversity of ways in which children experienced and adapted to their parents' separation and divorce. Some appeared more resilient and confident throughout the process, spending time with and talking to parents, friends and other relatives. Others appeared more solitary and withdrawn, dealing with their emotional distress alone, sometimes through quiet reflection.[231] Here space limits the range of examples that I have chosen from the 2003 publication.

Positive adaptation

Although for many of the children in the study their parents' divorce was still fairly recent, a number had evidently come to look back on it as having some positive benefits; some felt they had grown up rapidly. Thus, a 14-year-old girl told the researcher:

> 'I think I have changed ... I've grown up now. I'm much more mature than I was before, and I haven't got a silly attitude any more. I'm not saying I'm no more teenager, like, I still have my "fits" and everything, but in other ways I've grown up a lot.'[232]

Likewise, a 12-year-old girl said:

---

[229] Ibid at pp144–170 – see important chapter entitled 'Change and adaptation'.
[230] Ibid at p148.
[231] Ibid at p148.
[232] Ibid at p157.

'I think I have matured a lot through it. I have had to make decisions for myself and stuff. It's just made me more mature and understanding of things.'[233]

Others talked of the experience giving them a 'different view on life', and of becoming a better person. A 15-year-old described how the experience:

'made me more sort of open-minded of how families work. It's made me realise, it's not all sort of get married, have kids, live life happily ever after. I don't think it's affected me in a bad way. It hasn't made me go off the rails. I think it's just made me more open-minded about relationships and I think I understand more.'[234]

A number felt they had gained in self-confidence, made more friends and even that their school work had improved.

Some of the children considered that they had returned to what they felt was a 'normal' pattern of life. This was particularly so if their parents had come to terms with each other and if arrangements for contact had been agreed and were working satisfactorily. For example, a 14-year-old boy said that while he initially found his parents' separation difficult to cope with, he:

'gradually got pretty used to them and I don't feel there is anything wrong with them now at all. I think that we have all got used to it and it's just as though it's normal.'[235]

Likewise, when asked how she thought things were now, a 10-year-old girl said:

'Normal really. It was different when Mummy and Daddy split up but now they are just like normal. I like the way it is now. It's not going to make any change 'cos they still love me and they still won't love each other. They'll still live in separate homes and we still see our dad the same amount.'[236]

---

[233] Ibid at p157.
[234] Ibid at p157.
[235] Ibid at p158.
[236] Ibid at p159.

Children continuing to experience difficulties

Among those who were having difficulty coming to terms with and adjusting to their parents' separation were several who experienced the contact with the parent who had left as emotionally upsetting. For example, a 12-year-old boy told us that after each visit to his father he went up to his bedroom:

> 'to sit down and cry. Basically I sit down and try and read a book and go to sleep most of the time we come back from the weekends.'[237]

Some felt that their world had fallen apart or that what had happened was not real. For example, one 11-year-old said:

> 'I think it is all a dream and it's all going to be better tomorrow ... I'm still feeling really strange because sometimes I get really upset and cry in my room because I think everyone has gone: it's all gone away and I haven't got anything.'[238]

Adjustment: the overall picture

Of the 104 children interviewed in the Cardiff sample, the majority appeared to have adapted well to the parents' separation and divorce. Although, as one would expect, there was a range of experience, as a research team we wanted to understand which elements in the children's circumstances might have contributed to their adjustment. The team identified two groups at either end of the spectrum of adaptive modes: 14 children who appeared at the time they were interviewed to have adapted well, and 19 who were still having difficulty and experiencing emotional distress.[239] While of course the team were not suggesting that the experience of parental separation and divorce was the sole contributory factor influencing the children's adjustment – prior experience and personality traits were also likely influences – the fact remains that some children appeared to be coping better than others and statistically significant differences between the two groups emerged.

---

[237] Ibid at p159.
[238] Ibid at p159.
[239] Ibid at pp161–162 – a detailed statistical breakdown of these data is given in tabular form.

Those who at the time of the research interview appeared to have adapted well were:

- more likely to be a girl;
- more likely to be under 12;
- more likely to have been told by a parent about the separation/divorce, to have received an explanation, and to have been consulted about residence and contact;
- more likely to have sought and received support from others: parents, friends and so on;
- more likely to have a best friend to whom they had talked about the divorce;
- less likely to have kept it secret.

The research team noted that 'almost all the children who had not adjusted well to their parents' separation and divorce described generalised difficulties in their relationship with their non-resident parent'.[240] Many of these children evidently had a poor relationship with that parent previously, and this appeared to have become more difficult because of physical distance resulting from separation. Likewise, dissatisfaction with contact arrangements seemed more prevalent in the group of children who had adapted with difficulty.

With respect to the crisis of separation, which for many of these children, as we have seen, came as a shock, the research team noted:

> While they were attempting to regain some kind of psychological equilibrium, it was apparent that being left out of the discussions (ie of the family's future) tended to increase the children's anxiety and upset. Dissatisfaction with inflexible and irregular contact arrangements, which exacerbated problems in ongoing parent/child relationships, also made the children's adjustment more difficult.[241]

With respect to what mediated their experience of parental separation and divorce, the children consistently identified the role of accessible and effective empathetic support, particularly from close friends, resident mothers and some grandparents. All this pointed to the relevance of the crisis model of mental health as a means of understanding the processes of adapting to the temporary overwhelming stress of parental separation.

---

[240] Ibid at p165.
[241] Ibid at p169.

It is to that more theoretical subject I turn next, in preparation for outlining my ideas about practice and policy proposals to create a joined-up network of preventive support services specifically for the large annual army of children and young people grappling with this form of family crisis.

SIX

The crisis model of preventive mental health and its potential application for support services for children coping with parental separation

Introduction

This chapter considers the development of a conceptual framework modelled on Caplanian Community Mental Health principles, an approach which offers a readily understandable theoretical basis for early support for children and families undergoing stressful critical life experiences.[242] It also underlies my argument for a coordinated network of preventive services for children and young people facing

---

[242] (A) G Caplan (1961) *An Approach to Community Mental Health* Tavistock Press, London. See also G Caplan (1964) *Principles of Preventive Psychiatry* Tavistock Press, London; and G Caplan (1974) *Support Systems and Community Mental Health* Behavioural Publications, New York. Also G Caplan (1986) 'Recent developments in crisis intervention in the promotion of support systems' in M Kessler and S E Goldston (eds) *A Decade of Progress in Primary Prevention* University Press of New England, Hanover, NH. Also G Caplan (1989) 'Prevention of psycho-pathology and maladjustment in children of divorce' in M Brambring, F Losel and S Skowrock (eds) *Children at Risk: Assessment, Longitudinal Research and Intervention* Walter de Gruyter, Berlin. (B) Gerald Caplan was born and educated in Britain. Trained as a psychoanalyst, he began his practice at the Tavistock Clinic in London in 1945, with contemporaries such as John Bowlby and Michael Balint. Although he specialised in child and family psychiatry, it was at the Tavistock Institute of Human Relations that he began to question what more could be done to help forestall the onset of serious psychological disturbance following stressful life-changing events. The opportunity to explore this question came in 1952 when he took up a post at Harvard, first as Professorial Director of the Community Mental Health Training Programme at the Harvard School of Public Health, and then in 1964 as Director of the Laboratory of Community Psychiatry in the Harvard Medical School. Here he was responsible for the training of psychiatrists, psychologists, social workers and nurses specialising in preventive community mental health. One of his earlier collaborators was Erich Lindemann (see further below).

serious parental conflict and separation. In this respect, in subsequent chapters I shall concentrate first on the role of schools as 'first responders' (although this could apply equally to GPs and primary healthcare teams which are readily accessible, non-stigmatising and part of children's everyday lives).[243] Second, I shall look at the 'backup' preventive support services of the family justice system when parental conflict and separation result in potential litigation under the Child Arrangements Programme (CAP) (see Chapter Ten).

As mentioned in the Introduction to Part II of this book, my aim is to revive interest in preventive social psychiatry, and what became known in the 1960s and 1970s as the crisis model of mental health and the related practice of crisis intervention. In my opinion, this school of thought largely complements more recent empirical findings from the field of developmental psychology, advanced particularly in the United Kingdom by Professor Sir Michael Rutter and Professor Gordon Harold, to which I referred in Chapter Three.

Both theoretical approaches are concerned with reducing risk to children's mental health and with promoting the emotional resilience and social wellbeing of those affected by parental conflict and separation. Both take into account stressors, internal as well as external, which can seriously impact on a family's overall mental health and social functioning. Even so, I find it puzzling that, with the exception of an important paper concerning prevention by Caroline and Philip Cowan,[244] little reference is made to the obvious complementarity between these two important schools of thought – at least in the professional literature that I have considered. I suspect one reason for this is the well-known tendencies for professionals in various areas of specialist knowledge to build defensive 'silos' to protect their professional expertise and status in a competitive world – a point to which I shall return when considering interprofessional collaboration and training in the concluding chapters (Chapters Thirteen and Fourteen) of this book. At all events, I consider that in this particular

---

[243] M Balint (1957) *The Doctor, His Patient and the Illness* Harcourt Publishing, London. This classic study of general medical practice throws light on the crucial role of the GP as a first responder for patients whose physical presenting problems are frequently accompanied by anxiety and stress or may be psychosomatic in origin. This text was reproduced in 2000 with an updated introduction by John A. Balint, Michael's son, and published by Churchill Livingstone, London.

[244] C P Cowan and P A Cowan (2012) 'Prevention: intervening with couples at challenging family transition points' in A Balfour, M Morgan, C Vincent (eds) *How Couple Relationships Shape Our World: Clinical Practice, Research and Policy Perspectives* Karnac Books, London, pp1–14.

field both schools of thought should be brought into a much closer conceptual relationship with each other. But for now, in this chapter, I concentrate on exploring why the Caplanian approach to preventive mental health remains highly relevant for practitioners and policy makers alike.

To briefly recap, in the previous chapter I drew on qualitative research evidence with which I was closely associated. This illustrated, in children's own words, how they experienced episodes of for the most part intensely stressful conflict between their parents which led to parental separation and divorce. For many youngsters this was a 'crisis', a term used in a specific sense to mean a period of emotional turmoil. This temporarily disturbed their normal psychological equilibrium or homeostasis (the reasonably steady state of normal life). Therefore, in this chapter I outline the key elements of the crisis model of mental health, briefly explaining its development in the period following the Second World War. I then summarise the related practice of short-term crisis intervention, which can be used by various services offering support to children as they adapt socially and psychologically to challenges posed by stressful life-changing events – in this instance, parental conflict and separation.

I conclude the chapter by speculating as to why such a preventive approach has not caught on in the United Kingdom despite mounting evidence of the long-term risks to young people's mental health and wellbeing resulting from the breakdown of parental relationships.

An outline of the concept: the crisis model of mental health

Novelists and dramatists have known from time immemorial the significance of crisis periods which determine the fate of individuals and groups. Dramatic effect occurs because a crisis has a peak or sudden turning point reached after a period of mounting tension. Often, individuals 'rise to the occasion' and after a short while overcome the challenges posed by the stress-provoking event, but others fail to do so and subsequently encounter further difficulties and crises.

In the period following the Second World War, behavioural analyses of these situations led to the view that a crisis occurs when some stressful event produces a major disorientating psychological upset or disequilibrium within an individual, a small group, such as a family, or a social institution. As my co-authors and I put it:

Typically such crises occur when people are faced with a serious threat or sudden loss (often referred to as a stressor) such as bereavement, loss of job, onset of serious illness etc., which cannot be dealt with by the person's normal coping mechanisms.[245]

As we have seen in the previous chapter, in the context of parental separation, the loss that children experience is often most acutely felt in relation to the parent who moves out of the family home. However, they may also fear the loss of close friends, the possibility of moving house and school, and the loss of contact with relatives such as grandparents – in other words, the loss of all their important social support systems. I consider this point more closely in outlining key stages in a typical crisis response (see further below).

Post-war development of the conceptual building blocks

Homeostasis in family relations

While professionals who work psychotherapeutically in the field of couple and family relations will be familiar with the concept of homeostasis, originally developed in physics and physiology, others such as family lawyers, school teachers and policy makers may not be. So it needs a little explaining. Homeostasis refers to the self-regulating principle which preserves the intactness and continuity of the human organism in response to changing circumstances, for example, the maintenance of normal blood temperature as external temperatures fluctuate. Transposed by various social psychologists to family group relations, it explains the normal capacity to maintain coordinated psychosocial functioning under constantly changing conditions. It is therefore concerned with maintaining a sense of social and emotional balance in coping with and adapting to not too stressful change. By contrast, a 'crisis' response is triggered when a stressful event in effect temporarily overwhelms these normal coping mechanisms. This fundamental concept, based on observations of behaviour in the face of overwhelming stress, was explored in various contexts by social psychologists in the years following the Second World War.

---

[245] I Butler, L Scanlan, M Robinson, G Douglas and M Murch (2003) *Divorcing Children: Children's Experience of Their Parents' Divorce* Jessica Kingsley, London at p18.

The social psychiatry movement

In particular, there were two major areas of interdisciplinary research – anthropological and psychological – which, as it were, laid its conceptual foundation stones. First, there was a group of American psychiatrists and clinical psychologists who were exploring the social pressures associated with various kinds of mental illness (clinical depression, acute anxiety, schizophrenic conditions etc). Some of them, such as Alexander Leighton,[246] an anthropologist turned psychiatrist, formed part of a movement in the US in the 1960s known as social psychiatry. This in turn had been influenced by Kurt Lewin's field theory, which saw behaviour as a function of persons in their immediate social environment and the social norms (sometimes referred to as social rules) to which they are subject.[247]

Families and their social networks

Another important work building on Lewin's field theory was that of Elizabeth Bott, a social scientist with degrees in psychology and anthropology. Her seminal 1957 book *Family and social network* was based on field research in London concerning the relationship between conjugal partners and relatives, friends and neighbours (that is, their social networks). This demonstrated empirically that the type of relationship between husband and wife was related to the type of networks or social relationships within which they lived. Bott suggested that the degree and extent of a family's connectedness to their social network is 'a function on the one hand of a complex set of forces in the total environment and on the other of the family themselves and the reactions to these forces'.[248]

As we will see, the availability or otherwise of a network of supportive relationships is crucially important in understanding the way in which families and particularly children cope with stressful crises. Even so, it is fair to say that neither Elizabeth Bott nor the social psychiatry movement in the 1950s and 1960s focused specifically on children.

---

[246] A H Leighton (1959) *My Name is Legion: Foundations of a Theory of Man in Relation to Culture* Basic Books, New York.

[247] K Lewin (1936) *Principles of Topological Psychology* McGraw Hill, New York. See also K Lewin (1959) *Field Theory in Social Science* (ed D Cartwright) Tavistock Publications, London.

[248] E Bott (1957) *Family and Social Network* Tavistock Publications, London at p220.

Studies of bereavement and other critical stresses

Another important conceptual building block for what became known as the crisis model of mental health emerged from a series of post-Second World War studies concerning the impact of stressful events of various kinds on individuals and families. For the sake of brevity, I have here to be highly selective, choosing just two key seminal researches which Gerald Caplan (described as 'the father of community mental health'[249]) referred to in a series of workshops on crisis intervention which I attended, held at the Tavistock Institute of Human Relations, London, in the early 1970s. The first was by a sociologist, Reuben Hill. He studied what he termed 'crisis-prone families' during wartime following the conscription of husbands/fathers. He observed that while some families rode out the consequent hardship without apparent disorganisation, most families initially seemed, at least temporarily, 'paralysed' by the sudden absence of the father. Hill went on to produce a paper, 'Generic features of families under stress', which developed a conceptual framework for viewing families beset by various kinds of temporarily overwhelming stress – a framework which I shall outline below in diagrammatic form.[250]

The second seminal paper concerned the crisis of bereavement and grief reactions related to war casualties studied by a psychiatrist, Erich Lindemann. In particular, this considered cases where grief took the form of what he termed delayed reaction, manifested in the later emergence of various serious psychological disorders, particularly clinical depression.[251] As Lindemann wrote:

> If the bereavement occurs at a time when the patient is confronted with important tasks and when it is necessary to maintain the morale of others, he may show little or no reaction for weeks or even much longer.[252]

---

[249] D L Cutler (1993) 'Roots, trunks, branches and blossoms: a preface to Gerald Caplan's preventive psychiatry programme' in *Community Mental Health Journal* 29 pp263–265. See also G E Langley (1997) 'Meeting Gerald Caplan' *The Psychiatric Bulletin* 21 pp181–183.

[250] R Hill (1958) 'Generic features of families under stress' *Social Casework* XXXIX (2-3); reproduced in H Parad (ed) (1967) *Crisis Intervention: Selected Readings* Family Service Association of America, New York at pp32–52.

[251] Nowadays we term such delayed reactions 'post-traumatic stress disorders'. After the First Wold War the term 'shell shock' was frequently used.

[252] E Lindemann (1944) 'Symptomology and management of acute grief' *American Journal of Psychiatry* 101; reproduced in H J Parad (ed) *Crisis Intervention: Selected*

Lindemann described other forms of what he termed 'distorted reactions' to bereavements and other critical separations. These included overactivity without a 'sense of loss' and prolonged 'agitated depression' with sleeping difficulties and increased feelings of worthlessness.

Lindemann of course was not the first to study grief reactions. Freud in his *Mourning and melancholia* (1917) observed that the loss of someone important normally gives rise to grief accompanied by a mixture of emotions such as anger and sadness.[253] Freud realised that mourning involved a process of coming to terms with the reality of loss.

Following on from Lindemann, the whole subject of loss and separation has since been explored, most notably in the 1970s by John Bowlby in his classic three-volume text *Attachment and loss*.[254] This examined the way that *children* responded to the temporary or permanent loss of the mother figure. Also in the 1970s, Colin Murray Parkes produced a text bringing together various studies of *adult* grief, which in many ways complements Bowlby's work.[255] I mention Parkes here because in the mid-1960s he worked with Lindemann and Gerald Caplan in the Laboratory of Community Psychiatry in the Harvard Medical School. It was here that Caplan opened up the whole concept of community psychiatry and preventive mental health, linked conceptually to the crisis model of mental health and the practice of crisis intervention (see further below).

The conceptual strands of what Caplan and colleagues at Harvard sought to develop as a model for a comprehensive community programme for preventing mental disorders rested on a number of different empirical and clinical studies of major life-changing and stressful turning points in people's lives. These included not only bereavement, but other unexpected critical events, such as loss of job, maternal reactions to premarital birth and to the onset of sudden illness, as well as more common maturational and situational turning points such as becoming a parent for the first time and, for children, starting school and subsequent moves from primary to secondary school.

In one of his last publications Caplan himself describes the way that, over a period of some twenty years, the conceptual framework developed from both research and clinical practice. This culminated in

---

Readings Family Association of America, New York at p13.

[253] S Freud (1917) 'Mourning and melancholia' *Collected Works: Standard Edition* vol 14 pp243–258.

[254] J Bowlby (1973) *Attachment and Loss, Volume 2: Separation, Anxiety and Anger* Pelican Books, London. Also J Bowlby (1985) *Attachment and Loss, Volume 3: Loss, Sadness and Depression* Pelican Books, London.

[255] C M Parkes (1975) *Bereavement: Studies of Grief in Adult Life* Pelican Books, London.

a paper and book which stressed not only the importance of supportive networks to sustain and strengthen individuals experiencing the temporary disequilibrium of the crisis, but the need to 'support the care-giving supporters'.[256]

With respect to children, he observed that some crises could be associated with normal developmental phases, for example, hormonal changes on entering puberty in adolescence. He describes these as 'endogenous'. Another category of crisis termed 'exogenous' can be traced to particular problems in the child's environment. Into this category, of course, fall children's crisis reactions provoked by the loss of a parent and by intense interparental conflict and parental separation – a subject which Caplan addressed towards the end of his career while working as a clinician and Emeritus Professor of Child Psychiatry at the Hebrew University, Israel.[257]

In this context, he foresaw the need for some kind of triage mechanism which divided the potential population of children at risk into three groups: those low-risk children with no need for professional support, those who were in need of and could likely benefit from primary prevention and short-term crisis intervention, and those who needed longer-term psychotherapeutic help. In this respect, Caplan and his collaborators, working in both the clinical and Israeli family justice context, identified potential pathogenic factors as including high parental conflict, one parent recruiting a child to take sides, abandonment by the non-custodial parent, and a failure by parents to inform children of their separation and the likely consequences – all factors which, as we have seen in Chapter Three, have now been widely understood and confirmed by a number of empirical studies, particularly from the field of developmental psychology.

---

[256] G Caplan (1974) *Support Systems and Community Mental Health: Lectures in Concept Development* Behavioural Publications, New York at pp75–77. The idea of 'supporting the supporters' was elaborated in two publications: G Caplan (1970) *Theory and Practice of Mental Health Consultation* Basic Books, New York; and G Caplan and R Caplan (1993) *Mental Health Consultation and Collaboration* Jossey-Bass, San Francisco, CA.

[257] G Caplan (1989) 'Prevention of psychopathology and maladjustment in children of divorce' in M Brambring, F Lösel and H Skowronek (eds) *Children at Risk: Assessment, Longitudinal Research and Intervention* Walter de Gruyter, Berlin, pp367–393. See also G Caplan (1986) 'Preventing psychological disorders in children of divorce: guidelines for the general practitioner' *British Medical Journal* 292 pp1563–1566.

Simultaneous crises: 'double and triple whammies'

While the focus of this chapter is the application of this conceptual model of preventive mental health as it concerns children whose interparental conflict results in parental separation and divorce, and while I have illustrated such children's crisis reactions, drawn largely from the Cardiff *Divorcing children* study, it should be remembered that even children not subject to the problems of family dissolution and reconstruction can nevertheless be confronted with stressful experiences which temporarily overwhelm their normal coping mechanisms. For example, some find the transition from primary school to secondary school particularly challenging. especially if it means the loss of friends, trusted teachers and entry into a totally strange, rather frightening new setting (see further Chapter Thirteen). Similarly, some children find the onset of puberty, and its associated biopsychological tensions and hormonal changes, difficult to cope with, given that these may confuse their sense of identity and social relationships. Thus Reynolds et al assert that 'girls are more likely to find the challenges of puberty combined with the move to a larger more impersonal secondary school more stressful than boys'.[258] Such normal critical transitions may result in a range of psychosomatic disorders (eating problems, difficulties with sleep etc) and behaviours associated with feelings of acute anxiety, frustration and anger – all of which to the outsider may indicate that the child is grappling with a crisis. When these sorts of endogenous crises coincide or overlap with stress provoked by parental conflict and separation, they act as a 'double whammy', adding to emotional distress and tension. Being left alone and socially isolated in these circumstances increases the child's vulnerability to maladaptive and mentally unhealthy response. This may become so entrenched as to damage the child's education and life chances. Early preventive crisis intervention and supportive help therefore becomes all the more necessary.

Five key stages of crisis resolution

In the previous chapter I gave a number of verbatim extracts from interviews with children and young people which, one way or another, showed how they had reacted to violent rows between their parents and parental separation. As we have seen, for many of them this was a critical turning point in the trajectory of their family life, as indeed it may

---

[258] J Reynolds, C Houlston, L Coleman, G Harold (2014) *Parental Conflict: Outcomes and Interventions for Children and Families* Policy Press and One Plus One at p54.

well have been for their parents. At this point, having summarised the way the Caplanian conceptual framework developed, for those readers who may be unfamiliar with the crisis model, I summarise with the aid of Figure 1 the key features of a typical adjustment process to crisis.

Stage one: shock and disbelief

We have seen how most of the children in the Cardiff study described feeling shocked when they found out about their parents' separation, particularly when it was unexpected.[259] As with many other kinds of crisis – sudden bereavement, unexpected injury, loss of job etc – the initial stage is often one of disbelief and emotional distress. This brief initial reaction is usually quickly followed by a sense of grief, crying and a feeling of acute sadness. As we have seen, the majority of children said that they had cried when they first found out that their parents were separating. Nevertheless, a small number reported feeling relief, as they had been aware that the situation between their parents had become intolerable. But for those who were initially shocked and overwhelmed, a sense of confusion and uncertainty rapidly followed – again, this is typical of crisis responses in other kinds of stressful situations.

Stage two: onset of grief

Many who have experienced a sudden bereavement will remember that once the initial shock has worn off, a period of tense confusion and depressed irritability usually follows. The person is preoccupied with the precipitating event and the problems it presents. Often memories of similarly overwhelming problems from the past flood back, contributing further to a sense of hopelessness and depression. Difficulties with concentration and sleeping are common. So it was with the majority of children in the Cardiff study, who reported feeling very unsettled and worried, with disturbed sleep patterns. As the researchers put it:

> During this time they were trying to come to terms simultaneously with the changes happening in their family; with new living and contact arrangements; coping with their ongoing feelings of uncertainty about the future

---

[259] I Butler, L Scanlan, M Robinson, G Douglas and M Murch (2003) *Divorcing Children: Children's Experience of Their Parents' Divorce* Jessica Kingsley, London at pp43–45.

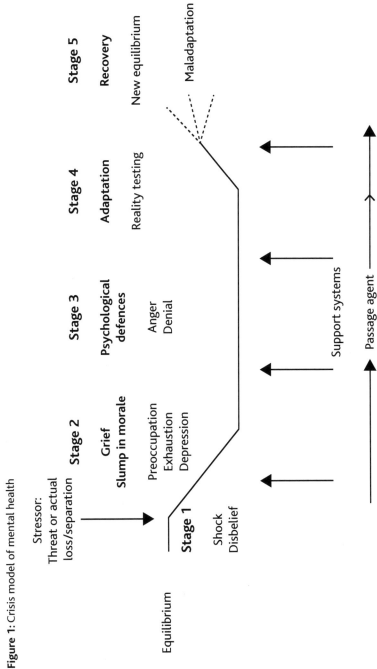

Figure 1: Crisis model of mental health

and dealing with the continued confusion and worry surrounding the breakdown.[260]

Many were trying to deal with strong feelings of loss, missing their absent parents. Again, as we have seen, some felt angry as well as confused and preoccupied. In addition, it should be remembered that since one or both of the children's parents may well have been simultaneously affected by the crisis, this could make for further communication difficulties within the family.

With respect to supporting children at this stage in the resolution of the crisis, it should also be remembered that not all of the children's schools had been made aware of what was happening at home. Yet, as Caplan pointed out, given that a child's school is such an important social setting, the well-trained teacher 'should be alert for signs that a particular student is beginning to show evidence of strain'.[261] This will probably be manifested in reduced classroom performance or in difficulties with other students. I return to this point in Chapter Eight and Chapter Thirteen, when considering the role of the school as first responder to children in crisis, within the broader context of crisis intervention as a primary preventive measure to foster children's resilience and wellbeing.

Christopher Clulow, while working as a psychotherapist at the Tavistock Centre for Couple Relationships, observed that for both children and adults parental breakdown and separation can be harder to come to terms with than a death in the family, partly because the continuing uncertainty prevents 'closure' and partly because parental conflict and separation can weaken trusts and confidence between the parents and child. He writes:

> the consequences of that can be that [the children] worry about their future security – if one parent leaves why not both? They may blame themselves for the rift or they may become angry about their powerlessness in a situation which is not of their choosing and where their wishes and feelings may be disregarded by those who are supposed to care for them. For in divorce the wishes and sometimes the interests

---

[260] Ibid at p47.

[261] G Caplan (1974) *Support Systems and Community Mental Health: Lectures in Concept Development* Behavioural Publications, New York at p170.

of parents and children are likely to diverge in a way that rarely happens in bereavement.[262]

This point was endorsed by the National Health Service in 1997.[263] This supports the view that children facing the crisis of interparental conflict and separation deserve particular attention and support. This is especially so if they are simultaneously grappling with other key transitional points, such as moving from primary to secondary school, when they may lose the support of former friends and teachers, and have to adapt to a new school setting.

Stage three: constructing psychological defences

We all have different ways of adapting to loss and enduring the emotional pain of grief. Anger and resentment at what has happened is a common reaction, and in family breakdown and separation these feelings are generally focused on the person perceived to have caused the event. When a person is in crisis, whether an adult or a child, it is normal to lose interest in the daily affairs of everyday life, to experience feelings of loneliness, loss of appetite, periods of weeping, sleeping problems, and a preoccupation with the events and separations that have precipitated the crisis. With respect to bereavement, Lindemann noted that psychic energy is withdrawn from everyday life and is concentrated on reviewing details and memories which were enriched by association with the deceased.[264] As we have seen in Chapter Five, a number of the children interviewed in the Cardiff *Divorcing children* study described feeling isolated, lonely and depressed, sometimes marked by disturbed

---

[262] C Clulow (1991) 'Making, breaking and remaking marriage' in D Clark (ed) *Marriage, Domestic Life and Social Change: Writings for Jackie Burgoyne (1944–1988)* Routledge, London at p176. See also D Black (1984) 'Sundered families: the effect of loss of a parent' *Adoption and Fostering* 8 pp38–43. In this research-based article, Dora Black, a distinguished British child psychiatrist, systematically compared and contrasted the child's experiences of parental death and parental divorce. She found that efforts to maintain psychological connection – described as 'remain fantasies' – were more common among children of divorce than among bereaved children.

[263] NHS Centre for Reviews and Dissemination, University of York (1997) *Effective Healthcare Bulletin: Mental Health Promotion in High-risk Groups* at p3.

[264] E Lindemann (1944) 'Symptomatology and management of acute grief' in H Parad (1965) *Crisis Intervention: Selected Readings*, Family Services Association of America, New York, pp7–21.

sleep patterns.[265] Of course they also had to learn to cope with the uncertainties of the future, including the often thorny issue of contact with the parent who had left home. This could have involved having to come to terms with any new partner that their now non-resident parent may have acquired. This could be further complicated if that partner had children from a previous relationship. In our Cardiff study there was a small group of children who seemed to be beset by particularly difficult feelings of upset, anger and confusion which had apparently lasted for some time. When interviewd, a few of these said that they continued to feel isolated and could see only the negative side of what had happened.[266]

Stages four and five: adaptive and maladaptive reactions towards recovery

It is fundamental to the Caplanian model that if later, more serious, mental health and behavioural problems are to be avoided, the crisis period has to result in a realistic and socially acceptable way of living. The person in crisis has to discover a new emotional equilibrium. Thus, summarised in Chapter Five, a number of children and young people referred to a wish to get back to normality, to re-establish some sort of stability in their relationship with both parents.

   In respect to the thorny issue of contact, my co-authors and I wrote that:

> We were impressed by the extent to which children were prepared to forego their own preferences in order to facilitate arrangements. Their own involvement in managing contact forced them to manage time in new ways and to a degree which children from 'intact families' seldom have to. They had to do so in situations that could be highly charged emotionally. Moreover, they had to balance a number of competing demands.[267]

In doing so, a number had discovered unexpected abilities and capacities within themselves. They had gained in self-confidence and acquired a

---

[265] I Butler, L Scanlan, M Robinson, G Douglas and M Murch (2003) *Divorcing Children: Children's Experience of Their Parents' Divorce* Jessica Kingsley, London at pp46–47.

[266] Ibid at pp48–49.

[267] Ibid at p143.

new more mature perspective on life.[268] Thus, for these children, once successfully worked through, the crisis appeared to have strengthened their resilience. Moreover, in order to achieve this successful outcome, it was clear that it had been important that during the crisis they had received reliable information regarding what to expect as their family circumstances changed and had access to sources of emotional comfort and support, to encourage them to deal with the consequent challenges and problems. As we have seen, support mostly came from important figures in their existing social network of close trustworthy friends and relatives – people who Caplan referred to as 'natural caregivers'.

On the other hand, there were a few children who, at least when interviewed, continued to harbour unrealistic expectations that their divorced parents would get back together, and who seemed to have resorted to magical thinking, believing that they were living through a nightmare from which they would one day wake up.[269]

Crisis intervention: a preventive community mental health approach

It is fundamental to the crisis model and the general framework of thinking based upon it, which gave rise to the concept of community-based preventive mental health, that both adults and children caught up in the throes of a crisis need support to encourage a realistic adaptation to radically altered circumstances. Caplan pointed to two key features of a crisis which are important for those undertaking preventive work.[270] First, a person in crisis usually feels a greater need for help than when in their normal psychological state. Moreover, the signs of emotional distress caused by crisis usually stimulate people around to respond empathetically. This applies to so-called 'natural caregivers', such as friends and relatives, as well as to those in the helping professions who might be on hand as first responders (for example, school teachers, school counsellors, GPs, health visitors and others in the primary healthcare services). Second, during a crisis, a person is more easily influenced than at other times. As Caplan graphically put it:

> He is in an unstable equilibrium like a person standing on one leg – a slight push tips his balance from one side to

---

[268] Ibid at p157.

[269] Ibid at p156.

[270] G Caplan (1974) *Support Systems and Community Mental Health: Lectures in Concept Development* Behavioural Publications, New York at p203.

the other ... a crisis therefore represents a leverage point ... the person can be more easily influenced at such times to choose a mentally healthy path ... This means that a small amount of help and effort will produce a much bigger effect if focused on people at crisis times than if applied to people in stable equilibrium.[271]

Likewise, Howard Parad, another American theorist and a professor of social work, explained in a nutshell the justification for short-term help and support:

Persons in crisis states are usually more ready for and amenable to interventive help if it is offered at the right time and at the right place; that is, during the throws of a crisis before rigid defences and related maladaptive solutions have become consolidated ... Therefore a minimal interventive force, administered by a skilled person with appropriate supporting services, can produce a maximum result in a relatively short period of time.[272]

For those wishing to support children in crisis resulting from interparental conflict and separation, this raises a number of practice and policy questions: how best to mobilise appropriate community preventive support resources, and how to deploy them at a time when they can make the maximum positive and economic impact?

The answer to these questions will depend on how to identify those children who are most at risk. This may require the use of some form of triage mechanism to distinguish between those who are coping well with the aid of their own psychosocial resources (for example, schools, friends, relatives etc) from those who need short-term 'passage agent' supportive crisis intervention (see further below) and those who are exhibiting signs of more serious behavioural and psychological disorder requiring longer-term psychotherapeutic help. As I show in the next chapter, to my knowledge at least one agency, Cafcass Cymru, is already successfully using a specially designed psychometric instrument with children subject to private law litigation in the local family courts in Wales. I argue that this or some similar tool should be deployed more

---

[271] Ibid at p123.

[272] H J Parad (1965) 'Preventive casework: problems and implications' in H J Parad (ed) *Crisis Intervention: Selected Readings* Family Services Association of America, New York at p289.

widely. For example, in terms of first responders in schools, it could be used by specialist trained school counsellors; it could also be used in the context of secondary prevention within the family justice system by Cafcass in England as well as in Wales.

A further point to remember is that children in these circumstances may well be in special need of preventive supportive crisis intervention. This is because unlike other stressful crises, such as bereavement or sudden onset of serious illness, parental conflict leading to separation and divorce is often a cumulative process. Many parents are ashamed to reveal this conflict to the outside world. When it does become more public, it can evoke decidedly ambivalent, even unhelpful responses from natural caregivers such as relatives, grandparents, friends and neighbours. Such persons may be tempted to take sides and thus reinforce the parental conflict or offer unrealistic solutions at the point of crisis adaption. Moreover, as we have seen, many children feel very isolated in these circumstances and are left feeling overwhelmed when the crisis strikes, particularly if their parents are also struggling and are unable to provide them with comforting support.

Crisis intervention: adjusting the approach to stages in the crisis resolution process

I do not intend to go into detail about the method of crisis intervention, but merely to outline the salient points. As mentioned above, the aim is to provide assistance to those in a crisis so that they can deal positively and realistically with the predicament they face. Of course, the assistance delivered will vary depending on whether the professional practitioner is dealing with the child's parents together, as a mediator or counsellor; dealing with a parent individually, as in the case of a family lawyer; or dealing with a child or young person, as might be the case with a school teacher, youth worker, GP or practice counsellor. The professional setting and role will thus shape the approach, but the essential technique of crisis intervention will be broadly the same.

Stage one: absorbing shock

The timing of intervention is another factor which should determine the nature of the support that should be offered. Thus in the early stages of a crisis when a person is in a state of shock, scarcely believes what has happened and is struggling to absorb the impact of the stressful event, all that can normally be done is to ensure that the individual has time and space to come to terms with what has happened. In these initial stages the person in crisis may feel quite overwhelmed and unable to cope with everyday life tasks. So for those caregivers wishing to help, the main concern at this stage may well be to take the pressure off and to find alternative ways to compensate for the subject's temporary inability to concentrate and cope. For example, this could be by helping with simple everyday tasks like making meals, accompanying children to school, asking teachers to excuse the child from homework and so on.

Stage two: grief and mourning

It may also be necessary to encourage the person to express grief rather than 'be brave and keep a stiff upper lip'. Grief is a lonely business. We have seen in the previous chapter how a number of children in the Cardiff *Divorcing children* study said they cried and felt bereft when their parents separated, sometimes retreating to their own room to do so. Parkes, in his classic study of bereavement, has written:

> There is an optimum 'level of grieving' which varies from one person to another. Some will cry and sob, others will betray their feelings in other ways. The important thing is for feelings to be permitted to emerge into consciousness. How they appear on the surface may be of secondary importance.[273]

Authorities in psychiatry seem agreed that bottling up feelings of grief carries serious dangers for subsequent mental health.[274] In the context of preventive mental health, Caplan has talked of the importance of 'grief work', which in most cultures evokes support from friends and

---

[273] C M Parkes (1975) *Bereavement: States of Grief in Adult Life* Penguin Books, London at p140.

[274] See E Lindemann (1944) 'Symptomology and management of acute grief' *American Journal of Psychiatry* 101; reproduced in H Parad (ed) (1967) *Crisis Intervention: Selected Readings* Family Service Association of America, New York at p13. This seminal article develops the observation based on clinical studies that 'morbid grief' reactions represent distortions of normal grief. See also Carhart-Harris, R Maybeg, A Melizia and D Nutt (2003) 'Mourning and melancholia revisited: correspondences between principles of Freudian metapsychology and empirical findings of neuropsychiatry' *Annals of General Psychiatry* 7 pp9–42; cited in D Hewson, C Clulow, H Drake (2014) *Couple Therapy for Depression: A Clinician's Guide to Integrative Practice* Oxford University Press at p13.

neighbours by way of condolence.[275] But as mentioned above, when parents separate, this may merely result in partisan support for one parent or the other. This may reinforce conflict, while the children in the middle may be thrown back to their own emotional resources, to cope as best they can with grief on their own. Indeed, some children interviewed in the Cardiff *Divorcing children* study who appeared to be adapting poorly reported that they were having to give support to a parent who was having more difficulty than them in coming to terms with the marriage breakdown. This raised questions among the research team of whether these children were more prone to later delayed grief reactions.

Establishing psychological defences

We have seen from the reactions of some of the children in the Cardiff study that they felt particularly angry about their parents' separation, and some expressed this anger at school. According to the crisis model, such expressions are not be to understood as in some way pathological, but as part of the normal grieving process, as psychological defences (in psychoanalytic terms, those of projection) are marshalled to ease the pain of grief. Even so, there are dangers for interveners to be aware of at this stage. Thus, according to Hewson et al this entirely healthy but temporary adaptation can be unhealthily redirected as self-blame and persistent depression. In this way, they write, the feelings of anger can get turned onto the self, 'resulting in the merciless self-criticism and self-abnegation that is characteristic of many depressive states'. According to this view, this maladaptive reaction serves to protect the depressed person from 'awareness of the reality of the loss as well as from expressing feelings of anger and hatred stirred up by it'.[276]

Another observed defence is that of denial, that is, acting as if the stressful event has had little or no effect or consequences. Again, as we have seen, a few children struggled with the notion that a parent had left for good. Some felt that they would wake up from what seemed to be a nightmare and that it would all be over. For others it was reported that 'some children coped by avoiding thinking about

---

[275] G Caplan (1974) *Support Systems and Community Mental Health: Lectures in Concept Development* Behavioural Publications, New York at p205.

[276] D Hewson, C Clulow, H Drake (2014) *Couple Therapy for Depression: A Clinician's Guide to Integrative Practice* Oxford University Press at p13.

what was bothering them either by sheer efforts of will or by escapist activities like watching television or sleeping'.[277]

Other forms of, often delayed, distorted maladaptive reactions, noted by Lindemann, Caplan and other social psychiatrists, include what they termed 'conversion symptoms'. These took the form of psychosomatic illness such as ulcerated colitis and asthma – conditions which have a psychical manifestation but which, according to these clinical theorists, may have been aggravated by suppressed emotional reactions to an earlier critical stressor such as bereavement.[278]

Reynolds et al refer to a number of studies which variously point to the impact on children's health, family social relationships and education. They report that with respect to health, parental conflict has been found to be associated with 'digestive problems, fatigue, reduced psychical growth, headaches and abdominal pains'. The research literature also suggests that some young people may attempt to 'self-medicate in order to manage the psychological distress arising out of their family environment'.[279] With respect to older children, various studies cited point to an association between parental conflict and 'risky' health and behavioural problems such as smoking, drug and alcohol misuse, and sexual promiscuity.

Michael Rutter has stressed the point that not only do parents influence children, but children can influence parents: that the interaction is a two-way process.[280] Perhaps this is no truer than in the case of sleep deprivation. Parents who lose sleep get 'ratty' with each other and function less well. Likewise, child sleep disturbance can be an indicator of family stress and can be associated with difficulties at school.[281]

---

[277] I Butler, L Scanlan, M Robinson, G Douglas and M Murch (2003) *Divorcing Children: Children's Experience of Their Parents' Divorce* Jessica Kingsley, London at p49 and at p156.

[278] I Butler, L Scanlan, M Robinson, G Douglas and M Murch (2003) *Divorcing Children: Children's Experience of Their Parents' Divorce* Jessica Kingsley, London at pp148–153.

[279] J Reynolds, C Houlston, L Coleman, G Harold (2014) *Parental Conflict: Outcomes and Interventions for Children and Families* Policy Press and One Plus One at p27.

[280] M Rutter (1999) 'Resilience concepts and findings: implications for family therapy', *Journal of Family Therapy*, 21, pp119–44 http://onlinelibrary.wiley.com/doi/10.1111/1467-6427.00108/pdf.

[281] M El-Sheikh, J A Buckholt, P Keller, E M Cummings and C Acebo (2007) 'Child emotional insecurity and academic achievement: the role of sleep deprivation' *Journal of Family Psychology* 21(1) pp29–38. Also M El-Sheikh, J A Buckholt, J Mize and C Acebo (2006) 'Marital conflict and disruption of children's sleep' *Child Development* 77(1) pp31–43.

As far as supportive crisis intervention is concerned, it may be necessary to sensitively challenge these sorts of maladaptive crisis responses by helping the subject, whether child or adult, to face up to the realities of what has happened. Certainly it is important for caregivers not to collude with the unreality of these responses when they first appear during the crisis. Indeed, as far as short-term intensive crisis intervention is concerned, the stage in the crisis process when the subject is beginning to look forward to find solutions to changed circumstances can be viewed as the key period when encouraging support is most necessary.

Support from natural caregivers

As we have seen, for most children in the Cardiff study, parents were the most obvious actual or potential providers of comfort and support throughout the critical process of family change resulting from parental separation and divorce (and sometimes re-partnering, which can bring its own crises for children). As was noted, where parents were on reasonable terms with one another or where the children felt able to sustain separate and positive relationships with both parents, children often considered their parents as an accessible and useful source of emotional support, information and advice. In addition, children often chose to go to their parents when they needed psychical comfort. It was further reported that 'children usually considered their resident parent best placed to provide them with support and a number of children regretted the more limited access they had to the other non-resident parent, particularly boys with non-residential fathers.'[282]

But not all children felt able to turn to their parents for support. Some felt that their parents would not understand what they were experiencing. Others thought their parents were too upset and confused themselves to be able to help. A few turned to grandparents for comforting support, but a number of children interviewed considered that their grandparents were also either too upset or too close to the family's problems to be able to provide support.

---

[282] I Butler, L Scanlan, M Robinson, G Douglas and M Murch (2003) *Divorcing Children: Children's Experience of Their Parents' Divorce* Jessica Kingsley, London at p149.

Support from school friends

As has been pointed out in Chapter Five, for most children in the Cardiff study it was their friends who provided their most significant supportive relationship, especially for those who found it difficult to draw support from their parents. Of course, it was the social context of the school which provided the best opportunity for these close peer relationships to be established – a point which I consider further below in Chapter Eight when considering the potential role of teachers and school counsellors in offering short-term crisis intervention, providing passage agent support (see further below) and facilitating children's friendship groups.

Taken overall, there is evidence from the Avon Longitudinal Study of Parents and Children (ALSPAC) examined by Judy Dunn, a distinguished British psychologist, which highlights the important supporting role of friends, grandparents and siblings in moderating the impact of separation on children.[283]

The techniques of crisis intervention: the role of the passage agent

One of the reasons why I have chosen to focus on the Caplanian school of thought in thinking about preventive intervention is that the technique of crisis intervention does not require specialised psychological training or sophistication. It has a common professional language based on the crisis model which is easy to understand. The approach may be used by a range of professionals in the health, educational, social welfare and family justice services – all of whom may encounter children and families beset by highly conflicted interparental relations, often leading to separation and divorce. Any of these practitioners may be called upon by the parents and the children separately or as a family unit to help them through the critical process of family status change consequent on the breakdown in the parental relationship. This supporting role is termed a 'passage agent': someone who acts as a supportive guide to children and parents when families break down and enter strange unfamiliar territory, invariably not knowing what to expect from day to day.

The term passage agent may need a little explanation. The processes of family breakdown, parental separation and divorce involve all family members in a change of social status. As Michael King has written:

---

[283] J Dunn (2008) *Family Relationships: Children's Perspectives* One Plus One, London.

A status passage occurs whenever an individual moves to a different part of the social structure involving a loss or gain of privilege or power and a changed identity or sense of self. The concept of status passage covers a wide variety of social transitions, from illness to promotion, from marriage to dying.[284]

Glaser and Strauss suggest that the task of assisting people in the change of status is one which many professions perform. As they explain:

Doctors, lawyers, social workers, counsellors and others see sections of the passage as rough and conceive of themselves as agents who are alert to unknown contingencies with consequences that can be softened. Passage agents make a profession of managing transitions to get passagees through without any bruises.[285]

They further observe that the clients of passage agents are often dependent on the agent for successful navigation of the status passage. This of course conceptually complements Caplan's clinical observation that times of crisis are often the point at which people are most likely to accept help and be influenced by the person performing short-term crisis intervention. In the context of family breakdown and parental separation, until civil legal aid was withdrawn, the parents' solicitors were often the most important passage agent, at least for divorcing parents,[286] although an earlier study suggested that when children's matters were the subject of litigation, this role could be performed to a lesser extent by a Divorce Court Welfare Officer.[287] A later 2005/06 study into the operation of separate representation for children in highly contested private law disputes, conducted for the Department for Constitutional Affairs (now Ministry of Justice) confirmed that this role was in fact performed well by a guardian from Cafcass, and in several instances from the National Youth Advisory Service (NYAS), while for some of the older children the specially appointed children's solicitor

---

[284] M King (1977) 'A status passage analysis' in *Warwick Law Working Paper No 3* at p8.

[285] B G Glaser and A L Strauss (1971) *Status Passage* Routledge and Kegan Paul, London at p51.

[286] G Davis (1988) *Partisans and Mediators: The resolution of divorce disputes* Clarendon Press, Oxford.

[287] M Murch (1980) *Justice and Welfare in Divorce* Sweet & Maxwell, London at p167.

emerged as the key figure.[288] It was reported that most of those who received such support appeared strengthened by it – a view confirmed by some of the children's parents. But there were also other children who appeared not to have found anyone they could trust and relate to, despite having a guardian. They appeared lost, withdrawn, depressed, intimidated or angered by their contact with the family justice system. Nevertheless, overall my research colleagues and I concluded that the findings of this study were an endorsement of the value of separate representation by the so-called 'tandem model' of Cafcass guardians working in partnership with a specialist children's solicitor. We argued for its wider application within the context of reformed child-friendly family courts. As will be seen in the second part of Chapter Eight and in Chapter Thirteen, I have taken on this idea to be developed in the context of the new family justice regime and an enlarged role for Cafcass, which I see as part of the joined-up network of preventive mental health services based on Caplanian principles that I advocate in the concluding chapters of this book.

---

[288] G Douglas, M Murch, C Miles, L Scanlan (2006) *Research Into the Operation of Rule 9.5 of the Family Proceedings Rules 1991* Department for Constitutional Affairs, London at p189. From a sample of 121 Rule 9.5 disputed family cases involving 224 children (45% boys and 55% girls), 15 were interviewed with respect to their experience of being separately represented. Many of their cases had been defined by the judge as 'intractable' and had involved a number of separate court hearings.

SEVEN

The pros and cons of the preventive mental health approach

Introduction

Before outlining in Chapter Eight a practice proposal to introduce a system of crisis intervention in schools, the best place from which to mount non-stigmatic primary preventive measures in this field, to be backed up in the context of secondary prevention by a similar 'passage agent' support role for children from Cafcass when parents commence litigation in the family justice system, I need to consider various points. First, some of the reasons why Caplanian principles of preventive mental health have not generally as yet found their way into practice and policy in England and Wales; second, why services for children in this field, such as they are remain largely uncoordinated and focused on remedial services when problems have become acute and entrenched; and third, why the development of preventive services in particular has proved so difficult.

Obstacles hindering the preventive crisis intervention approach

Over and over again for many years numerous official reports and studies have called for early intervention, particularly in the area of child abuse and neglect. Invariably these inquiries and serious case reviews use hindsight to look back on errors in social work intervention and highlight a serious lack of interagency coordination. Since the 1960s this has led to calls to tighten up managerial supervision and bureaucratic compliance. Yet, as the Munro Report explained, in child protection this produced a compliance culture 'where meeting performance management demands became the dominant focus rather than meeting the needs of children and their families'.[289]

---

[289] E Munro (2011) *The Munro Review of Child Protection: Final Report: A Child-centred System* www.gov.uk at pp19 and 20 paras 1.16–1.21.

Not only has this approach contributed to defensive organisational behaviour and low morale among many social workers, but it has inevitably directed priorities and resources to the most challenging and vulnerable cases where a child's safety is at stake and where removal from a dangerous family situation has to be considered. The problem is that such policy responses invariable come at the expense of early supportive intervention in what are seen as less risky cases. Moreover, when resources are severely restricted and cut as they are when government pursues an austere economic policy with a view to eliminating the public deficit, it is even more difficult for care-giving organisations to make adequate provision for preventive work, even though it is recognised that failure to do so will lead later to even more serious acute emergencies. In this way a vicious circle is established. One could say that this is one of the major social policy dilemmas of our age. Even so, I think there is much more to it than that. There are a number of factors which perpetuate this unfortunate state of affairs.

First, acute emergency services, such as existing local authority children's services and child and adolescent mental health services, are not geared up to developing an effective preventive first responder crisis intervention approach. Instead, existing resource pressures encourage defensive status quo policies, meaning that such services only get involved when behavioural problems have become established and difficult to treat.

Second, there are no obvious professional 'brownie points' to reward a preventive approach under existing managerial practices to ensure compliance with performance indicators – as Eileen Munro explains in her Review of Child Protection.[290] Besides, it is likely that measurable results from a preventive approach almost by definition take time to emerge. Reducing demand on acute services, even if demonstrable in the medium to long term, also risks reducing available resources for those services unless sufficient staff can be redeployed and retrained for preventive work. Such an organisational shift in priorities might well be resisted by staff committed to established practices and fearing dilution of their specialist skills. Some might fear, at least in the current economic climate, that the prime motivation for such a change is a political desire to cut the size and cost of a service with its established way of doing things. Such considerations work to maintain an organisation's status quo.

---

[290] E Munro (2011) *The Munro Review of Child Protection: Final Report: A Child-centred System* www.gov.uk at pp15–20, paras 1.5, 1.16–1.21

Third, in any case, it can be difficult to prepare and organise a rapid reaction crisis intervention service for children experiencing stressful family change. It involves, for example, a capacity to identify and target that section of the child population while it is particularly at risk, and to be so organised as to make a rapid supportive response. This is not an easy managerial task. Some managers may fear that, rather like a fire brigade or ambulance service, too much staff time will be spent waiting at a moment's notice for a call to action. Of course, one may reply that such times need not be unproductive, but rather provide much needed opportunities for preparatory training, continuing professional development, supportive professional consultation and the like.

This last point is necessary because dealing empathetically with children and families going through a crisis is 'emotionally hot' work. As Caplan pointed out many years ago:

> In the same way that families get upset when helping their members cope with crisis, professional care givers might themselves become upset while they are supporting families.[291]

Too much exposure day in and day out to children experiencing intense distress and anxiety can make heavy demands on a caregiver's own emotional resources. I found that out, for example, some years ago when Douglas Hooper (a clinical psychologist who had studied with Caplan at Harvard) and I were involved in the setting up, in a small voluntary social work agency in a large city, an experimental short-term crisis intervention service for fathers suddenly left alone with dependent children through the death or desertion of the mother.[292] Two well-trained female social caseworkers were appointed to set up and run the project. They were successful in identifying and targeting the relevant section of the population. So much so that soon a steady stream of distressed fathers contacted the agency.[293] Both workers

---

[291] G Caplan (1974) *Support Systems and Community Mental Health: Lectures in Concept Development* Behavioural Publications, New York at p ix.

[292] M Murch (1973) 'Motherless Families Project: Bristol Council of Social Service: Report of first year's work' *British Journal of Social Work* 3(3) pp365–376.

[293] Analysis of the first 30 cases referred to the agency, in which the reasons included 23 cases of desertion and six caused by the death of a mother, revealed that the majority of fathers came to the agency in a state of emotional distress, being particularly worried about arrangements for the care of the children. The agency case workers recorded their impression of the emotional state of the father on each

rapidly became fully engaged in offering crisis intervention support; providing information about welfare benefits, childcare support and so on; and encouraging the men to find ways of realistically adapting to the family's sudden change of circumstances.

Before long, however, it because apparent that both social workers needed professional consultation and support as they came to terms with the emotional demands placed upon them day–to-day. This was provided on a weekly basis by Douglas Hooper, then a senior lecturer in Bristol University's Department of Mental Health – a department then led by Professor Russell Davies, who was committed to the social psychiatry approach.

Caplan himself recognised that professional caregivers engaged in regular crisis intervention work would need consultative support, particularly if certain situations that they were dealing with stirred up through projective identification problematic aspects in the professional caregiver's personal life. As the Caplans explained:

> The effectiveness of a professional worker – physician, nurse, a school teacher – who is dealing with mental health problems of a client, is likely to be influenced by personal subjective factors, longstanding personality difficulties, personal or cultural prejudices or sensitivities and current emotional upsets in the professional worker's life. Any of these may distort his perceptions of his client and his remedial efforts.[294]

It is important to distinguish mental health consultation from supervision and various forms of psychotherapy. Caplan developed a form of consultative support for coalface workers using a technique he termed 'theme interference reduction'. This is not the place to go into this aspect in detail. It is sufficient to make the general point that those engaged in regular crisis intervention preventive work, particularly

---

occasion they met, which, over a short period of two or three months, could be several times a week. Analysis of this aspect confirmed the general rollercoaster pattern of a typical crisis response. In at least half of the cases the fathers concluded their contact with the agency in a much calmer state, being more accepting of the family situation, and with a more positive and realistic approach to coping with it. There were, however, two or three cases where the case workers noted that the father appeared locked in a state of unrealistic denial – two of which were later known to have been admitted to a psychiatric hospital.

[294] G Caplan and R B Caplan (1993) *Mental Health Consultation and Collaboration* Jossey-Bass, San Fransisco, CA at p16.

with children, will need backup access to professional support of a mental health consultant trained in this approach. This will depend on collaboration with the caregiving agency – school, health centre, family justice support service etc. I will develop these points in the next chapter, where I will suggest that schools and Cafcass should consider adopting a more preventive mental health crisis intervention approach. I also suggest that this is a consultative approach which CAMHS should consider providing if and when they can devote more resources to preventive work.

But it should be noted that at the end of 2017 while I was writing this book all was not doom and gloom. The Government Green Paper *Transforming Children and Young People's Mental Health Provision* proposed a broad organisational and structural framework to strengthen collaboration between schools and Child and Adolescent Mental Health Services as well as endorsing three specific interventions (cognitive behavioural therapy in schools and colleges for young people showing signs of acute anxiety and depression, family based behavioural change and group based intervention). As already mentioned, my proposals for school based crisis intervention outlined below in Chapters Eight and Thirteen, should complement these measures. Moreover, the then Secretary of State for Education, Justine Greening MP, said: 'These would be backed by £300 million of "new money"[295] in addition to making an additional £1.4 billion available for children and young people's mental health over five years.'[296]

But note she left the Government in January 2018 in a so-called Cabinet reshuffle. This raises the question whether her successor as Secretary of State for Education, Damien Hurst MP, will be equally committed to implementing the Green Paper's proposal. (For consideration of the general problem of ministerial "churn" see Chapters Eleven at p255-259 and Chapter Twelve at p285-288 below.

Before considering how the preventive crisis intervention approach can be developed in schools and the family justice context, there are several other key points to note. First, careful selection and preparation of the professional caregiver is important. They have to be emotionally secure and empathetic. Second, they will need to have an adequate understanding of the conceptual framework underpinning the crisis intervention approach and be able to relate it to their own experience of

---

[295] In BBC interview with Andrew Marr in the Andrew Marr Show December 2017.

[296] Department of Health and Department for Education (December 2017) *Transforming Children and Young People's Mental Health Provision: a Green Paper* CM 9523 p3.

normal everyday life. Third, they will need to be able to recognise the way the child is working through the various stages in crisis resolution and be able to adapt their supportive work appropriately. In this respect, as the child recovers equilibrium and seems to be facing up realistically to the altered circumstances in their home life, the caregiver needs to be able to disengage sensitively. Crisis intervention is essentially an intensive, short-term form of support. Fourth, the crisis interveners will need to be able to spot those children who are not coping and whose behaviour risks becoming more seriously problematic: children who will need more specialist mental help. In this respect, crisis first responders, whatever their setting, play an important early warning role and a triage system can be helpful. Fifth, given the danger that unremitting exposure to families in crisis can easily overtax the psychological resources of the caregiver with the risk of 'burnout', it is important that services developing a preventive crisis intervention facility ensure that such exposure is regulated. This can be achieved, for example, by weaving in other less emotionally demanding work so that a practitioner (school teacher, general medical practitioner, health visitor or family justice social worker etc) is only expected to use their crisis intervention skills from time to time in the normal run of their professional practice, when the need for it is recognised and an appropriate response can be made quickly. This means, of course, that the caregiving employing agency has to be so organised as to facilitate this form of preventive work.

In the light of the 2017 Green Paper this could be achieved by the proposed: 'Mental health support teams supervised by the NHS Children and Young People's Mental Health staff to provide specific extra capacity for early intervention and ongoing help.'[297]

It goes without saying that professional caregivers undertaking this sort of work with children need to have the skills and aptitude for communicating effectively with children. They need to be able to give children *time* to establish trust, and to find appropriate space in the setting for the children to unburden their private thoughts and feelings. These are all crucial points to which I shall return in the next chapters when considering the potential role of schools and family justice support services as agencies to undertake supportive crisis intervention for children experiencing family breakdown.

---

[297] Department of Health and Department for Education (December 2017) *Transforming Children and Young People's Mental Health Provision: a Green Paper* CM 9523 at p4.

The case for the early intervention preventive approach[298]

As we have seen, a fundamental tenet of the Caplanian crisis model of mental health has been the observation based on clinical and experimental research that crisis intervention helps to buffer the impact of a stressful event, assists in the process of adapting realistically to it, and thereby may strengthen resilience and capacity to cope with future life-changing events.[299]

As Professor Eileen Munro asserts in her *Review of child protection,* the case for prevention is clear in respect of child neglect and child abuse, particularly in early childhood years.[300] Likewise, in my opinion it applies to children facing serious parental conflict where the sequilae in terms of their education and life chances can be just as serious. First there is a moral case to minimise adverse experiences for children. This was explicitly endorsed by the United Nations Convention on the Rights of the Child, in particular Article 19. This requires states to:

> Take all appropriate legislative, administrative, social and educational measures to protect the child from all forms of psychical or moral violence, injury or abuse ... while in the care of parents, legal guardians or any other person who has care of the child.

Second, Munro argues that there is an obligation to prevent harm to children and young people that might otherwise become irreversible – what she terms the 'now or never' argument. In this respect she referred to:

> Compelling neuroscience evidence on the enduring damage to babies by unresponsive and neglectful adults.[301]

---

[298] For a classification of prevention into primary, second and tertiary, see E Munro (May 2011) *Review of Child Protection: Better Frontline Services to Protect Children* CM8062, Department for Education – see Chapter 5 at p79. See also M Little and K Mount (1999) *Prevention and Early Intervention With Children in Need* Ashgate, Aldershot. See C P Cowan and P A Cowan (2012) 'Prevention: intervening with couples at challenging family transition points' in A Balfour, M Morgan, C Vincent (eds) *How Couple Relationships Shape Our World: Clinical Practice, Research and Policy Perspectives* Karnac Books, London at p3.

[299] G Caplan (1964) *Principles of Preventive Psychiatry* Tavistock Press, London.

[300] E Munro (May 2011) *Review of Child Protection: Better Frontline Services to Protect Children* CM8062, Department for Education – see Chapter 5 at p69.

[301] E Munro (May 2011) *Review of Child Protection: Better Frontline Services to Protect Children* CM8062, Department for Education – see para 5.7 at p70.

But for older children too I argue that time lost, for example, in education, when they are stressed and preoccupied while coping with serious interparental conflict, can equally turn out to be difficult to make up later.

Munro's third argument concerning the cost benefits of early preventive intervention draws heavily on the economic modelling work in the field of mental health of Martin Knapp and colleagues for the Department of Health.[302] In particular, this concerned schemes to prevent persistent conduct disorders in children; school-based social and emotional learning programmes, which proved to be particularly good value and may have direct applicability to children facing parental conflict; and GP screening for alcohol misuse.

Furthermore, the Cowans raise the important question, seldom asked by politicians and policy makers: how much would it cost *not* to fund preventive programmes?[303] It was therefore particularly depressing to learn in March 2014 that a number of child and adolescent mental health services had had their funding for early intervention schemes substantially cut. As the Munro Report itself pointed out, even in 2010, early support and preventive services were the target for cuts, with a quarter of 72 Children England member organisations experiencing cuts of more than 25%. Since then there have been further cuts to the budgets of CAMHS.

For example, a Young Minds investigation reported that more than half of the local councils in England had cut or frozen budgets for child and adolescent mental health between 2010/11 and 2014/15. Moreover, as reported in the *Observer* newspaper, a health select committee warned in 2014 that:

> In many areas early intervention services are being cut or are suffering from insecure or short-term funding.[304]

The Institute of Public Policy's study demonstrates that: 'The only way to achieve sustained long-term improvements in mental health is

---

[302] M Knapp, D McDaid and M Parsonage (eds) (April 2011) *Mental Health Promotion and Mental Illness Prevention: The Economic Case* www.lse.ac.uk, Department of Health and LSE PSSRU.

[303] C P Cowan and P A Cowan (2012) 'Prevention: intervening with couples at challenging family transition points' in A Balfour, M Morgan, C Vincent (eds) *How Couple Relationships Shape Our World: Clinical Practice, Research and Policy Perspectives* Karnac Books, London at p13.

[304] D Boffey (22 December 2015) 'A&E hit by children's mental health crisis' *The Observer*.

to invest more in early intervention and prevention in order to stem the flow of people who need access to more prolonged and expensive forms of treatment.'[305]

The question that therefore needs answering is this: if as a nation we now accept the concept and effectiveness of a preventive approach to reduce known risks in a range of community services, from flood prevention to public health (through inoculations against disease, clean water supply etc), why when it comes to preventing psychosocial dysfunction in conflicted family relations, where the causes and consequences are increasingly well understood through research, are we apparently reluctant to invest in preventive services until matters have reached an emergency level? As my former colleagues and I pointed out elsewhere:

> One might use a medical diagnosis analogy here: we do not wait for a tumour to get very big before taking action to excise it. Of course early diagnosis does not prevent fatality in every case but it certainly improves the chances of survival.[306]

The importance of a shared intellectual arena and 'common language' for both professional and non-professional caregivers

The conceptual model underpinning crisis intervention was built on what one might call anthropological observations of the way people normally react and adapt to critical stressful turning points in their lives and to the supportive responses from those in their immediate social network, such as family friends, neighbours and so on. Yet there are many occasions when these informal caregiving systems fail or are unavailable. For example, I have shown in Chapter Five how many children with conflicted and separated parents felt isolated, especially if they felt unable to turn to either parent for comfort, information and support. This was especially so if they did not have anyone else, such as a close friend, to confide in.

---

[305] C Thorley (May 2016) *Education, education, mental health: Supporting secondary schools to play a central role in early intervention mental health services* Institute of Public Policy Research Ch5 para 5.1 p21.

[306] G Douglas, M Murch, C Miles, L Scanlan (2006) *Research Into the Operation of Rule 9.5 of the Family Proceedings Rules 1991* Department for Constitutional Affairs, London at p204 para 7.55.

It is when there are no available so-called 'natural' caregivers that a range of more formal occupations may be called upon to support children and parents through the crisis of family breakdown. For children this may involve engaging with first responders such as childminders, school teachers, GPs and health visitors. Any of these may make referral to backup, more specialist, services, such as school counsellors, family mediators or, if a child's behavioural problems seem seriously persistent, psychologists or psychiatrists in CAMHS. Moreover, if parents take their child-related disputes to the family court then, as we will see, mediators conducting the initial Mediation Information and Assessment Meetings (MIAMs) will be involved, as might officers from Cafcass, either in preparing welfare reports or, in particularly difficult disputed cases, acting as guardians for the child (see further Chapters Eight and Thirteen).

It will clearly promote interprofessional understanding and collaboration between all these different kinds of service if, in addition to their specialist areas of knowledge, they share an understanding of normal psychosocial responses to crisis and are able to spot warning signs when things are going wrong and more specialist intervention may be needed.

Later, in the concluding Chapter Fourteen of this book, I will look more closely at the shortcomings of what Gillian Tett, in her book *The silo effect*, refers to as the 'peril of expertise', that is, the way specialists tend to work in silos (or ghettos) of assumptive thought, which cut them off even from colleagues from a different discipline working within the same organisation.[307] Theodore Zeldin argued that specialists, despite their many advantages, tend to reinforce one another's assumptive worlds within 'fortresses in which specialists cut themselves off from the distractions of other forms of knowledge'.[308] Thus, I argue that the promotion of a common language based on a shared intellectual framework between caregiving occupations in the service of children involved in family breakdown is one important way of overcoming the limitations of undue specialism – to use Gillian Tett's phrase, 'busting open' the professional silos in which they develop.

---

[307] G Tett (2015) *The Silo Effect: The Peril of Expertise and the Promise of Breaking Down Barriers* Simon and Schuster, New York.

[308] T Zeldin (1994) *An Intimate History of Humanity* Minerva Paperbacks, London at p197.

Short-term intensive crisis intervention can save lengthy and more expensive specialist intervention later

It is the essence of crisis intervention that it focuses short-term on the events that trigger the crisis and adaptive responses to it. As Caplan put it, the model is useful because:

> Individuals in crisis are more susceptible to influence than during periods of stable equilibrium, so that crisis times are points of leverage. Also the kind of influence which can tip the balance is essentially that of supportive human relations and so can be practiced on a widespread scale by interested key people where usually there is no demand for specialist knowledge which would restrict its use to a relatively small number of highly trained experts.[309]

In this way it offers a guide to primary prevention by encouraging mentally healthy ways of helping people going through a critical life-changing event. It can thus be targeted at specific groups in the populations whose wellbeing is at risk, the incidence of which can usually be anticipated by those providing community support services.

However, as I have mentioned, to be effective, supportive help needs to be provided during the crisis, not weeks or months after unrealistically maladaptive defences have been erected and when related problems have escalated – when, for example, a girl reacting to parental conflict and separation has resorted to a pattern of self-harming behaviour or a boy has persistently acted out his anger on fellow pupils and school teachers, possibly resulting in exclusion from school.

In enabling frontline community care agents such as school teachers to undertake, with suitable training and support, crisis intervention when it is needed, the need for more expensive specialist therapeutic intervention is reduced later. In any case, such 'hard end' services are expensive, in short supply and frequently have waiting lists while the child or young person's maladaptive behaviour problems become more difficult to deal with. This, as we have seen, is the problem currently facing CAMHS.

---

[309] G Caplan (1974) *Support Systems and Community Mental Health: Lectures in Concept Development* Behavioural Publications, New York at p247.

Crisis intervention can be part of a community's normal non-stigmatic support mechanism

An important point is that this form of support can be employed by a range of caregiving organisations, many of which carry no stigmatic associations. Therefore, turning to them for help through crisis need not in itself involve the risk of being labelled as some kind of 'mental health patient' or welfare case.

We have seen how children may be concerned about privacy when choosing whom to tell about their parents' relationship problems and separation. It is not exactly something to boast about! Parental separation and its aftermath involves the family in a critical status passage and calls into question members' notions of family identity, of what is normal, what is socially acceptable. For adolescents experiencing the normal maturational process of questioning identity, this can be an additional burden. Therefore, the confirmational response of outsiders as either accepting or disapproving can be crucial. The avoidance of stigma is an important part of a child's successful adaptation to the crisis of parental separation.

Such considerations have major implications for those caregiving agencies which might seek to provide early preventive crisis intervention support. For example, schools as organisations are generally not seen as stigmatic. In contrast, many people consider that to be regarded as a patient of quasi-psychiatric or social welfare support is tantamount to admitting personal failure to manage one's own life according to the prevailing standards of the day. This important point needs to be remembered when considering the Green Paper's proposals to tackle mental health issues in schools. Thus it states: 'The school environment is non-stigmatising, making interventions offered in this context more acceptable to children and young people and their parents.'[310]

I return to this point when considering the broader question of how parents and children find socially acceptable forms of information and support from some of the more established caregiving agencies, particularly now that civil legal aid has been withdrawn from most private law cases.

---

[310] Department of Health and Department for Education (December 2017) *Transforming Children and Young People's Mental Health Provision: a Green Paper* CM 9523 para 23 p10.

EIGHT

Providing short-term primary preventive crisis intervention for children in schools

Introduction

In the first part of this chapter I offer for discussion some ideas about how the Caplanian approach to preventive mental health – specifically the method of crisis intervention (explained in Chapters Six and Seven) – might be applied in state schools, a non-stigmatic site for primary prevention.[311] Like the 2017 Green Paper, I envisage this as part of a developing programme to promote social and emotional wellbeing using a 'whole school' approach. Even so, I recognise that this, although gaining wider acceptance, is still a contentious concept since it challenges the traditional view of the purpose of education, namely, that its sole purpose is to pursue academic excellence and to control the school environment so as to manage disruptive pupil behaviour. There is a view that much of our existing public sector school system still largely operates on this basis. But that is increasingly open to question: is the purpose of schooling simply about gaining qualifications and preparing young people for adult working life? Or do schools have a wider purpose in supporting young people at critical moments in their educational journey from infancy to adulthood, so that as far as possible they can develop into well-rounded emotionally secure and resilient citizens able to develop their individual talents for the wider benefit of society?

As I will outline below, these basic questions underlie a vigorous social policy debate which developed throughout the Cameron

---

[311] I should point out that most of the remainder of this text concerned with social and educational policies refers to mainstream government-funded schools. But it should not be thought that privately educated children are, as it were, immune from behavioural and mental health disorders triggered in reaction to interparental conflict. On the contrary, some such children can suffer badly by being 'sent away to boarding schools', as Joy Schaverien reveals in her (2015) book *Boarding School Syndrome: The Psychological Trauma of the Privileged Child* Routledge, London. See further Chapter Thirteen in Part IV.

government years (2010–16) and continued throughout 2016–17 under the Conservative administration led by Theresa May, up to the point when on 18 April 2017 she called a general election. It so happens that in the month following May's earlier announcement of 8 February that there was to be a Green Paper on Child and Adolescent Mental Health Services published in the autumn, the House of Commons Education and Health Committee produced a report on children and young people's mental health and the role of education.[312] I return to the proposals advanced by this committee when reviewing the policies adopted by David Cameron's administration, especially as in many ways they take a more progressive 'whole school' approach in which it should be possible to embed the preventive mental health crisis intervention method, given the appropriate preparation and training of school-based staff (see further below and Chapter Thirteen). The principle of this approach has now been endorsed by the Green Paper.[313]

Why focus on primary prevention in schools?

As I have mentioned earlier, schools are the most obvious site from which to mount primary preventive mental health programmes.[314] First, they contain a large proportion of the child and young person population which is potentially at risk. Second, schools are readily accessible to children and young people at critical turning points in their lives. Sensitively handled supportive intervention could therefore be woven into the normal part of school life as part of a broader whole school approach to education, health and wellbeing for all children as part of schools' normal Personal, Social, Health and Economic educational programmes (PSHE). Third, as I have already mentioned

[312] House of Commons Education and Health Committees (2 May 2017) *Children and Young People's Mental Health: The Role of Education* https://publications.parliament. uk – this was the first joint report of the Education and Health Committees session 2016–17.

[313] Department of Health and Department for Education (December 2017) *Transforming Children and Young People's Mental Health Provision: a Green Paper* CM 9523 at p10, where it is stated 'A whole school approach, with commitment from senior leadership and supported by external expertise, is essential to the success of schools in tackling mental health'.

[314] See, for example, Department for Children, Schools and Families and Department of Health (2010) *Keeping Children in Mind: The Government's Response to the Independent Review of CAMHS*. This acknowledged that where children and young people experience mental health problems and difficulties, we must identify and address these as soon as possible to help ensure they do not worsen and that problems do not become entrenched.

above, school-based supportive intervention is culturally a non-stigmatic form of help that is potentially accessible at a time when it is most needed by the children concerned.

Fourth, it also provides an opportunity for schools to apply a triage screening system by which to identify those who are coping well with the problems between their parents; those who are temporarily experiencing a normal short-term crisis response which will affect their educational performance and who, I argue, will benefit from crisis intervention in the school context; and those who are experiencing more serious long-term mental and behavioural problems meriting immediate referral to CAMHS.

Fifth, as far as social and education policy is concerned, it has been recognised professionally for some years that much more needs to be done to improve training for school teachers in understanding children's social and emotional development.[315] This would enable them to teach more effectively, to develop their communication skills with children so as to listen more effectively to the voice of the child, and thus to be in a position as 'first responder' to offer supportive individual help if the child seeks it.

---

[315] In July 2007 the Labour government announced a £60 million fund for the Targeted Mental Health in Schools (TaMHS) project, with an aim of improving the emotional wellbeing and mental health outcomes for children and young people through evidence-based interventions (para 2.22, see also Department for Education (2011) *Me and My School: Findings from the National Evaluation of Targeted Mental Health in Schools 2008–2011*, Department for Education, London). This programme aimed to develop 'a range of models of integrated early intervention and targeted support delivered through schools and building better links with specialist CAMHS for those children, young people and their families who need it most', see Department for Children, Schools and Families and Department of Health (2010) *Keeping Children and Young People in Mind: The Government's full response to the independent review of CAMHS*, DCSF Publications, Nottingham, para 2.21–23 p32. See also NHS Centre for Reviews and Dissemination (June 1997) *Effective Health Care: Mental Health Promotion in High Risk Groups* vol 3 no 3, p1. This research review reported that: '(i) high quality pre-school education and support visits for new parents can improve mental health in children and parents in disadvantaged communities; (ii) school-based intervention and parent training for children showing behavioural problems can improve conduct and mental wellbeing; (iii) mental health problems in children of separating parents can be reduced by cognitive skills training and emotional support.'

A brief outline of the broader picture of schools' promotion of children's social and emotional wellbeing

In advancing the suggestion that the primary preventive model of crisis intervention should be woven into a school's broader skillset to foster pupils' wellbeing, I of course recognise that, building on a large volume of educational research, for a number of years several schemes have already claimed to use a variety of interventions to promote positive mental health for pupils.[316] Professor Kathleen Weare, a prime mover in promoting social and emotional wellbeing in schools, has pointed out that the last 30 years have seen 'an experiential growth in programmes and interventions in schools under a wide range of titles' – for example, the Targeted Mental Health in Schools (TaMHS) and Primary and Secondary Social and Emotional Aspects of Learning (SEAL) programmes.[317] Weare observes that, in general, 'this field has been the focus of a considerable amount of evaluation, including several comprehensive reviews and meta-analyses, including four in the UK covering all phases of schooling by the National Institute of Clinical Excellence'.[318] She considers that taken together these well-conducted reviews demonstrate that there is a solid group of approaches, programmes and interventions which 'when well designed and implemented show repeated and clear evidence of positive impacts' concerning:[319]

---

[316] See H Taggart, S Lee, L McDonald (December 2014) *Perceptions of Wellbeing and Mental Health in English Secondary Schools: A Cross-sectional Study* CentreForum, London.

[317] K Weare (2015) *What Works in Promoting Social and Emotional Well-being and Responding to Mental Health Problems in Schools?* National Children's Bureau, London at pp1–2. Kathleen Weare is an emeritus professor of education at Southampton University and a visiting professor at Exeter University. She is reported as saying, "Mental health has always been the Cinderella service. The services for children are drastically underfunded. Waiting lists (for CAMHS) are insanely large. As need is growing the response is getting less well financed." See S Weale (27 January 2016) 'Schools trying to help children shut out by mental health services' *The Guardian*.

[318] The two most relevant are (i) Y Adi, A Killoran, K Janmohamed, and S Stewart-Brown (2007) *Systematic Review of the Effectiveness of Interventions to Promote Mental Wellbeing in Children in Primary Education. Report 1: Universal Approaches: Non-violence Related Outcomes* Warwick University Medical School and Centre for Public Health and NICE; and (ii) L Blank, S Baxter, E Goyder, L Guillaume, A Wilkinson, S Hummel, J Chilcott and N Payne (2009) *Systematic Review of the Effectiveness of Universal Interventions Which Aim to Promote Emotional and Social Wellbeing in Secondary Schools* NICE, London.

[319] K Weare (2015) *What Works in Promoting Social and Emotional Well-being and Responding to Mental Health Problems in Schools?* National Children's Bureau, London.

- academic learning
- pupil wellbeing
- the development of social and emotional skills and attitudes
- improving school behaviour
- reductions in 'risky behaviour'.

Given the sweep of Weare's NCB (National Children's Bureau) paper and the detail and rigour of the NICE reviews, to which I have already referred in Chapter Three, I do not propose to dwell further on them apart from observing that I have not found any specific reference in the educational research literature to the Caplanian preventive mental health approach. Nor have I found very much reference to the extensive psychological research literature concerning risk and resilience in children associated with parental conflict and separation, as advanced in the UK by Professor Sir Michael Rutter and Professor Gordon Harold, and others in the field of developmental psychology.

I should also mention that another important psychological school of thought adopted by several leading educationists such as Heather Geddes and James Wetz,[320] and of course familiar to most social workers and psychoanalysts, is that often termed 'attachment theory', the leading theoretical exponent of which was John Bowlby. His research, to which I have referred above in Chapter Six, was based on clinical research and published in his three-volume *Attachment and loss*.[321] I suspect that one reason for this is that these separate fields of research, practice and policy, all of which are relevant to the wellbeing of children, develop in their own exclusive academic and policy domains, or silos. I address this problematic issue further in the final chapter of this book.

A summary of policy concerning the development of mental health provision in schools 2010–16: a story of damage limitation?

Before offering some suggestions as to how schools might apply Caplanian concepts of preventive mental health and crisis intervention

---

[320] H Geddes (2006) *Attachment in the Classroom: The Links Between Children's Early Experience, Emotional Well-being and Performance in School* Worth Publishing, London. J Wetz (2009) *Urban Village Schools: Putting Relationships at the Heart of Secondary School Organisation and Design* Calouste Gulbenkian Foundation, London.

[321] J Bowlby (1969, 1973 and 1980) *Attachment and Loss*, 3 vols Hogarth Press, London at pp137–158.

for children facing stressful problems of serious parental conflict, violence and separation, I outline the policy background. This followed the economic recession of 2007/08 and the coalition government's deficit reduction measures, which resulted in many local authorities reducing their CAMHS budgets. In subsequent years there was mounting and widespread concern about the deteriorating state of these services. Organisations such as Young Minds and the National Children's Bureau (NCB) produced strong evidence of growing numbers of children not knowing where to turn to for mental health support, with mental disorders in children reaching 10% of the general population. Waiting times to obtain CAMHS treatment increased to such an extent that the numbers of children and young people with serious mental health problems going to hospital Accident and Emergency departments almost doubled from 2010/11 to around 17,000 in 2013/14.

As the number of children and young people with serious mental health problems continued to rise, there developed growing concerns that much more attention needed to be focused on early *intervention* within the state educational system. Back in 2009, James Wetz, a former secondary school head teacher, had conducted a study for the Calouste Gulbenkian Foundation into the reasons why more than 35,000 young people left school in the UK each year with few if any qualifications.[322] Many of these so-called disaffected children, often with turbulent family backgrounds, had failed to adapt to the critical move from small primary schools, where they had felt cared for by particular teachers, to much larger secondary schools. Here they felt lost and had not developed any encouraging supportive relationships with a particular teacher.

Wetz's solution was radical, influenced by educational policy in Denmark and some educational schemes in the US. He advocated fundamental reorganisation of the educational system so that primary and smaller-scale secondary schools could be integrated into what he termed 'urban village schools'. This would avoid the critical hiatus that occurs when, under existing arrangements, children make the sudden transition from primary to secondary school – a transition which can break meaningful supportive attachments established with friends and staff at the primary level. As we have seen, when this transition coincides with a breakdown in parental relationships, children unsupported in the crisis at home face a double whammy. This can

---

[322] J Wetz (2009) *Urban Village Schools: Putting Relationships at the Heart of Secondary School Organisation and Design* Calouste Gulbenkian Foundation, London.

set in train a series of mental health and behavioural problems which escalate and damage children's educational attainment and longer-term life chances.

The results of Wetz's study coincided with the work of the Targeted Mental Health in Schools Project to which I have referred above.[323] But the Labour government's initiative seems to have stalled following the financial crisis of 2007/-08 and the advent of Cameron's coalition government. Nevertheless, pressure for reform and improvement in mental health awareness among the teaching profession continued, aggravated by the cuts to CAMHS mentioned above.

The Carter review of initial teacher training

In April 2014, the then Secretary of State for Education, the Right Honourable Nicky Morgan MP, asked Sir Andrew Carter to undertake an independent review of Initial Teacher Training (ITT).[324] The aim was to examine 'core elements of high quality' training across stages in the educational process to equip trainees with the required skills and knowledge 'to become outstanding teachers'. Carter submitted his report in January 2015. The report observed, in respect to child and adolescent development:

> the fact that more and more children are presenting in schools with difficult and disruptive behaviour that is interfering with their learning. Respondents [to the review] emphasised that teachers well trained in children's emotional development and the impact of trauma and loss are likely to be more confident and effective in providing a safe setting for all students, including the more vulnerable and challenging, leading to better pupil outcomes.[325]

Later, the review reported that:

> Experts like those from the school-based mental health organisation Place2Be and the Consortium of Emotional

---

[323] See Department for Education (2011) *Me and My School: Findings from the National Evaluation of Targeted Mental Health in Schools 2008–2011*, Department for Education, London.

[324] A Carter (January 2015) *Carter Review of Initial Teacher Training (ITT)* www.gov.uk/government/publications

[325] Ibid at p29 para 2.3.24.

Wellbeing in Schools have highlighted a lack of training in child development ... there is evidence to suggest that there is a widespread perception amongst teachers in England that although they believe they have a duty to help identify and support pupils with mental health problems, they feel inadequately prepared to do so.[326]

The review further observed that teachers should be trained to identify when and how to refer appropriately to more specialist support.

It is significant that although in her response to the Carter Review (12 July 2016), the then Secretary of State generally welcomed the report, there was no clear commitment to improve this aspect of teacher training. In the meantime, pressure for radical reform continued to mount following the Carter Review.

In November 2015, in a short House of Lords debate on mental health introduced by the cross-bencher, the Earl of Listowel and Baroness Tyler of Enfield, while acknowledging that in a rapidly changing world, children and young people face a wide range of risk factors, it was commented that:

'It is salutary to note that in an average classroom 10 children will have witnessed their parents separate, eight will have experienced psychical violence, sexual abuse or neglect and seven will have been bullied.'[327]

To give the coalition government its due, as these mounting concerns became increasingly apparent, it responded by establishing in September 2014 a Children and Young People's Mental Health and Wellbeing Taskforce. Also, in November 2014 an additional £7 million was made available to NHS England to provide more CAMHS hospital beds, and £150 million was pledged over the five years 2015–20 to improve services for the treatment of children and young people with eating disorders and for those that self-harm.

The priority dilemma: acute treatment or early intervention?

These were all welcome policy measures, but note that the promised financial resources, if they materialise by 2020, are targeted at children

---

[326] Ibid para 2.3.23 p29.
[327] House of Commons Hansard (25 February 2015) *Debate on Mental Health Services* https://hansard.parliament.uk

and young people suffering acute and chronic behavioural and mental health disorders. It appears that they will do little to advance preventive early intervention, even though numerous organisations and official parliamentary publications over the years have stressed the importance of early invention and prevention. It is also worth noting that in 2010 the previous Labour government recommended in its response to the independent review of CAMHS, a £60 million Targeted Mental Health in Schools programme plus £58 million for the colocation of health services incorporating mental health provision alongside schools and in youth centre settings.[328] Given the change of government in 2010 and cuts following the subsequent strategic Spending Review, it is questionable whether any of this money materialised. Nevertheless, in 2011 at least £60 million was invested by the coalition government in the Children and Young People's Improving Access to Psychological Therapies programme (CYPIAPT).

In March 2015, in the final days of the coalition government, the *Times* newspaper launched a campaign to improve access to child and adolescent mental health services, which coincided with the task force report.[329] The campaign provoked a vigorous supportive correspondence.[330] A number of points were made. I quote:

> Just announcing more money does not magically conjure up the extra qualified experts needed. It takes time and experience to deliver the effective care and treatment needed.
>
> Early intervention does not stop the demand for services dealing with the highest levels of need.
>
> The treatment for children with mental health problems was well covered in your report. However, guides and manifestos do not address the causes.

Jenny Edwards, CEO of the Mental Health Foundation, wrote:

> As a society we have an obligation to provide adequate support to children experiencing mental health problems and to promote resilience among all children and young

---

[328] Department for Children, Schools and Families and Department of Health (2010) *Keeping Children in Mind: The Government's Response to the Independent Review of CAMHS.*

[329] See *Times* leader (12 March 2015) Manifesto Time to Mind.

[330] See *Times* newspaper (13 and 17 March 2015) 'Letters to the editor'.

people. Most adolescent and adult mental health problems can be traced back to childhood, with the annual cost to society estimated to be in excess of £100 billion.

One family judge from Surrey pointed out that although the *Times* campaign was welcome:

> CAMHS will not provide services for children while they are the subject of legal proceedings – leaving thousands of children without support at times when they most need it. These include vulnerable children when families are struggling to cope and who are the subjects of care proceedings, and those children whose parents bitterly dispute issues of residence and contact. Despite recent reforms, these proceedings can take many months or even years to resolve, and during this time the children are denied access to mental health services on the grounds that the children's futures need to be decided before help is given to them.

He went on to add:

> Unsurprisingly, children frequently display signs of acute anxiety and distress and many have been exposed to very traumatic events. A faster, more responsive and more easily available system of mental health provision for these children is vital if they are not to be severely affected into their adult lives.

Such a view is likely to be confirmed by many family court judges throughout the country.

Taskforce support for early intervention

At all events, by the end of the Coalition government, when the Children and Young People's Mental Health and Wellbeing Taskforce reported in March 2015[331] its recommendations were supported by the

---

[331] Department of Health and Social Care (2015) *Future in Mind: Promoting, Protecting and Improving our Children and Young People's Mental Health and Wellbeing* www.gov.uk/government/uploads/system/uploads/attachment_data/file/414024/Childrens_Mental_Health.pdf

then Liberal Minister of State for Care and Support, Norman Lamb, and then Parliamentary Under Secretary of State at the Department for Education with specific responsibility for Child and Adolescent Mental Health, Sam Gyimah MP.[332] This report, like its predecessor five years earlier,[333] also emphasised the need to promote resilience, prevention and early intervention, not just focusing on mental illness and diagnosis. The 2015 report was succinct in its statement of the issues and in making a compelling, moral, social and economic case for improvement in the provision of mental health services for children and young people. Thus it stated:

> Mental health problems cause distress to individuals and those who care for them. One in 10 children needs support and treatment for mental health problems. These range from short spells of depression or anxiety through to severe and persistent conditions that can isolate, disrupt and frighten those who experience them. Mental health problems in young people can result in lower educational attainment (for example, children with conduct disorder are twice as likely as other children to leave school with no qualifications) and are strongly associated with behaviours that pose a risk to their health such as smoking, drug and alcohol abuse and risky sexual behaviour.[334]

It further pointed out that:

> The economic case for investment is strong. 75% of mental health problems in adult life (excluding dementia) start by the age of 18. Failure to support children and young people with mental health needs costs lives and money. Early intervention avoids young people falling into crises [but note that here the report may not be using the term 'crisis'

---

[332] Department of Health and NHS England (March 2015) *Future in Mind: Promoting, Protecting and Improving our Children and Young People's Mental Health and Wellbeing* www.gov.uk at pp33–40.

[333] Department for Children, Schools and Families and Department of Health (2010) *Keeping Children and Young People in Mind: The Government's Response to the Independent Review of CAMHS*.

[334] Department of Health and NHS England (March 2015) *Future in Mind: Promoting, Protecting and Improving our Children and Young People's Mental Health and Wellbeing* www.gov.uk para 1.4 at p13.

in the Caplanian mental health sense] and avoids expensive and long term intervention in adulthood.[335]

The taskforce comprised numerous representatives of organisations from health, social work and education. It also consulted a wide range of people and organisations in these fields, and some young people and their parents. With respect to prevention and early intervention, it pointed to the important role that universal services, 'including some Sure Start children's centres, schools, school health services including school nurses, colleges, primary care and youth centres',[336] can play. In particular, it highlighted the roles of GPs and schools, both of which were recognised as being non-stigmatic. The importance of this emerged from the taskforce's discussions with young people. Thus GP practices were seen as having 'significant potential' because they were seen as being 'a less stigmatising environment than a mental health clinic'. While I recognise this important point and see that GPs and primary healthcare teams are potentially well placed to offer crisis intervention support using the Caplanian model, in this book, as I have explained above, I have chosen to focus on the educational system and the role of schools. This is partly because, as pointed out in the 2015 taskforce report, 'many are already developing whole school approaches to promoting resilience',[337] improving emotional wellbeing with a view to preventing mental health problems from arising and providing early support where they do. Citing research in the annual report for 2012 of the Chief Medical Officer,[338] the taskforce claimed that 'interventions taking a whole school approach to wellbeing have a positive impact in relation to both physical health and mental wellbeing'.[339]

Even so, the taskforce reported that many young people themselves stated that 'their school was not an environment in which they felt safe to be open about their mental health concerns'.[340] I suspect this is because of the way the school is organised. I describe further below in this chapter how some schools are developing opportunities for students to have a private consultation with a member of staff.

---

[335] Ibid, para 1.5 at p13.

[336] Department of Health and Social Care (2015) *Improving Mental Health Services for Young People*, para 4.2 at p33.

[337] Ibid at p36 para 4.13.

[338] F Brooks (2012) 'Life stage: school years' Chapter 7 in Department of Health *Annual Report of the Chief Medical Officer 2012: Our Children Deserve Better: Prevention Pays* www.gov.uk.

[339] Department of Health and Social Care (2015) op cit, para 4.13 at p36.

[340] Ibid para 4.8 at p35.

Reinforcement for the idea that schools should play a central role in providing early intervention mental health services for children and young people came in the form of a major report from the Institute for Public Policy Research (IPPR) in May 2016.[341] This IPPR report also highlighted what it termed 'a perfect storm' in the gap between rapidly accelerating demand for CAMHS services at the same time that NHS and local authority early intervention services received cuts of 55% – with budgets falling from £3.2 billion per year in 2010/11 to £1.4 billion in 2015/16. Investigation by the IPPR found that as a result of these cuts:

> Specialist CAMHS are, on average, turning away 23 percent of children and young people who are referred to them, and the average maximum waiting time to access services has more than doubled since 2011/12 (data reported by E Frith from the *Centre Forum Commission on Children and Young People's Mental Health* 2016).[342]

The IPPR report thus stated that 'an immediate rejuvenation of early intervention services is necessary in order to help the CAMHS system escape from the current vicious circle'.[343]

While acknowledging that the Coalition government responded to the Department of Health and NHS England's taskforce report of 2014, *Future in mind*, by committing to spend an additional £1.26 billion on mental health services up to 2019/20, the IPPR report raised serious doubts as to how much would go to CAMHS services, adding:

> While funding is being directed towards these services, too little is finding its way to schools which lack established mechanisms by which they can influence NHS commissioning gaps.[344]

This could be another one of those problems resulting from the silo effect which I will consider in the concluding Part IV of this book.

---

[341] C Thorley (May 2016) *Education, Education, Mental Health: Supporting Secondary Schools to Play a Central Role in Early Intervention Mental Health Services* Institute for Public Policy Research www.ippr.org.uk see para 3.2 at p16 and para 3.3 at p18.

[342] Ibid at p23.

[343] Ibid at p23.

[344] Ibid at p53–4.

Academisation

A further problem to which the IPPR report drew attention was the Coalition government's and its successor's drive to increase the number of English schools classified as academies.[345] Under the Academies Act 2010 schools were transferred from the local authority to direct central government funding. Academies have greater freedom to commission a range of services according to their particular preferences and how they view children's education and needs. Not all might therefore appreciate the need to build into the school's culture adequate preventive mental health provision. The IPPR report noted that:

> Local authority's role in coordinating mental health provision across local schools and providing the link between health provision and commissioners has been increasingly scaled back ... On top of this, the increasing fragmentation of the school system can mean that individual schools lack the internal commissioning expertise required to design effective school-based mental health provision.

So clearly the question of *how* schools approach the issues of early intervention and preventive support is key. In this respect, it is necessary to make two cautionary observations about the way that recent policy in this field is presented to the general public.

Offers of money and fine aspirations are not enough

We live in an age when governments, and indeed many established organisations, are very skilled at putting a fine gloss on the presentation of facts and figures to obscure social realities. As Amitai Etzioni pointed out many years ago:

> One of the most disconcerting phenomena of our time is the elaborate and encompassing attempts to cover social realities with elaborate facades which make society seem even more appealing, humane and participatory than it really is.[346]

---

[345] Ibid at p28.

[346] See Professor Etzioni's Foreword to E Stanton (1969) *Clients Come Last: Volunteers and Welfare Organisations* Sage Publications, Beverly Hills, CA. See also A Etzioni (1969) *The Active Society* Free Press, New York, Chapter 21. Stanton's study

We need to remember this at a time when those working in public and voluntary services are facing an increasingly competitive market to secure funds while government seeks to reduce the deficit and pursue selective austerity measures for those departments which are supposedly not ring-fenced. This is especially so when it is hard to prove evidence of 'what works'. It is tempting, then, for statutory and voluntary services to rely on exaggerated aspiration and morally good intent to make a claim for both continued funding and for new funds for experimental initiatives. Unfortunately, in the past there have been instances when large amounts of public money were assigned to services which had difficulty in showing that it had been money well spent. The Kids Company fiasco is a case in point. This voluntary organisation received many millions of pounds from the Cameron government but was unable to demonstrate that it was producing value for money. It was subsequently closed down. I return to this issue in Chapter Thirteen when I argue that the new services to support children and parents through the crisis of parental conflict, separation and divorce will need to be carefully designed, monitored and evaluated by rigorous 'independent' researchers (by which I mean investigators who have no special interest, financial or otherwise, in proving a positive outcome).

A second point to note concerns the way that government announces the provision of 'extra' financial resources in response to criticism of failing service provision, particularly when continuing to pursue so-called deficit reduction measures. Thus although the headline figure frequently appears large – usually tens of millions – this is often promised over the length of the whole five-year parliamentary period, and so may not materialise until the fourth year. Also, there is seldom any explanation as to how the promised extra provision matches up to a measurement of need, which may outstrip the amount promised, as seems likely to be the case with respect to mental health needs in general, and for child and adolescent mental health in particular.

A third related point concerns the way that funding is provided from particular government departments, so it is not easy to discern how, say, health budgets affect education and vice versa. The picture is further complicated by devolution of these services to Wales and Scotland.

These cautionary points need to be borne in mind as we consider how the overall policy picture unfolded under David Cameron's

---

impressed me when I was working with several voluntary organisations as a young lecturer in social administration. I became aware of the way they manipulated their image, consciously and unconsciously, in the constant struggle to raise funds and convey an impression of agency effectiveness.

Conservative administration concerning children coping with serious parental conflict and separation and its impact on their social, emotional and educational wellbeing. The 2017 Green Paper set out how Theresa May's government intends to approach these issues (see further below).

Continued pressures on resources for CAMHS

After the election of May 2015, when the Coalition government was replaced by David Cameron's Conservative administration, public concern for the state of CAMHS continued unabated. For example, over the winter of 2015/16 a series of press reports expressed alarm at the increased number of children with psychiatric conditions who attended major hospital Accident and Emergency departments. The *Observer* newspaper reported that the number of such attendances rose 8% in 2014/15 to 18,673, from 17,278 the previous year.[347] The paper quoted Sarah Brennan, Chief Executive of Young Minds (a charity working with children suffering mental illness), saying that this increase should have been foreseen when CAMHS were being run down in certain areas. A Young Minds survey had found that half of the councils in England and Wales had cut or frozen child and adolescent mental health budgets between 2010/11 and 2014/15. Indeed, the *Observer* report further pointed out that a Health Select Committee had warned about this the previous year.

In February 2016 the *Independent,* commenting on a recently announced NHS England *Five year forward view for mental health,* pointed out that 24/7 community-based mental health crisis care was then only available in half the country. Children and adolescents consequently could be sent 'anywhere in the country for in-patient treatment, forcing families to travel long distances'.[348] The taskforce report, chaired by Paul Farmer, Chief Executive of Mind, and accepted by the government, called for access to mental health care to be available seven days a week, and stated that new funding should be provided so that crisis resolution and home treatment can be offered as an alternative to acute inpatient admission.

---

[347] D Boffey (22 December 2015) 'A&E hit by children's mental health crisis' *The Observer* at pp1 and 5.

[348] H Stubbs (15 February 2016) 'Young people and mothers to get better mental health care' *The Independent* at p11.

Pioneering schools: helping children unable to access mental health services

One response to the problems created by limited access to CAMHS has been for schools all over the country to explore new experimental ways of helping their pupils with mental health and behavioural problems within the school itself. A good example of this was reported in the *Guardian* newspaper in January 2016, concerning the Childeric Primary School in New Cross, South East London, which covers a large multi-ethnic catchment area.[349] More than half of the pupils are entitled to free school meals and many of the rest come from families working long hours in low-paid jobs or on zero hours contracts. A number of parents were reported as struggling with drug dependency and a significant number of pupils were the subject of child protection plans. There is a fair amount of gang culture in the area and according to the head teacher, Ann Butcher, some children act out scenes of violence in role play.

To address the needs of pupils who have mental health problems but do not qualify for help from CAMHS the head teacher has enlisted the help of the children's mental health charity Place2Be to provide additional in-school help. This is reported as providing:

> a lunchtime service for children who want to talk. Pupils post a slip in a special box and are given an appointment with Maria Valdivia, a qualified psychotherapist who works at the school two days a week. She is in demand; she has a waiting list. Most children ask to see her to discuss friendship issues, which may reflect wider difficulties they are suffering. As well as the lunchtime service, Place2Be provides regular weekly therapy for children – 12 Childeric pupils are being helped at the moment – which has also led to therapy for parents.[350]

This is a school where, despite the enormous social pressures faced by parents, children are reported as making greater progress than the national average and leave it 'at or above national expectations, having begun at a much lower starting point'.[351]

---

[349] See S Weale (27 January 2016) 'Schools trying to help children shut out by mental health services' *The Guardian*.

[350] Ibid.

[351] Ibid.

This is achieved by the school having a strong pastoral team, including two learning support mentors to help children with barriers to learning and the presence of a dedicated community worker who helps with parents' needs, around everything from housing to food banks. Nevertheless, at the time of writing this book, an informant has told me that Lewisham Borough Council is being forced to make cuts to the school budget which will result in the removal of a number of teaching assistants and possibly other vital support staff.

The involvement of voluntary organisations like Place2Be is significant. They can pioneer new ways of supporting individual children and parents, helping them through periods of stress in their daily lives, which can of course include family breakdown and parental separation. Another such organisation is Family Links, a national charity 'dedicated to empowering children, parents and families and schools to be emotionally healthy'.[352] Among other projects, the charity runs a 10-week Nurturing Programme, targeted at parents and designed to 'provide adults and children with the understanding, skills and ability to lead emotionally healthy lives, build resilience, empathy, self-esteem and support positive relationships'.[353] It also contributes to initial teacher training at several universities in partnership with the Teach First programme, running workshops for students taking the PGCE or BA degrees in education. The charity has established a network of schools and teachers who have all signed up to promoting emotional health and wellbeing in the whole school approach. It may be that for the immediate future, progress in developing early preventive intervention will have to depend on pioneering voluntary charities such as these to prove the viability of this approach. But this is no long-term substitute for properly financed state provision.

2017: Prime Minister Theresa May – what prospects for much needed reform?

In spring 2017 there was growing public and professional alarm about the deteriorating state of children's mental health and wellbeing in schools, and this was manifested in media reports that one in 10 children and young people aged 5–16 suffers from a mental health disorder,

---

[352] www.familylinks.org.uk
[353] Ibid.

three children in every secondary school class have a serious mental health condition and 'rates of self-harm are sky-rocketing'.[354]

On 17 April 2017, shortly after Theresa May announced her intention to call a general election, the House of Commons Education and Health Committee produced its first joint report: *Children and young people's mental health – the role of education*. This followed the Prime Minister's announcement on 9 January of its intention to publish a Green Paper on children and young people's mental health later in the year (now published in December 2017),[355] as mentioned in the Preface of this book. Of course, Green Papers do not necessarily signify a major shift in policy, especially if to make such a shift would involve increased public spending, but as the Joint Education and Health Committee report observed:

> with half of all mental illness starting before the age of 15, it is a false economy to cut services for children and young people that could help improve wellbeing, build resilience and provide early intervention.[356]

The joint committees endorsed the whole school approach to promoting pupils' wellbeing and rejected an apparent 'trade-off' between a focus on an academic achievement as a 'false dichotomy'. It accepted the view that 'wellbeing increased pupils' capacity to learn by lessening anxiety, improving confidence and equipping them to better deal with stress'.[357] Although acknowledging that the government was committed to making personal, social, health and economic (PSHE) education mandatory in schools and colleges, it noted with concern that despite the £1.25 billion of extra funding for young people's mental health, state schools were facing an increasing number of funding cuts 'due to inflation and pension pressures'. Accordingly, in the light of the general election on 8 June 2017, the committees stated that they would:

---

[354] See letter in the *Guardian* (17 April 2017) 'Mental health illness at school' from the Chief Executives of Young Minds, National Children's Bureau, Samaritans, Mental Health Foundation, Girlguiding, British Youth Council and 10 others. See also letter in *The Times* (17 April 2017) 'Mental health crisis for more than 25 consultant psychiatrists and clinical psychologists'.

[355] Department of Health and Department for Education (December 2017) *Transforming Children and Young People's Mental Health Provision: A Green Paper*, CM9523.

[356] House of Commons Education and Health Committees (2 May 2017) *Children and Young People's Mental Health: The Role of Education: First Joint Report of the Education and Health Committees of Session 2016–17* HC849 para 39 p12.

[357] Ibid para 17 p8.

strongly urge the government to review the effect of budget reductions on the in-school provision of services to support children and young people's mental health and wellbeing.[358]

In addition, the committees urged Ofsted to ensure that schools' inspection ratings are linked to the promotion of better mental health rather than simply academic achievement. Reflecting the joined-up nature of the two committees, they recommended that:

> a structured approach to referral from education providers
> to CAMHS must be developed across the country.[359]

This is an obvious point, but of course its effectiveness will be totally dependent on the government reversing the cuts that have already been made to CAMHS by Conservative-led governments. And it is it not just a question of money. CAMHS need to be able to recruit the necessary trained specialists to staff the service. However, demand on CAMHS will only continue to grow, possibly exponentially, unless measures are in place to ensure that alert-minded teachers spot children in crisis and provide early preventive intervention.

Sadly, at the very time that the Joint Education and Health Committees report was published, it had received reports from around the country that schools were having to lay off teachers of non-core subjects as well as various support staff, including counsellors, because of reductions in their budget, with financial pressures affecting schools' ability to bring in external support from such pioneering voluntary child mental health services as Place2Be and the Anna Freud National Centre for Children and Families.[360]

The Green Paper, signalled by Theresa May in January 2017, finally emerged in December 2017. It was issued for consultation so it does not necessarily mean that all its recommendations will be followed. Nevertheless it was in tune with the approach of the Joint Education and Health Committee's Report and I very much welcome the emphasis it gives to preventive work and its proposals for structural organisation. This should lead to closer collaboration between schools and Child and Adolescent Mental Health Services. It also seeks to substantially reduce waiting times for access to specialist NHS services trialling a four week target in some areas. As mentioned already in

---

[358] Ibid at p12.
[359] Ibid para 8 p17.
[360] Ibid at p12 para 39.

the Preface the two key organisational proposals are; first a Designated Senior Head for mental health in every school and college,[361] building on successful practice in certain parts of the country and designed to foster the 'whole school' approach to mental health and wellbeing with links to local mental health services. Secondly, the establishment of mental health support teams to work with clusters of schools and colleges across the country.[362] These teams, supervised by NHS children and young person's mental health staff, are intended to provide new capacity locally to address 'the needs of children with mild to moderate mental health issues' and to link up with specialist mental health services 'so that children that swiftly access help if that is necessary'.

With respect to those young people presenting conditions such as 'anxiety, low mood and common behavioural difficulties', these support teams will employ interventions such as Cognitive Behavioural Therapy (CBT), family based behavioural change and group based intervention.[363] The Green Paper envisages these new support teams training other professionals such as social workers, school nurses, educational psychologists, counsellors and local troubled families' teams in the use of these methods.

Although no mention is made of children reacting adversely to parental conflict, separation and divorce, the Green Paper does expect the new mental health support teams 'to support young people who have experienced trauma (such as bereavement) or traumatic incidents'.

So if these aspirations of the Government materialise by 2020/21 together with a promise of extra money, then a new organisational framework of coordinated services between schools and NHS specialist services will come into being – a major step forward from existing much criticised fragmented provision. This could therefore provide an opportunity for the Caplanian crisis intervention approach to be incorporated into the other forms of intervention mentioned in the Green Paper.

---

[361] Department of Health and Department for Education (December 2017) *Transforming Children and Young People's Mental Health Provision: a Green Paper* CM 9523 paras 65–80 pp19–22.

[362] Department of Health and Department for Education (December 2017) *Transforming Children and Young People's Mental Health Provision: a Green Paper* CM 9523 paras 65–80 pp19–22.

[363] Department of Health and Department for Education (December 2017) *Transforming Children and Young People's Mental Health Provision: a Green Paper* CM 9523 paras 65–80 pp19–22.

Weaving the primary preventive Caplanian model of crisis intervention into a whole school wellbeing programme: a challenge to innovate

So far I have argued that there is a strong prima facie case, based both on evidence from children and young people and from theory, for finding ways and means to apply crisis intervention methods of support for children in schools to help them cope with stressful upheavals associated with intense interparental conflict, separation and divorce. I am not arguing that this is the only method, but simply that it could form part of an armoury of short-term school-based primary preventive support methods to help children through a critical turning point in their family life, to strengthen their emotional resilience, and to lessen risk of longer-term educational and life path disadvantages, including serious behavioural and mental health problems. The main challenge is how to persuade practitioners and policy makers and educational and school health services that this is a promising approach worth developing, particularly in the light of the recommendations of the Joint House of Commons Education and Health Committee's report of 2 May 2017 and the Green Paper of December 2017 to which I have referred above.[364]

Despite the ongoing tough economic climate for public finances, I am convinced that attempts should be made to explore the feasibility of such an approach. The questions that must be answered are whether adequate funds can be found to set up a carefully prepared and evaluated exemplar scheme in an experimental area, with support from local educational and mental health authorities. After which, if successful, could some kind of strategic plan be developed? Might this be a project that falls within the remit of the Early Intervention Foundation set up by David Cameron's Coalition government following the Graham Allen report of 2011 for the Cabinet Office?[365] (See further Chapter Twelve). I will develop this idea in Chapter Thirteen. I do not underestimate the difficulties of getting something along these lines off the ground, but as I will show in Chapter Thirteen, the pressure for reform is growing strongly in health and education circles.

All I can say about this comes from other projects that I have been involved with using initiatives which developed from research studies (for example, in helping to launch the first out-of-court mediation

---

[364] Ibid.

[365] G Allen (January 2011) *Early Intervention: The Next Steps: An Independent Report to HM Government* Cabinet Office, London.

service in Bristol and being involved in the early days of the Guardian Ad Litem service).[366] Both involved persuading a very cautious legal profession and reluctant government administration to take an interest. But through the perseverance of a small but committed group of practitioners, both of these kinds of service eventually took off within the context of the family justice system and its Children and Family Court Advisory and Support Services. It is in this context I will consider the potential secondary preventive 'passage agent' support role of these services, utilising the Caplanian approach to which I will turn in Part III of this book. Before this, I need to explain the evolutionary way in which the family justice system has slowly attempted to address the welfare of children in divorce proceedings and the setbacks this process has received in recent years.

---

[366] M Murch (2004) 'The germ and gem of an idea' in J Westcott (ed) *Family Mediation: Past, Present and Future* Jordan's Family Law, Bristol at pp21–32. M Murch and K Bader (1984) *Separate Representation for Parents and Children: An Examination of the Initial Phase* Department of Health, London and University of Bristol. See also M Murch (1998) 'The guardian at litem service in the family justice system: retrospect and prospect' in *Social Services Inspectorate of Panel Managers Annual Workshop Briefing: Approaching the Millennium – children and the guardian service within the family justice system* Department of Health Social Care Group, London at pp3–22.

Part III
Secondary prevention

Introduction to Part III:
Family justice policy under the Coalition government (2010–15): how will a new regime meet the needs of children with separating and divorcing parents?

Introduction

The overall direction of thinking in this book is to consider ways and means of embedding the crisis model of preventive intervention into policies and practices that support children and young people facing serious interparental conflict and separation. In Part II I examine the relevance of this approach in the context of primary prevention in schools and, by implication, other first responder support services. I now turn to what, in mental health terms might be called a secondary preventive backup service for children and families when parental disputes take the form of litigation in the family courts, that is to say, when the interests of the child become the primary concern of the judicial system governed under the constitutional principles of the rule of law and an independent judiciary. As we will see, this raises the important issue of where the boundary of the family court system should be drawn so as to distinguish it from the state's executive services. Perhaps controversially I argue that the family court's welfare arm in the form of the Children and Family Court Advisory and Support Service (Cafcass) should be viewed constitutionally as part of the judicial system, since ultimately its officers are accountable to the family court judge when carrying out the duties to children. By contrast, unless mediators are undertaking work within the court system, their services lie outside of the court. In terms of Cafcass practice, I wish to see its officers equipped to understand and apply the crisis intervention approach whenever appropriate. I develop this line of thinking later in Chapter Thirteen, but first I need to review the emerging family justice policy background.

In the next three chapters I turn to policy and family law reform, an area with which I have been most closely associated in my academic career. I review major policy changes, introduced by the previous Coalition government and the senior judiciary, in the way the family justice system seeks to meet children's needs. It is a story of initial government blunders followed by attempts at emergency repair once it became apparent that substantial and hastily introduced cuts in civil legal aid had produced a number of unintended consequences. Some of these I have already highlighted in the Preface and Chapter One. In particular, I explain that a number of mediation services, intended by government to provide a cheaper and better form of service, were forced to close for financial reasons. At the same time there was an unexpected rise in the number of parents who pursued their disputes as litigants in person. This put extra pressure on the courts. Moreover, an unknown (but probably substantial number) of conflicted parents were deterred altogether from seeking help and redress from the system, thus denying their children any support they might have received from the family court's welfare service, Cafcass.

Overall, in May 2015, at the end of the Coalition government led by David Cameron, we appeared to have returned to a two-tiered system of family justice reminiscent of the period before the introduction of legal aid for divorce in the 1950s. Nevertheless, as this book was being prepared there were a few signs that the incoming Conservative administration was becoming aware of the dangers of a two-tiered system of justice. Thus, to many people's surprise, the then new Minister of Justice and Lord Chancellor, the Rt Hon Michael Gove MP, reviewing the legal system as a whole, spoke of a "dangerous inequality" at the heart of the system.[367] He acknowledged that "legal aid is a vital element in any fair system," adding, "There is a responsibility on government to make sure those in the greatest hardship at times of real need are provided with resources to secure access to justice."

With respect to family justice in particular, he evidently agreed with Sir James Munby, President of the Family Division, that the:

---

[367] M Gove (23 June 2015) 'What does a one nation justice policy look like?' Lecture to the Legatum Institute www.gov.uk/government/organisations/ministry-of-justice

'sometimes fraught and certainly disorientating process ... of dealing with family separation or divorce could be far more quickly and sensitively handled. By using plain English rather than legalese, replacing paper forms with simple questions online and automating much of the administrative process, many issues could be resolved far more quickly, often without administrators or the judiciary. This would free the time of Sir James and his colleagues for the vital work of the family court in deciding what is in the best interests of children.'[368]

So Michael Gove, the then minister, appeared in this speech to commit himself and the government to a further major reform programme, investing in modern technology to:

'deliver faster and fairer justice for all citizens; to make sure our system of family justice safeguards children, especially those at risk of abuse and neglect, more effectively than ever; to make sure the laws we pass provide protection for the weakest.'

One might say these were fine aspirations. Compared with some of the measures of the previous Coalition government, they might even represent a U-turn. However, Michael Gove stood down from the government in the run-up to the EU Referendum when, on 23 June 2016, David Cameron lost the 'remain campaign' and resigned. The new prime minister, Theresa May, then appointed Liz Truss MP to the position of Minister of Justice and Lord Chancellor, and she was subsequently replaced after the general election of June 2017 by David Lidington MP, and now after a cabinet reshuffle in January 2018 by David Gauke MP.

Therefore, at the time of writing (October 2017), it is not known what view the new minister is likely to take concerning family justice matters, although it may be encouraging to know that Theresa May said in an interview on the BBC *Today* programme (3 October 2016)[369] that her primary motivation for coming into politics had been to tackle 'injustice'. Nevertheless, I suspect that the new minister will probably have to give priority to penal reform and possibly concerns arising from the controversial independent inquiry into child abuse.

---

[368] Ibid.
[369] BBC Today (3 October 2016) Interview with Prime Minister May.

Moreover, given the rapid turnover of officials and ministers in the Ministry of Justice in past decades, it is very likely that neither they nor the minister will have much knowledge of the recent evolution of the interdisciplinary family justice system, and the role it should share with educational and mental health services, when addressing the needs of children caught up in the turmoil of parental separation and divorce. This is one reason why we should look more closely at the number of measures introduced by the Coalition government. Accordingly, I go into the matter in some detail partly to outline the historical context. This illustrates shifting social values concerning marriage, divorce and children, and the growing appreciation that it is the institution of parenthood rather than marriage which has come to have the greatest significance in contemporary society where, as we have seen in Chapter Two, many parents cohabit rather than marry.

Each of the next three chapters takes the form of a separate essay with a specific focus concerning the evolving nature of these measures. Even so, there is overlap between them and therefore a certain amount of unavoidable repetition, particularly with respect to cuts in legal aid. Also, as will become apparent, there are a number of consistent themes and arguments running through each chapter which form the basis of some of the policy and practice proposals which I set out in the conclusions of this book.

I take first, in Chapter Nine, the decision to remove the child welfare check in undefended divorce proceedings. In Chapter Ten I examine the way in which the current Minister of Justice's predecessors set about dismantling much of the old private family law regime. I then consider whether new measures might enable children coming into contact with the family justice system to receive reliable impartial information to help them understand the legal process regulating family change following the breakdown of their parents' relationship; how, if at all, their voice might be heard in the family justice process; and what support, if any, they receive during the course of proceedings from the system's practitioners, including some mediators working as gatekeepers to the family courts' welfare support service and Cafcass.

In Chapter Eleven I examine a number of obstacles to reform, some recent, others longstanding, which have frustrated previous attempts to improve the efficiency and sensitivity of the family justice system service for children and their parents going through the upheavals of parental separation and divorce, to which Michael Gove referred in his June 2015 lecture to the Legatum Institute.[370]

---

[370] Ibid.

It will be seen that I take the view that these issues have to be considered not just from the perspective of orthodox family jurisprudence, but from the viewpoints of preventive community mental health and social policy. This is because the specialist interdisciplinary work of the family justice system in which the children's interests are paramount must aim to promote children's positive social and emotional wellbeing, and where possible to strengthen their resilience in the face of critical and stressful family change. In this respect the family justice system needs to be seen as part of the community's network of preventive public services backing up, as a second line of support, the role of schools and primary healthcare services. These, as we have seen in Part II, are usually the first responders when children and young people begin to manifest mental health symptoms such as depression, anxiety and poor school behaviour in reaction to stressful difficulties they may be encountering at home.

I should just add by way of an introductory caveat to the three family justice-related chapters, that in my experience there is little evidence so far that the majority of policy makers and law reformers in this field have been guided by both the extensive and growing behavioural science knowledge base to which I have referred in Chapters Three and Four or by principles of early intervention and preventive mental health which I have addressed in Part II. Rather, the approach of most concerned law reformers and social policy makers seems to me essentially pragmatic and short–term, and to have been largely conditioned and shaped by their own specialist professional experience – be it as lawyers, economists, social workers or as official bureaucrats – and not infrequently set against their own subjective experience of family life, whether or not they are consciously aware of it. Moreover, as is the English way, there is a certain distrust of academic thinking and what is sometimes dismissed as mere theorising. Readers may need to hold these points in mind in order to link Part II to what follows here in Part III.

NINE

The repeal of Section 41 of the Matrimonial Causes Act 1973 and related reforms: is the state turning a blind eye to the needs of children in divorce proceedings?

Introduction

Section S.18 of the Children and Families Act 2014 repealed s41 of the Matrimonial Causes Act 1973. Generally known as the welfare check in undefended divorce cases where there were no accompanying applications for child-related orders, these provisions had required a district judge to scrutinise a Statement of Arrangements for all the dependent children of the family (set out in Form 4) in order to determine whether the court should exercise any of its powers under the Children Act 1989.

In addition, the 2014 act repealed the unimplemented s11 of the Family Law Act 1996, which would have amended s41 so as to require a divorce court to treat the child's welfare as the paramount consideration and to have regard to a checklist of factors, including the wishes and feelings of the child in light of his/her age and understanding. Thus Lowe and Douglas point out:

> The 2014 reforms effectively deny children a voice in divorce proceedings. It can be seen as the ultimate adoption of the non-interventionist policy espoused by the Children Act 1989, which in turn has been said to rely upon the assumption that parents may be trusted, in most cases, to plan what is best for their children's future, and that where they are in agreement on this, it is unnecessary and potentially damaging for the State in the guise of the court to intervene.[371]

---

[371] N Lowe and G Douglas G (2015) *Bromley's Family Law* (11th edition) Oxford University Press at p447.

Nevertheless, Lowe and Douglas observe that the 2014 reform, while it may be:

> in line with the general policy of discouraging recourse to the courts in family matters ... the signals sent out by the 2014 reform ... run counter to the general trend of involving children more rather than less in proceedings that concern them.[372]

Indeed, it might run counter to the provisions of Article 12 of the United Nations Convention on the Rights of the Child.[373] Moreover, Lowe and Douglas point out that:

> a parent wishing to apply for what is known as a Child Arrangement Order[374] (previously specifying orders for residence or contact) must first attend a Mediation and Assessment meeting (MIAM) conducted by a mediator – in effect now a gatekeeper to the family justice system – except in cases where there are substantive allegations of domestic violence or child abuse.[375]

As we will see, it is debatable that there is no current requirement for children capable of forming their own views to attend a Mediation Information and Assessment Meeting (MIAM), even though they might wish to have their say before a decision about their future is arrived at.

But it is not just an issue concerning children's rights – important though that is. There is a social paradox raised by the abolition of s41

---

[372] Ibid.

[373] Article 12 of the UN Convention on the Rights of the Child 1989, to which the UK is a signatory, states that: '(i) States' Parties shall assure to the child who is capable of forming his or her own views the right to express those feelings in all matters affecting the child, the views of the child being given due weight in accordance with the age and maturity of the child;' and '(ii) The child shall in particular be provided the opportunity to be heard in any judicial or administrative proceedings affecting the child either directly or through a representative or appropriate body in a manner consistent with procedural rules of national law.'

[374] A Child Arrangement Order under s12 of the Children and Families Act 2014 means an order regulating any of the following: (a) with whom a child is to live, spend time or have contact, and (b) where a child is to live, spend time or have contact with any person.

[375] N Lowe and G Douglas G (2015) *Bromley's Family Law* (11th edition) Oxford University Press at p447.

and the failure to give children a voice in the new MIAM procedure. As we have seen in Part I, at least since the 1980s a whole series of British and international social and behavioural science studies have produced compelling evidence to show that when their parents' relationship breaks down, many children are plunged into an emotional upheaval and their education is disrupted. Indeed, some parents are themselves so stressed that they do not appreciate the full impact of the breakup on their children. Moreover, as we have seen, it is clear from research that a significant number of these children, particularly in high-conflict cases, will suffer prolonged reactive psychological dysfunction, with serious consequences for their behavioural and educational development.

The repeal of s41 therefore raised the question of whether the state should attempt to safeguard these children's welfare in some other more effective way. Under the reforms of the 2014 act, in cases where a parent seeks a Child Arrangement Order (replacing 'contact orders and 'resident orders' under s8 of the Children Act 1989) it might have been possible to do so when the compulsory MIAMs came into force (see further below).[376] But, as we shall see in the next chapter, at least as far as hearing the voice of the child is concerned, mediators conducting MIAMs are not expected to involve children directly.

In this chapter, therefore, I examine the matter from the perspective of a socio-legal researcher who over the years has studied the operation of the welfare check in its various guises,[377] and who with colleagues has conducted several other child-related divorce studies, including some high-conflict cases where the children were separately represented.[378] As we have seen in Chapter Five, these include children's own accounts of how they experienced the breakdown of their parents' relationship. In these studies children were viewed as actors during the divorce process in their own right, rather than as appendages of the adults. This was

---

[376] Cl 12 the Children and Families Act 2014.

[377] E Elston, F Fuller and M Murch (1975) 'Judicial hearings of undefended divorce petitions' *Modern Law Review* 38(6) at p609. G Davis, A Macleod and M Murch (1983) 'Undefended divorce: should s41 be repealed?' *Modern Law Review* 46 at p121. M Murch, G Douglas, L Scanlan, L Perry, C Lisles, K Bader and M Borkowski (September 1999) *Safeguarding Children's Welfare in Uncontentious Divorce: A Study of s41 of the Matrimonial Causes Act 1973: Report to the Lord Chancellor's Department* Cardiff Law School.

[378] G Douglas, M Murch, C Miles and L Scanlan (March 2006) *Research Into the Operation of Rule 9.5 of the Family Proceedings Rules 1991* Department for Constitutional Affairs, London. See also I Butler, L Scanlan, M Robinson, G Douglas and M Murch (2003) *Divorcing Children: Children's Experience of Their Parents' Divorce* Jessica Kingsley, London. This is a more discursive text bringing together the findings of earlier Cardiff studies.

in line with the principle set out in Article 12 of the United Nations Convention on the Rights of the Child 1989 (see note above).

The slow demise of the welfare check in undefended divorce

The principle and assumptions behind the former s41 of the Matrimonial Causes Act 1973: why should the state attempt to safeguard children's welfare in divorce?

In the post-war period, one can trace two distinct strands of thought offering different justifications for a welfare check in undefended divorce petitions: first, a dominant legal/moral set of arguments, and second, an emergent psychosocial line of thought. To some extent both of these persist to this day in policy discussions about how the needs of children in separation and divorce proceedings should be approached, although the balance between the two may be shifting in favour of the second, in view of the modern recognition that family justice matters should be thought about less in strictly legal terms and more in holistic interdisciplinary terms.[379] Nevertheless, I will argue later that in some respects the repeal of the welfare check in undefended divorce risks taking us back to the situation that existed before it was first introduced. Therefore, it is necessary to examine the principles and assumptions upon which it was based, and to consider its genesis.

The beginning of the story: the orthodox legal/moral justification

A check on the welfare of children whose parents were divorcing was first introduced in 1958 under s2(i) of the Matrimonial Proceedings (Children) Act.[380] This followed the concern of the Denning Committee on Procedure in Matrimonial Causes and the Royal Commission on Marriage and Divorce (the Morton Commission) that the needs of children were not adequately safeguarded in divorce proceedings.[381]

---

[379] For a discussion of the concept of 'autopoiesis' in legal thought, see M King and C Piper (1995) *How the Law Thinks About Children* Gower, London; and M Murch (1995) 'The cross-disciplinary approach to family law: are we trying to mix oil with water?' in D Pearl (ed) *Frontiers of Family Law* Wiley, Chichester.

[380] The provision was re-enacted by s33 of the Matrimonial Causes Act 1965 and then by s41 of the Matrimonial Causes Act 1973, now subject to the proposed repeal.

[381] The Committee on Procedure of Matrimonial Causes (1947) Cmnd 7024. The Royal Commission on Marriage and Divorce (the Morton Commission) (1956) Cmnd 9678 – see paras 368–407.

These had increased following family disruption caused by the Second World War and the return of demobbed service personnel to changed and unfamiliar family circumstances.

Indeed, the Denning Committee noted that no subject caused them greater concern than the welfare of children. As Cretney observed, the 1956 *Report of the Royal Commission on Marriage and Divorce (the Morton Commission)* was even more outspoken about the effect of divorce on children than the Denning Committee.[382] He cites the Royal Commission report, which stated:

> there is a wealth of testimony as to the effect on children of the breakdown of normal family relationships. When family relationships break down there is always the risk of failure to meet fully the child's needs for security and affection. If in fact there is such failure the child may become so emotionally disturbed as to reject the influence of the family and this may result in anti-social behaviour ... Where divorce takes place it is essential that everything which it is possible in the circumstances should be done to mitigate the effect upon the child of the disruption of family life.[383]

The Denning Committee took the view that divorced parents had 'disabled themselves from fulfilling their joint responsibility', and consequently proposed that a court welfare officer should have access to all petitions and should report to the court, and that in all cases the judge should deal with the children's future on the same day as the court dealt with the divorce. Cretney noted that although a number of years were to pass before any of the committee's recommendations were followed:

> it can reasonably be claimed that the Denning Committee marked a decisive shift in the approach taken by the law to the legal consequences of divorce in relation to children" and "was influential in the gradual development of the divorce court welfare service.[384]

---

[382] S Cretney (1998) *Law, Law Reform and the Family* Oxford University Press at p150. Report of the *Royal Commission on Marriage and Divorce* (the Morton Commission) (1956) Cmd 9678 at paras 366(ii) and 370; quoted in S Cretney (2003) *Family Law in the Twentieth Century: A History* Oxford University Press at p579.

[383] S Cretney (1998) *Law, Law Reform and the Family* Oxford University Press at p150

[384] Ibid at p150.

These concerns were followed up in some measure by the Morton Commission, which recommended a procedure:

> which firstly will ensure that the parents themselves have given full consideration to the question of their children's future welfare and, secondly, to enable the control of the court over the welfare of the child to be made more effective.[385]

The Morton Commission thought that in undefended divorce petitions a written statement, to be followed by a few oral questions and answers on oath from the petitioner parent in the witness box, would normally suffice to enable the judge to assess the soundness of the proposed arrangements.[386] I consider below criticisms that were made of this procedure. Here it is sufficient to probe a little more into the rationale. The clearest articulation for some sort of welfare check was given some years later by Gerald Caplan, a mental health expert, who wrote:

> by voluntarily approaching the courts to dissolve their marriage, parents explicitly open up their private domain to public scrutiny and intervention. Their request for a divorce is a formal statement that their marriage has broken down.[387]

Subsequently, the view of the Finer Committee was that since 1958 the law recognised that children involved in matrimonial proceedings needed to be given 'special protection'. The committee found that this was underlined:

> by the fact that it is expressly enacted that a divorce decree made absolute where this order (i.e. Certification of Satisfaction) has not been made will be void.[388] (See further below)

---

[385] *Royal Commission on Marriage and Divorce* (the Morton Commission) (1956) Cmd 9678 at para 383.

[386] B Mortlock (1972) *The Inside of Divorce* Constable, London at p68. See Also Morton Report (1956) Cmd 9678 para 383 op cit at n219.

[387] G Caplan (1989) 'Prevention of psychopathology and maladjustment in children of divorce' in M Brambring, F Lösel and H Skowronek (eds) *Children at Risk: Assessment, Longitudinal Research and Intervention* Walter de Gruyter, Berlin at p367.

[388] *The Report of the Committee on One Parent Families* (The Finer Committee) (1974) Cmnd 5629 HMSO, London at para 4.406.

The social context of post-war divorce reform

In order to appreciate why this provision was enacted when it was we need to understand something of the broader socio-legal context in the post-war period, in particular, the interplay between the conflicting social values concerning children. On the one hand, there was an argument that family life, whether or not it is affected by marital tensions, is essentially a private matter, and thus divorcing parents can normally be expected to make appropriate arrangements for their children. On the other hand was a view that the state has a residual responsibility to safeguard the welfare of children – a legal concept that can be traced back to the early days of wardship when the sovereign, as parens patriae, had a duty to protect children unable to protect themselves.[389] To this day, the tension between these two opposing arguments are held, as it were, in dynamic suspension; this is seen in the practices and policies of both so-called 'private' and public family law. As we shall see, the balance between the two has fluctuated according to political and economic considerations, set against a growing understanding of children's developmental, welfare and educational needs as revealed by social and behavioural research and clinical practice.

We also need to remember that in the immediate post-war period when the welfare check was first introduced, divorce was viewed very differently from today. Being divorced still carried a social stigma, particularly for those seen as the 'guilty party'. This was a time when the concept of the matrimonial offence held sway. Even in undefended suits the 'innocent petitioners', mostly women, had to endure what many felt to be a public degradation ritual in open court in order to prove the grounds for the divorce petition.[390] Indeed, right up to the early 1960s, in disputed children's cases, although the court had come to accept that an adulterous mother should not be barred from having care and control, on the basis that the child's interests were the first and paramount consideration, this could still be qualified as 'not the sole consideration' and that 'the claims of justice' should not be overlooked.[391] Thus Harman LJ thought it necessary to declare that a

---

[389] N Lowe and R White (1986) *Wards of Court* (2nd edition) Butterworth, London at p126.

[390] L Elston, J Fuller and M Murch (1975) 'Judicial hearings of undefended divorce petitions' *Modern Law Review* 38, pp609–40.

[391] See Re L (Court of Appeal) per Lord Justice Harman (1962) 1 Weekly Law Report pp889–890; quoted in S Cretney (2003) *Family Law in the Twentieth Century* Oxford University Press at p577.

woman guilty of deserting the husband might be deprived the care of her children, observing:

> If a wife chooses to leave her husband, for no ground which she chooses to put forward, she must be prepared to take the consequences. She is a curious woman in that she seems to have no consciousness that she has duties as well as rights.[392]

A further point to remember is that at this time, in comparison to today, the scale of divorce was relatively small.[393] Even so, as Cretney observed, the upheavals to family life occasioned by war led to what was regarded at the time as 'a massive increase' in divorce. As he put it, this was:

> a source of grave anxiety to conventional opinion, which saw in the 'insidious growth' in the divorce rate a tendency to take the duties and responsibilities of marriage less seriously than formally and a threat to the whole stability of marriage.[394]

Although in this post-war period the main focus of law reform concerned the growth of divorce and whether the notion of the matrimonial offence should give way to the concept of irretrievable breakdown of marriage (a fierce debate skilfully chronicled by Cretney)[395] many from both sides of the argument shared an intuitive unease about the position of children caught up in the turmoil and uncertainties of their parents' marriage breakdown. Even so, until the Denning Committee's recommendations were introduced in 1958, opinion was that these matters were best left to the parents and not to the state, even when parents were disputing custody. Indeed, given adversarial proceedings, such disputes were still referred to as 'ancillary matters' (as indeed they often still are).

It is sometimes asserted that the availability of legal aid for divorce cases under the Legal Aid and Advice Act 1949 led to a major increase in divorce. Yet, Colin Gibson showed that:

---

[392] Ibid.

[393] According to the Council of Europe the divorce rate in England and Wales increased 20-fold since between 1956 and 1993 to reach the highest rate in Western Europe – in the 1960s and increased from 20,000 or so in the 1960s to a peak of 163,000 in 1993.

[394] S Cretney (1998) *Law, Law Reform and the Family* Oxford University Press pp34–35.

[395] Ibid at pp38–72.

the new system of legal aid greatly improved poor petitioners' access to divorce. The number of legally aided practitioners rose threefold between 1949 and 1950, while there was a 9% rise in the number of petitions filed. But it was a 21% rise in the number of wives petitions which accounts for this increase; the number of husbands petitioning in 1951 declined by 3% over the 1949 figure ... poverty had hindered often more wives than husbands from access to the divorce courts and wives were the most numerous beneficiaries of the legal aid scheme.[396]

This historical point is particularly important in the light of cuts in civil legal aid introduced by the Legal Aid, Sentencing and Punishment of Offenders Act 2012, since once again proportionally more women than men will suffer from the absence of legal aid to pursue their claims in the family courts in child-related litigation.

Returning to the immediate post-war period, there is a further point to make. This concerns the view of Mortlock, a reformist practitioner, that at that time judges were mostly dealing with divorcing parents who broadly came from the same socioeconomic background as themselves. Thus, in the days before legal aid became available, divorce and related children's proceedings affected a comparatively small social class of well-to-do people – a class from which High Court and Appeal Court judges themselves were mostly drawn. So they were 'dealing for the most part with people who lived in an environment the habitual assumptions and ethos of which were substantially their own'.[397]

Moreover, judges as well as divorcing couples were generally accustomed to sending their children to private boarding schools – an educational provision which provided a useful if sometimes stoical, even harsh, refuge from the daily tensions of their parents' collapsing marriage. As Royston Lambert, who with colleagues Spencer Millham and Roger Bullock conducted research in the 1960s for the Public Schools Commission, pointed out, 'only in England has boarding rather than day school been the style of education long favoured by the governing classes'.[398] This is probably one reason why, as we shall see,

---

[396] C Gibson (1994) *Dissolving Wedlock* Routledge, London at p180.

[397] B Mortlock (1972) *The Inside of Divorce* Constable, London at p71.

[398] R Lambert and S Millham (1967) *The Hothouse Society: An Exploration of Boarding-school Life Through the Boys' and Girls' Own Writing* Weidenfeld and Nicolson, London. They also pithily observe that 'some children in boarding schools were sent away to avoid the tensions of a broken home but absence does not necessarily lessen their anxiety' (at p269).

when the welfare check was finally introduced in 1958, its operation was at best cursory. Judges generally felt that children's interests were being taken care of in a setting with which they themselves were familiar – even though this was not a view shared by Lord Denning and his colleagues, or even the members of the much criticised Morton Commission.[399]

Some might wonder why Lord Denning and the Commission under Lord Morton of Henryton should not share the general view of judges at the time. The answer probably lies in Lord Denning's well-known empathy with the common man due to his own upbringing. Another factor was probably the pressure from the Attlee government's Committee on Legal Procedure.[400] As far as the Royal Commission was concerned, their view on the matter may well have been influenced by the arguments of Dame Irene White, a well-known social reformer, notwithstanding the trenchant criticisms made by Professor O. R. McGregor that the Morton Commission made inadequate use of available social statistics.[401]

An emerging child and family mental health approach

While in the post-war period High Court divorce and matrimonial proceedings in magistrates' courts were still largely seen as the province of the lawyers (as some would claim they have been until very recently), there was among behavioural and social scientists a separate but parallel field of thought and concern for children of broken homes. This was particularly influenced in the 1950s and 1960s by the British School of Psychoanalysis at the Tavistock Institute of Human Relations, where attachment theory was developed by John Bowlby.[402] His work was

---

[399] O R McGregor (1957) *Divorce in England: A Centenary Study* Heinemann, London at pp187–193.

[400] This distrust of the influence of lawyers may have surfaced again in the membership of the Norgrove Review panel, which only had one lawyer, Mr Justice (as he then was) McFarlane.

[401] O R McGregor (1957) *Divorce in England: A Centenary Study* Heinemann, London at pp186–187. Committee on Reform of Legal Procedure (1946) *Minutes* referred to by S Cretney. This did not want the Denning Committee to be dominated by lawyers; thus the Legal Procedure Committee recommended that membership should include 'a working class woman', believing that while such a person would be unable to contribute much, if anything, to legal matters, she could be expected to make a valuable contribution to the discussion of the social issues involved. S Cretney (1998) *Law, Law Reform and the Family* Oxford University Press at p142.

[402] J Bowlby (1953) *Childcare and the Growth of Love* Pelican Book, London at p93. Also J Bowlby (1980) *Attachment and Loss Volume 1 and Volume 3* Pelican Books,

particularly influential in childcare social work in this period, as indeed it is today. Supported by clinical and empirical research studies from both the UK and US, this school of thought focused on the insecurities caused to children of all ages through broken attachments and discontinuities of parenting caused by ill-health of a parent, unhappy marriage, desertion, separation and divorce. The main proposition which Bowlby drew from a number of such studies was that the emotional life of the adult was largely conditioned by love relationships during childhood, and that 'deprived and unhappy children grow up to make bad parents,[403] reflecting the social values of the age echoed in the concept of the matrimonial offence. Some modern readers may be surprised by the judgemental tone of some of Bowlby's earlier writing. This also occurs in the work of another influential post-war Tavistock thinker – again, a former wartime army psychiatrist – Dr Henry Dicks.[404] His seminal work focused on the dyadic marital relationship and was based on object relations theory, associated with the work of Melanie Klein and W.D.A. Fairbairn. Dicks's work influenced the setting up of the Tavistock Family Discussion Bureau (FDB) (later to become the Tavistock Centre for Couple Relationships and now Tavistock Relationships).[405] The theory and practice of marital therapy as developed at the FDB in the 1950s and 1960s was drawn upon extensively by the probation service in its training for domestic court conciliation work, particularly when, following the Denning Committee's recommendations, it began to undertake child welfare reports for the divorce court.[406] The probation service's interests in part stemmed from the belief that much juvenile delinquency could be traced back to marital and parental discord and therefore justified a preventive approach to the service's intervention.

There were of course a number of other sociological and social policy developments taking place in the post-war period before the

---

London. See also J Bowlby (1979) *The Making and Breaking of Affectional Bonds* Tavistock, London at pp126–160.

[403] J Bowlby (1953) *Childcare and the Growth of Love* Pelican Book, London at p93.

[404] H V Dicks (1967) *Marital Tensions: Clinical Studies Towards a Psychological Theory of Interaction* Routledge and Kegan Paul, London.

[405] K Bannister, A Lyons, L Pincus, J Robb, A Shooter and J Stevens (1955) *Social Casework in Marital Problems* Tavistock, London. A Balfour, M Morgan and C Vincent (eds) (2012) *How Couple Relationships Shape Our World: Clinical Practice, Research and Policy Perspectives* Karnac, London.

[406] M Murch (1980) *Justice and Welfare in Divorce* Sweet and Maxwell, London. C Clulow and C Vincent (1987) *In a Child's Best Interest: Divorce Court Welfare and the Search for Settlement* Tavistock, London.

introduction of the welfare check in undefended divorce which, as it were, brought about a favourable climate for its development. Some of these have been outlined elsewhere.[407] Perhaps the most important concerned the policy development following the Curtis Committee's inquiry into the care of children, which reported in 1946.[408] Cretney observes that this 'was the first inquiry in the country directed specifically to the care of all children deprived of normal home life and covering all groups of such children'. Potentially it covered children whose parents had separated, though in fact it was deemed to apply mainly to children in the care of the local authority and children's charities.

The recommendations of this committee, fuelled in part by the tragic death of Dennis O'Neill, who was killed by his foster parents, revealed a serious lack of supervision by the local authority. But the general experience of wartime evacuation had also raised concerns about the care of children separated from their parents, particularly those who were made homeless when the evacuation scheme was wound up.[409] Among other things, the committee's recommendations led to the Children Act 1948 and the establishment of local authority children's departments led by a named children's officer.[410] The 1948 act gave statutory recognition to the principle that the state had a responsibility to provide for children in need. Professionally trained welfare officers, many with good university degrees, developed an understanding of attachment theory as advanced by Bowlby and his followers. Also building on the voluntary social work of organisations such as the Quaker Family Service Units and the Family Welfare Association, the concept of preventive social work was established.

Three relevant points need to be made here in relation to the subject of this book, namely, the needs of children caught up in disputes between their parents leading to separation and divorce. First, the notion of preventive work with children and their families – a theme continued in the report of the Ingleby Committee, which was

---

[407] M Murch (2009) 'Cultural change and the family justice system' in G Douglas and N Lowe (eds) *The Continuing Evolution of Family Law* Jordan's Family Law, Bristol at pp119–125.

[408] *Report of the Care of Children Committee* (1946) Cmd 6922.

[409] See S Cretney (2003) *Family Law in the Twentieth Century* Oxford University Press at pp671–692.

[410] For a detailed exposition of the background to the Children Act 1948 see R A Parker (1983) 'The gestation of reform: the Children Act 1948' in P Bean and S Macpherson (eds) *Approaches to Welfare* Routledge and Kegan Paul, London, p202.

primarily concerned with the problem of juvenile delinquency.[411] That committee accepted that the problems of neglect and delinquency were:

> more often than not the problems of the family and that the need for positive preventive action is needed to ensure that children get the best possible upbringing.[412]

As we shall see, I return to the fundamental theme that 'prevention is better than cure' in the final part of this book.

Second, it should be noted that in the gestation to the Children Act 1948 and all that followed in relation to local authority children's departments in the 1950s and 1960s, the emphasis went on what we now term *public* family law proceedings (that is, dealing with the chronic problems of mostly impoverished families where the children were deemed to be in need of care and protection). In my opinion this set up an organisational and constitutional split between those child protection agencies with state powers to bring proceedings (that is, local authority children's departments and the NSPCC), and what later emerged in 2001 from the civil work of the probation service, namely, the court-based Cafcass, which had responsibilities to provide court welfare reports in both public and private law proceedings as well as court based conciliation services.[413]

Third, another point to bear in mind is that before legal aid became available for divorce, the jurisdiction of what we now term private family law was characterised by a structural division based essentially on social class: on the one hand there was the High Court and county court providing divorce for the well-to-do, and on the other there was the local magistrates' court providing 'separation orders' (known technically as partial relief) for the poor and labouring classes. The existence of this structural division was strongly criticised by many social reformers in the 1950s and 1960s, not least by the distinguished academic O. R. McGregor.[414]

---

[411] *Report of the Committee on Children and Young Persons* (the Ingleby Report) (1960) Cmnd 1191.

[412] Ibid, Chapter 1.

[413] See further M Murch (2009) 'Cultural change in the family justice system' in G Douglas and N Lowe (eds) *The Continuing Evolution of Family Law* Jordan's Family Law, Bristol at pp111–145.

[414] O R McGregor (1957) *Divorce in England: A Centenary Study* Heinemann, London at pp91–128. See also O R McGregor, L Blom-Cooper and C Gibson (1979) *Separated Spouses: A study of the Matrimonial Jurisdiction of Magistrate's Courts* Duckworth, London.

The history of the welfare check: progressive disillusion in legal effectiveness

To return to the welfare check, following its inception this judicial checking mechanism underwent several important changes. Its character altered from (a) a procedure applied in open court hearings of undefended divorce petitions; to (b) a 'special procedure' whereby before granting the divorce decree circuit judges interviewed petitioner parents privately in chambers about the content of the Statement of Arrangements before declaring that these arrangements were satisfactory or the best that could be devised in the circumstances; and then to (c) the now repealed, quasi-administrative exercise under the provisions of s41 of the Matrimonial Causes Act 1973, as amended by the Children Act 1989, whereby a district judge scrutinised the Statement of Arrangements along with the undefended divorce petition with a view to deciding whether the court should exercise any of its powers under the Children Act 1989 before granting the divorce decree. I summarise below the influence that socio-legal research may have played in assessing the effectiveness of each of these stages. As today, the major drive for these reforms was the need to reduce escalating costs, particularly civil legal aid, which having become available for divorce in the early 1950s, was substantially cut by the removal of legal aid for most divorce cases by the provisions of the Legal Aid, Sentencing and Punishment of Offenders Act 2012.[415]

The initial scheme: open court hearings

Taking the view that law reform and social policy should be preceded by empirical research, very soon after the creation of the Law Commission in 1965, its chairman, Sir Leslie Scarman (as he then was) in the context of an examination of divorce reform, requested a Cambridge law lecturer, Mr John Hall, to ascertain how the legislative safeguards to protect children in undefended cases were working in practice.[416] Questionnaires were sent to judges, registrars, court welfare officers and children's officers to sound their views. Hall also conducted interviews with solicitors. He found that in only about 5% of cases the judges refused the decree nisi and adjourned the case for a welfare officer to see each parent at home and report. Hall concluded that judges had

---

[415] LASPO 2012 Schedule 1 para 12(9), as amended by SI 2017/748.

[416] J Hall (1968) 'Arrangements for the care and upbringing of children: s33 of the Matrimonial Causes Act 1973' *Law Commission Working Paper No 15*.

insufficient time and facilities, and sometimes insufficient relevant experience, to conduct a wholly satisfactory enquiry into the proposed arrangements and that in consequence the procedure was 'something of a formality.[417] Even so, he reported that 80 out of 98 judges thought that the system was working satisfactorily.

The Law Commission continued its interest in undefended divorce proceedings and the operation of the welfare check after the introduction of the Divorce Reform Act 1969. One of Scarman's earlier objectives on becoming Chairman of the Commission was that it should harness the findings of social research to the process of law reforms.[418] Accordingly, it responded positively to my research proposal, supported by the then Social Science Research Council, into the circumstances of families in divorce proceedings. This included a court observation study and follow-up interviews with a sample of petitioners. This research confirmed Hall's findings and found that of the 470 relevant cases observed in three county courts, the judge withheld a certificate of satisfaction in only 2.8% (21 cases) and sought welfare reports in only 1.6% (12 cases), and then only in extreme circumstances where the children were already subject to other sorts of inquiry by local authorities.[419] Most cases lasted no more than 10 minutes. In most the questioning by the judge, if it occurred at all, was perfunctory. In over half the cases the judge asked no questions about the child. The majority of parents, who gave evidence on oath in open court with members of the public looking on, found the whole procedure stressful and often embarrassing. They were surprised that such little impartial care and attention had been paid to their children's welfare. Many felt that there should have been a more rigorous check in every case and were amazed that the court had taken their word without further corroboration. The researchers concluded that open court hearings of undefended divorce petitions, representation for which was often funded through civil legal aid, was an expensive ritual experienced by the majority of petitioners, mostly women, as a public degradation ceremony and totally ineffective as a child welfare check.

---

[417] Ibid at p13. See also M Murch, G Douglas, L Scanlan, L Perry, C Lisles, K Bader and M Borkowski (1999) *Safeguarding Children's Welfare in Uncontentious Divorce: A Study of s41 of the Matrimonial Causes Act 1973: Report to the Lord Chancellor's Department Research Series 7/99* at p7.

[418] See Law Commission (1966) *First Annual Report 1965–1966*, https://www.jstor. org/stable/1093013?seq=1#page_scan_tab_contents.

[419] E Elston, J Fuller and M Murch (1975) 'Judicial hearings of undefended divorce petitions' *Modern Law Review* 38(6) pp608–640.

It was not surprising, therefore, that the Lord Chancellor's Department, seeking savings in the legal aid budget, should justify the introduction in 1973 of the so-called special procedure whereby open court hearings were abolished. Instead, postal applications for undefended divorce petitions were permitted, no longer requiring legal representation in open court. It was estimated that this measure saved £6 million on the civil legal aid budget in the first year.[420] In 1981 McGregor described this change of procedure as:

> the only fundamental change in divorce procedure since it ceased to be obtained by act of Parliament. It was in fact established by fiat of judges and officials, an example of the strong influence procedure can exert on the substantive law itself, which in Maine's famous phrase 'has the look of being gradually secreted in the interstices of procedure'.[421]

The operation of the special procedure

Private children's appointments by which a judge interviewed petitioner parents (with or without the respondent and sometimes in the presence of a court welfare officer) marked the introduction of a more inquisitorial approach. The hope was that 'greater informality would improve communication between judge and parents and help uncover problems as well as enable the judges to offer parents advice and encouragement'.[422] A study of 1,500 appointments and follow-up interviews with 374 parents published in 1983 revealed that although courts and judges varied in their approach, with up to a dozen or more appointments dealt with in a morning, 60% heard in a courtroom, a certificate was granted in 90% of the cases.[423] Welfare reports were ordered in only 4% of cases, usually because the family was already

---

[420] See M Murch (2009) 'Cultural change in the family justice system' in G Douglas and N Lowe (eds) *The Continuing Evolution of Family Law* Jordan's Family Law, Bristol at p129. Before then, as Cretney records 'young barristers could make substantial incomes by appearing in a series of brief undefended divorce cases'. See S Cretney (2000) *Family Law in the Twentieth Century: A History* Oxford University Press at p287.

[421] O R McGregor (1981) *Social History and Law Reform* Stevens, London at p44.

[422] M Murch, G Douglas, L Scanlan, L Perry, C Lisles, K Bader and M Borkowski (September 1999) *Safeguarding Children's Welfare in Uncontentious Divorce: A Study of s41 of the Matrimonial Causes Act 1973: Lord Chancellor's Department Research Series* 7/99 at p11.

[423] G Davis, A Macleod and M Murch (1983) 'Undefended divorce: should s41 of the Matrimonial Causes Act 1973 be repealed?' *Modern Law Review* 46 at p121.

known to social services. Many parents were nevertheless favourably impressed by the judge's manner and by being able to briefly discuss matters such as contact arrangements, the children's day care and general wellbeing. Even so, it was concluded that the procedure remained ineffective as a welfare check, because there was little real scope for the judge to probe the evidence presented.

In 1985 the committee chaired by the Honourable Dame Margaret Booth made various criticisms of this procedure: the Statement of Arrangement was often filled in with minimal information, no encouragement was given to the respondent to attend or file a separate statement, and information was often out of date by the time the appointment was held.[424] In 1986, as part of its review of child law, the Law Commission concluded that the appointment procedure 'had not been successful in any of its declared aims', while its 'most discernable value appears to be symbolic or incidental'.[425] While it should not be abolished according to the Law Commission, since this might create the impression that the law does not value protecting children's interests,[426] in a subsequent paper,[427] the commission recommended that the court should be required to consider (rather than approve) the arrangements for the children. Recommending that the Statement of Arrangements should be improved and considered by the court at an earlier stage, the commission nevertheless recommended that the children's appointment system should be abolished, since insisting that every divorcing couple with children should discuss their proposed arrangements for the children with a judge could be seen as simply singling out parents who divorce as more irresponsible than others.[428] In contrast to the views of the Denning Committee and the Morton Commission, this clearly marked a major shift in social values to a less paternalistic approach which placed the responsibility for children's interests primarily on the parents,[429] and perhaps a growing recognition that the law does not in any case seek to protect in a similar fashion those increasing numbers of children whose unmarried parents separate.

---

[424] The Booth Report (1985) *Report of the Matrimonial Causes Procedure Committee* HMSO, London.

[425] Law Commission (1986) *Review of Child Law: Custody* Working Paper No 96 at para 4.10.

[426] Ibid.

[427] Law Commission (1988) *Review of Child Law: Guardianship and Custody* Law Comm No 172.

[428] Ibid at para 3.10.

[429] J Eeklaar (1991) 'Parental responsibility: state of nature or nature of the State' *Journal of Social Welfare and Family Law* 37.

Children Act Reform

Consequently, the Children Act 1989 (Schedule 12 Paragraph 31) amended s41 and set up the basis of a system (now repealed by s17 of the Children and Families Act 2014) whereby a district judge scrutinised the filed Statement of Arrangements with a view to deciding whether the court should exercise any of its powers under the Children Act with respect to any children of the family. If there were any exceptional circumstances making it desirable to do so, the court could direct that the granting of a divorce decree absolute could be withheld until the court ordered otherwise.

Further available research

In 1997 the then Lord Chancellor's Department, as part of its preparation for the possible implementation of the Family Law Act 1996, commissioned the Cardiff Law School to undertake a detailed research study to illuminate and evaluate the working of the s41 procedure as revised by the Children Act 1989.[430] A systematic random sampling technique was employed, giving a sample of 350 undefended divorce petitions drawn representatively from 10 courts in the Midlands, South West England and South Wales. Once special measures were taken to protect confidentiality, data were gathered from Form 4 (the Statement of Arrangements) concerning details of the family. The courts then invited a selection of petitioner parents to take part in the research and be interviewed. A total of 63 parents agreed. Also, 28 district judges and seven deputy district judges were interviewed, plus 40 solicitors – four from each of the 10 court areas in the study.

The following key points concerning the now defunct s41 procedure emerged:

- There was general scepticism as to its utility, but a general acceptance (shared by parents, district judges and solicitors) that the state *does* have a role to play in safeguarding children's welfare in divorce.
- District judges rarely took action under s41 after scrutinising the documents because they did not consider they could usefully 'solve' any problems that this might have identified.

---

[430] M Murch, G Douglas, L Scanlan, L Perry, C Lisles, K Bader and M Borkowski (September 1999) *Safeguarding Children's Welfare in Uncontentious Divorce: A Study of s41 of the Matrimonial Causes Act 1973: Lord Chancellor's Department Research Series* 7/99.

- The Statement of Arrangements form was not well designed to elicit information which might be expected to enable the court to gain a clear picture of the children's welfare.
- The study did not suggest any significant attempt by either parents or solicitors to 'conceal' information or to present a misleading picture to the court, and it found no evidence of collusion between parents to do so.
- Respondents did not usually contribute to the completion of the petitioner parent's statement.
- Parents interviewed would have welcomed more support and advice during the divorce process and would have been happy for 'someone' to talk directly to the children about their wishes and feelings.

A further point reinforced by later research (see further below) was that, as a child welfare safeguarding measure, s41 was generally applied too late. As was seen in Part II, children need support most of all during the critical period when their parents separate, when the family is often in a state of emotional turmoil and when contact and financial arrangements are still being worked out – not many months or even years later when the divorce petition itself is being filed.

It has to be remembered that this study was undertaken in the expectation that Part II of the Family Law Act 1996 would be implemented. Following the Law Commission's paper the *Ground for divorce*,[431] this would have introduced divorce following a 'period of reflection' to deal with children and financial matters, and would have finally removed all traces of the matrimonial offence from substantive divorce law. As Cretney explains, during the 1980s there had been much criticism that because the Divorce Reform Act 1969 had not in fact achieved the clear concept of no fault irretrievable breakdown of marriage as the only grounds for divorce, the parties were in effect still required to think in terms of wrongdoing and blameworthiness in a way which perpetuated images of the 'innocent and guilty'.[432]

---

[431] The Law Commission (October 1990) *Family Law: The Ground for Divorce* Law Comm No 192 HMSO, London. The Law Commission had available to it a number of studies from the divorcing population which had exposed the shortcomings of the current law even though public opinion as a whole appeared evenly divided on the issues. See also G Davis and M Murch (1988) *Grounds for Divorce* Oxford University Press. See also Lord Chancellor's Department (April 1995) *Looking to the Future: Mediation and the Ground for Divorce* HMSO, London.

[432] S Cretney (2003) S Cretney (2003) *Family Law in the Twentieth Century* Oxford University Press at pp386–389. Cretney also gives an illuminating account of the reasons why the Family Law Act 1996 was so modified by its parliamentary

It is interesting to remember in view of the new provisions under the Children and Families Act 2014 to make attendance at a MIAM compulsory for those seeking child arrangement orders, that in the hotly debated passage of the 1996 act there was much discussion about the place of mediation and whether it could be made in some way compulsory.[433] I consider below in Chapter Ten whether the MIAM procedure could provide an opportunity for mediators conducting such meetings to explore the question of children's welfare in any other than a superficial ritualised fashion – the main shortcomings of the s41 procedure in all its watered-down stages of development.

In the latest edition of *Bromley's family law* Lowe and Douglas give a clear account of the various efforts made to further reform the law of divorce and how these were frustrated even after the principle of divorce over a period of time for reflection had been legislated for in Part II of the Family Law Act 1996.[434] At first not implemented, it was repealed altogether by the Children and Families Act 2014. In this context Lowe and Douglas note significantly how the attitude of the legislators concerning the welfare of children in divorce proceedings appears to have changed between 1996 and 2014: a major purpose of the Family Law Act 1996 had been to ensure that parents should be required to take more time to consider the children's interests before embarking on divorce. It was also hoped that finally getting rid of the last traces of the matrimonial offence would bring about less adversarial attitudes, with consequent benefits for the children. But, as Lowe and Douglas noted:

> It is striking how attitudes have changed again as evidenced by the repeal of the Children and Families Act 2014 of the s41 Statement of Arrangements for Children.[435]

They observe:

> the abolition of the Statement of Arrangements delivers the opposite message that the state is not actually very interested in children's welfare at all except where parental

---

opponents as to render it virtually unworkable – in view of it becoming 'an exceedingly complex legislative construct'.

[433] See Children and Families Act (2014) s18 Repeal of the un-commenced provisions of Part II of the Family Law Act 1996.

[434] N Lowe and G Douglas (2015) *Bromley's Family Law* (11th edition) Oxford University Press.

[435] Ibid at p240.

disagreement forces this to the attention of the family justice system.[436]

They might well have added that in many cases, following the withdrawal of civil legal aid (and even then all but those who are financially able to litigate the child-related dispute), parents now have to go through the rigmarole of a MIAM (although with a limited amount of legally aided advice), followed by possibly fruitless attempts at mediation, before arguing their case as litigants in person before the family court's district judge or a bench of magistrates (see further Chapter Eleven). One could be forgiven for thinking that this is all an obstacle course for those of limited means designed to deter all but the most determined from seeking justice as they perceive it. Furthermore, while all this is going on, children, usually lacking a voice in the process, look on, as it were, from the wings.

Renewed calls for Divorce Law reforms

It should also be noted that since the non-implementation in 2001, and now repeal of Part II of the Family Law Act 1996, divorce law reform is decidedly not on the government's agenda. Nevertheless, a certain amount of pressure for reform of the grounds for divorce is still being pursued by professionals working within the system. This is because they see at close quarters the antagonisms and misunderstandings that can result from the old fault-based elements retained in the current law. As Resolution, a professional organisation of family solicitors, mediators and other professionals, observed in a briefing paper on the Children and Families Bill 2013:

> a fault-based divorce system is out of step with many other jurisdictions and is contrary to the government's objective of directing parties away from conflict enabling the focus on making arrangements for the future that put the interests of children first.[437]

A further push for divorce law reform occurred in the autumn of 2017 while I was putting the finishing touches to this book. This followed the publication of a Nuffield study by Professor Liz Trinder and colleagues

---

[436] Ibid at p240.
[437] Resolution briefing paper obtainable from resolution.org.uk

at the University of Exeter.[438] After extensive empirical research this concluded that: 'Current laws increased conflict and suffering for separating couples and their children, encourages dishonesty and undermines the aims of the family justice system.'

It further pointed out that the law of England and Wales is now out of step with Scotland and most other countries in Europe and North America. There was no evidence that the current law protects marriage. Subsequent to this research *The Times*[439] newspaper launched a campaign to 'overhaul divorce and protect children'. This is supported by a number of MPs and peers including Lord Mackay of Clashfern, the Lord Chancellor who had piloted the Family Law Act 1996 onto the statute book before its implementation was subsequently blocked and later repealed. The current campaign is supported by the Marriage Foundation, senior judges and a number of leading family law experts.

Herring, Probert and Gilmore, in their text *Great debates in family law*, give a clear account of the moral and legal arguments that continue to surround and bedevil the question of divorce law reform, and of the events that led first to the non-implementation of Part I of the Family Law Act 1996, with in essence its single concept of divorce after reflection, and has more recently led to its repeal.[440] One cannot help observing that in this particular debate, at least as was advanced by a group of respected academic lawyers, the position and wellbeing of children appears to be somewhat marginalised, although they do provide a useful chapter on disputes about children.[441] Nevertheless, as has traditionally been the case in legal circles and politics, the institution of marriage receives far more attention than that of child development and the social institution of parenthood, which in a secular society appears in reality to be the new foundation of modern family life.

It should be noted that at the time of writing this book, in the summer of 2017, it was reported that the Ministry of Justice had amended the forms accompanying a divorce petition so that petitioners could, if they so wish, name the co-respondent in cases relying on the fact of adultery (s1(2)(a) of the Matrimonial Causes Act 1973) to

---

[438] L Trinder et al (30 October 2017) *Finding Fault ? Divorce Law and Practice in England and Wales*

[439] *The Times* (17 November 2017) leading article "Modern Marriage". See also letters to the editor *The Times* (29 November 2017).

[440] J Herring, R Probert and S Gilmore (2012) *Great Debates in Family Law* Palgrave Macmillan, Basingstoke at pp170–195.

[441] Ibid at pp76–98 – but note that this chapter, too, highlights legal and moral questions with little or no reference to the extensive relevant behavioural science research literature which should inform the debate.

establish irretrievable breakdown of the marriage. By so doing the co-respondent could be liable for a share of the cost. It is argued that this apparently simple alteration to a form is likely to aggravate further marital tensions and division between the parties and, if those parties are parents, is likely to have adverse repercussions for the children. In short, a cynical short-sighted retrograde step, perhaps driven by the Ministry of Justice's wish to recoup costs for the taxpayer at the expense of the interests of children.

TEN

Demolition and reconstruction in the family justice regime: what can be salvaged for children whose parents separate and divorce?

Introduction

The main focus of this chapter concerns the needs for children coming into contact with the family justice system to receive impartial information, to have a voice in proceedings if they so wish and to receive support during the course of proceedings. I consider these issues in the context of fundamental changes in the system. The story underlying this chapter is one where the old regime of family justice administering private family law has been dismantled by radical measures introduced by the Coalition government between 2010 and 2015.[442] I outline the development of these measures in the first part of the chapter (Part A). In the second (Part B) I focus on the new policy framework based on what has been termed the Child Arrangements Programme (CAP), which replaces the old regime. The problems caused by cuts in legal aid are considered separately in Chapter Eleven along with a number of other obstacles which over the years have hindered the development of an efficient, child-friendly family justice system.

Part A: Out with the old

The Family Justice Review, chaired by Sir David Norgrove, described:

> a poorly performing system characterised by delay, expense, bureaucracy and lack of trust. A system where unnecessary

---

[442] Ministry of Justice (March 2011) *Family Justice Review: Interim Report.* Ministry of Justice and Department for Education (February 2012) *The Government's Response to the Family Justice Review: A System with Children and Families at Its Heart.* Ministry of Justice Department for Education and the Welsh Government (November 2011) *Family Justice Review: Final Report.* All available at www.gov.uk

delay in public law cases meant that children were denied stability in their lives, where too many separating parents argued in court over the children's arrangements, and where children and adults were often confused about what was happening to them and why.[443]

Based on a recognition that the family justice system 'makes life-changing decisions which affect many thousands of couples, children and families every year', the ambitious vision of the government, stated by its Family Justice Board in 2013, was for 'a family justice system that effectively supports the best possible outcomes for all children who come into contact with it'.[444] To this, all one can say is that as of the spring of 2015 (when the Coalition government came to an end) there was still a long way to go to turn this sort of aspirational rhetoric into practical reality nationwide.

As I will explain, the new system being reconstructed from parts of the old aims to divert many separating and divorcing parents in dispute about the future care of their children away from expensive adversarial litigation and to promote greater use of mediation. It has done this first by cuts in civil legal aid, except where there are serious allegations of domestic violence and/or child abuse.[445] This has had the effect for most parents of removing the partisan solicitor as gatekeeper and guide to the system, except for those who can still afford it. Instead, the gatekeeping function is now performed by independent mediators conducting Mediation Information and Assessment Meetings (MIAMs), attendance at which is now compulsory for all parents seeking resolution of their disputes. The MIAM mechanism was intended not only to act as a filter, rationing access to court, but instead aimed to encourage greater use of mediation. A second hoped-for improvement to the system has been the establishment of a unified system of local family courts administering a number of legislative provisions introduced by the Children and Families Act 2014, some of which were covered in the previous chapter.

Another point to note when considering these developments is that there is an underlying constitutional tension between the responsibilities

---

[443] Ministry of Justice (August 2013) *Family Justice Board: Action Plan to Improve the Performance of the Family Justice System* www.gov.uk at p5 para 11.

[444] Ibid at p5 para 10.

[445] The definition of domestic violence was amended during the passage of the LASPO Bill to reflect that which is used by the Association of Chief Police Officers (ACPO). It covers not just physical violence but psychological abuse and other forms of controlling behaviour which make for a repressive relationship.

of the Executive and those of the Judiciary, the boundaries between which are not always clear. This issue is seldom openly acknowledged in the official reports associated with these innovations. My colleague Julie Doughty and I have explored it more fully elsewhere.[446] Here suffice to say it can be inferred from the respective initiatives which, as we shall see, were taken to implement change on the one hand by the Ministry of Justice's Family Justice Board and its ad-hoc Mediation Task Force, and on the other by those establishing the new family court and Child Arrangements Programme (CAP) being driven forward by Her Majesty's Courts and Tribunal Service (HMCTS) and by the President and senior judges of the Family Division of the High Court (see further below). Of course, when challenged, all those involved will invariably say they collaborate effectively, but I invite the reader to be sceptical until the new regime has been properly established and is shown to be working satisfactorily.

A further point which I shall elaborate and challenge in the conclusions to this book is that up until now family justice issues have been largely framed within the orthodox domains of family law and child welfare social policy. The important child and adolescent mental health perspective is seen as a separate policy area of more concern to the fields of education and public health. By contrast, I argue that the family justice process, because of its impact on child and family processes, has to be viewed in broader community mental health terms as much as in orthodox legal terms.

My aim in this chapter, therefore, is to question how well in reality the combined effect of the new regime is likely to measure up to the government's Family Justice Board 'high-level vision' stated above and to advance the wellbeing of children given the state of knowledge derived from socio-legal and behavioural science research outlined in Chapters Two to Eight.

A yardstick against which to evaluate the new regime

As I see it there are three fundamental questions to be considered when evaluating the future performance of the new regime in this respect:

- First: Will children and young people receive sufficiently reliable independent information while their families are engaged with the

---

[446] See J Doughty and M Murch (2012) 'Judicial independence and the restructuring of family courts and their support services' *Child and Family Law Quarterly* 24(3) at pp333–354.

family justice system regulating the critical changes resulting from parental conflict, separation and divorce?
- Second: Will they have a voice in the decision-making process about their future care?
- Third: Will the new system be able to identify and support those most at risk of abuse, longer psychological dysfunction and social disadvantage associated with the breakdown of their parents' relationship so as to boost their resilience to cope with it? In this respect, will it be able to utilise where appropriate the preventive crisis intervention approach?

In what follows I consider these matters in the context of the main legislative and social policy changes which altered the whole character of the private family law regime during the lifetime of the Coalition government (2010–15). I argue that these were driven by four, to some extent, contradictory factors: the need to save public money as part of the government deficit reduction measures; the need to reduce the perceived harmful consequences for families of adversarial litigation; the need to provide for the wellbeing of children more effectively and, in particular, the need to give them a stronger voice in the family justice process.

As foreshadowed in the Preface, I argue that the haste with which the Ministry of Justice, at the behest of the Treasury, introduced cuts to its civil legal aid budget (which might be more appropriately termed Family Legal Aid – see further below) has had the unintended consequence of damaging the fragile network of out of court publicly funded mediation services as well as increasing pressure on overburdened family courts through the increase of litigants in person. There is also a risk that the combined effect of these measures, which aim to deter many disputing parents from using the family justice system, will in effect deprive children and young people of the help they might otherwise have received from the system. Furthermore, with restricted budgets, Cafcass and Cafcass Cymru have had to give priority, for understandable reasons, to public law proceedings dealing with cases of child neglect and abuse. Where private law disputes are concerned, as well as the aim of there being fewer cases in which welfare reports would be required, a more focused approach has meant that Cafcass officers are expected to give less time to support children when undertaking s7 welfare reports or acting as guardians in cases where the court orders that the children should be separately represented. This is, as we shall see, inevitably restricted even under the enlightened Child Arrangement Programme introduced in April 2014 (see further below).

Before developing this line of argument, I first set out, for readers who may be less familiar with this subject, a chronology of the principal policy reviews which have preceded legislation and a summary of their purpose.

Six steps to regime change

During the lifetime of the Coalition government led by David Cameron, there were six important reports: the Norgrove Family Justice Review (2011); the Munro Review of Child Protection (2011); the House of Commons Justice Committee's Pre-legislative Scrutiny of the Children and Families Bill (2012); the Ryder Review concerning the modernisation of family courts (2012); the Cobb Report of the Private Law Working Group set up by the President of the Family Division of the High Court (2013); and the Report of the Family Mediation Task Force (2014) chaired by David Norgrove under the guidance of Simon Hughes, MP, the then Minister of State for Justice and Civil Liberties. I consider each separately.

The Norgrove Family Justice Review interim and final reports (2011)

The Family Justice Review was set up in 2010 in the final days of the Labour government led by Gordon Brown.[447] It was chaired by the economist David Norgrove. Its specific terms of reference were to examine:

- the extent to which the adversarial nature of the court system is able to promote quality family relationships and what alternative arrangements would be more effective in fostering lasting and positive solutions;
- the options for introducing more inquisitorial elements into the family justice system for both public and private law cases;
- whether there are areas of family work which could be dealt with more simply and effectively via an administrative rather than court-based process and the exploration of what that administrative process might look like;

---

[447] Ministry of Justice, Department for Education and the Welsh Government (November 2011) *Family Justice Review: Final Report* TSO, London.

- how to increase the use of mediation when couples separate as a preferred alternative to court processes;
- how to promote further contact rights for non-resident parents and grandparents;
- the roles fulfilled by all the different agencies and professionals in the family justice system, including consideration of the extent to which governance arrangements, relationships and accountabilities are clear and promote effective collaboration and operational efficiency. This will include looking at the roles carried out by Cafcass England and Cafcass Cymru.[448]

The final report of the Norgrove Review was published on schedule in November 2011.[449] It was a progressive and far-sighted document covering the whole spectrum of work covered by the family justice system. It produced an extensive list of recommendations, including those they wanted to see driven forward by an interdepartmental Family Justice Service (see further below). The list starts by focusing on the need to consider the *voice of the child*, so that 'children's interests are truly central to the whole operation of the family justice system.[450] In this respect the review made four key points:

- Children and young people should be given age-appropriate information to explain what is happening when they are involved in public and private law cases.
- Children and young people should as early as possible in the case be supported to make their views known and older children should be offered a menu of options, to lay out the ways in which they could – if they wish – do this.
- The proposed Family Justice Service should take the lead in developing national standards and guidelines on working with children and young people in the system. It should also:
  - ensure consistency of support services, of information for young people and of child-centred practice across the country, and
  - ensure the dissemination of up-to-date research and analysis of the needs, views and development of children.

---

[448] Ministry of Justice, Department for Education and the Welsh Government (March 2011) *Family Justice Review: Interim Report* TSO, London, p36.

[449] Ministry of Justice, Department for Education and the Welsh Government (November 2011) *Family Justice Review: Final Report* TSO, London, see Appendix A at p182.

[450] Ibid pp26–37.

- There should be a Young People's Board for the Family Justice Service, with a remit to consider issues in both public and private law and to report directly to the service on areas of concern and interests.[451]

Further private law recommendations

Many of the report's recommendations concern public law proceedings and therefore fall outside the scope of this book. But with respect to parents who are in conflict over the future arrangements for their children, the review made a number of key recommendations 'intended to enable parents to reach agreements following separation while ensuring the child's welfare remains paramount'.[452] These include:

- encouraging parents to develop and stick to a Parenting Agreement which could have evidential weight in any subsequent dispute;
- scrapping the provision of separate orders for residence and contact under the Children Act 1989 and substituting a new Child Arrangement Order;
- encouraging parents wherever possible to 'resolve their disputes safely outside the court'.
- proposing to extend and make compulsory a Mediation Information and Assessment Meeting (MIAM) as part of a Pre-Application Protocol.

I consider these proposals in the context of the new Child Arrangement regime further below. Here it is only necessary to flag up Norgrove's somewhat controversial proposal for an executive mechanism, subsequently termed the Family Justice Board, to administer its proposals to ensure that the voices of children and young people are heard by the system and to encourage out-of-court settlement of parental disputes.

Thus, with respect to the review's proposed Family Justice Service, it recommended that it should be 'sponsored by the Ministry of Justice with strong ties at both ministerial and official level with the Department for Education and the Welsh government'. The service should have

---

[451] It also recommended that the UK Government should closely monitor the effects of the Welsh Rights of Children and Young Person's Measure 2011.

[452] Ministry of Justice, Department for Education and the Welsh Government (November 2011) *Family Justice Review: Final Report* TSO, London, at paras 101–14 pp20–22.

'strong central government and local government arrangements'. Among the Family Justice Service's other responsibilities, the review recommended that it should administer the budget for the court social work services in England, develop an integrated IT system, and coordinate a 'wide approach to research supported by a dedicated research budget" and 'consider how research should be disseminated around the country'.[453]

The following year, 2012, the Coalition government published its response to the Norgrove Report, much of which formed the basis of what became, after extensive consultation and parliamentary debate, the Children and Families Act 2014.[454] A review by the House of Commons Justice Committee was part of this pre-legislative process. As far as executive action was concerned, in order to improve the overall performance of the family justice system in line with many of the Norgrove Review's recommendations, the government established in March 2012 a Family Justice Board (see further below).

House of Commons Justice Committee: Pre-legislative scrutiny of the Children and Families Bill (2012)

This committee, then chaired by the Rt Hon Sir Alan Beith MP, over the years kept a watchful parliamentary eye on developments in the family justice system. With respect to the new Family Justice regime emerging from various measures brought forward by the Coalition government, it produced two reports. The first, in 2011, entitled *The operation of the family courts,* supported the idea of a unified local family court, subsequently established by the Courts and Crime Act 2013. The second, published in 2012, addressed the draft legislation concerning the Children and Families Bill, having taken evidence from a number of stakeholders and individuals.[455]

Later in this chapter I will particularly refer to what the committee had to say about MIAMS and the issue concerning the voice of the child at such meetings. Here I only mention two general remarks

---

[453] Ministry of Justice, Department for Education and the Welsh Government (November 2011) *Family Justice Review: Final Report* TSO, London, paras 24–25 at pp8–9.

[454] Ministry of Justice and Department for Education (February 2012) *The Government's Response to the Family Justice Review: A System with Children and Families at Its Heart* TSO, London.

[455] House of Commons Justice Committee (14 December 2012) *Pre-legislative Scrutiny of the Children and Families Bill: Fourth Report of Session 2012–13* TSO, London at p7 para 15.

the committee made about the legislative process leading up to the enactment of the Children and Families Act 2014. The first concerns the speed of legislative change. Thus the committee observed:

> Legislative change in an area which affects so many children and families *ought* to be considered in an orderly and measured way, and Parliament cannot ensure this unless government at every level acts accordingly.[456]

As we shall see, this comment is particularly pertinent with respect to the rapidity with which government forced through major cuts in civil legal aid with damaging unintended consequences for local mediation services.

The second observation concerns the collection of management information linked to the operation of family legislation. As we shall see in the next chapter, this is a longstanding problem which has seen governments of all complexions fail lamentably to invest and introduce appropriate modern data collection methods – a point also made by the Norgrove Review.[457] On this the Constitution Committee observed:

> This is a period of great change for all involved in the family justice system, and it is important to consider draft clauses in the light of other proposed changes. Of equal importance is the establishment of comprehensive data collection processes in order that the effect of individual clauses and combined clauses can be recorded and analysed.[458]

The Munro Review of Child Protection

A parallel development to the Norgrove Family Justice Review was the Munro Review of Child Protection.[459] This reported in May 2011. It was set up in June 2010, by Michael Gove, then Secretary of State for Education in England, in the wake of the Baby P child abuse tragedy. It was led by Eileen Munro, a professor of social work at the London School of Economics. After consulting widely and making an analysis

---

456 Ibid (emphasis in original).
457 M Murch (2011) 'Special feature: Family Justice Review; the interim report: investing in information systems and interdisciplinary training' *Seen and Heard* 21(2) pp42–47.
458 Ibid pp42–7.
459 Review of Child Protection (May 2011) *Munro Review of Child Protection: Final Report – A Child-centred System* Department of Education, Cm 8062.

of many deeply entrenched problems facing child protection workers, Professor Munro's report concluded with 15 recommendations. Taken together, these are intended to:

> Shift the child protection system from being over-bureaucratised and concerned with compliance to one that keeps a focus on whether the children are being effectively helped and protected.

Professor Munro further stated:

> This move from compliance to a learning culture will require those working in child protection to be given more scope to exercise professional judgement in deciding how best to help children and their families. It will require more determined and robust management at the front line to support the development of professional confidence.[460]

In the context of this book's concern for children with conflicted and separated parents, the Munro Report is particularly useful for the emphasis it gives to preventive work. Moreover, it stresses the need for professionals to give sufficient time to listen carefully to what children and young people have to say. It emphasises that social workers need to develop better skills and understanding to respond appropriately.

Referring to children subject to child protection measures, Munro reported that children:

> said that above all they want a trusting and stable relationship which provides them with help and information when they need it. Yet for the many this is not achieved.[461]

Here are key messages not only for the child protection services but for mediators, Cafcass officers, solicitors and barristers working within the family court system.[462]

---

[460] Ibid at para 8.5. By the term 'learning culture' I take it she meant an organisation which monitors and analyses its operation, learning from mistakes as well as from what works best in the interests of children. This would include provision for feedback from children themselves.

[461] Ibid para 8.5 at p129.

[462] For a useful critique and comparison of the Norgrove and Munro Reviews see E Lloyd-Jones (2011) 'Back to the future: the battle of ideas over children's justice' *Seen and Heard* 21(2) pp34–39.

The Ryder Review and Family Justice Modernisation Programme

This was established by Her Majesty's Courts and Tribunal Service (HMCTS), a next step board within the Ministry of Justice set up under the terms of a negotiated framework agreement between the Lord Chancellor and the Lord Chief Justice to secure and underwrite the constitutional principle of judicial independence in the courts. The senior judiciary had been concerned that there was a danger that this principle could be eroded by the Executive when the Ministry of Justice was set up by the Blair New Labour government, which apart from administering the courts, took over the administration of the penal system. Thus HMCTS was established after the Report *Relations between the Executive, the Judiciary and Parliament* was published by the Constitution Committee of the House of Lords.[463] In this report concern was expressed that there would be conflicts of interest when the traditional role of Lord Chancellor to protect the principle of judicial independence was incorporated with that of the newly created office of Secretary of State for Justice, who thus also had executive responsibility for prisons.[464] In my opinion this is a tricky constitutional issue giving rise to awkward priority questions, which will continue to rumble underneath the family justice system unless a much clearer distinction is made between the family court system and the responsibilities of executive departments.

It became clear, following the recommendations of the Norgrove Review, that as government would legislate to unify local family courts (achieved by the provisions of the Crime and Courts Act 2013) it would become necessary to engineer changes in the structure and processes of the courts. Accordingly, HMCTS, with the full support of the President of the Family Division, established a special Family Business Authority (FBA), not to be confused with the Ministry of Justice's Family Justice Board.[465] This was to be the decision-making

---

[463] House of Lords Select Committee on the Constitution (July 2007) *Sixth Report of Session 2006-07: Relations between the Executive, the Judiciary and Parliament* TSO, London.

[464] For a more detailed explanation of these constitutional changes see J Doughty and M Murch (2012) 'Judicial independence and the restructuring of family courts and their support services' *Child and Family Law Quarterly* 24(3) pp333–354. Under the Cameron government this post was held for the first time by a non-lawyer, Christopher Grayling MP, following the retirement to the back benches of the Rt Hon Kenneth Clarke MP.

[465] Note in the article by J Doughty and M Murch (2012) ibid there is discussion as to whether the responsibilities of the Family Justice Board – recommended by

forum for HMCTS' part of the family justice system. Under the FBA's Terms of Reference its responsibilities included:

> developing a strategy for the modernisation of family justice; developing a prioritised jurisdiction work plan focused on improving outcomes, including performance and efficiency; developing robust management information to support improved outcomes through better process, and ensuring effective communication between HMCTS staff at all levels, the judiciary and stakeholders.[466]

It fell to Mr Justice Ryder (as he then was) to develop a work plan for the FBA by the end of July 2012. Following widespread consultations with field agencies concerning the practical improvements needed, he produced two reports for consideration by the senior judiciary and the HMCTS. The overall aim of his proposal was to speed up the court process and avoid unnecessary delay in children's cases.

In 2013 the President of the Family Division, Sir James Munby, announced the new structure for the forthcoming unified local family courts.[467] In each local court area there was to be a designated family centre headed by a designated family judge. All applications for court orders were to be allocated to a 'gatekeeping team' consisting of a district judge and a legal advisor to the court's specially selected magistrates, so that the applications could be dealt with expeditiously by the appropriate level of judge (including magistrates) and allocated to the appropriate hearing centre within the court area.

The Ryder proposals were followed up by a special implementation working group, chaired by Mr Justice Cobb, considered next.

The Private Law Working Group, chaired by Mr Justice Cobb

With the advent of a unified system of local family courts created by the Crime and Courts Act 2013, the President of the Family Division set up a Private Law Working Group, chaired by Mr Justice Cobb. Among other things this was to review the arrangements and processes for what is now known as the Child Arrangements Programme (CAP)

Norgrove and set up within the Ministry of Justice – would overlap or even conflict with those of the judiciary's Family Business Authority.

[466] Published by the Judicial Communications Office (12 January 2012).

[467] Sir James Munby and K Sadler (2013) *The Single Family Court: A Joint Statement* HMCTS, London www.judiciary.gov.uk.

(see further below). The subsequent report clarified the procedural steps that follow the compulsory MIAMs before an application for a Child Arrangement Order can be made to the local family court.[468] One clear objective was to reduce delay by speeding up the procedure. For example, in a draft guidance on *allocation and gatekeeping*[469] most applications were expected to be dealt with by district judges and magistrates, and applications were expected to be allocated within one working day of receipt.

Moreover, in an even more revolutionary statement of objectives, legal advisors (formally Justices' Clerks) to magistrates and district judges were expected to 'fit their availability around the case and not the other way around'.[470] Courts are expected to set tight time schedules between various stages in the procedure – for example, five to six weeks between the issue of an application to the First Hearing and Dispute Resolution Appointment (FHDRA) – again, to minimise the risk of delay which bedevilled the previous regime.

A further notable point was the expectation that there would be fewer cases in which the court would require welfare reports by Cafcass under s7 of the Children Act 1989. Under a Practice Direction Order, the previous revised Private Law Programme,[471] Cafcass officers met the parties before the first hearing to assess risk and attempt conciliation. The court was urged to avoid ordering s7 reports unnecessarily. Now when these are needed they are expected to be more focused than hitherto, directed specifically at particular issues which concern the court.[472] Nevertheless, while this might save some Cafcass time, the increase in the number of litigants in person seems likely to mean that the family court will require the regular attendance of a Cafcass officer at the FHDRA.

One should also note that in England up to 2014 the overall number of private law cases remained fairly constant at around 4,000 cases per month, the total for the year 2013–14 being 46,636.[473] After the full operation of cuts in civil legal aid this only showed a small decrease of

---

[468] *Report to the President of the Family Division of the Private Law Working Group* (the Cobb Report) (November 2013).

[469] Ibid para 45.

[470] Ibid para 10.

[471] FPR 2010. Practice Direction 12B.

[472] Practice Direction (CAP14) paras 11, 12, 16 www.justice.gov.uk/courts/procedure-rules/family/practice_directions.

[473] Cafcass (12 November 2014) *Cafcass Private Law Demand* 12 November 2014 [press release].

about 5% according to the annual report of the Family Justice Board,[474] but then for year 2014/15 there was a sharp decrease of 26.3%, to result in 34,357 – still a substantial workload for a hard-pressed service.[475] (For the latest figures see Chapter Thirteen.)

I consider below in this chapter further aspects of the Cobb Report's influence on the Child Arrangements Programme concerning the role of the court and Cafcass in monitoring and enforcing contact under a Child Arrangement Order where there is a risk of non-compliance under s11 of the Children Act 1989. Later, I do so again in relation to the role of the court and Cafcass in the broader context of the matrix and coordination of preventive community services, which I dealt with in Part II, Chapters Five, Six, Seven and Eight.

The Family Mediation Task Force

Set up in March 2014 and reporting in June 2014, this was in effect a damage limitation exercise following the blunder of hastily removing legal aid from most domestic disputes (discussed further in Chapter Eleven). Thus its authorising document states:

> The immediate reason for the creation of the Task Force is that publicly funded mediations have in practice fallen by over a third as an unintended consequence of the implementation of the Legal Aid, Sentencing and Punishment of Offenders Act 2012 (LASPO) and the loss of a major referral mechanism from legal aid lawyers to mediators (previously attendance at a MIAM had been for most people a pre-requisite to being able to obtain legal aid to engage a solicitor). One result has been an increase in a number of litigants in person in the family courts, many not representing themselves through choice. In addition, too many people including even some solicitors do not understand that legal aid is still available for mediation. So the government's objective is not being achieved – the reverse in fact.[476]

---

[474] Ministry of Justice (2014) *Family Justice Board Annual Report 2013–14* www.gov. uk at p4 para 3.

[475] Cafcass (2015) *Annual Report and Accounts 2014–15* www.cafcass.gov.uk.

[476] See Family Mediation Task Force (2014) *Report of the Family Mediation Task Force* www.justice.gov.uk/downloads/family-mediation-task-force-report.pdf at p5

The task force was chaired by David Norgrove who also chairs the Family Justice Board. But unlike the Ministry of Justice's Family Justice Board (see further below) and indeed the Family Justice Review, membership of the task force (set up under the guidance of Simon Hughes MP, then Minister of State for Justice and Civil Liberties) contained a good number of practising mediators and family lawyers. It also took evidence from the Family Justice Young Peoples' Board, an increasingly important innovation in the policy-making process.[477] Further references to the findings of this task force and its specialist reports by Professor Jan Walker and Angela Lake-Carroll will be made below in this chapter.

The evolving family justice system: the broader context of regime change

Having outlined and summarised the main official reviews and legislative developments which are, in effect, seeking a change in the professional culture in order to establish a new family justice regime, I consider next the broader contexts of the issues involved, particularly as they affect children and young people. As far as possible I focus on the three key questions posed at the beginning of this chapter: namely, the issues of providing them with independent information, a voice in the family justice process and individual support.

The first point to acknowledge is that the family justice system as a distinct interdisciplinary branch of civil justice is a relatively new system (indeed, the Norgrove Review questioned whether it could described as a system at all!) It came into being in the period after the Second World War when family law began to be viewed as a specialist branch of civil jurisprudence.[478] This reflected major social, economic and technical change in the post-war period, the rapidity of which has increased over the last 30 years in what has been termed postmodern Britain.[479]

As far as its courts are concerned, despite recent organisational changes, the system is still fundamentally based on the common law

---

[477] Ibid at para 84.

[478] M Murch and D Hooper (1992) *The Family Justice System* Jordan's Family Law, Bristol. This publication and the interdisciplinary conferences to which it gave rise is credited with establishing general use of the term 'the family justice system'. See *Family Justice Review Interim Report* (March 2011).

[479] See further M Murch (2009) 'Cultural change and the family justice system' in G Douglas, N Lowe (eds) *The Continuing Evolution of Family Law* Jordan's Family Law, Bristol at pp111–145.

adversarial mode of justice, although it has inquisitorial elements and applies the civil law's evidential tests based on the balance of probabilities. Even so, it has a number of features which distinguish it from criminal and other civil jurisdictions. These have been explained more fully elsewhere.[480] Here it is only necessary to emphasize the following:

- Most important decisions impact on the family's future, including the separation of children from their parents via care proceedings and adoption, the regulation of contact and residence following parental separation and divorce, the removal of violent spouses from the family home and other protective orders, and of course the division of family assets and orders for financial support following separation and divorce.
- In dealing with family disputes, the emotions of everyone including mediators and court personnel are likely to be more deeply engaged than in most other forms of litigation. This puts a premium on practitioners' self-awareness.
- Despite the principle of open justice, respect for family privacy and treating the identities of children and the parents as confidential is an important value regulating the conduct of the family justice process. While accredited journalists can attend family courts they must not publish anything without leave of the court.
- Family proceedings should have no stigmatic association with criminality – a point strongly held by the Finer Committee on One Parent Families.[481]

This is particularly important where children and young people are concerned, especially as some, as we have seen, can blame themselves for their parents' relationship problems. Courts are frequently erroneously associated by children with crime and punishment and are thus seen as a powerful social stigmatising mechanism.[482]

For example, in a study of separate representation of children in family proceedings it was observed:

---

[480] Ibid.

[481] *The Report of the Committee on One Parent Families* (The Finer Committee) (1974) Cmnd 5629 HMSO, London at paras 4.360–4.364.

[482] See, for example, C Thomas, V Beckford, N Lowe and M Murch (1999) *Adopted Children Speaking* British Agencies for Adoption and Fostering at pp67–73.

It is important to note that most of the children in our study recognised the need for judicial authority to take difficult decisions when their parents are unable to do so; but quite apart from those young people who want to participate more directly in proceedings (seeing the judges etc) the prevailing image seems to be of the courts as scary places with a punitive ethos which could, in intractable cases, lead in fantasy at least, to the child believing he/she could be separated not only from the non-resident parent but from the resident parent as well.[483]

To avoid this it is crucially important that special counter measures are taken to make the family courts of the future 'child friendly', a point to which I return in the conclusions to this book.

The second point to note is that the system that evolved in the post-war period was essentially paternalistic and in respect of private law proceedings largely adult-focused. As Nigel Lowe and I pointed out elsewhere:

Historically the great shift in English law governing parent and child was the move from the position where children were of no concern at all to one where their welfare was regarded as the court's paramount concern ... Traditionally under English law, the children's futures have been decided upon the views of the adults, that is, parents and professionals. In other words the welfare principle itself is adult-centred and paternalistic. Even so, what we have been witnessing over the last decade or so is the equally significant cultural shift in which children are no longer seen as passive victims of family breakdown but increasingly as participants and actors in the family justice process.[484]

So the question that then arises with all the legislative and policy changes that are taking place aimed at achieving a new family justice regime, is: how likely is it that children and young people will become genuine centre-stage participants if they so wish? This is difficult to

---

[483] G Douglas, M Murch, C Miles, L Scanlan (2006) *Research Into the Operation of Rule 9.5 of the Family Proceedings Rules 1991* Department for Constitutional Affairs, London at p206 para 7.60.

[484] N Lowe and M Murch (2001) 'Children's participation in the family justice system: translating principles into practice' *Child and Family Law Quarterly* 13 pp137–158.

achieve when procedures are still essentially based on the traditional common law adversarial model of justice. Nevertheless, despite the restrictions of resources (cuts in legal aid etc) at least in principle the signs are moderately encouraging. Take, for example, the aspirations of the Family Justice Board, established in March 2012, following the government's response to the Norgrove Family Justice Review. Chaired by David Norgrove and accountable to the Secretaries of State for Justice and Education, its overall aim is 'to drive significant improvements in the performance of the family justice system where performance is defined in terms of how effective (and efficient) the system is in supporting the delivery of the best possible outcomes for children who come into contact with it'.[485] Moreover, the Norgrove Review and the Senior Family Division judiciary have pointed to the need to moderate the culture of the family courts with a view to enabling children, if they so wish, to express their wishes and feelings.

The Family Justice Board

Firmly embedded, therefore, in the Executive arm of government, rather than as part of the judicial system under the aegis of the Lord Chief Justice and President of the Family Division, the Board's Terms of Reference focus on four aspects of system performance:

- reducing delay in public law cases, where there is now a 26-week limit in accordance with s14 of the Children and Families Act 2014;
- resolving private law cases where appropriate;
- building a greater cross-agency coherence;
- tacking variations in local performance.

To achieve these aims the board is supported by a network of 46 local Family Justice Boards, a Family Justice Young People's Board (FJYPB) and the Family Justice Council (an interdisciplinary consultative body chaired by a senior judge). In addition, a Family Justice Network for Wales was established to advise on specific Welsh issues and deliver specific actions on devolved aspects of the family justice system in Wales. Of these, the Young People's Board may in time come to have the most influence. The FJYPB was originally created by Cafcass as a

---

[485] Ministry of Justice (2013) *Family Justice Board Annual Report 2012–13* www.gov. uk at p2.

sounding board.[486] It is now being consulted regularly by the Ministry of Justice Family Justice Board.

As part of its work plan for the first year, the Family Justice Board set itself a number of key performance measures (KPMs), including one designed to check the timeliness of progressing child-related family law proceedings involving parents who, following separation or divorce, are unable to agree future arrangements for their children. Another was intended to measure the take-up and initial effectiveness of publicly funded family mediation.

In August 2013, the board published an ambitious *Action plan to improve the performance of the family justice system 2013–15*.[487] Nevertheless, it should be noted that the work of the board is being hampered by the reluctance of government to invest in a comprehensive, modern case-based system of management information, linking mediation services, Cafcass and Cafcass Cymru, and the family courts. This longstanding problem is considered further in the next chapter.

Specifically, to ensure that the children and young people's views inform the work of the Family Justice Board and the family justice system more widely, the board aimed (under Action Plan 14) to:

- 'Provide relevant information to children and young people involved in the family justice system, including child-friendly explanatory material and an online forum for those involved in family cases.'
- 'Develop improved ways in which children and young people can be supported to make their views known as early as possible in a case and receive updates on their cases.'
- 'Hold Voice of the Child Conferences to explore the experiences of the children and young people who have experience of the family justice system and disseminate learning accordingly.'

At the time of writing this book, the board had not reported on how well these aims were being achieved, although at the two Voice of the Child conferences held respectively in July 2014 and in early 2015, Simon Hughes MP, then Minister of State for Justice and Civil Liberties, announced the Coalition government's intention to ensure

---

[486] The Family Justice and Young People's Board currently consists of around 43 children and young people 'who have been through or have a keen interest in the family justice system' – see Department for Education and Ministry of Justice (August 2014) *A Brighter Future for Family Justice: A Round-up of What's Happened Since the Family Justice Review* www.gov.uk at p9.

[487] Ministry of Justice (August 2013) *Family Justice Board Action Plan to Improve the Performance of the Family Justice System 2013–15* www.gov.uk.

that young people were heard more effectively in court proceedings: an objective he elaborated in a letter circulated to Dispute Resolution Professionals in March 2015, a few weeks before the General Election of that year (see further below).[488]

Issues of voice, information and support for children and young people

It is appropriate at this point to consider more closely the policy debate between 2010 and 2015 concerning the provision of independent information for children and young people, the questions of whether and how to give them a voice in the family justice process, and the issues of impartial support for them during that process. As things stood in early 2015, one has to say that questions concerning voice have been considered and translated into policy more effectively than the issues concerning information and support, factors which are important when considering ways of bolstering children's emotional resilience in dealing with stressful parental conflict, as I explained in Part II of this book.

To understand how these policy issues have been approached in the policy-making process, one must first consider the way they were dealt with in the final report of the Norgrove Family Justice Review.

The Family Justice Review's approach concerning children in private law proceedings

The whole thrust of the review's approach was to advance measures to encourage parents to mediate rather than litigate. So it is not surprising that its main focus seems to have been on parents and how to encourage them to show greater responsibility to the children.[489] Nevertheless,

---

[488] S Hughes (18 March 2015) 'Letter to Dispute Resolution Professionals: the Voice of the Child: Dispute Resolution Advisory Group' – available from www.gov.uk/moj

[489] Ministry of Justice, Department for Education and the Welsh Government (November 2011) *Family Justice Review: Final Report* TSO, London – see paras 4.5–4.16 under the heading 'Making parental responsibility work'. Para 4.7, in particular, states: 'all our recommendations on the process of separation are governed by the aim to strengthen shared parental responsibility and to emphasise its importance as parents make arrangements for their child's upbringing post separation. The aim is to focus both parents on the needs of their child and where they both have parental responsibility that they each share equal status as parents of the child. But note that this does not mean that children have to spend an equal

the separate rights and interests of children were considered in two main respects: the mediation process and in-court proceedings. The review stated its acceptance of the principle of giving children a voice in proceedings as follows:

> It is now generally accepted, as indeed we do, that it must be right for children and young people to be given every opportunity to have their voices heard in cases about them. Yet many children and young people may not even be aware that a case is underway, let alone how their view is heard as part of it.[490]

How then did the review attempt to translate this principle into practical proposals?

Information through an online information hub and through schools and community-based services

Perhaps because such services fell outside the review's terms of reference, its mention of these services was cursory and limited to the view that:

> It is important that children and young people should be given access to materials and support through both the online hub and through the local and community based services such as schools and children's centres that enable them to understand the process and the decisions that are likely to be made.[491]

It added:

> The content of the hub should be both age appropriate and realistic. It should be made clear to young people the intention is that they should be heard if they wish but that their views will be considered alongside other factors.[492]

---

amount of time with both separated parents as urged by some fathers' groups.' It should be noted that I consider the important role of schools in Part II.

[490] Ibid para 4.132 at p166.
[491] Ibid para 4.135 at p166.
[492] Ibid para 4.136 at p166.

Here I should point out that in February 2015, Resolution, the professional organisation representing 6,500 family lawyers, published a *Manifesto for family law*, concerning six key areas where they identified the need for change in the family justice system.[493] In this they encouraged parents to recognise that children have what Resolution considers to be a list of children's rights. These include the right to 'be kept informed about matters in an age-appropriate manner', a recognition that a number of researches had recorded that many children felt they were kept in the dark or were misinformed during the breakup of their parents' relationship. Yet, on a more contemporary note, in the age of the internet, which children and young people invariably use as a source of information, the Resolution manifesto suggests that children have a right to 'protection from information and material including that found online which might be harmful to them'.[494]

It is therefore disappointing that, at least until spring 2015, the Family Justice Board made no mention of these two important points in its annual report – possibly leaving them to the Young People's Board and the Family Justice Council to consider further how they might be translated into policy.[495] Thus, in his letter to Dispute Resolution Professionals in March 2015, Simon Hughes, the then minister, urged that the FJYPB should be 'involved in the creation and distribution of child-focused information so that it is created by young people for young people.[496]

Professor Walker and her colleague, in Appendix D of the Mediation Task Force report, stressed the need to provide young people with a range of good information in a 'child-friendly' way. They reported that this should include changes in family circumstances that were likely to happen, 'coping strategies, what to expect, the emotions they might experience and how conflict might be resolved'.[497] Relevant to my proposals for a coordinated network of preventive support services

---

[493] Resolution (February 2015) *Manifesto for Family Law* www.resolution.org.uk

[494] Ibid.

[495] Ministry of Justice (2014) *Family Justice Board Annual Report 2013–14* www.gov.uk.

[496] S Hughes (18 March 2015) 'Letter to Dispute Resolution Professional: the Voice of the Child: Dispute Resolution Advisory Group' – available from www.gov.uk/moj www.gov.uk/moj (Emphasis in original).

at p3.

[497] Department for Education and Ministry of Justice (June 2014) *Report of the Family Mediation Task Force* Appendix D at p27.

which I outline in later chapters, Professor Walker and colleague further wrote:

> Young people want access to a range of professionals, not just mediators or judges, as most parents will most probably not consult a mediator or come before a judge ... The clear message is that children and young people would like to be given greater options so that each child can choose how they would like to communicate with the professionals involved and to do what is most comfortable for them. The young people expressed clear views about the importance of confidentiality and would not want mediators and judges [and I would add a wide range of other professionals too] relaying information to parents unless the young person had given permission.[498]

I agree.

I have already argued in Part II (and will again later in Part IV of this book) for a more active involvement of schools, general medical practices, and child and adolescent mental health services so that such preventive 'first responder' public services can be on the lookout across the board for children and young people who are stressed by their parents' relationship tensions and conflicts, whether or not these have led to separation and divorce. I do so because I argue for a preventive community mental health approach not only to provide information but to support children when they need it to help them cope with the problems at home. As will become apparent, I would prioritise skilled empathetic support rather than simply a surveillance/safeguarding approach.

The voice of the child and mediation services – distinction between child-centred and child-inclusive mediation – variation in practice

Although in this book I am primarily concerned with the family court and its welfare support services, it would be misleading not to mention the mediation process with respect to children's participation in it, since many of the practice issues are similar. Yet, in their current state of development, mediation services are primarily adult-centred in the sense that the children and young people generally do not

---

[498] Ibid at p43.

normally take part in the mediation process. Of course the Family Justice Review pointed out:

> All mediation in which disputes about children are being discussed should be child-centred – that is, the child should be central to it.[499]

One might nevertheless ask, what about those cases where dispute does not revolve around the children? There are many bitter intractable disputes about finance and property, particularly in high net worth families where children are caught up in the backwash even if they are being educated in private boarding schools. Indeed, some of these children may worry even more because they are 'kept" in the dark' about the troubles between their parents back at home (see further in Chapter Thirteen).

Because it has been recognised that it can be very difficult to judge the real impact on children and young people without meeting them when only the parents are engaged in mediation – parents whose perception of the children's views may range from exaggerated to being denied altogether – some mediation services have been developing what has become known as child-inclusive mediation, a practice recognised by the review. Thus it stated:

> Mediators may consult children, where children want this, in a process known as child inclusive mediation. This mediation should be available to all families seeking to mediate, provided that it is appropriate and safe and undertaken by well-trained mediators. There are early suggestions that it can be successful.[500]

However, as it is not generally available, the review wanted to encourage 'a consistent, evidence-based development'.

The voice of the child in mediation

Marian Roberts, a leading authority on mediation, stated that:

---

[499] Ministry of Justice, Department for Education and the Welsh Government (November 2011) *Family Justice Review: Final Report* TSO, London at para 4.105.
[500] Ministry of Justice, Department for Education and the Welsh Government (November 2011) *Family Justice Review: Final Report* TSO, London at para 4.106.

the vexed question of children's direct participation in the mediation process – whether, when and how this should take place – has excited controversy rather than consensus.[501]

In her textbook she clearly and fairly sets out the arguments in favour and against involving children, and reviews the nature of the debate against the history of the UK's mediation movement. Lisa Parkinson, another key authority on mediation, also considers the potential benefits and disadvantages of including children directly in the mediation process. Very usefully she sets out a long list of prerequisite guidelines that have been accepted by the Family Mediation Council's member organisations (the Family Mediators Association, National Family Mediation and Resolution). Parkinson also cites some small-scale studies of child-inclusive mediation in Devon and Scotland, the second of which reported that 24 out of 28 children 'felt they had benefited from seeing the mediator' and that most of the parents consulted agreed. Overall she reports that research experiences of practitioners in Britain and Australia suggests that 'children are more competent to take part in family decision-making that adults generally believe'.[502]

In an important review article on the subject, Professor Janet Walker, like both Marian Roberts and Lisa Parkinson, pointed out that the weight of the available research evidence supports greater participation of children in the mediation process.[503] This evidence included an important Australian study from the Australian Institute of Family Studies.[504] This compared outcomes for children and parents who had experienced parental mediation in which the child was the focus of discussion (CFM) with those who experienced child-inclusive mediation (CIM). It was found that on a number of measures the child-inclusive approach did rather better. A similar finding emerged

---

[501] M Roberts (2014) *Mediation in Family Disputes: Principles of Practice* (4th edition) Ashgate Publishing, Aldershot at p249.

[502] L Parkinson (2014) *Family Mediation* (3rd edition) Jordan's Family Law, Bristol at pp215–216.

[503] J Walker (February 2013) 'How can we ensure that children's voices are heard in mediation?' *Family Law* vol 43 pp191–195.

[504] J M McKintosh, B Sythe, M Kelaher, Y Wells and C Long (2011) 'Post-separation parenting arrangements: patterns of developmental outcomes' *Family Matters* No 86 Australian Institute of Family Studies, Melbourne. See also P Parkinson and J Cashmore (2003) *The Voice of the Child in Family Law Disputes* Oxford University Press at pp106–115.

from a New Zealand study of child-inclusive mediation.[505] Although a relatively small qualitative piece of research of 17 families where parents agreed to the children taking part in the mediation process, the survey results suggested that by being included children were:

> more relaxed and had adapted significantly better to the situation after having been given the opportunity to have a 'voice' and having been listened to by their parents ... in every case there appeared to be an enhancement of parents' awareness of the impact of the conflict and the impact of conciliation on their children's lives.[506]

Even so, despite these Australian and New Zealand studies, Professor Walker concluded that in the United Kingdom, children's recent involvement has been patchy; a finding confirmed by the report of the Family Mediation Task Force published in June 2014 to which I have referred earlier.[507] As Professor Walker pointed out in her article published the previous year:

> the decision to include children has been based less on the right and needs of the children and more on arbitrary factors to do with the personal position of each mediator on the matter.

She concluded:

> there is widespread international agreement that giving children a voice must be embedded in processes and not regarded as a one-off event; using a variety of approaches enables interventions to be tailored to the needs of the

---

[505] J Goldson (2006) *Hello, I'm a Voice, Let Me Talk: Child-inclusive Mediation in Family Separation* Innovative Practice Report No 1/06 Families Commission of New Zealand and Auckland University.

[506] Ibid at p16

[507] Department for Education and Ministry of Justice (June 2014) *Report of the Family Mediation Task Force* www.justice.gov.uk at p27 – Appendix D by Professor Jan Walker and Angela Lake-Carroll it is reported: 'our discussions with a number of mediation services revealed that very few children and young people participate in any way in the mediation process'. Reasons given include insufficient training and supervision, that legal aid payments as currently provided 'act as a disincentive to work with children', and worries that one or both parents might refuse consent and that child participation 'would place too much pressure on the child'.

child; and including children cannot be left to individual discretion based on arbitrary factors. Lack of opportunity for real participation marginalises children and increases alienation and distrust.[508]

Subsequently, as members of the Mediation Task Force, Professor Jan Walker and Angela Lake-Carroll were asked to enquire whether and how children's voices are heard in current arrangements for mediation. They reported that:

> the incontrovertible evidence from England and Wales and across the globe is that children and young people want the opportunity to be heard and participate in a variety of ways.[509]

Likewise, in an article on the implementation of recent developments in 'private' child and family law proceedings, Gillian Douglas wrote:

> Very little mediation in the UK is child *inclusive* as distinct from child *focused*. The distinction is important – child inclusive mediation involves the child directly in the mediation process, enabling the child to express their wishes and feelings to the mediator who thereby knows at first hand what the child is thinking and feeling and who can also act to protect and promote the child's welfare in the handling of the parents' mediation sessions. Child focused mediation, by contrast, simply relies on bringing home to parents the importance of taking their children's welfare and feelings into consideration when negotiating their agreements. It has no direct mechanism for direct involvement and no guarantee that the parents will in fact address what their own children actually want or need.[510]

She further pointed out that the ability to take the child's individual welfare into account in the mediation process as predominantly practised in the UK is therefore 'much reduced in comparison to a court process

---

[508] J Walker (February 2013) 'How can we ensure that children's voices are heard in mediation?' *Family Law* vol 43 pp191–195.

[509] Ibid p27.

[510] G Douglas (2013) 'Implications of recent developments in private child and family law for children's rights' *Seen and Heard* 23.4 at p29.

in which a Cafcass officer may be involved and who will investigate from the child's welfare perspective and make recommendations to the court'.[511] Especially, one might add, when the court appoints the child to be separately represented by a Cafcass guardian under Rules 16(2) and (3) of the Family Procedure Rules 2010.

What happens when mediation fails?

Douglas also makes a further critically important observation concerning the consequences for children when their parents either reject or fail to reach agreement at mediation. She suggests that many of these cases 'may reach the court in a more confrontational frame of mind than would have been the case had they been able to proceed directly to court'.[512] Given that since 2014 one or both parents may not be legally aided and will appear as litigants in person, this is likely to make the task of the judge to promote amicable settlement that much harder and increase the chance that one parent will consider an imposed court order unfair. All of which is likely to mean ''that the effect on the couples' children will be an even more acrimonious atmosphere and further damage the parents' ability to communicate and cooperate with each other to the detriment of the children'.[513]

In the conclusion of this book I return to this issue, arguing for its further development as part of a wider approach to the selection and training of practitioners who offer support and information to children in a whole range of preventative services, including Cafcass officers and mediators.

Mediation Information and Assessment Meetings (MIAMs): an opportunity to consider the voice of the child?

It was suggested by the Constitutional Select Committee that the compulsory MIAM procedure introduced under the Children and Families Act 2014 should provide an opportunity for children and young people to directly participate and express their views. Yet, as we shall see, this view was opposed by the government. The final report of the Family Justice Review itself was largely silent on the issue, although it came up rather obliquely under the heading 'safeguarding

---

[511] Ibid at p29.
[512] Ibid at p29.
[513] Ibid at p29.

children'[514] in considering suggestions by Cafcass and the Family Justice Council that safeguarding checks with local authorities should be carried out in advance of the MIAM as part of the mediator's role to make assessments of suitability for mediation and to screen and assess the risk of domestic abuse and child protection issues. The review itself was not convinced about this, fearing that it might deter couples from taking part in mediation, and it merely recommended that it was an issue which government should keep under review.[515]

It should be noted that neither the report of the Mediation Task Force nor the Ministry of Justice response to it, published in July 2014 addressed the issue of whether children should take part in MIAMs.[516] Even so, the task force clearly supported the principle of hearing children's voices in the Family Dispute Resolution process in the future. For the time being the task force limited itself to recommending that options to include children 'should be urgently reviewed and a small interdisciplinary group is established to improve training and supervision and registration in this area'.[517] Subsequently, at a Cafcass conference on the Voice of the Child the then Minister of State for Justice and Civil Liberties, Simon Hughes MP, announced the government's plans with respect to court proceedings:

> from the age of 10 children and young people... will have access to the judge, in an appropriate way... to make clear their views as to what is the best resolution of the family dispute in their interest.

But concerning mediation, he added:

> We will also work with the mediation sector to arrive at a position where children and young people of 10 years old and over have appropriate access to mediators too in cases which affect them.[518]

---

[514] Ministry of Justice, Department for Education and the Welsh Government (November 2011) *Family Justice Review: Final Report* TSO, London – see paras 4.111 – 4.114 pp161–61.

[515] Ibid at para 4.115 p162.

[516] See letter from Rt Hon Simon Hughes MP (7 July 2014) 'Family mediation: latest developments' www.gov.uk/moj/family

[517] Department for Education and Ministry of Justice (June 2014) *Report of the Family Mediation Task Force* at p4.

[518] Cafcass Conference (July 2014) 'Voice of the Child Conference 2014' www.gov.uk/government/speeches/simon-hughes-speech-at-the-voice-of-the-child-conference.

This of course was an implicit recognition that as Lowe and Douglas put it in their latest eleventh edition of *Bromley's family law* 'many practitioners in the family justice system lack the necessary skills and understanding for effective face to face work with children'.[519] Many mediators particularly may currently be deficient in this respect, at least in comparison to Cafcass officers. I consider this further below in the section of this chapter concerning the Child Arrangements Programme.

Safeguarding and representing children in court proceedings: the role of Cafcass

In its interim report the Family Justice Review recommended that safeguarding checks with the police and local authority should be completed at the point of entry into the court system, following which the case will proceed to the First Hearing and Dispute Resolution Appointment (FHDRA) – in short, the current practice. Then, if unresolved, the issue could be allocated, according to its complexity, priority and seriousness, to a 'tracking' system within the court system.[520] The Private Law Programme (current at the time before being replaced by the Child Arrangements Programme) allowed the court to request a report from Cafcass if the court felt unable to make a final order at that stage. The review recommended that courts specify what kind of report is required, and whether it should address a single issue, whether it should make a safeguarding risk assessment, and whether it should ascertain the wishes and feelings of the child.[521]

With regard to separate representation for children and young people under the so-called interdisciplinary 'tandem' system by a children's guardian and solicitor under r16.4 of the Family Procedure Rules 2010 (formally r9.5 of the Family Proceedings Rules 1991), the review pointed out that although this only occurs in cases of special difficulty (in 2010, for example, it occurred in 1,512 cases out of a total of 43,738 private law cases handled by Cafcass, or 3.5% of the total) there are signs that judges consider it a valuable provision and may wish to make greater use of it in the future, particularly as more parents represent themselves following reductions in legal aid.[522] Rule

---

[519] N Lowe and G Douglas (2015) *Bromley's Family Law* 11th Edition Oxford University Press at p473.

[520] Ministry of Justice, Department for Education and the Welsh Government (November 2011) *Family Justice Review: Final Report* TSO, London – see paras 4.116–4.130 at p163.

[521] Ibid see para 4.122 at p164.

[522] Ibid see para 4.143 at p168.

16.4 appointments increased by 6.6% from 1,571 in 2013/14 to 1,674 in 2014/15.[523] Again, the review advised government to keep this matter under consideration and to commission further research as the previous government had done.[524]

Part B: Salvage and reconstruction: the Child Arrangements Programme (CAP)

In April 2014, based on the proposals of the Cobb Report and in tune with much of the Norgrove Family Justice Review, the President of the Family Division, Sir James Munby, issued a Practice Direction entitled the Child Arrangements Programme (hereafter termed the CAP).[525] It is intended as a guide for both separated parents in dispute about their children's future – some of whom will become litigants in person – and for family justice practitioners, that is, mediators; Cafcass officers and their Welsh equivalents, family proceedings officers (WFPOs); solicitors and barristers; and judges working within the new unified local family courts. It sets out in clear non-technical language and diagrammatic form, reproduced here as Figure 2, the procedural framework and various routes through the system which have to be followed for court-based dispute resolutions.

[523] Cafcass (2016) *Annual Report and Accounts 2014–15* www.cafcass.gov.uk/media

[524] G Douglas, M Murch, C Miles, L Scanlan (2006) *Research Into the Operation of Rule 9.5 of the Family Proceedings Rules 1991* Department for Constitutional Affairs, London.

[525] Practice Discretion (2014) *The Child Arrangement Programme*, PD 12(B): (CAP 2014) issued on 22 April 2014 http://flba.co.uk/downloads/ms_6482.pdf.

Figure 2: The Child Arrangements Programme

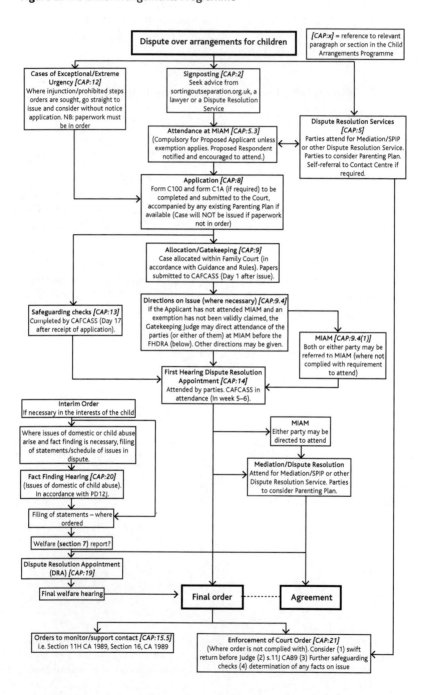

Source: Child Arrangements Programme: flowchart from Practice Direction 12B – Associated Documents. Contains public sector information licensed under the Open Government Licence v3.0..

As far as children are concerned, the CAP gives their welfare 'the highest priority' in two major respects. First, it sets out a timetable to minimise delay, and second, it emphasises the need to enable children to feel 'that their wishes and feelings have been considered in the arrangements which are made about them'.[526]

In the context of the CAP I consider these two points further below. As we have seen, they indicate a growing policy emphasis given to hearing the child's voice, which developed between the senior Family Division judiciary and – in its final years (2014-15) – the Coalition government. In particular, I draw on an important speech given by Mr Justice Cobb to the Annual Conference of the Association of Children's Lawyers in November 2014; to an official letter from the then Minister of State for Justice, the Rt Hon Simon Hughes MP to Dispute Resolution Professionals in March 2015; and to the judiciary's *Report of the Vulnerable Witnesses and Children Working Group*, published in February 2015.[527] First, it is necessary to highlight the essential features of the CAP.

The aim of the CAP

The overall aim of the programme is stated as being:

> to assist families to reach safe and child-focused agreements for their child, where possible out of the court setting. If parents/families are unable to reach agreement and a court application is made, the CAP encourages swift resolution of the dispute through the court.[528]

Thus it encourages parents to negotiate agreements, taking the view that such agreements 'enhance long-term cooperation for the benefit of the child'. This implicitly recognises that psychologically it can be difficult for parents to separate themselves from an unsatisfactory 'marital' relationship while at the same time preserving a workable parental coalition. Resolving such a difficult conflict makes demands on a person's emotional maturity and stability – the more so when a family's living arrangements may be in a state of flux causing

---

[526] Ibid at para 4.1.
[527] Mr Justice Cobb (2015) 'Seen but not heard' *Family Law* 45 pp144–157. S Hughes (18 March 2015) 'Letter to Dispute Resolution Professional: the Voice of the Child: Dispute Resolution Advisory Group' – available from www.gov.uk/moj
[528] PD 12(B): (CAP 2014) p1.

acute anxiety. In the past, parents often received a degree of positive emotional, as well as legal, support from their own partisan solicitors when navigating their way through this period in their lives. That has now been taken away from many as a result of the cuts in civil legal aid. Instead, for those who cannot afford it, the CAP suggests a number of 'signposts' to websites of various services offering 'advice and support'. Yet of course there is a world of difference between a face-to-face meeting with a knowledgeable empathetic lawyer, who will be a 'passage agent' through a life-changing process, and accessing an impersonal objective website, however well designed it might be.

Altogether some fifteen websites are listed in the document. These cover help in accessing mediation services (including those providing MIAMs); how to contact local Cafcass services; and how to find out about eligibility for the limited amount of legal aid available to pay for non-court dispute resolutions and/or separation, for example, negotiating the terms of a settlement. For those taking a case to court without a lawyer, parents are referred to the website of the Personal Support Unit.[529] If those who can afford it wish to seek advice and representation from a family law solicitor and/or barrister, they are also referred to several websites.

The document is clearly written, if in idealistic, aspirational terms. It also includes a useful section concerning Parenting Plans, which are described as 'a tool for separated parents to identify, agree and set out in writing arrangements for their children', which could be used 'as the basis for discussion about a dispute which has arisen'. Pointing out that it is 'designed to help separated parents (and their families) work out the best possible arrangements for the child', it stresses that the plan 'should be understood by everyone including (where the child is of an appropriate age and understanding) the child concerned'. Of course, it remains to be seen in future how often and in what ways Parenting Plans are used in reality. Nevertheless, the admonition to involve the child is welcome and accords with the view taken by the drafters of the document that 'the child and young person should feel that their needs, wishes and feelings have been considered in arrangements which are made for them' in accordance with their age and level of understanding.

---

[529] See www.thepsu.org – this innovation, with the support of the Lord Chief Justice, operates with volunteers to help litigants in person put their case and to provide a degree of moral support in court. At the time of preparing this book it was not clear how widespread the new charitable service was.

Mechanisms to hear the voice of the child in disputed family court hearings (s4 of the CAP)

The senior judiciary has clearly taken on board the views of both Simon Hughes MP and those of the Family Justice Young People's Board, that 'children and young people should be at the centre of all decision-making'.[530] Thus the document encourages the involvement of children and young people when arrangements are being worked out, whether through negotiations leading to a Parenting Plan; in the context of dispute resolution outside of court, that is, through mediation; or in the litigation process itself. In this last respect, the Practice Direction gives specific guidance on how judges may wish to learn about the child's view,[531] which may be communicated to the judge in a number of ways:

- in a Cafcass s7 Welfare Report, 'by the child being encouraged (by the Cafcass Officer or WFPO or parent or relative) to write a letter to the court';
- in the 'limited circumstances where a child is made a party to the proceedings under Rule 16.4 of the Family Procedure Rules 2010 and a guardian appointed (see further below);
- and/or 'by the judge meeting with the child in accordance with approved guidance (currently the Family Justice Council's *Guidelines for judges meeting children who are subject to family proceedings)'*.[532]

Safeguarding: the role of Cafcass and Cafcass Cymru when child proceedings are to be commenced

The CAP Practice Direction sets out the duties of the Cafcass officer and WFPO to undertake certain safeguarding checks *before* the First Hearing and Dispute Resolution Appointment (FHDRA). It states that 'such steps shall be confined to matters of safety'. That is to say, 'the parties will *not* be invited to talk about other issues, for example, relating to the substance of applications or replies or about issues

---

[530] Providers in the Family Disputes Practice Discretion (5 April 2004) IFLR at 1188 para 4.2 www.justice.gov.uk/courts/procedure-rules/family/practice_directions/pd_part_12b.

[531] Ibid at para 4.5.

[532] See Family Justice Council (April 2010) *Guidelines for judges meeting children who are subject to family proceedings* www.judiciary.gov.uk – for full reference see Appendix A at p5.

concerning matters of welfare or the prospect resolution'.[533] They should be advised that such matters will be deferred until the FHDRA.

This needs to be understood in the context of the strict timetable which the CAP sets for the completion of proceedings, and as a measure to ensure that Cafcass officers and their Welsh counterparts stick closely to their role in this respect. Similarly, when it comes to the preparation of s7 welfare reports, the president has let it be known that they should address particular issues that concern the court in order that the FHDRA can only normally take place in week five, following the issuing of the parents' application, and at the latest in week 6. Some professionals may find these tight time schedules tiresome, but they need to remember the reasons for them:

Timetable for the child

The argument for strict timetables was first advanced as long ago as 1973 when Goldstein, Freud and Solnit published their highly influential little book *Beyond the best interests of the child*.[534] It has since become accepted that a child's sense of time is different from that of an adult. Indeed, the younger the child the more difficult it becomes for them to comprehend the passage of time. In the context of separation from an adult to whom the child is emotionally attached, Goldstein et al wrote prescriptively:

> Procedural and substantive decisions should never exceed the times that the child-to-be placed can endure loss and uncertainty ... the courts, social agencies and all adults concerned with the child's placement must greatly reduce the time they take for decision.[535]

With respect to separation and divorce proceedings, these authors wrote:

> The child's sense of time guideline would require that all disputes between the parents about the placement of their children be resolved by separate and accelerated proceedings

---

[533] Practice Direction (CAP 2014) at para 13.2 www.justice.gov.uk/courts/procedure-rules/family/practice_directions/pd_part_12b.

[534] J Goldstein, A Freud, A J Solnit (1973) *Beyond the Best Interests of the Child* Free Press, New York at pp43–52.

[535] Ibid.

prior to and without waiting for a determination on the issues of the divorce and separation itself.[536]

This principle has long been accepted in reformist family justice circles. (Indeed, it was one of the reasons for the ill-fated Family Law Act 1996, which would have put the settling of children's arrangements before the granting of a divorce petition.) It is also a basic tenet of the Children Act 1989 that delay is normally to be regarded as detrimental to the child. Even so, the Norgrove Family Justice Review found that in child-related private law proceedings, 'the average case duration was 32 weeks in 2010', and reported that:

> this has not changed. The longer these cases take to resolve, the more entrenched and embittered the dispute is likely to become. It is also more likely that default contact arrangements will become the norm for a child in longer cases, which may not be in their interests.[537]

According to the Family Justice Board, reporting 'provisional data from HMCTS', there was a decrease of 5% in the number of private law cases in the year 2013 to March 2014 – the year that cuts in civil legal aid came into force – compared with the year before.[538] Nevertheless, the average time from application to first full order in s8 child-related cases actually increased to 16.8 weeks in that year compared with 15.7 weeks in the year April 2012 to March 2013.

Of course the average length of proceedings does not show the full range and variability of the sample. Complex cases may take much longer. For example, a court file sample of 115 cases taken in the summer of 2004 in which children were separately represented revealed an average duration of 22 months, with the shortest being concluded after four months and the longest recorded case lasting more than six and a half years. More than half this sample lasted between one and three years.[539]

---

[536] Ibid at p42.

[537] Ministry of Justice, Department for Education and the Welsh Government (November 2011) *Family Justice Review: Final Report* TSO, London at p42 para 2.11.

[538] Family Justice Board (2014) *Annual Report 2013–14* www.gov.uk at p4 paras 13 and 14(b).

[539] G Douglas, M Murch, C Miles and L Scanlan (2006) *Research into the Operation of Rule 9.5 of the Family Proceedings Rules 1991* Department for Constitutional Affairs, London para 6.16 at p180.

Given such a background, one can only applaud the efforts of the President of the Family Division and the senior judiciary to set firm timetables under the CAP for child-related proceedings. Moreover, it is clear that judges have accepted the behavioural science messages about the child's sense of time. Thus, in paragraph 15, entitled 'Timetable for the child', we find the important guideline that:

> the judge shall, at all times during the proceedings, have regard to the impact which the court timetable will have on the welfare and development of the child to whom the application relates. The judge and the parties shall play particular attention to the child's age and important landmarks in the immediate life of the child, including:
>
> (a)   the child's birthday;
> (b)   the start of nursery/schooling;
> (c)   the start/end of the school term/year;
> (d)   any change of school; and/or
> (e)   any significant change in the child's family and social circumstances.[540]

Not only have the judges accepted the significance of a child's sense of time related to age and psychosocial developmental stage, it is to be noted that this section of the CAP draws attention to potentially critical turning points or transitions in the child's life, such as moving from nursery to school and changes in the school year. As we have seen in Part II of this book, these critical transition points can provoke or aggravate a 'crisis response', overwhelming at least temporarily a child's capacity to cope with everyday life tasks – an important aspect of mental health. At such times, it is important that the child understands the nature of the changes and feels well supported while adapting to them. It is in these respects (that is, the provision of information and support for the child in the family justice process) that the CAP is perhaps less clear than it might have been, although it may be implicit in what it has to say about the role of Cafcass and the appointment of guardians under

---

[540] Practice Direction (CAP 2014) at para 15.2 www.justice.gov.uk/courts/procedure-rules/family/practice_directions/pd_part_12b.

r16.4 of the Family Procedure Rules 2010 in complex cases necessitating separate representations for the child.

The role of Cafcass officers and WFPOs in preparing s7 reports for the family court

As will be seen from the flow chart accompanying the Practice Direction (Figure 2), those cases which proceed to court after the MIAM and after Cafcass has carried out the necessary safeguarding checks of the police and local authority (all to be completed by day 17, after receiving the application) will go forward to the family court for a FHDRA to be held in weeks five or six. At this hearing, at which a Cafcass officer will normally be in attendance, the CAP requires the judge to consider whether the parents 'can safely resolve some or all of the issues with the assistance of a Cafcass Officer, WFPO or a mediator'. Also at this hearing the judge may ask the officer to prepare a welfare report for the court before the next hearing.

At this point it may be helpful to remind the reader about the duties of Cafcass and Cafcass Cymru under the provisions of s12(1) of the Criminal Justice and Court Services Act 2000.

The functions of Cafcass are to:

- safeguard and promote the welfare of the child;
- give advice to any court about any application made to it in any such family proceedings;
- make provision for the child to be represented in such proceedings; and
- provide information, advice and other support for the child and their family.

Notwithstanding the limitations of the CAP timetables, it is in respect of this last sub-section that Cafcass officers and WFPOs have discretion to provide information and support to children subject to court proceedings. It is an important if currently largely undeveloped role to which I will turn in Part IV of this book when considering the coordination of preventive support services. Here, I only need to point out that the opportunity to do so arises in two contexts, namely, the preparation of s7 reports, and when a Cafcass officer is asked to represent a child (usually with the help of a specially appointed solicitor) under r16.4 of the Family Procedure Rules 2010 (formerly r9.5 of the Family Proceedings Rules 1991).

Section 7 welfare reports: ensuring a more sharply focused approach

In recent years, because of the resource pressures on Cafcass and local authorities to which I have referred earlier, there has been some reluctance on the part of family court judges to request s7 reports. Indeed, as long ago as 2004 the government proposed that Cafcass should reduce the proportion of its resources that are devoted to report writing in order to create the capacity to deliver conciliation and support services.[541] Likewise, the Cobb Report suggested that 'in order to reduce the duration of a private law case', s7 reports if ordered should be subject to 'a stepped phasing in of arrangements for the child (i.e. recommendations for the medium and longer term future of the children) so that there is no need to return to court at each stage insofar as the officer is able to do so safely in the interests of the child'.[542]

However, with respect to providing information by meeting the child or young person to ascertain their views, wishes and feelings, the Cafcass officer has an opportunity to explain the nature of the court proceedings and the nature of conciliation, if that is to be attempted, as well as to explain how the family court differs from the hearing of stigmatic criminal proceedings.

Rule 16.4 Guardians

As we have seen above, there are signs that judges dealing with child-related court proceedings often see merit in appointing a guardian to arrange representation for the child under r16.4 of the Family Procedure Rules 2010, when the interests of the parents and child may diverge, particularly in high-conflict cases. Nevertheless, in issuing his Practice Direction setting out the procedure for the CAP, the President was clearly mindful of the need to avoid undue demands on the resources of Cafcass. Thus the CAP[543] makes three points for the guidance of the judges. First, that they should be 'vigilant in identifying cases where a guardian should be appointed'. Second, that the court should consider with a relevant Cafcass manager 'any advice

---

[541] See G T Harold and M Murch (2005) 'Inter-parental conflict and children's adaptation to separation and divorce: theory, research and implications for family law, practice and policy' *Child and Family Law Quarterly* 17(2) at p202.

[542] *Report to the President of the Family Division of the Private Law Working Group* (the Cobb Report) (November 2013) at p17 para 82.

[543] Practice Direction (CAP 2014) paras 18.1–3 www.justice.gov.uk/courts/procedure-rules/family/practice_directions/pd_part_12b.

in connection with the prospective appointment and timescale' and in doing so be mindful 'of the demands on the resources of Cafcass'. Moreover, 'the court should also make clear on the face of the order [i.e. the appointment of a guardian], the purpose of the appointment and the timetable over any work to be undertaken'.

I will refer more fully in Part IV of this book to the value of separate representation in complex child-related litigation as revealed in research conducted with colleagues in 2004/05 for the Department for Constitutional Affairs.[544] Here it is only necessary to point out that such appointments provide much needed opportunities not only to inform anxious children about the family justice process but to provide them with support and reassurance (see Chapters Six and Seven).

Enforcement of Child Arrangement Orders

Finally, in respect of the CAP, a word about the enforcement of orders. These illustrate the powers and authority of the court, which are held in reserve until disputes show signs of becoming intractable. Thus, the CAP sets out very clearly how an allegation of non-compliance with a Child Arrangements Order is to be dealt with.[545] Sanctions available to the court range from referral to a Separated Parents Information Programme (SPIP), the making of a contact enforcement order under s11j of the Children Act 1989, a fine or in the last resort committal to prison (para 21.6). When such an application is made, the court is obliged to ascertain the facts and reasons for non-compliance and, most importantly, to consider how the wishes and feelings of the child are to be ascertained. In doing so, it will normally turn to Cafcass for advice as to the best way forward. The gatekeeping team in the court (a judge and a Cafcass officer) are required to list the hearing of the application within 20 days of the issue of proceedings and as far as possible to have the case allocated to the judge who originally made the order. For a more in-depth consideration of the issues concerning enforcement the reader is recommended to consult the study by Trinder, Hunt, Macleod, Pearce and Woodward.[546]

---

[544] G Douglas et al (2006) op cit.

[545] Practice Direction (CAP 2014) paras 21.1–8 www.justice.gov.uk/courts/procedure-rules/family/practice_directions/pd_part_12b.

[546] L Trinder, J Hunt, A Macleod, J Pearce and H Woodward (2013) *Enforcing Contact Orders: Problem-solving or Punishment?* University of Exeter and the Nuffield Foundation.

Cafcass preventive community mental health thinking and the family justice system

I turn now to consider the role of Cafcass viewed as part of the network of potential preventive community mental health services for children and families. This is not a conceptual framework within which its services are normally understood. Rather, in conventional terms, Cafcass and its Welsh counterpart, Cafcass Cymru, are defined as the social work arm of the family justice system – itself a specialist interdisciplinary branch of the civil justice system. Up to now such behavioural science and mental health thinking as has permeated jurisprudential and court social work processes and practices has often been more implicit than explicit, though obviously decisions about the future of children and the assessment of risk invariably involve the weighing of evidence against a range of behavioural and social considerations – not infrequently from differing theoretical backgrounds.

In this part of the book, therefore, my aim is to highlight the relevance of the Caplanian model of preventive mental health and the related practice of short-term support crisis intervention to Cafcass and its direct work with children and their parents within the new CAP operated by family courts. I see this as essentially a key backup secondary preventive role when disordered family relationships enter the family court. It complements such primary prevention that might develop in schools (and of course primary healthcare) and other 'first responder' services along the lines that I have suggested in the first part of this chapter. In particular, I suggest that there is a good case for Cafcass to apply this sort of short-term supportive 'passage agent' casework for children caught up in the stresses and strains of family litigation, particularly when it appears to a mediator or a Cafcass officer that the child is in crisis or manifesting longer-term mental health problems.

As things stand at present, I recognise that this is a controversial view which needs explanation. Under the CAP regime, the first opportunity to identify such children should occur when parents attend MIAMs. As I explained above, the problem is that even if children are of an age to express their views and wish to attend the MIAM, it is doubtful that they will be allowed to do so. There are a number of reasons for this. First, many mediators lack the experience and training in direct face-to-face work with children even when a MIAM leads to mediation. There is also a time pressure on those conducting a MIAM which could be aggravated and made more complex by the presence of children. Yet, judging from the Mediation Task Force report, ministerial announcements, the recommendations of the Voice of the Child Advisory Group,[547] and subsequent conferences with young people themselves, it is clear what the longer-term direction of travel for policy should be if we are to hear the voice of the child so as to give them a more inclusive participatory role in the family justice process. Current reality suggests that we are a long way from achieving it with respect to MIAMs and mediation in general.

Moreover, there remain some experienced practitioners who argue that children should not be drawn further into their parents' conflict by taking part, as this could add to their emotional burden.[548] Eventually MIAMs might evolve to a point where at least some children take part and where an alert-minded mediator could respond to a child's need to be heard. They might also be in a position to recognise that a child needs an independent source of reliable information and support, although this may be difficult to provide in the context of a MIAM and any subsequent mediation. But for the time being Cafcass and Cafcass Cymru are the most obvious sources to meet these needs once the litigation process is commenced, both in the context of s7 welfare reports and when a Cafcass officer is appointed by the court to act as a guardian.[549]

As I explained above, once an application for child-related proceedings concerning contact or residence has been made to the court, the case has to be considered according to the specific CAP time schedule in weeks five to six at an FHDRA where the parents come before a judge. This has to occur once the case has been allocated to a judge within the family court and Cafcass has made its safeguarding checks of the police and local authority. A Cafcass officer is expected to be in attendance at this appointment and so in a position to make a preliminary assessment of the need for an s7 welfare report. It has become the practice for judges to specify the kinds of issue that need to be covered by the children and family reporter in this report, although of course the reporter is expected to exercise independent professional judgement as to the content.

---

[547] Voice of the Child Dispute Resolution Advisory Group (March 2015) *Final Report* www.gov.uk

[548] B Cantwell and S Scott (1995) 'Children's wishes, children's burdens' *Journal of Social Welfare and Family Law* 17(3) at p337.

[549] For a clear account of the legal responsibilities of Cafcass and Cafcass Cymru see N Lowe, G Douglas (2015) *Bromley's Family Law* (11th edition) Oxford University Press pp451–464.

With respect to welfare reports under the provisions of the CAP (2014) (para 11.12.6(c)) several points need to be remembered. First, the Cafcass officer carrying out the investigation of the court is now known as the children and family reporter; second, occasionally the local authority can be asked to prepare the report; and third, whichever service prepares the report, it is to act independently of both the parents and the child. As Lowe and Douglas point out:

> It is important to emphasise that the reporter's duty is to report on the child's welfare rather than a child's wishes and feelings as such, though in discharging this duty, the reporter will investigate those wishes and feelings. In other words, a welfare report provides an indirect voice for the child.[550]

Furthermore, having made all the necessary enquiries and prepared the report for the court, the officer:

> Must notify and explain to the child such contents (if any) as the officer considers appropriate to the child's age and understanding, including any reference to the child's own views and the recommendations [in accordance with Practice Direction 16A para 9.3].[551]

A further point that should be noted is that in the past officers preparing welfare reports could on occasion use the period of inquiry to mediate between the parents in an attempt to get them to settle their differences, sometimes after having seen the child. As explained by Lowe and Douglas, this practice should no longer occur since the role of the reporter is different from that of a mediator.[552] If the reporter considers that mediation might be helpful then Cafcass service principles require that a referral to another practitioner should be considered.

So it seems clear that under existing practice the opportunities for a Cafcass reporter to provide direct short-term support to children in crisis during the litigation process are very limited. However, it has to be recognised that for many children just meeting a knowledgeable outsider who is prepared to listen to their worries, and being given reliable, unbiased information about the family court process, can be

---

[550] N Lowe and G Douglas G (2015) *Bromley's Family Law* (11th edition) Oxford University Press at p456.

[551] Ibid at p456.

[552] Ibid at p457.

helpful. The position is very different if the court makes the child a separate party and appoints a guardian under Rule 16.4 of the Family Procedure Rules 2010 (formerly Rule 9.5 of the Family Proceedings Rules 1991).

The Role of the Cafcass Guardian

There is an argument that in order to be human rights compliant under Article 6 of the Human Rights Act 1998 (the right to a fair trial) where there is dispute between parents in so-called 'private' proceedings, children should have automatic party status enabling them to be separately represented by a guardian and/or solicitor.[553] Given the potential numbers involved, this would under current circumstances be impractical and costly. In fact, as we have seen above, this is a provision only to be used in cases of special difficulty, typically where there is a so-called intractable dispute between the parents, where contact has ceased, where the child may be suffering harm, or in a dispute where the child has a standpoint or interest which is inconsistent with the views of the parents.[554] In these circumstances the court must appoint a guardian who may also on behalf of the child appoint a children's solicitor under what is known as the tandem model of representation. Given that the numbers of private law cases involving initial assessment by Cafcass England rose by 10.4%, from 35,302 in 2014/15 to 37,649 in 2015/16, it is notable that the number of r.16.4 cases actually dropped by 2.6%, from 1,667 in 2014/15 to 1,623 in 2015/16, and this reflects the increased pressure to contain Cafcass expenditure which the judges are aware of.[555]

As far as children and young people as well as their parents are concerned, there is research evidence that the provision of a guardian is valuable. We can deduce this from an investigation which I and my Cardiff Law School colleagues conducted back in 2004/05 for the Department for Constitutional Affairs (now the Ministry of Justice).[556] The numbers of families involved in the interview programme were by necessity fairly small because of the limited use of the provision

---

[553] Ibid at p469.

[554] See President of the Family Division's Practice Direction accompanying the CAP Practice Discretion (2014) *The Child Arrangement Programme*, PD 12(B): (CAP 2014) issued on 22 April 2014 http://flba.co.uk/downloads/ms_6482.pdf.

[555] Cafcass (7 July 2016) *Annual Report and Accounts 2015–16* www.gov.uk at pp16–18.

[556] G Douglas, M Murch, C Miles and L Scanlan (2006) *Research Into the Operation of Rule 9.5 of the Family Proceedings Rules 1991* Department for Constitutional Affairs, London.

at the time. They were drawn from five major courts believed to make relatively high use of the provision in the four years preceding April 2005, yet a survey of court records produced only 121 cases. From these were drawn qualitative interviews with 15 children (eight boys and seven girls) between the ages of seven and 17, and from 23 parents as carers – all of whom elected to take part from the larger sample of 121 court records. Because the researchers could not be sure how representative this interview sample was, they concluded that the messages reported from these 15 children 'should be regarded as suggestive rather than conclusive'. Even so, although the family circumstances which led to the court proceedings varied considerably, a number of consistent messages emerged from the children's interviews.[557] These are summarised as follows:

- Most of the children liked the idea of someone being appointed by the court to help them have their say in proceedings.
- A number needed someone accessible to them apart from their parents to support them through the litigation process. That person had to be trustworthy and able to relate to them with empathy.
- Most of them believed that if their parents could not resolve their differences in any other way a neutral judicial authority of some sort was needed.
- Children wanted the court to be 'child friendly', so that if they wanted to they could put their views to the judge directly.
- A number of children were clearly ignorant, confused and made anxious by the knowledge that their parents were going to court to contest residence or contact. They imagined courts to be 'scary places', with judges who had the capacity to punish their parents for behaviour for which they themselves felt responsible, such as refusing to go on contact visits.
- The children generally had clear ideas what constituted a 'good' guardian, that is:
  - The person appointed should give the child enough time to get to know them.
  - They wanted someone they could trust who could communicate with them at their level and who was not patronising.
  - They disliked hasty interrogations and preferred a friendly conversational style of interviewing.
  - They wanted clear explanations not only about the guardian's role but of the whole court process.

---

[557] Ibid at pp7–9 and pp112–113.

- They particularly wanted guardians or their solicitor to report what they had told them accurately to the court.
- They wanted to be kept regularly informed about the progress of the case.

Where most or all of these elements were present in the children's relationship with the guardian, most reported feeling more confident both in terms of coping with the court proceedings and more generally as a young person. Overall, although the samples in this study were small, for reasons which I have already explained, the researchers concluded that a good guardian was one who was able to relate with empathy to children and young people and generally act as a guide through a critical, turbulent family transition.

This was confirmed by a number of the custodial parents. Like their children, the majority believed the intervention of the guardian had had a positive effect on their child and thus favoured the idea of separate representation. Among the positive effects noted was the recognition that their child felt reassured and supported, that their child's behaviour had 'calmed down', and that the process had enabled some parents to see things in a different light and so recognise the validity of the child's perspective.[558]

Of course there was a minority of disgruntled parents. Most of these had lost their case and believed that the guardian had taken a partisan stance in the dispute between the parents. In highly inflamed parental disputes, for a guardian to remain impartial is easier said than done, although as agents of the court, Cafcass staff have to be mindful of the report of HM Inspectorate of Court Administration that 'courts need to demonstrate clearly that it is neither biased against or in favour of one party'.[559]

A further important point that emerged from parent interviews in this study was that a number of the parents wished that the guardian had been appointed much earlier to help them short-circuit escalating conflict and costly litigation. It has to be remembered that this study occurred before the CAP with its much shorter timetables (see Chapter Four). On average these cases, admittedly a small and specialist group of high-conflict ones, had been before the courts for four and a half years, ranging from nine months to 14 years! Many of these disputes had thus been protracted and defined by the judge as 'intractable'. It

---

[558] Ibid at p192 paras 7.23 and 7.24.

[559] HM Inspectorate of Court Administration (October 2005) *Domestic Violence, Safety and Family Proceedings* HMICA Secretariat, London at para 4.26.

seemed from the court records in the 121 cases sampled, that in the majority of cases Rule 9.5 was applied as a measure of last resort because the judge feared the welfare of the child was worsening as a result of the interparental dispute and recurrent court hearings.[560]

This retrospective wish on behalf of parents for a guardian to have intervened earlier is reminiscent of my early research in the 1970s into parents' reactions to the Divorce Court Welfare Officer – the equivalent of today's Cafcass children and family reporter.[561] Of those parents, 60% found the court welfare officer helpful, while only 20% found them unhelpful. Indeed, it was on the basis of this early study that I convened a small group of Bristol family lawyers, social workers and academics which ultimately led to the setting up in 1979 of the Bristol Family Courts Conciliation Service, the first pioneering mediation service in the country.[562]

Cafcass opportunities for short-term crisis intervention to support children

I have spent some time considering the findings of the Rule 9.5 study because it illustrates the value to both children and parents of a form of impartial yet empathetic supportive intervention. This is especially so in cases where interparental conflict has become intense and prolonged. Many of these children seem to be crying out for independent help in coping with it. The arrival of the guardian and/or children's solicitor appointed and backed up by the independent authority of the family court has provided a way of responding to this need, in addition, of course, to providing the court with evidence of the child's wishes and feelings. What I am suggesting here is that the role played by the guardian appears in many instances to involve an element of supportive crisis intervention in community mental health terms – though I doubt whether many Cafcass officers or their managers realise this.

I am not the first to suggest this sort of supportive role. Like myself, Brian Cantwell, whose early professional experience was that of a Divorce Court Welfare Officer in the Probation Service, has long argued the need for Cafcass to develop what he terms 'private family law

---

[560] Ibid at p202 para 7.52. See also *Re M (Intractable Contact Disputes: Courts Positive Duty* [2005] EWCA Civ 1090, noted at [2015] *Fam Law 938* by Rebecca Bailey-Harris.

[561] M Murch (1980) *Justice and Welfare in Divorce* at p59–63 and 205Sweet and Maxwell.

[562] M Murch (2004) 'The germ and gem of an idea' in J Westcott (ed) *Family Mediation: Past, Present and Future* Jordan's Family Law, Bristol at pp21–32.

case work'.[563] Cantwell argues that Cafcass (and its Welsh counterpart, Cafcass Cymru) has failed to adequately develop the support element in its title where the interests of children are concerned.[564] He makes a number of points relevant to this theme. Thus he asserts that:

- Cafcass staff have been more confident in 'assessing physical risk such as allegations of domestic violence than in assessing and responding to emotional risk to children that arise through enduring parental and family conflict'.[565]
- Cafcass 'should focus on issues of high conflict parental separation and its impact on children – itself a significant emotional safeguarding issue'.[566] He consequently envisages 'a prioritisation of these cases where reference might be made under Rule 16.4 for a guardian appointment' (formerly r9.5 of the Family Proceedings Rules 1991).[567]
- 'Cafcass is an agency with the deepest knowledge base in terms of the assessment of post-separation parental conflict and its impact on the children involved. In these cases of very high or entrenched conflict – where emotional safeguarding concerns arise – the agency could further develop its own specialist casework in relation to Rule 16.4 appointments and by creative use of the Family Assistance Order (FAO)',[568] that is, under Section 16 of the Children Act 1989 (see further below).

---

[563] B Cantwell (2015) 'Developing contemporary private law case work in Cafcass' *Seen and Heard* 15(1) pp38–42. He refers to his early probation caseload as including a number of children on what were termed Matrimonial Supervision Orders (MSOs) and also of his undertaking 'kindred social work' cases, which as I recall usually involved a matrimonial problem referred from the local domestic magistrate's court for matrimonial conciliation. This usually happened when a wife sought a so-called 'separation order' for maintenance in the days before civil legal aid became available and before there was a child support agency. I shall return to a consideration of these and similar practices in my conclusions in Part IV, since they may become relevant again now that legal aid has been withdrawn from most divorce proceedings.

[564] B Cantwell (2010) 'The emotional safeguarding of children in private family law' *Family Law* vol 10 pp84–90. See also B Cantwell (2014) 'The Review of private law: a role for Cafcass in the change process' *Seen and Heard* 24(1) pp38–44.

[565] B Cantwell (2014) 'The Review of private law: a role for Cafcass in the change process' *Seen and Heard* 24(1) at p42.

[566] Ibid at p42.

[567] Ibid at p43.

[568] Ibid at p41.

- Cafcass is well placed to promote (in collaboration with other agencies) services of 'a short-term therapeutic nature', so as to ensure that troubled families and their children receive help and services that are tailored to their needs rather than by being offered on a 'one size fits all' (mediation) basis as the alternative to court proceedings. I pick up this important point over designing services to wrap, as it were, around the individual needs of children and their families later in my conclusions in Part Four.

The use of Family Assistance Orders

The key to Cantwell's suggestion for an extended short-term casework role for Cafcass lies in greater use of FAOs. Such an order requires either a Cafcass officer to be available or the local authority to make an officer of the authority available 'to advise, assist and (where appropriate) to befriend any person named in the order' (s16(1)).

Lowe and Douglas point out that this power replaced the former power to make supervision orders in private law proceedings. They cite the Department of Health guidance and regulations in relation to the Children Act 1989, which states that:

> A family assistance order aims simply to provide short-term help to a family to overcome the problems and conflicts associated with their separation and divorce.[569]

Lowe and Douglas further note that under the Children and Adoption Act 2006 an FAO may be made in 'any family proceedings' and may be exercised by the court acting on its own motion. Moreover, a former requirement that the circumstances of the case had to be exceptional was removed by the 2006 act as 'part of a policy to enable such orders to be used more often to facilitate more contact'.[570] Revised guidance requires the court to make plain why an FAO is needed and what it is hoped to achieve by it. Before such an order is made, the opinion of the appropriate officer has to be obtained as to whether it would be in the child's best interest and, if so, how it should operate and for how long. Furthermore, it is not necessary for a child to consent to the order and there is no specific requirement to ascertain the child's wishes and feelings about the matter.

---

[569] N Lowe and G Douglas G (2015) *Bromley's Family Law* (11th edition) Oxford University Press pp547.

[570] Ibid at p548.

Although the power to support children and families through a critical period of family change and adjustment is clearly provided by this provision, it has been relatively rarely used. According to *Cafcass annual report 2012–13*, cited by Lowe and Douglas, only 355 orders were made in that period – a drop from 590 the previous year. Although equivalent numbers rose in 2014/15 to 491, they fell again in 2015/16 to 458 – a decline of 6.7%.[571] As Lowe and Douglas observe, 'clearly a key factor is the availability of resources'.[572] But I think there is much more to it than that: greater use would stem from a better appreciation of the child's needs for passage agent support in these circumstances, and by Cafcass itself realising, as Brian Cantwell argues, that it is so well placed to perform this critically important preventative role.

This is the reason why I have earlier spelt out in this part the potentiality of the conceptual framework of the Caplanian model of short-term crisis intervention in these circumstances, as well as indicating the scale of the issues in Part I of this book. As I see it, the advantage of appointing a Cafcass officer rather than someone from the local authority is that the officer is backed by the authority of the family court. I will develop this point in Part IV when I consider the role and authority of the family court judge and the concept of participant family justice, which needs to be viewed in preventive community mental health terms as much as from the perspective of orthodox family jurisprudence.

I should emphasise that I am *not* here viewing family justice as a branch of social work or in psychotherapeutic terms; rather, I am suggesting that just as a child's education has to be concerned with a child's social and emotional wellbeing, so must a family court when it seeks to do justice according to law and to use its independent judicial authority sensitively to contain and if possible resolve interparental conflict in the primary interests of the children. The FAO provides an important mechanism to do so, sometimes enabling, among other things, the child's and the parents' grief at the breakup of existing family relationships to be acknowledged in the process of working out, with short-term help from a Cafcass officer, a new homeostatic pattern of family relationships in which the symbolic power of family justice has a crucial part to play.

Of course I realise that in times of austerity, when existing services are being severely constrained, it is a tall order to expect Cafcass and family

---

[571] Cafcass (7 July 2016) *Annual Report and Accounts 2015–16* www.gov.uk

[572] N Lowe and G Douglas G (2015) *Bromley's Family Law* (11th edition) Oxford University Press p549.

courts to develop new approaches. These will inevitably raise questions about how to draw and maintain the constitutional boundaries between, on the one hand, the family court and its support services as a specialist interdisciplinary system of civil law, and on the other, the role of executive services such as provided by primary healthcare teams and local authority social services and the like. In what follows in my conclusions (in Part IV, Chapter Thirteen) I intend to explain how this should be done.

I next consider more closely the role of the family court judge, particularly the contentious question of whether judges should meet with children who wish to do so.

Some thorny practice issues: listening to the voice of the child in the family court context

In an article based on a speech given in November 2014 to the Annual Conference of the Association of Lawyers for Children, Mr Justice Cobb, (a highly experienced family law practitioner and author of the report which formed the basis of the CAP) drew attention to the downturn in private law applications following the implementation of the Legal Aid, Sentencing and Punishment of Offenders Act 2012.[573] As already explained, this cut in legal aid led to a reduction in the number of referrals to mediation services, one of the unintended consequences which I consider further in the next chapter. But Mr Justice Cobb focused on another consequence – namely, that fewer children will have an opportunity to have their views heard directly both in court proceedings and in the context of mediation. Thus he observed that:

> Many children who prior to 2013 would probably have had their own situation considered by either a judge and/or Cafcass and/or another professional are no longer receiving that sort of attention. While recognising that family law litigation brings with it many disadvantages for children, I nevertheless have a concern that those children that were former private law cases on the cusp of public law (where there are safeguarding elements) are escaping without scrutiny, potentially exposing children to the risk of harm.[574]

---

[573] Mr Justice Cobb (2015) 'Seen but not heard?' *Family Law* 45 pp144–157.
[574] Ibid p147.

In so far as there has been a reduction in referrals to mediation services, the same point obviously applies, together with other problems which I consider below. But here sticking with court proceedings, Mr Justice Cobb in his article makes the further point concerning listening to the voices of children, that:

> There is risk that the clamour of adult conflict can cause them to be ignored or drowned out.'[575]

First, he expects Cafcass to 'remain the "eyes and ears" of the court and will remain the primary frontline service for children and families in the court system'.

Children meeting the judge: a challenging issue

Second, with respect to the question of judges seeing children, he points out that this raises a number of challenging questions and requires very careful handling, even though he is, in general, 'persuaded of its value'. For example, it may not be appropriate for some children with learning or other disabilities who might not understand its purpose or for those who simply do not want to see the judge. In his view, in such cases the Cafcass worker can act as a valuable liaison between child and judge and should be able to assess the suitability of the judge meeting the child.

Next he stresses that it is 'important that children are reassured that the judge who decides the case is the one who they meet', hence the importance of judicial continuity.

Perhaps the most difficult aspect of judge/child communication is how to draw the boundary between listening to the child whilst not eliciting information from the child 'in a way that ultimately fashions judicial analysis, opinion and/or findings'. (Here he cites various cases.) As the *Report of the Vulnerable Witnesses and Children's Working Group* points out:

> This is a difficult concept for any young person to grasp at best; and is misleading as it amounts to saying that the judge is here to listen to you but cannot take any notice of what you say.[576]

---

[575] Ibid p148.

[576] *Report of the Vulnerable Witnesses and Children Working Group* (March 2015) The Judicial Office of the Judiciary of England and Wales www.judiciary.gov.uk at paras

Yet this report does not expressly advise how this particular problem should be dealt with. It was recognised that judges are having to feel their way in this respect, perhaps learning ways of doing so from practice in the Criminal Crown Court. Thus the working group states:

> The dissatisfaction of children and young people expressed by those on the Family Justice Young People's Board and others revealed their underlying belief that they are not being listened to and heard. These young people that the Working Group heard from do not expect, or even want, the judge to do as they say; they want to know that they have been listened to and this perceived (and in many cases actual) defect cannot be cured by meeting the judge or tribunal alone if at all.[577]

One might think that the working group might be being too influenced by the experience of taking evidence from children in adversarial criminal proceedings, not sufficiently recognising that family courts are becoming more inquisitorial and have a quite different ethos. This may explain why, significantly, the working group added:

> To hear a child must mean to hear her/his evidence and if the child/young person is not going to give oral evidence there must be provision for their evidence to be heard as directly as possible without interpretation by the court appointed officers or others.[578]

Consequently, the working group argues for better training for advocates and judges and recommends the use of the Advocate's Gateway Toolkit proposed by the Advocacy Training Council. This seeks to ensure that children understand the questions they are asked – necessary if they are to be considered competent witnesses – and are enabled to give their answers in an understandable fashion. Intimidating questioning must be avoided. The possibility of using video links to the courts should be developed. All this is necessary to ensure compliance with the principle of Article 6 of the European Convention on Human Rights (the right to a fair trial) incorporated into the Human Rights Act 1998, so that evidence can be tested on behalf of *all* the litigant

---

24 and 25.
[577] Ibid at para 35.
[578] Ibid at para 36.

parties to the case.[579] Overall, the working group concluded that further work will be needed to be carried out on:

> Modernising the ways in which evidence of children is gathered and put before the family courts. This will ultimately require a substantive change in the prevailing culture in respect of evidence of children on the part of judges, social services, Cafcass and others who work with children in the family courts.[580]

It is easy enough to call for 'cultural change', whatever that may mean, but as we will see in Chapter Eleven, there are many obstacles to be overcome, not least the need for a sustained, well-thought out programme of *shared interdisciplinary training* of all family justice practitioners to achieve it – the mechanisms for which barely exist at present when resources are so restricted.

Reading between the lines, I suspect that Mr Justice Cobb would not altogether agree with the traditional orthodox views of the working group. Rather, by referring to guidelines formulated by the Family Justice Council's Voice of the Child Committee, produced in 2010, he stressed in his article that the meeting between the child and the judge is *not* for the purpose of gathering evidence; that is the task for Cafcass and other experts in this field. The purpose is to enable the child to gain some understanding of what is going on and to be reassured that the judge has understood him/her. Judges should be reasonably 'passive recipients' of the child's views and should not set out to probe or seek to test what the child is saying.

This is the view taken by Sir Mark Hedley, an experienced former High Court Family Division Judge.[581] I quote from his reflective lecture on the subject, which distils legal concepts and principles into clear language. Having stressed the important role of the Cafcass reporting officer, without which a judge might be dependent on what parents say, he observes that often those parents have only been told what the child thinks they want to hear:

---

[579] For extensive consideration of these and other related International Conventions, see N Lowe and G Douglas G (2015) *Bromley's Family Law* (11th edition) Oxford University Press at pp21–29.

[580] *Report of the Vulnerable Witnesses and Children Working Group* (March 2015) The Judicial Office of the Judiciary of England and Wales www.judiciary.gov.uk at para 39.

[581] Sir Mark Hedley (2016) *The Modern Judge: Power, Responsibility and Society's Expectations* Lexis/Family Law, Bristol at pp54–55.

I favour seeing children in principle, where parents, guardians and child all support it, but I have been very reluctant to further embroil a child in a dispute by seeing them if to do so is controversial, unless there is some special strong ground like a strongly expressed view by an older child, although even there communication by letter might be sufficient.

He observes that the official view is increasingly in favour of direct communication between judge and child'. He points out:

> 'this does not have to be a face–to-face meeting. Many children would find that intimidating and most do not want physical involvement in the court process. However, where a child wants it, more judges will now be happy to meet in person. I think it is difficult to insist that a judge should meet a child as if the judge is ill at ease the child is likely to feel the same. Letters to the judge are now encouraged and no doubt other forms of communication will find favour too. The key issues are: does the child feel they have been heard? Does the judge fully appreciate the child's wishes and feelings?[582]

Overall, I favour the line taken by Mr Justice Cobb and Sir Mark Hedley rather than the more orthodox view of the working group, influenced as it is more by advocacy practice in the criminal justice system.

Communicating with children: skills required

A further important point that Mr Justice Cobb makes concerns the manner in which judges communicate with children: they must do so in language that children understand. Quoting the Family Justice Young People's Board Charter, he points out that this must be 'clear, understandable, age appropriate and jargon free'.[583] This is surely a message for all professionals working within the family justice system and has obvious implications for training when it comes to face-to-face work with children and young people. With respect to family court judges, this admonition particularly concerns the importance of giving

---

[582] Ibid – see Foreword by Sir James Munby, President of the Family Division.

[583] Mr Justice Cobb (2015) 'Seen but not heard' *Family Law* 45 pp153.

accurate, honest *feedback* to the child about the decision which the judge has made – all the more important if that decision goes against the express wishes and feelings of the child. It is a question of treating the child with respect and being accountable. As Mr Justice Cobb put it:

> A child benefits from knowing that their views have been heard, more so by reassurance that their views have been understood. A meeting with the judge fulfils (or should fulfil) this objective immediately and vividly. But if the meeting takes place, it is perhaps even more important than at the conclusion of a case, or after a critical decision has been made, the direct message is sent to the child – ideally from the judge – whether by letter or otherwise explaining what has happened and why.[584]

Should family court magistrates be barred from meeting children in private law proceedings?

One problem, not mentioned by Mr Justice Cobb, concerns the role of lay magistrates in the family court. First, meeting a group of lay magistrates may be even more intimidating than meeting a single judge. Moreover, many magistrates will not have had the experience or training to deal sensitively and appropriately with the challenges proposed by the direct participation of children in private law proceedings. This point was picked up by Lowe and Douglas in their latest edition of *Bromley's family law*, following an article by Baroness Hale of the Supreme Court.[585] There she had pointed out that in the past there was a reluctance on the part of the higher courts to allow lay magistrates to interview children in private, even though under the Children Act 1989 they have comparable powers as judges in the higher courts. Second, as far as one can tell the most recent consideration of this issue seems to assume that, if it seems the child's direct participation is requested or, if in any event, it seems desirable in the circumstances of the case, the case will be allocated a judge at or before the FHDRA, given that the CAP requires the court to ask specifically (a) whether the child is aware of the proceedings, (b) whether the child's wishes and feelings are available, (c) how the child

---

[584] Ibid p154.
[585] N Lowe and G Douglas G (2015) *Bromley's Family Law* (11th edition) Oxford University Press at p465. Baroness Hale (2007) 'The voice of the child' *International Family Law* 171 at p172.

is to be involved in proceedings, if at all, and (d) who will inform the child of the outcome of the case where appropriate.[586]

The selection of family court judges

There is a further point resulting from the need to enable children and young people to participate more directly in the family court process – which is crucial to the idea of making more 'child friendly' what to them is often an unfamiliar experience. This concerns the need to select family court judges with suitable temperament and understanding. Not all judges, particularly those conditioned by the daily cut and thrust of adversarial trial in other forms of non-family civil litigation, can adapt their approach and language so as to establish sufficient rapport with children and young people, and to overcome the gap in age and culture which separates the judge from them. Most will come from a very different social background; besides, the modern generation of young people may also be much more familiar with electronic means of communication, with its own specialist language codes, than many judges. All of which points to the urgent need to have training in the new child-friendly family court craft. Fortunately, there are many experienced family court judges that have already developed the necessary skills who can act as the necessary role models. For example, much could be learnt from former Judge Nicholas Crichton and colleagues who pioneered in London the successful specialist Drug and Alcohol Court now being replicated in other parts of the country.[587] I deal with this issue further in the conclusion of this book.

The voice of the child in mediation: unresolved policy and practice issues

It seems to me that many of the points made by Mr Justice Cobb with respect to court proceedings should ideally apply equally to child-inclusive mediation and possibly also to MIAMs if a child of suitable age and understanding wishes to attend. But here the CAP document is largely silent. As already mentioned, this is not surprising given that the report of the Mediation Task Force found that under existing practices 'children and young people are rarely provided ...

---

[586] N Lowe and G Douglas G (2015) *Bromley's Family Law* (11th edition) Oxford University Press at p475.
[587] N Crichton (2015) 'FDAC Works' *Family Law* 45 at p449.

with the opportunity to be heard and that child inclusive mediation is rarely undertaken'.[588]

The Mediation Task Force observed:

> when children are included in mediation it is usually as an aid to parental decision-making rather than as an opportunity for children to express their views. The decision to include children is driven by adults (parents and practitioners) and not by children's rights to participate in proceedings that impact on their future.[589]

This was a point made by Professor Jan Walker in her article the previous year.

The reasons for this state of affairs are given as:

> inadequate training, supervision and resources; uncertainty about the availability of legal aid funding for child inclusive work; out of date standards and protocols; the lack of a coherent framework for hearing children's views; concerns about confidentiality and privilege; and polarised views about the efficacy and purpose of involving children in adult matters.[590]

The task force report therefore recommended that the 'issue should be urgently reviewed and steps taken to improve training and supervision for dispute resolution practitioners'.[591]

Hearing the voice of the child in child-inclusive mediation: the need for consistent practice between Cafcass and mediation services

It seems to me that this undeveloped aspect of mediation practice could learn quite a lot from the experiences of Cafcass and Cafcass Cymru of involving children – a point I shall return to below in Part IV of this book where I suggest an expanded coordinating role for these two services in a matrix of preventive community services for children with separating or divorcing parents. Suffice here to say there is

---

[588] Department for Education and Ministry of Justice (June 2014) *Report of the Family Mediation Task Force* www.justice.gov.uk at p27 paras 83–86.

[589] Ibid at p27 paras 83–86.

[590] Ibid para 83 at p27.

[591] Ibid at p27 para 85.

in my view a strong argument for bringing mediators, who in MIAMs now act as gatekeepers to the family justice system, into a much closer organisational relationship with Cafcass and Cafcass Cymru – at the very least in terms of their training and supervision in direct face-to-face work with children and young people. In this respect, the task force report recognised that:

> perhaps the most important change ... is one which addresses the barriers to hearing children's voices and professional concerns which inhibit child inclusive approaches.[592]

The issue about whether the child's voice should be heard in the mediation process continued to be hotly debated in professional circles in the closing months of the Coalition government. In August 2014, Simon Hughes MP, then Minister of State for Justice, set up on the recommendation of the Family Mediation Task Force the specialist Voice of the Child Dispute Resolution Advisory Group to consider the matter. This had a remit to bring forward proposals to ensure that the voice of the child – particularly those over the age of 10 – would be heard in the mediation process.[593] Although there were some who thought this should be a legal presumption, the advisory group, including Professor Jan Walker and Angela Lake-Carroll, stopped short of this. Consequently, in March 2015, in his official letter to Dispute Resolution Professionals, Simon Hughes limited his view to being 'that children and young people should routinely have the opportunity to have a say in matters which affect their future and agree that this should be a <u>non-legal</u> presumption'. Even so, he endorsed the advisory group's proposal that 'where any form of out of court dispute resolution has involved a child or young person, and the parties achieve agreement, any Memorandum of Understanding or agreement should reflect the participation of the child. This should be reflected in any subsequent court consent order'.[594]

This advisory group's report contains altogether a list of some 34 recommendations which the then Minister endorsed, for example:

---

[592] Insert footnote: Ibid p44.

[593] For a full list of recommendations see www.gov.uk/moj

[594] S Hughes (18 March 2015) 'Letter to Dispute Resolution Professionals: the Voice of the Child: Dispute Resolution Advisory Group' – available from www.gov.uk/moj emphasis in original.

that information about hearing the voices of children and young people should be incorporated in all materials about mediation and dispute resolution services and should be included in all relevant products for separated parents and their children, and websites run by the relevant agencies.[595] (Recommendations 25–29)

One further important point concerns the issue of confidentiality (Recommendations 12 and 14). Mediators should respect the child's wishes if they do not want information about them to be disclosed, unless there are exceptional circumstances and good reasons to override them.

What is very clear, however, is that both this advisory group and the then minister recognised first that the participation of children in child-inclusive mediation requires practitioners to be suitably qualified and 'fully trained and skilled in working sensitively with families to ensure constructive outcomes for children'. And second, that to bring about a situation where child-inclusive mediation becomes the established norm 'will require a change of culture within the dispute resolution sector'.[596] This of course won't happen unless there is investment to sustain long term the necessary family justice training programmes.

With respect to the implementation of the advisory group's recommendations, there is a clear statement (Recommendation 34) that 'young people should play a central role in the implementation of child-inclusive processes and that the Family Justice Young People's Board Charter should reflect the presumptions and recommendations made in this respect'.[597]

Furthermore, the then minister, Simon Hughes MP, acknowledged that an increase in child-inclusive mediation is likely to result in additional work for the mediators conducting the process. This is because sessions are likely to take longer and may also result in more work for the lawyers who assist parents in drawing up agreements to be endorsed in court orders. Unsurprisingly therefore, given the imminence of the 2015 General Election and the prospect of further substantial cuts in the Ministry of Justice's budget, he announced that he was 'unable to make a formal commitment to funding at this time',

---

[595] Ibid – see Appendix A attached to Simon Hughes' letter.
[596] Ministry of Justice (March 2015) *Final Report of the Voice of the Child Dispute Resolution Advisory Group* para 205 at p53.
[597] Ibid para 219 at p55.

stating merely that 'further consideration'[598] should be given to the funding requirements for child-inclusive mediation and that officials should consider the issues when they are reviewing the Legal Aid Agency's contract later in the year.

All this shows that ultimately the issues under consideration are political, dependent on the prevailing political and economic philosophy of the government of the day and its view about the role of state support for public services, the family justice system, and the extent to which 'private' markets should, if at all, play a part – big questions which I consider in the conclusions of this book.

Developing skills in communicating with children and young people

Throughout this chapter I have referred to the need for family justice practitioners to develop skill in working directly with children and young people in the usually highly charged emotional circumstances of parental conflict. Here I just want to flag up a particularly useful article on the subject by Paul Bishop – an independent social worker and former family court advisor – which appeared in *Seen and Heard* (the journal for children's guardians, family court advisors and independent social workers).[599] In it he gives a number of illustrations of just how complex it can be to ascertain children's wishes and feelings, which may change, appear contradictory or be in other respects unclear. The challenge for the professional is to be able to establish sufficient rapport and trust with the child, given that children are often worried about talking to a stranger about the family. In such circumstances it is critically important for children to be given sufficient time to establish this trust.

In the next chapter I examine many obstacles which currently hamper the development of the social and legal policy issues addressed in this chapter.

---

[598] S Hughes (18 March 2015) 'Letter to Dispute Resolution Professionals: the Voice of the Child: Dispute Resolution Advisory Group' available from www.gov.uk/moj.

[599] P Bishop (2015) 'Ascertaining the wishes and feelings of children' *Seen and Heard* 25(1) 31–37.

ELEVEN

Changing the culture of family justice: barriers to be overcome

Introduction

This chapter broadens the focus to consider a number of underlying problematic issues – some recent, others longstanding – which make it difficult to change the culture of the family justice system so as to put the needs of children centre stage and see the system as part of a matrix of public services to promote children's wellbeing and strengthen their emotional resilience.

As Sir David Norgrove, now Chair of the Family Justice Board, wrote in the Foreword to the *Family Justice Review final report*:

> changes in structure, rules and processes will not by themselves measure up to the strains and problems we diagnose ... Much of the improvement for children will have to come from the way people choose to work, from change in the culture of family justice and change in the culture of delay.[600]

It is relatively easy to state the overall objective of a new strategic approach, but of course far harder to achieve it in practice. Both the former President of the Family Division Sir Nicholas Wall and Mr Justice (now Lord Justice) Ryder, Judge in Charge of the Modernisation of Family Justice, as well as David Norgrove, have spoken of the need for a 'cultural change' in the family justice system. I will argue that one needs to unravel what this really entails. For a start, I believe that to achieve significant change in this field, one must first ask the question: if we have known now for a number of years what children's needs in these circumstances are, and if – as is the case and as I explained in Part II of this book – the elements of an effective preventive programme have been articulated and understood, why is it that we do not already have in place the necessary policy and practice measures?

---

[600] Ministry of Justice, Department for Education and the Welsh Government (November 2011) *Family Justice Review: Final Report* TSO, London atp3.

The barriers to be overcome

To address this fundamental question one must consider some of the barriers that have inhibited the development of such a strategic approach in the past. I suggest that these were added to by some of the measures introduced by the Coalition government (2010–15), some of which I have already touched on in the previous chapters and the Preface.

As I have explained, two major factors are currently shaping the character of the evolving family justice system as it concerns children of separated and divorcing parents. The first is the need to find major cuts in public expenditure and to reduce the deficit in government finances following the economic crisis of 2007/08 and the subsequent recession. The second is the previous Coalition government's legislative response to the Norgrove Family Justice Review, particularly the subsequent Child Arrangements Programme (CAP) designed and introduced by the senior judiciary in the Family Division of the High Court. Of these, the withdrawal of legal aid from family litigation, except where there is a risk of domestic violence or child abuse, has had the most profound impact on the system. As explained in the Introduction to Part III, this had two unintended consequences: damage to the economically fragile network of mediation services and an increase in the number of litigants in person appearing in hard-pressed family courts. Of course it is conflicted parents who suffer when erected barriers such as these prevent them from accessing services intended to help them resolve their disputes, but it is the children who have to put up with the emotional backwash. So, while this chapter focuses on broader socio-legal policy problems, the reader should constantly hold in mind the likely impact on the children.

The removal of legal aid in most 'private' family law cases: should the term 'civil legal aid' be changed to 'family legal aid'?

In this section I examine more closely the way the Coalition government set about cutting legal aid from most private family law proceedings. In doing so I invite readers to consider my suggestion that it would be better to refer to this aspect of the legal aid scheme as 'family legal aid'. (Please note that in Chapter Thirteen I develop a mental health argument for this change of terminology and suggest that the Department of Health might share responsibility for funding it with the Ministry of Justice.) In other words, might a change of terminology alter the way people perceive its purpose, thereby bringing about a greater appreciation that supportive partisan legal help, given by solicitors to parents in most cases, implicitly serves a psychosocial function in helping them cope with and adapt to critical family change while also facilitating the settlement of conflicting interest?

As mentioned earlier, the removal of civil legal aid in most divorce cases where children's arrangements are disputed is provided for by Schedule 1 of the Legal Aid, Sentencing and Punishment of Offenders Act 2012 (referred to as LASPO). According to the Ministry of Justice family court statistics, in only 24% of private law cases are both parties now legally represented.[601] Legal aid for representation may still be available provided there is clear evidence of domestic violence, defined as 'any incident or pattern of incidents of controlling, coercive or threatening behaviour, violence or abuse (whether psychological, physical, sexual, financial or emotional) between individuals who are associated with each other'.[602] Proving domestic violence within this definition can be difficult. Thus two surveys quoted by Lowe and Douglas found that of 377 cases almost half (49.5%) did not have any of the prescribed forms of evidence (such as corroborative medical or police evidence) and so the complainant could not apply for legal aid.[603] Moreover, if they proceed as litigants in person to court, they have to have the emotional strength and clarity of mind to cross-examine the alleged abuser – no easy task. So there is a strong incentive to take no further action.[604]

It should, however, be pointed out that a limited amount of legal aid (about £110 worth of legal advice) was made available to those who are financially eligible for mediation so that parents might receive a solicitor's help in drawing up an agreement (for example, over contact with children or financial provision) which can be endorsed by a family court as a consent order.[605] More recently this was extended

---

[601] Ministry of Justice (2014) *Family Court Statistics Quarterly* January to March www.gov.uk.

[602] LASPO (2012) Schedule 1 para 12.9 as amended by Statutory Instrument 2013/748.

[603] N Lowe and G Douglas (2015) *Bromley's Family Law* (11th edition) Oxford University Press at p13.

[604] L Truss MP, the previous Minister of Justice, has suggested (March 2017) that women alleging domestic violence should be able to pre-record their evidence before the trial in order to avoid cross-examination by the alleged abuser. But this has been strongly criticised by the Lord Chief Justice (23 March), in evidence to the Parliamentary Justice Select Committee, as being contrary to due process principle.

[605] Public Accounts Committee (4 December 2014) *Oral Evidence: Implementing Reforms to Civil Legal Aid* Evidence of Peter Hancock, Chief Executive of Her Majesty's

to cover both parents, as a step to encourage greater use of mediation (see further below).

Of course, apart from saving public money, the stated intention of this measure was to encourage those in dispute to reach settlement out of court. Nevertheless, as we have seen in the Preface and the previous chapter, the withdrawal of civil legal aid – as I have suggested, it might be more appropriately termed family legal aid – has had a number of unintended consequences. Not only did it seriously reduce referrals to mediation services, but as Lowe and Douglas point out:

> the potential impact is to increase the number of litigants in person who feel they have no alternative but to take the case to court, with consequential difficulties for themselves in terms of trying to conduct a legal case and examine witnesses; for their family members (i.e. including children) in the hostility and distress this may engender, and for the courts in having to assist such litigants so that they can receive justice.[606]

An indication of the problems that have occurred was revealed by a BBC *Panorama* programme on 30 March 2015. This illustrated two cases in which litigants in person struggled (one successfully, the other not) to present their case. The BBC programme also interviewed two experienced judges. Both expressed the view that the legal aid restrictions had effectively limited access to justice by deterring many, particularly women, from attempting to overcome the obstacles now placed before them when seeking orders concerning children. These judges also referred to the problem that litigants in person posed for judges who had to help them conduct their case, particularly where one parent is skilfully represented and the other not. In the judge's experience this took much longer – a point defensively disputed by officials in the Ministry of Justice giving evidence to the Public Accounts Committee, although it was admitted that the ministry does not collect data on the length of hearings.

Courts and Tribunal Service, questions 66–70 Hansard HL808 https://hansard. parliament.uk.

[606] N Lowe and G Douglas (2015) *Bromley's Family Law* (11th edition) Oxford University Press at p13.

The consequence of increasing numbers of litigants in person

It was entirely predictable that the withdrawal of civil legal aid for all disputes, save those involving allegations of domestic violence and/or child abuse, would lead to an increase of litigants in person. Official figures showed that family courts in England and Wales dealt with 19,140 more unrepresented parents in the year 2013/14 compared with the previous year – an increase of 54%. According to judges, this situation had led to serious courtroom delays as well as serious concerns about access to justice. For the first time mothers made up more than half (53%) of parents without lawyers attending court to contest child arrangements. In a short speech in a House of Lords debate on the legal system and the rule of law, initiated by Lord Wolf, Dame Elizabeth Butler-Sloss, a former President of the Family Division, described the way government had misunderstood the relationship between lawyers and mediators before the legal aid cuts had taken effect. She explained the situation thus:

> 'Barristers and solicitors who did this private law work did not earn large amounts. Their desire has always been to seek settlement of the issues between the parties and their protocols require them to put the welfare of children first. They now do very little of this work because most litigants have no money, so men and women, untrained in the law, but fighting their failed relationships through the arena of the courts, appear unrepresented before judges and magistrates. The task of the courts, faced with carrier bags of unsorted and disorganised papers in child cases and even more so in financial disputes over the former matrimonial home and maintenance is huge and unmanageable. On a practical note it clogs the courts and creates delays, so I hope that the government will listen to the fact that it is not cost effective.'[607]

There is some doubt over whether the judges are right about their intuitive perception that cases are taking longer. 'The Ministry of Justice has published experimental statistics on the length of hearings before and after LASPO which don't show any evidence that they take longer. Those are based on estimated rather than actual hearing

---

[607] House of Lords, Hansard (10 July 2014) *Motion to Take Note: Legal Systems: Rule of Law* Col 348.

duration ... The statistics on the progress of cases through the system are more robust and do show an increase in the average length of a private law case but that it is the case whether or not there are lawyers involved. While it makes intuitive sense that, as the judges say, litigants in person take more court time and make cases go on longer, there isn't conclusive evidence of this at present.'[608]

Liz Trinder and Rosemary Hunter have pointed out that:

> the difficulty with interpreting these figures is that they do not give an indication of the nature and complexity of the cases. Full representation cases are now very much in the minority and are more likely to involve two highly conflicted parties who can afford to litigate. Further, rather than an indicator of efficiency, short hearings and proceedings may simply reflect the absence of lawyers filtering out non-meritorious cases or the inability of the LIPs to put their case.[609]

Given the substantial rise in the number of litigants in person, it is reasonable to suppose that, as observed, 'most people without a lawyer would have one if they could afford it or if legal aid were available to pay for it'.[610]

An example of the way that withdrawal of legal aid leads to additional expense for courts appeared in the *Times law reports* on 7 April 2015. The Court of Appeal case of *Lindner v Rawlins* (CA.TLR7.4.2015) concerned an appeal of a litigant in person. This involved complex legal issues arising in the context of divorce which meant that the judges in the Court of Appeal were obliged, in the absence of representation, to assist the appellant. Thus, Lady Justice Black observed inter alia:

> 'the task that would normally have been fulfilled by the parties' legal representatives, of finding relevant documents amongst the material presented and researching the law and its application to the facts of the case, had to be done by

---

[608] *Full Fact* (2015) '"DIY justice" or vital reform – what do we know about legal aid?' 23 April, https://fullfact.org/law/diy-justice-or-vital-reform-what-do-we-know-about-legal-aid/. The Ministry of Justice statistics were published as Ministry of Justice (2014) *Experimental Statistics: Analysis of Estimated Hearing Duration in Private Law Cases, England and Wales* www.gov.uk.

[609] L Trinder and R Hunter (2015) 'Access to justice? Litigants in person before and after LASPO' *Family Law* 45 at p538.

[610] *Full Fact* (2015) op cit.

the judges of the Court of Appeal instead. This was not a satisfactory state of affairs as the time taken to attend to that had been considerable and could not be spared in what was already a very busy court.'

Lord Justice Aikens, in his concurring judgment added:

'The court has had to trawl through a large amount of documents on the file. All that involved an expensive use of judicial time, which was in short supply already. Money might have been saved for the legal aid funds but an equal amount of expense if not more had been incurred in terms of the costs of judges and court time. The result was that there had in fact been no economy at all. Worse, that way of dealing with cases ran the risk that the correct result would not be reached because the court had not had the legal assistance of counsel that it should have had and the court had no other legal assistance available to it.'

This last point suggests that if legal aid continues to be unavailable even in complex family law cases, the courts should be able to draw on some other form of publicly funded legal representation to assist the litigants to prepare and put their case on the order of the court itself.

In this respect, Trinder and Hunter argued that 'there should be wider availability of free or low cost legal services, including law centres, pro bono schemes and unbundled and fixed price packages to help litigants in person prepare their case'. Perhaps optimistically, they wish to see 'a uniform and well organised response to pre-court support needs which would enable parties: (i) to receive initial legal advice; (ii) to be referred to mediation if appropriate; (iii) to be assisted to prepare for court'.[611]

Furthermore, they are almost certainly right to suggest that the court process should become more inquisitorial, which would mean changing the traditional role of the judges – a point I return to in Chapter Thirteen. There is also an argument for using the court itself as a 'hub' from which to mount a range of help, including legal advice provided by a court-appointed lawyer for the parents disputing child-related issues. This might well limit the problems that litigants in person create for themselves and the court – a point I develop in

---

[611] L Trinder and R Hunter (2015) 'Access to justice? Litigants in person before and after LASPO' *Family Law* 45 at p541.

Part IV in the context of family legal aid. At the very least this should be considered in any future government review of the legal aid scheme.

In the report of the National Audit Office (NAO) it was estimated that litigants in person had cost HM Courts and Tribunal Service as much as £3 million per year plus direct costs to the Ministry of Justice itself of approximately £400,000. To compensate for these additional costs the ministry was reported as committing £2 million for additional support for litigants in person over the next two years. Further, the NAO report observed:

> there may also be costs to the wider public sector if people whose problems could have been resolved by legal aid suffered consequences to their health and wellbeing as a result of no longer having access to legal aid.[612]

In a valuable review article based on a study of litigants in person *before* the legal aid cuts took effect, Liz Trinder and colleagues reported that:

> cost shifting fell on all associated within the system ... There were instances where court staff were having to deal with extensive correspondence from LIPs [litigants in person] or having to pick up the errors of omissions in LIP paperwork. We observed cases where Cafcass officers were taking on roles formerly undertaken by lawyers, including helping the parties to negotiate, outlining the case in hearings and occasionally drafting orders.[613]

As things stood in the spring of 2015, at the end of the Coalition government, one could not say with any confidence how many disputing couples took the alternative routes of attempting settlement through mediation or simply avoiding dispute resolution mechanisms altogether.

---

[612] National Audit Office Report of the Comptroller and Auditor General (20 November 2014) *Implementing Reforms to Civil Legal Aid* HC784 www.nao.org.uk at p6 para 6 – see also paras 1.17 to 1.34.

[613] L Trinder, R Hunter, E Hitchings, J Miles, R Moorhead, L Smith, M Sefton, V Hinchly, K Bader and J Pearce (2014) *Litigants in Person in Private Family Law* Ministry of Justice www.gov.uk.

Did political philosophy override a realistic appraisal of the likely consequences of withdrawal of legal aid?

It soon became apparent that this indeed might have been the case since, as mentioned in the Preface, it was also in tune with a political philosophy dedicated to reducing the size of the state. It might also have reflected a superficial, ill-informed understanding of the emotional complexities of parental disputes: of individual parents' need for partisan support and the psychological pressures (sometimes appearing to outsiders as irrational) which drive people to seek impartial justice in the family courts – points which I have already explained in Part II.

Here, to get some idea of the initial rationalisation for cuts in civil legal aid in the early days of the Coalition government, it is instructive to turn to the text of a speech which the then Lord Chancellor and Minister for Justice, Kenneth Clarke MP gave to the Centre for Crime and Justice Studies on 30 June 2010. Although the speech was mostly concerned with penal affairs, he indicated that major reforms would be needed in two areas affecting the family justice system: the courts and legal aid. He talked of trying "to turn financial stringency into some constructive and sensible policies". With respect to legal aid, he stated, "it is clear to me we must make major changes while acknowledging the right and desire of people to use the law to settle disputes and assert claims". He indicated that people might well have to pay more from their own resources, implying that if they could not do so they would have to do without. In a significant comment on family law, he had this to say:

> 'nor am I convinced that in many private family cases the traditional adversarial system is necessarily the best for the parties involved or the best use of public funds. In the worst cases bitter disputes between spouses and partners are actually in my opinion made worse by repeated and fruitless battles between lawyers in court hearing after court hearing. Might we be better off in focusing on better, less legalistic ways of seeking to resolve highly charged emotional disputes between former partners in broken relationships?'

Of course Kenneth Clarke, as the responsible minister at the time and a former Chancellor of the Exchequer, was under pressure from the Treasury to quickly find savings within the Ministry of Justice. This was subsequently revealed in evidence given to the Public Accounts

Committee by Ursula Brennan, then Permanent Secretary, Ministry of Justice on 4 December 2014. She told the committee:

> 'we knew very clearly that there was an imperative to cut legal aid funding. The government was absolutely explicit about that from the start ... It needed to make these changes swiftly. Therefore it was not possible to do research about the current regime before moving to the cuts.'[614]

Eekelaar and Maclean, in their latest book, suggest that the Coalition government's cuts to civil legal aid were driven by more than just financial expediency: underneath lay a neoliberal philosophy based on market-driven principles where people have to take responsibility themselves for the personal choices they make.[615] As they see it, such a policy:

> can only be seen as an indirect way of announcing that the neo-liberal policy stance considers the rule of law to be at best irrelevant in the family context and at worst undesirable in building a society where self-reliance and self-sufficiency are prioritised.[616]

How cuts in legal aid adversely affect mediation services

At the time the government aimed to reduce the legal aid bill (that is, criminal legal aid and civil legal aid) by about £300 million per year. Although no careful previous research had been undertaken, the ministry estimated that about 10,000 cases a year would be diverted through mediation. As events turned out, this was an unfulfilled estimate, because the ministry had not realised that cuts in legal aid would reduce the number of solicitors able to make referral to mediation services, as I have shown in the Preface and the Introduction to this part of the book. Thus, as the *Report of the National Audit Office* stated in November 2014:

---

[614] Public Accounts Committee Hansard (4 December 2014) *Oral Evidence: Implementing Reforms to Civil Legal Aid* HC808 questions 42–48.

[615] M Maclean and J Eekelaar (2016) *Lawyers and Mediators: The Brave New World of Services for Separating Families* Hart Publishing, Oxford at p8.

[616] Ibid at p8.

Significantly fewer family law cases were diverted to mediation following the reforms than the Ministry expected. The Ministry expected that removing funding for civil legal aid for private family law matters, but retaining funding for mediation, would divert people away from courts and lead to additional 9,000 mediation assessments and 10,000 mediation cases per year. However, there were 17,248 fewer mediation assessments in 2013–14, a 56% decrease from 2012–13. In addition the number of mediation cases starting fell by 5,177 cases or 38% in the same period.[617]

Even so, the NAO report acknowledged that, following the Mediation Task Force report, the Ministry of Justice decided to increase the take-up of mediation by, for example, funding one mediation session for *both* parties in cases where previously only one party was receiving the limited amount of legal aid funding for help in drafting an agreement. The ministry also funded an ongoing mediation public awareness campaign. These measures helped to increase the number of mediation assessments by 12%.

Misunderstanding the nature and complexity of parental disputes

I will return later to the problem of undertaking a major policy initiative in haste without preceding it with careful research upon which to estimate its likely consequences. Here I want to pick out some other assumptions made in 2010 by Kenneth Clarke when, as Lord Chancellor and Minister of Justice, he indicated that legal aid would be cut.

First, the assumption that disputes between spouses and partners (note he did not call them parents) are made worse by 'repeated and fruitless battles between lawyers in court hearing after court hearing'.[618] I challenge two aspects of this. First, the implication that lawyers aggravate parental dispute. As Lady Butler-Sloss (quoted above) indicated, this is an outdated view. It may be true of a few 'big money cases' involving high net worth couples who engage the help of certain

---

[617] National Audit Office Report of the Comptroller and Auditor General (20 November 2014) Implementing Reforms to Civil Legal Aid HC784 www.nao. org.uk at para 2.8 at p23.

[618] K Clarke (2010) 'The Government's vision for criminal justice reform' Speech at the Centre for Crime and Justice Studies, London, 30 June 2010.

expensive firms of London solicitors, but it was certainly not true of the vast majority of solicitors taking on legally aided family cases. On the contrary, a number of studies had shown that solicitors sought to restrain the parties and promote settlement through negotiation, and to use mediation where the parties failed to agree.[619] Solicitors 'cool out' their clients to reduce hostile emotion and strike bargains in the shadow of the law.[620]

Second, Kenneth Clarke referred to 'highly charged emotional disputes', as if experienced family lawyers were not the right people to cope with and contain such feelings. Of course, mediators as well as many other helping professionals, such as GPs and psychotherapists, get involved in helping in various ways people caught up in emotional disputes. But that is not to assume that family lawyers have no role when so much research evidence points to the contrary. Nor does such a view acknowledge that the authority of the court process itself may help to contain and constrain emotional conflict, as I explain below.

Of course there is a small minority of cases – sometimes labelled 'intractable' – where to the outside observer there are repeated battles in court which appear, as Kenneth Clarke says, 'fruitless'. But this merely raises the question of why so often, despite the reluctance of their lawyers who advise against it, the parents involved insist on going back to court. In my opinion, this can best be seen as a behavioural problem in which the symbolic authority of the impartial judge may have for these parents particular powerful psychological (if unconscious) significance, leading to the perception that the resort to a powerful impartial judicial authority is the only way to free themselves from the intense emotional pain of loss and injustice they feel from the breakdown of their relationship. In this sense the resort to court proceedings may be seen as the only way to regain a sense of emotional balance or equilibrium linked symbolically to a concept of justice. I have written about this elsewhere.[621] Here, I merely suggest that this

---

[619] G Douglas, M Murch, A Perry, K Bader and M Borkowski (1990) *How parents cope financially on marriage breakdown* Family Policy Studies Centre and Joseph Rowntree Foundation, London. J Ekelaar, M Maclean, S Beinart (2000) *Family Lawyers: The Divorce Work of Solicitors* Hart Publishing, Oxford at pp57–80. M Maclean and J Ekelaar (2009) *Family Law Advocacy: How the Barrister Helps the Victims of Family Failure* Hart Publishing, Oxford.

[620] A Sarat and W Felstiner (1995) *Divorce Lawyers and Their Clients: Power and Meaning in the Legal Process* Oxford University Press at pp108–141.

[621] M Murch (2012) 'The role of the family court system in England and Wales in child-related disputes: towards a new concept of the family justice process' in A Balfour, M Morgan and C Vincent (eds) *How Couple Relationships Shape our World:*

is the most plausible way to explain those apparently irrational family law cases, which recur regularly in the press, when all the assets are apparently wasted on litigation costs. Baroness Ruth Deech drew attention to this in support of her Divorce (Financial Provision) Bill.[622]

In these cases it is not just the financial costs that have to be considered but the emotional costs, immediate and long term, which can impact on the children. To me this indicates that simply viewing family litigation through the prism of orthodox family jurisprudence is basically a mistakenly limited approach. Rather, one has to think in terms of the family justice system as a mechanism to help children and their families cope with emotionally charged, critical life-changing events associated with separation and broken emotional attachments which give rise to strained and conflicted relations. This is particularly apparent in high-conflict parental disputes concerning children where parents feel that their very identity is under threat. In such cases the resort to justice in the courts usually contains within it an implicit search to restore or discover a new equitable equilibrium in the family's strained relationships. In this respect the impartial authority of the judge and the symbolic significance of the 'scales of justice' may well be experienced, possibly at an unconscious level, as the only way to safely contain the powerful emotions engendered by the breakdown of the parents' relationship. I suspect that most experienced family law practitioners – solicitors, judges and Cafcass officers – have an intuitive understanding of this even if they are not familiar with psychological frameworks of knowledge which suggest this way of viewing things. This is yet another less obvious reason why the withdrawal of civil legal aid and its unfortunate unintended impact on mediation services has caused so much alarm and misgiving among interdisciplinary family justice practitioners.

It may also explain why without the partisan support, advice and restraint which legally aided solicitors used to provide, so many parents proceed to court as litigants in person, with all the problems for themselves and the family courts that I have explained above. This point may well be ignored even if the Ministry of Justice eventually takes account of the many sensible recommendations from the research

---

Clinical Practice, Research and Policy Perspectives Karnac Books, London pp91–128. See also C Clulow 'Commentary' at pp129–135.

[622] R Deech (2015) 'Money and divorce' *Family Law* 45 at p110. In this article Deech gives an example of a case of 'a husband who was awarded £50,000 but was left with a bill of £490,000 in costs. In another case, the couple's assets were £25 million, costs £1.7 million ... and there was one where the costs swallowed up the entire assets.'

into litigants in person by Professor Liz Trinder and colleagues, which was based on practice before the full impact of the withdrawal of legal aid came into force in April 2013.[623] These recommendations included better information services for parents before proceedings commence, acceptance of the usefulness of a 'paid' professional McKenzie friend to provide moral support in court, and for the ministry to consider other forms of legal and procedural assistance with a possibility of judges being able to recommend publicly funded legal representation 'in the interests of justice'.

Are we moving towards a more inquisitorial mode of trial?

There is one further critically important point concerning the financial costs of family legal aid, which before the cuts resulting from the LASPO reforms consumed two thirds of the civil legal aid budget. This issue is how far the adversarial mode of trial forces up unnecessary costs? As an article on the *Full Fact* website pointed out, under our adversarial mode of justice 'judges expect parties to a case (through their lawyers) to present the best possible evidence for their side and attack the opposing evidence'.[624] By contrast, continental systems of justice which are more inquisitorial 'give judges greater responsibility for finding and testing evidence'. Yet of course, in practice, 'private' family law disputes concerning children have for years been evolving a more inquisitorial approach through, for example, the use of the court's welfare arm now administered by Cafcass and in Wales by Cafcass Cymru. Moreover, one can argue that the recent increase of litigants in person forces family court judges to take on a more inquisitorial role in partnership with the court's Cafcass officer.

In the next part of this book I will develop the argument that the point has now been reached in the evolution of the interdisciplinary family justice system when it is no longer appropriate or realistic to view it simply as a specialist branch of civil jurisprudence – say, administering family law on a par with the law of contract or tort. Rather, given our increasing understanding of behavioural aspects of family interaction, child development and parental breakdown, it should be viewed not

---

[623] L Trinder, R Hunter, E Hitchings, J Miles, R Moorhead, L Smith, M Sefton, V Hinchly, K Bader and J Pearce (2014) *Litigants in Person in Private Family Law* Ministry of Justice www.gov.uk

[624] See *Full Fact* (2015) 23 April '"DIY justice" or vital reform: what do we know about legal aid?', https://fullfact.org/law/diy-justice-or-vital-reform-what-do-we-know-about-legal-aid/

just in orthodox if specialist legal terms but as a distinct hybrid system. Thus, while retaining the constitutional independence of the judicial system with its related support systems,[625] it should also be seen as part of the community's preventive mental health services aimed at promoting children's emotional resilience and wellbeing within a context of helping parents recover from the emotional turbulence associated with the breakdown of their relationship. At a second level of preventive child and mental adolescent mental health services, the various components of the family justice system should also be viewed from this perspective.

I turn now to a completely different set of obstacles hindering the development of a modern system of participant family justice, namely, repeated and longstanding failures to invest in information technology.

Repeated failures to invest in and modernise management information systems: a shortage of money or an official mindset problem?

This is an area where it is all too easy to forget that the need for efficient management information is not just about getting value for money, but a vital tool for assessing how effectively the various components of the family justice system meet the needs of children with whom it is concerned. Yet, so often in the past when faced with calls for reform, the knee-jerk response of politicians and officials has been to object that there is no money available for new developments. So it was in the 1970s, after the oil shock crisis following the Yom Kippur War, when Barbara Castle turned down the Finer Committee's proposals for local family courts – now of course, almost forty years later, introduced by the provisions of the Crime and Courts Act 2013. Similarly, in the 1980s the then Lord Chancellor's Legal Aid Advisory Committee, and committees charged with introducing the Children Act, repeatedly called for a modern system of information technology to link legal aid expenditure to the length of cases in individual courts in order to identify some obvious drivers which had contributed to delays and the escalating costs of the legal aid budget.[626] Again, officials

---

[625] See See J Doughty and M Murch (2012) 'Judicial independence and the restructuring of family courts and their support services' *Child and Family Law Quarterly* 24(3) at pp333–354.

[626] See Lord Chancellor's Department (1981) HC 160 *30th Legal Aid Annual Report (1979-80)* HMSO; also (1984) HC 137 *33rd Legal Aid Annual Report (1982-1983)*; *34th Legal Aid Annual Report (1983-1984)* HC 156; *35th Legal Aid Annual Report (1984-1985)* HC 87.

refused the money for investment which would have saved millions of pounds, despite the fact that research had shown that courts of a similar kind varied considerably in the time they took to deal with similar sorts of children's cases.[627] It was thus difficult to identify causes of delay which not only added to costs but were detrimental to the welfare of children and thus contrary to one of the basic principles of the Children Act 1989. Indeed, it may come as a surprise to current officials and ministers to know that as far back as 1986 the Committee of Public Accounts, having taken evidence from both the Lord Chancellor's Department and the Law Society (then responsible for legal aid administration) expressed 'astonishment that neither the Lord Chancellor's Department nor the Law Society had the management information to identify precisely the causes of the increase in legal aid expenditure over the years'. In addition, it pointed out that 'it is not only lack of information but also failure to analyse available material which prevents any ongoing examination'.[628]

Compare this with similar astonishment from the more recent Family Justice Review in both its interim report and its final report which stated that 'current IT systems are wholly inadequate ... fundamental and sustainable improvement in performance is unlikely to be achieved until improvements are made and this will need investment'.[629] But note also that the review had evidently been told again, as official committees had been on previous occasions, that no such investment was likely in the current economic conditions. Thus it had to qualify its statement by urging an 'urgent review of how better use could be made of *existing* systems', a task that the new Family Justice Board and its Performance Improvement Sub-Group (PISG) are evidently grappling

---

[627] M Murch, M Borkowski, R Copner, K Griew (June 1987) *The Overlapping Family Jurisdiction of Magistrates' Courts and County Courts: A Study for the Inter-departmental Review of Family and Domestic Jurisdictions* Socio-Legal Centre for Family Studies, University of Bristol. See also M Murch, R Copner, K Griew (October 1988) *Management Information and the Family Jurisdictions: Deficiencies and Their Consequences: A Working Paper for the Lord Chancellor's Department* Socio-Legal Centre for Family Studies, University of Bristol.

[628] HM Government (1986) *Report to the Comptroller and Auditor General* HC 182 at para 1768.

[629] Family Justice Review (March 2011) *Interim Report* Ministry of Justice, Department for Education and Welsh Assembly Government at paras 2.60; 3.130; 3.137. Ministry of Justice, Department for Education and the Welsh Government (November 2011) *Family Justice Review: Final Report* TSO, London para 2.101 at p61 and Appendix E at p137.

with.[630] One can only hope that it will be more successful than a similar committee known as the interdepartmental Family Law and Administration Working Party (FLAWP) and its specialist information subcommittee (FISC [Family Information Sub-Committee]), set up to provide Parliament with statistical information on the workings of the Children Act 1989. These were quietly 'put to sleep' in the early 1990s when the necessary investment in modern IT failed to materialise.

True, the subsequent introduction of the Family Man system of data recording was a step forward, but its shortcomings were soon exposed: its design merely reflected a traditional way in which information was collected for purposes of compiling judicial statistics, rather than acting as a case management tool to track the progress of individual cases and hence expose unacceptable delay and unnecessary costs. It is also not linked to legal aid expenditure; nor does it reveal an individual child's court career, which would make it easier to distinguish between those children and families that have relatively short-term contact with the family justice system and those that come back repeatedly.[631]

Nevertheless, despite the shortcomings of the Family Man system and the apparent reluctance of the Coalition government to invest in a more comprehensive modern IT system in the family courts – possibly waiting for arrangements for the new system of local family courts to become established – renewed attempts are being made to squeeze better management information from existing systems so as to provide more reliable information to monitor the progress of at least public law cases. Thus the 2013 annual report of the Lord Chief Justice states that the judiciary and HMCTS have begun to pilot a scheme:

> jointly designed at no additional cost ... The system was refined ... and now provides reports to managing judges on caseload, delays, reasons for adjournment and requests for expert evidence.[632]

[630] Family Justice Board (January 2013) *Action Plan to Improve the Performance of the Family Justice System* Ministry of Justice www.gov.uk at p4, emphasis in original.

[631] G Douglas, M Murch, C Miles and L Scanlan (2006) op cit at n7 at pp197–198. See J Hunt and L Trinder (February 2011) *A Report for the Family Justice Council*. The need to identify the number of characteristics of chronic litigation cases led to this important research review. The authors conclude that "our best estimate is that in England and Wales, cases represents something like 1% of litigated cases and probably about 0.1% of the separated and divorced population" (at p27) Family Justice Council.

[632] Baron Judge (2013) *The Lord Chief Justice's Report 2013* Royal Courts of Justice at pp43–43.

Similarly, as part of the government's response to the Family Justice Review, the new Family Justice Board, chaired by David Norgrove, established in March 2012 a so-called Performance Improvement Sub-Group. This has set up a system of key performance measures (KPM) designed to establish the proportion of both public and private child-related cases that achieve specific completion targets, apparently again relying on the piloted HMCTS Case Monitoring System (CMS) in public law cases and existing Family Man data in respect of private law cases.[633]

A further fundamental problem, which is widespread across the civil service where IT is concerned, as the House of Commons Public Administration Select Committee has shown, is:

> the inability of the Civil Service to develop, recruit and retain key skills ... which successive governments and the leadership of the Civil Service have failed to address.[634]

The most hard-hitting general criticism of government IT failures has been made by Anthony King and Ivor Crewe, in their disturbing but entertaining policy review book *The blunders of our governments*.[635] They quote numerous examples where British government's grand but mismanaged schemes for expensive IT systems, such as that of the Child Support Agency, have failed to deliver the goods. They observe:

> the amount of harm they have done to individuals and firms is literally incalculable. The amount of public money wasted could in principle be calculated but apparently has never been. [Since 1979] it cannot have amounted to less than £50 billion and was probably a great deal more. Of course not all British government IT schemes have been disasters ... the customers of both HMRC and the Driver Vehicle Licensing Agency have benefited hugely from successful exploitation of IT. But the offsetting list of expensive failures has grown so long as to be grotesque.[636]

---

[633] Family Justice Board (August 2013) *Action Plan to Improve the Performance of the Family Justice System 2013–15* Ministry of Justice, London at p5 para 14.

[634] House of Commons Public Administration Select Committee (PASC) (September 2013) *Truth to Power: How Civil Service Reform Can Succeed: Eighth Report of Session 2013–14* TSO, London at p61 para 28.

[635] A King and I Crewe (2013) *The Blunders of Our Governments* OneWorld, London. See particularly Chapter 13 'IT – Technology and Pathology' at pp183–200.

[636] Ibid at p184.

This is a salutary warning indeed to officials, ministers and advisers who need to design and implement a modern IT system for the family justice system and its family courts. Here much has been written, notably by Richard Susskind (IT Adviser to the Lord Chief Justice), about the failure of successive governments to invest in modern information technology to aid case management in the courts.[637] Suffice to say, a similar sorry tale could also be said about the failure over the first twenty years or so to resource a national network of mediation services,[638] that is until the late 1990s when the Legal Services Commission assisted with funding under Part III of the Family Law Act 1996, as amended by the Access to Justice Act 1999 s8(3).[639] Since then, as we have seen, government seeking substantial cuts in the civil legal aid budget, in a complete change of tune, have pinned their faith on mediation services without properly understanding their links with solicitors as first responders, settlement seekers and referrers to mediation.

The 'normalisation' of divorce and the problem of scale

Today there must be very few families who do not have at least one member who has been through divorce or a breakup in a cohabiting relationship. We have seen how rapidly the incidence of children with divorcing parents grew in the 1960s and 1970s. With this increase, social values began to change: the social stigma attached to divorce in the post-war period has largely disappeared, though there is a general recognition that for the people involved (children as well as adults) the breakup is usually an emotionally exhausting and turbulent experience. This shows that there comes a point when the rising incidence and scale of parental breakdown effects a cultural change in the way it is viewed and understood.

As explained in Chapter Two, as far as children in divorce are concerned, we have witnessed a shift from a period just after the war when their rising numbers were viewed as a social problem that had to be addressed through a welfare mechanism linked to the divorce

---

[637] R Susskind (1996) *The Future of Law: Facing the Challenges of Information Technology* Oxford University Press. Also R Susskind (2010) *The End of Lawyers: Rethinking the Nature of Legal Services* Oxford University Press.

[638] B Hale (2012) '30 years of National Family Mediation: past, present and future' *Family Law* vol 42 pp1336–1343. J Westcott (2004) 'The origins and development of family mediation in the UK' in J Westcott (ed) *Family Mediation: Past, Present and Future* Jordan's Family Law, Bristol at pp4–6.

[639] This made legal aid available for mediation in family matters provided applicants had attended an Information Meeting to learn about mediation.

process itself. But as the annual numbers grew from the low tens of thousands to a hundred thousand or more, and as research showed that there was little practical consequence of the so-called welfare check (as we have seen in Chapter Nine), so that mechanism became more and more diluted and ritualised. The cost of any more rigorous investigative approach–– in every case, as was once suggested – would have been prohibitive and contrary to changing social values. Instead, the state in effect shrugged its shoulders, and left the responsibility for the children's welfare to the parents unless there was a litigated dispute about contact or residence. Even then, the large numbers of families involved put mounting pressure on the courts. They also threatened to overstretch the resources of Cafcass England, which from August 2009 was put on an emergency footing dealing with a flood of public law cases following the publicity given to the Baby P case. Understandably enough, the need to safeguard children at risk of abuse or neglect and subject to 'public law proceedings' had to be a priority, particularly when public expenditure was being so severely restricted. Nevertheless, as I will argue in the conclusion of this book, such a view is likely to be mistaken. In the long term the wellbeing of *all* children and young people is a common concern and responsibility – what Michael Sandel has termed 'a common good'.[640] From this viewpoint it is misleading to distinguish between public and private child-related proceedings. This takes us to the next point concerning the concept of privacy associated with interparental conflict, which still causes difficulty for both practitioners and policy makers in this field.

The problem of labelling interparental disputes as 'private law' cases

In our society privacy is a fundamental social value conferring on individuals and families the freedom to determine the shape of their own lives, having something to do, therefore, with a sense of autonomy.[641] A right to privacy is based on the idea that there is a conventionally defined zone within which individuals should feel free to do what they like.[642] Reisman argues that acknowledging a person's privacy is tantamount to acknowledging and confirming a

---

[640] M J Sandel (2009) *Justice: What's the Right Thing to Do?* Allen Lane, London at pp244–269.

[641] R Ingham (1978) 'Privacy and Psychology' in J B Young (ed) *Privacy* Wiley, New York at p53.

[642] J Thompson (1975) 'The rights to privacy' *Philosophy and Public Affairs* 4 at p295.

person's sense of self.[643] As Borkowski et al observed, when we speak of a couple's or a family's private life and of not wanting to intrude upon it, we are in effect acknowledging that the couple or family has a distinctive identity, maintained by a psychological and social boundary, which family members control and regulate in their dealings with the outside world.[644]

This is something which young children learn intuitively from an early age, along with the value of family loyalty and the need to keep secrets even in situations where they may be at risk of abuse, family violence or neglect. For them the price of help inevitably means giving information to a wide range of outsiders (school teachers, doctors, social workers, lawyers, as well as friends and confidants) with potentially unpredictable, even frightening, consequences, such as being 'taken away' to an unknown place. This is why they are so often reluctant to disclose what has happened – a point which unscrupulous abusers exploit.

For professionals working with children, this means winning the trust of those who are vulnerable so that they disclose 'private' information. As Borkowski et al put it:

> knowing when and how to ask the appropriate questions to elicit it, and recognising possible clues about the nature of that information are all part of the range of skills that practitioners develop to gain access to private information. These skills are usually backed up by actual or implied promises of confidentially and codes of ethics which help practitioners neutralise the defensive boundary of privacy.[645]

Although one should note that in modern times, with the increasing publicity given to many serious cases of child abuse, practitioners of all kinds feel much more constrained about offering promises of confidentiality, explained or implied, not least in the context of family litigation.

Nevertheless, when we define certain social constructs as 'private' – such as 'private family law' – we are in effect erecting a no-go sign; in this case saying that this is a province on which state authorities should

---

[643] J Reisman (1976) 'Privacy, intimacy and personhood' *Philosophy and Public Affairs* 6 at p39.

[644] M Borkowski, M Murch and V Walker (1983) *Marital Violence: The Community Response* Tavistock, London at pp107–110.

[645] Ibid.

be cautious about intruding, even when the welfare and wellbeing of children might be at stake. Indeed, for years, lawyers have become accustomed to referring to family disputes arising from divorce and separation as 'private' family proceedings, to distinguish them from 'public' law cases dealing with child neglect and abuse in which the welfare authority of the state is a party bringing the proceedings to protect the interests of the child. Jane Fortin, in her lucid, well documented text *Children's rights and the developing Law* explained how:

> the law over the last century has reflected an underlying uncertainty experienced by policy makers over finding an appropriate compromise between obliging the state to find and protect every child who is abused and maintaining family privacy.[646]

She further pointed out that unlike those who are subject to public law proceedings, when it comes to providing support for children in separation and divorce, the Children Act 1989 in effect discriminates against them, 'since the legislation contains no presumption that the child will be separately represented'.[647]

Acknowledging that the issue is complex, I nevertheless take the view that one of the reasons for this distinction stems from the assumption that in child-related separation and divorce proceedings, respect for family privacy carries a much greater premium, as well as the related but questionable assumption, made by the Law Commission in the run up to the Children Act 1989 that parents can be safely expected to act responsibly in the best interests of the children unless they actively dispute future arrangements for contact and/or residence.[648] This laissez-faire approach, as Fortin points out, was also reflected by the Children Act's no order/non-intervention principle (s1(5)).[649] Lowe and Douglas explain that the underlying philosophy of the act was to respect the integrity and independence of the family, save where court orders have some positive contribution to make towards the

---

[646] J Fortin (2003) *Children's Rights and the Developing Law* LexisNexis Butterworths, London at p448.

[647] Ibid at p212.

[648] Law Commission (1988) *Report on guardianship and custody law* Law Com No 178. See also N Lowe and G Douglas (2015) *Bromley's Family Law* (11th edition) Oxford University Press at pp438–439.

[649] See also A Bainham (1990) 'Privatisation of public interest in children' *Modern Law Review* 53 at p206.

child's welfare.[650] Yet of course the no order principle applies to both public as well as private law cases, even though in accordance with the paramountcy of the welfare principle under the act, the welfare checklist has to be applied in *all* contested s8 applications. However, the problem of using the term 'private' in public law remains, since many people assume that the state does not have the same degree of responsibility for children as in public law cases – an assumption which I question.

The problem of 'churn' in civil service staffing policy: striking the balance between stasis and change

There is nothing like a crisis to trigger a rethink. We all like to stay in our comfort zone, to potter along coping in our usual way with our daily life tasks in the home and at work and/or, in the case of children, at school. One could say that this is all part of the psychosocial homeostatic mechanism that helps us to cope with the everyday demands of life in a fast-changing world (see Part II). In the same way, where interdisciplinary family justice practice is concerned, professional training helps to socialise and familiarise practitioners with their particular fields of activity, allowing them to feel more confident in dealing with the daily run of complex and emotionally challenging family dramas. But there is a downside to this: comfort zones can encourage us to run on autopilot, to fail to adapt sufficiently to changing circumstances, to bury our heads in the sand, to erect defensive walls of denial, even to ossify into what has been referred to as the 'tyranny of a dead mind' – a particularly corrosive mindset that can afflict people who have responsibility for the wellbeing of others.[651] Moreover, those who fear that change will involve them in loss of some kind are more likely to fight tenaciously to preserve the status quo than those who see themselves as change agents advocating reform and development.

Indeed, it sometimes seems that this can infect the whole institution or organisation, as those of us who have been encouraging the development of a system of interdisciplinary family justice in tune with

---

[650] They cite the adoption case of *Re B (Adoption leave to appeal)* [2014] 1 WLR 563 at (23) in which Sir James Munby established that when considering what orders to make, if any, the court should adopt the least interventionist approach.

[651] B Mortlock (1972) *The Inside of Divorce: A Critical Examination of the System* Constable, London at pp3–16. This phrase was borrowed by Mortlock to challenge the traditional lawyer's approach to divorce. He took it from Leonard Woolf's (1937) book *After the Deluge* Pelican, Books London.

modern times have often observed. It seems to occur particularly with certain officials, policy makers and practitioners, especially those who are insufficiently familiar with knowledge of the needs of families and children. Even if they have understood, some appear to have chosen to do nothing, evading the responsibility that knowledge has placed upon them.

Yet, at an institutional level, the practice of regularly rotating staff in government departments – what is sometimes referred to as the 'churn' – can be used defensively to resist change.[652] This has sometimes been rationalised in the traditional civil service as a belief that the gifted high-flying 'amateur' will always quickly pick up the essence of a problem.[653] While this may be all very well in theory, it often means that a person who starts work on a major task never stays in post long enough to finish it and a successor has to come in to pick up the task, often without a proper understanding of what has gone before. In that way the institutional status quo prevails until a crisis is encountered when emergency action is taken, often with ill-considered consequences, as was the case with the hasty cuts in family legal aid. Indeed the problem of 'churn' and its consequences has been highlighted in the 2013 report of the All Party Parliamentary Public Administration Select Committee. This observed:

> there is a persistent lack of key skills and capabilities across Whitehall and an unacceptably high level of churn of lead officials, which is incompatible with good government.

Furthermore, in its main report it states:

> the rapid turnover of senior civil servants and in particular of lead departmental permanent secretaries, at a faster rate

---

[652] For example, in a two-year (1985–87) research project jointly funded by the Lord Chancellor's Department, the Home Office and the Joseph Rowntree Foundation, and set up to inform the interdepartmental Review of Family and Domestic Jurisdiction (termed the Family Court Review), which had a research advisory committee that met quarterly, the Lord Chancellor's Department was represented at almost every meeting by a different official – no fewer than 10 over a two-year period. See M Murch, M Borkowski, R Copner, K Griew (June 1987) *The Overlapping Family Jurisdiction of Magistrates' Courts and County Courts: A Study for the Inter-departmental Review of Family and Domestic Jurisdictions* Socio-Legal Centre for Family Studies, University of Bristol.

[653] In my experience, in the 1980s this practice was carried to the extreme by the then Permanent Secretary, Sir Derek Oulton at the Lord Chancellor's Department.

than Secretaries of State, begs the question: why do we still use the term 'permanent civil service'?

According to the committee, evidence received from several leading academics in the field of government studies suggests that:

> 'internal civil service churn and turnover' was an even more fundamental issue than the turnover of permanent secretaries, as it undermined any notion of any institutional memory and weakened accountability.[654]

This crucial point has been brilliantly examined by Anthony King and Ivor Crewe in their groundbreaking look at three decades of government blunders and mishaps.[655] They point out how relatively rapid turnover of ministers and their senior civil servants effectively creates a system to avoid accountability for failure. Very often where there have been major blunders, ministers have been promoted, moved to other cabinet jobs or given life peerages, or in the case of civil servants, knighthoods.[656] Here it is only necessary to point out that since the key elements of the new family justice regime were put in place during the lifetime of the Coalition government, both Kenneth Clarke, Lord Chancellor and Minister of Justice, and his junior minister, John Djanogly, were moved in a cabinet reshuffle. Since then three further junior ministers responsible for family justice have become involved, the last under David Cameron's coalition being Simon Hughes MP. The same rapid rotation of ministers has continued under Theresa May's premiership (see Part IV), with Liz Truss MP, following her short tenure as Minister of Justice and Lord Chancellor, being replaced by David Lidington MP. Since then, at the time of writing, after a mere six months he too has been replaced by David Gauke MP in Theresa May's January 2018 cabinet reshuffle.

---

[654] House of Commons Public Administration Select Committee (PASC) (September 2013) *Truth to Power: How Civil Service Reform Can Succeed: Eighth Report of Session 2013–14* TSO, London Vol 1 at paras 88–92..

[655] See A King and I Crewe (2013) *The Blunders of Our Governments* OneWorld, London at p321. Here it is reported that 'during the three decades covered by our study there were thirteen Home Secretaries with an average tenure of little more than two years, thirteen Cabinet Secretaries responsible for education, also with an average tenure of little more than two years, and fourteen Cabinet Ministers responsible for pensions.'

[656] Ibid Chapter 24 'Accountability – lack of it' at p347.

Of course, to compensate for these shortcomings, government sometimes sets up advisory committees of 'experts' or establishes special inquiries such as the Family Justice Review. But even when their reports have been published, the experts usually depart and civil servants move on to new tasks, so that knowledge acquired often dissipates and the government machine with its traditional mindset rolls on, unless special measures are taken to establish machinery to implement the findings. With luck this is what will happen in the case of family justice with the establishment of the Family Justice Board (FJB) (chaired by Sir David Norgrove, who chaired the Family Justice Review). Yet, as this is comprised largely of officials from a number of different government departments rather than expert and experienced practitioners from the field, one wonders whether the board will suffer also from the institutional problems of 'churn' considered above.[657]

Nevertheless, the Family Business Authority (FBA) – set up by HMCTS and led by Mr Justice (now Lord Justice) Ryder, appointed Judge in Charge of Modernisation in the Family Courts at the time of the Family Justice Review – is evidently continuing its work and may thereby avoid some of these problems. Moreover, Lord Justice Ryder and Sir James Munby, President of the Family Division, sit on the Family Justice Board as 'observers'. Yet precisely how these two bodies, the FJB and the FBA, will function remains open to question.[658]

Attempts to overcome obstacles to interprofessional understanding and collaboration

As already mentioned, the new system of local family courts with a single point of entry will work through judicially led interdisciplinary teams. Specialist locally designated family court judges will have to ensure, wherever possible, that there is effective case management working within clear time limits and that the same judge will deal with the case throughout. As we have seen in the previous chapter, this forms the basis of much of the Child Arrangements Programme (CAP) and is in line with the recommendations of the Family Justice

---

[657] Family Justice Board (January 2013) *Action Plan to Improve the Performance of the Family Justice System* Ministry of Justice www.gov.uk – for a complete list of members see p3, but note that no representatives of mediation organisations or practising family lawyers are included.

[658] J Doughty and M Murch (2012) 'Judicial independence and the restructuring of family courts and their support services' *Child and Family Law Quarterly* 24(3) pp333–354.

Review.[659] Effective judicial case management will depend on efficient support services – not just from court social workers provided by Cafcass – to provide the roles of guardians, family court advisers and in-court mediation. Vital to the whole operation will be the backup of a specialist family court administration, which hopefully will eventually use IT in case management to ensure good liaison with a range of public services, such as local authority children's services, paediatricians, and child and adolescent mental health specialists. One hopes that most family courts will appoint specialist case progressing officers and listing officers to combat delay and keep cases running to time.

As has been argued elsewhere, all this will require good interprofessional collaboration in so-called 'private' law child-related parental disputes.[660] It will also need effective liaison between the family courts and the mediation services running MIAMs. This will therefore involve family justice practitioners at every level having to develop a better understanding of each other's roles, assumptions, methods of working and professional languages. This, too, is easy to state but difficult to achieve in practice. This is where the realities of trying to bring about the cultural change in practice, referred to in the review, and by the former President of the Family Division, Sir Nicholas Wall, will have to be grappled with.

It will not be enough to hope that simply through familiar experiences of rubbing shoulders with other professions in the workplace, some kind of osmosis will take place to promote better interprofessional understanding; one major reason being that much basic professional training and socialisation for lawyers, social workers and mediators, medical specialists and the like takes place in single disciplinary professional 'ghettos', or 'silos' as they are sometimes termed.[661] Here the specialist interdisciplinary practice requirements of family justice are marginalised or not recognised at all. The term 'ghetto' is used to refer to a group of people who are trained to use the same universe of discourse and who feel more at home with each other than with practitioners from other 'ghettos'.[662] (See further in Chapter Fourteen.)

---

[659] Ministry of Justice, Department for Education and the Welsh Government (November 2011) *Family Justice Review: Final Report* TSO, London at paras 2.106–2.172.

[660] M Murch (2011) 'Investing in information systems and interdisciplinary training' Special Feature Family Justice Review *Seen and Heard* 21(2) pp42–47.

[661] G Tett (2015) *The Silo Effect: The Peril of Expertise and the Promise of Breaking Down Barriers* Simon and Schuster, New York.

[662] For further explanation of the use of the term 'ghettos' see M Murch and D Hooper (1992) *The Family Justice System* Jordan's Family Law, Bristol at p43; also Chapter

Of course specialism has many advantages and has pushed the boundaries of knowledge wider and deeper. But as Theodore Zeldin, a historian of ideas, cautions, it can so easily limit perception of wider related fields, restrict individual curiosity and become defensive.[663] With an observation which could apply equally to law and to the behavioural and social sciences, as well as to the natural sciences, he states:

> The more organised, expensive and specialised science is the more curiosity is fettered ... withdrawal into a fortress of limited knowledge meant that one could defend oneself on home ground; it gave oneself confidence of a limited kind; but left one helpless in vast areas of one's life particularly the emotional kind.[664]

He asks therefore whether:

> many people might be better off if they began looking again for the road that leads beyond specialization, if they tried seeing the universe as a whole.[665]

This is the challenge that faces those specialists who seek to practise in the wider interdisciplinary field of family justice. It also presents a real challenge to those who seek to train specialist practitioners at a post-professional level for family justice work. The problem is that once one has become trained and socialised in the professional 'ghetto', it becomes, as Zeldin points out:

> second nature for all to follow accepted usage and tendency, which since the implanting has become deep rooted. To such an extent are men swayed by pardonable respect for ancient authors.[666]

One might add that lawyers, particularly in the past, seem to some to have had an exaggerated institutional respect for the concept of precedent and the idea that the older a juridical concept the more the valid its authority. Indeed, there is a school of thought, drawing on

---

10 at pp110–122.
[663] T Zeldin (1995) *An Intimate History of Humanity* Minerva, London at pp195–198.
[664] Ibid at p197.
[665] Ibid at p198.
[666] Ibid at p196.

the writings of the German legal sociologists, Niklas Luhmann and Gunther Teubner,[667] and supported by Michael King and Christine Piper,[668] which advances the proposition that law is essentially a powerful, closed, self-referring and self-sustaining (autopoietic) system which 'enslaves' all other disciplines which come within its portals and distorts other views to fit its own particular discourse.

The authors cited above argue: first, that the legal discourse oversimplifies the child's social world, generally excluding from consideration environmental factors such as poverty, bad housing, social security provision and taxation – matters which the judicial process generally cannot address in any meaningful way: second, that the legal approach traditionally individualises parent/child relationships and tends to 'root' them in notions of individual morality and responsibility; third, that the legal process concentrates decision-making on dyadic relationships – child/mother, mother/father and so on. In addition, like many others, they point out that our essentially adversarial model of justice encourages distortion and exaggeration, with parties obliged to defend their corner and press their case to the limit. I have examined this view and argued elsewhere that law was not the only discourse to suffer from autopoietic tendencies.[669]

The difficulty is that these single disciplinary educational structures tend to create in the young professional attitudes of mind that subsequently inhibit interprofessional collaboration and understanding – an 'us and them' mentality reinforcing unhelpful stereotypes or myths of other professional competences.

There is a further point which reinforces this tendency and which helps us understand the institutional barriers (and the barriers in the mind) to collaboration between different professional groups within the interdisciplinary family justice system and between that system and other services. I have in mind the seminal work of both Isabel Menzies Lyth,[670] and Woodhouse and Pengelly who, adopting a psychoanalytic approach, suggested that:

---

[667] G Teubner (1993) *Law as an Autopoietic System* Blackwell, Oxford.

[668] M King and C Piper (1990) *How the Law Thinks About Children* Gower, London.

[669] M Murch (1993) 'The Cross-disciplinary approach to Family law – Trying to Mix Oil with Water?' in A Bainham and D Pearl (eds) *The Frontiers of Family Law*, J Wiley and Sons, Chichester, pp195–207.

[670] I Menzies Lyth (1985) 'The functioning of social systems as a defence against anxiety' in *Containing Anxiety in Institutions: Selected Essays* Vol 1 Free Association Books, London p43–85.

major impediments to inter-professional collaboration originate in the unconscious needs of practitioners to use structures of their agencies and professional groups to manage task-related anxiety.[671]

Of course nearly all family proceedings have the potential to provoke acute anxiety, touching raw nerves in practitioners called upon to deal with them: child neglect and abuse, domestic violence, the breaking and remaking of family relationships, separation and loss with resulting grief and anger, and much more. Menzies Lyth, based on a study of nursing management in hospital, showed how rigid institutional procedures developed as an unconscious means of protecting nurses from the anxiety provoked by dealing with seriously ill and dying patients. I suggest that in the family justice context, one can find similar institutional defences at work, for example, the often depersonalised isolation of litigant parents and their children in the court room, while professionals act out their respective roles in the litigation drama using a 'clubby' professional language which can be quite baffling and alienating to the family. So in developing a new family justice regime that inevitably will involve more litigants in person and a greater concern to ascertain and listen to the voice of the child, practitioners, especially family court judges who, as it were, 'hold the ring', should be alert to this tendency and guard against it. It is one of the areas where interdisciplinary training at a post-professional level is called for (see further in Chapter Thirteen).

Apart from the occasional interdisciplinary conference, such as being promoted with limited resources by Nagalro and the Association of Lawyers for Children, opportunities for shared or mutual learning within the family justice system remain rare, particularly at an initial training level, where these defensive myths could have been tested under supervision in the field.

Nevertheless, it would be unfair to give the impression that there are no interdisciplinary forces at work trying to develop shared learning between lawyers, mediators, family court social workers and the like. Great credit must go to the respective editors of journals such as *Family Law, Child and Family Law Quarterly*, and *Seen and Heard*, which continue to carry research-based material drawn from the social and behavioural sciences as well as updating practitioners with recent case reports, practice directions from the President of the Family Division,

---

[671] D Woodhouse and P Pengelly (1991) *Anxiety and the Dynamics of Collaboration* Aberdeen University Press at p228.

topical articles on the latest legislation and so on. Mention must also be made of the heroic efforts throughout the 1990s and early 2000s of Lord Justice Thorpe and previous Presidents of the Family Division, Sir Stephen Brown, Dame Elizabeth Butler-Sloss, Sir Mark Potter and Sir Nicholas Wall, all of whom fostered the interdisciplinary approach, first through the President's Interdisciplinary Committee and later its successor, the Family Justice Council. Lord Justice Thorpe, in particular, as chair of these organisations put a great deal of effort into organising and securing funding for a series of highly successful interdisciplinary conferences held on a biannual basis at Dartington Hall, Devon. These resulted in a number of influential and informative interdisciplinary publications of conference papers.[672] All these initiatives represented a sustained effort over several decades to change the culture of family justice towards one of shared interdisciplinary post-professional learning.

But of course there is much more that needs to be done. For example, there should be established one or two interdisciplinary training centres to develop post-professional training programmes on a cross-disciplinary basis, where practitioners can learn more about the various disciplines and schools of thought which underpin each other's practices, and where, for example, they can develop the skills needed in face-to-face work with children. We have already come a long way from the time in 1989, as the Children Act became law, when the then Lord Chancellor, Lord Mackay of Clashfern, said in the Joseph Jackson Memorial Lecture:

'This [family law] is not an area where knowledge of the black letters of law takes one very far ... in my view we must exert ourselves to ensure that the studies of judges and magistrates, social workers and other professionals, and not least the lawyers are informed by each other's disciplines

---

[672] See, for example, (i) The Hon Mr Justice Wall (ed) (1997) *Rooted Sorrows: Psychoanalytic Perspectives of Child Protection Aassessment, Therapy and Treatment* Jordan's Family Law, Bristol; (ii) Lord Justice Thorpe and E Clarke (eds) (1998) *Divided Duties: Care Planning for Children Within the Family Justice System* Jordan's Family Law, Bristol; (iii) Lord Justice Thorpe and E Clarke (eds) (2000) *No Fault or Flaw: The Future of the Family Law Act 1996* Jordan's Family Law, Bristol; and (iv) Lord Justice Thorpe and J Cadbury (eds) (2004) *Hearing the Children* Jordan's Family Law, Bristol.

and views, and that the study itself is based on a common core and common perceptions.'[673]

Unfortunately with the recession and continuing substantial cuts in the Ministry of Justice budget there has been little government investment in continuing professional development. It was not possible, for example, to continue the Dartington Family Justice conferences.

Thus the conceptual and educational barriers to learning for better interprofessional collaboration and teamwork which were explored elsewhere some years ago will still have to be grappled with, because the specialist single disciplinary cast of mind remains a strong countervailing force.[674] The new Family Justice regime, despite being rolled out in times of major financial cuts, will thus have to face this problem anew (see further below). In the final part of this book I offer some suggestions as to how it may be tackled.

Here suffice to say that the problems of poor interprofessional collaboration remain acute, as recurrent child protection special case reviews and related inquiries demonstrate all too clearly. The causes are complex and deep-rooted. Not only can they often be traced back to early professional socialisation in the single disciplinary ghettos (after which mindsets can easily become reinforced in practice), they can also be attributed to a corresponding failure to develop compensatory training at the post-professional level, where continuing professional development and specialisation also still largely proceed in the single disciplinary mode. Moreover, as I have suggested above, such mindsets are often developed and tenaciously clung to as an unconscious defence against anxiety provoked by the need to deal with emotionally difficult and challenging client/family situations.[675] Of course sometimes these can be mitigated in practice when needing to work with professionals from other disciplines – for example, in the health service, where many

---

[673] Lord Mackay (14 April 1989) 'The Joseph Jackson Memorial Lecture' *New Law Journal* vol 139 at p505.

[674] Indeed, during the 1990s the Family Justice Council, then chaired by Lord Justice Thorpe, on behalf of the President of the Family Division of the High Court, engaged June Thoburn, a professor of social work at the University of East Anglia, to prepare a specialist syllabus for interdisciplinary family justice studies. This covered both common law and specialist knowledge fields for those whose work involved the family justice system. It could still be obtainable on the Family Justice Council's website but when last enquired, uptake had been poor.

[675] I Menzies Lyth (1985) 'The functioning of social systems as a defence against anxiety' in *Containing Anxiety in Institutions: Selected Essays* Vol 1 Free Association Books, London p43–85. Also D Woodhouse and P Pengelly (1991) *Anxiety and the Dynamics of Collaboration* Aberdeen University Press at p10.

specialist firms and clinics work through multidisciplinary teams, teams which have grappled with these issues.[676] In child protection too there are serious attempts to develop closer multiagency working by sharing information across different services between social workers, GPs, health visitors, school nurses, police officers and others – for example, in Devon and Cornwall, as acknowledged by the Munro Report and encouraged by central government.[677]

As far as the family justice system is concerned, the idea of judicially led teams in the new family court regime is probably too much of a novelty for us to be clear yet how they will work in practice and to know whether problems around collaboration will emerge. Outside of the court context, under pressure from cuts in the legal aid budget, there are signs that mediators and family lawyers are working more closely together in the accreditation process, as has happened in Canada.[678] In England and Wales the recent study by Eekelaar and Maclean is a valiant early attempt to chart this process.[679] Within the court, where major cuts in legal aid have also led to an increase in litigants in person, judges and magistrates supported by Cafcass officers are having to deal directly with the emotionally hot conflicts without the previous restraining influence of legally trained representatives acting as intermediaries between the clients and the bench.

Moreover, how and in what ways the voice of the child will be heard in these circumstances is, as we have seen, another challenge for the judiciary and their Cafcass colleagues, as together they assess the best options to avoid the risk of harm and promote the child's wellbeing. These judgments will again depend not only on professionals' understanding of the evidential facts of the case, but on the extent of their knowledge and experience of normal and dysfunctional family interaction; their knowledge of what to expect in the future following family breakup; and upon their ability, singly or together, to sensitively

---

[676] K Soothill, L Mackay and C Webb (eds) (1995) *Inter-professional Relations in Health Care* Edward Arnold, London. See also particular essay therein by J Horder 'Inter-professional education for primary health and community care: present state and future needs'. Also J Gill and J Ling 'Inter-professional shared learning: a curriculum for collaboration'.

[677] See, for example, www.devonsocialwork.co.uk/working-children/.

[678] J Macfarlane (2008) *The New Lawyer: How Settlement is Transforming the Practice of Law* University of British Columbia pp237–239. For recent developments concerning collaboration between solicitors and mediators see M Maclean and J Eekelaar (2016) *Lawyers and Mediators: The Brave New World of Services for Separating Families* Hart Publishing, Oxford.

[679] J Eekelaar and M Maclean (2013) *Family Justice: The Work of Family Judges in Uncertain Times* Hart Publishing, Oxford.

handle displays of emotional distress and anxiety which may erupt within the courtroom.

I return to a number of these matters in Part IV, where I shift the focus to broader social policy and practice issues concerned with the provision of preventive support services for children whose conflicted parents separate and divorce. There I propose new policies and practices in the secondary preventive realm of the new family court regime, concerned specifically with incorporating the crisis intervention support role for Cafcass officers.

Part IV
Embedding the crisis intervention approach

Introduction to Part IV: The future policy and practice challenge

Introduction

My overall objective in this book has been to highlight the relevance of community mental health thinking in relation to primary prevention in schools and secondary prevention in the context of the family justice system's so-called private family law proceedings. In particular, I have drawn attention to this neglected form of early intervention when children are facing critical family change. In Chapter Twelve I consider some barriers which will need to be overcome before such an approach can be implemented. In Chapter Thirteen I outline some new policies and practices needed as a way of doing this. Before doing so, it may help readers if I briefly recap the social values which underlie my thinking in these matters:

- It is apparent from demographic change over the last half century that the social institution of parenthood has superseded in importance the institution of marriage (see Chapter One).
- If the family is riven by stressful interparental conflict and is unable to provide its children and young people with secure, consistent and loving support on their journey through childhood to adulthood then other social, educational, health and family justice services should compensate as far as possible.
- The fostering of children's mental health and resilient wellbeing is as much a community as a family responsibility and every bit as important as ensuring their physical health and academic attainment – indeed, the two are inextricably related.

- The provision of non-stigmatic early supportive intervention provided directly to the child or young person experiencing critical family change can help prevent the later onset of more serious problems affecting their mental health, educational attainment and other life chances.
- Helping children and young people through critical life-changing family experience involves having the time to establish a trusting rapport with them, listening empathetically and giving them a voice when decisions about their future are being taken. Translating this principle into practice remains a particular issue for the family justice system, as I have explained in Chapter Ten, but also obviously applies to other services in direct contact with children, such as schools, primary healthcare and other children's welfare services.

In the following chapters, as a background to my proposals which seek to inject community mental health thinking into future policy and practice, I need first to consider further major policy and practice developments which have occurred since 2010 under the Coalition government and its Conservative successor led by David Cameron following the economic crisis of 2007/08. This is important since these developments continue to set the broader political context against which my idea for a new approach to early intervention in this field will have to be set.

Early intervention: high hopes dashed

In June 2010, in the early days of the Coalition government, the then Prime Minister, David Cameron, requested Graham Allen MP to undertake a review of early intervention, which is defined as:

> An approach which offers our country a real opportunity to make lasting improvements in the lives of our children, to forestall many persistent social problems and end their transmission from one generation to the next, and to make long-term savings in public spending.[680]

---

[680] G Allen (January 2011) *Early Intervention: The Next Steps: An Independent Report to HM Government* Cabinet Office, London pvii.

Supported by the Prime Minister, Deputy Prime Minister and the Leader of the Opposition, Graham Allen's review reported in 2011.[681] It contained a large number of wide-ranging recommendations based on the need for effective evidence-based services. It observed that such early intervention programmes for children and families as do exist:

> [R]emains persistently patchy and dogged by institutional and financial obstacles. In consequence there remains an overwhelming bias in favour of existing policies of *late* intervention at a time when social problems are well-entrenched – even though these policies are known to be expensive and of limited success.[682]

It therefore argued that a move to successful early intervention requires 'new thinking about the relationship between central government and local providers'.[683]

Although one recommendation has since come into being – the Early Intervention Foundation – the subsequent contrast between the aspirations of the Allen report and what was to follow in relation to cuts to family legal aid, child and adolescent mental health services, and family relationship support services could hardly be more stark.

As I explained in the Preface, the initial impetus for me to write this book was a sense of frustration and dismay at the hasty and ill-considered way the Coalition government had set about cutting civil legal aid for most divorce cases under the provisions of the Legal Aid, Sentencing and Punishment of Offenders Act 2012 (LASPO). As we have seen, this had predicable consequences of restricting many parents' access to advice and support from solicitors. It also had knock-on adverse effects on many mediation services: of increasing the number of litigants in person and thereby adding to the pressures on already over-burdened family court judges, and above all of depriving many children of the potential support they might otherwise have received from Cafcass when warring parents were dissuaded by reason of cost from availing themselves of the dispute resolution services of the family justice system.

I was also concerned by the Coalition government's repeal of the so-called welfare check in undefended divorce cases. This was done

---

[681] G Allen (January 2011) *Early Intervention: The Next Steps: An Independent Report to HM Government* Cabinet Office, London.

[682] Ibid pvii, emphasis added.

[683] Ibid pvii.

without introducing any more effective alternative provision to safeguard the interests of these children. What was particularly galling was that all this occurred at a time when there was a large and growing volume of research to show that over a quarter of all children will have experienced the separation of their parents by the time they have reached 16 years of age; that serious parental conflict and separation is a destabilising crisis for many of these children; and that a significant minority of them will suffer serious stress-related consequences, in terms of both their educational performance (and hence damage to their future life chances) and their psychological and social wellbeing. Moreover, we know that many will carry over emotional scars into their adult relationships, with further sequilae.

Furthermore, as I worked on family justice aspects of these ill-considered measures, I realised that as far as these children were concerned, the impact of government cuts to welfare provision, together with much stricter control of financial provision to the health and educational services (supposedly protected by being ringfenced) were also having a knock-on effect on support services for children more generally. This was particularly in respect of children and adolescent mental health services dealing with those most in need of psychological treatment.

What I found particularly frustrating was that despite much professional rhetoric on the value of early supportive interventions in social work, child health and family justice literature, particularly in respect of serious child abuse and neglect of young children under three years of age,[684] little priority was given to helping children of separating parents make more realistic adjustments to the complex process of critical family change, so as to bolster their resilience in coping with future life challenges.

As was pointed out in the Munro Report concerning statutory child protection services, even in 2010 early intervention and preventive services were the target for cuts, with a quarter of the 72 Children England member organisations experiencing cuts of more than 25%.[685]

As I have explained in Part II, my former colleagues and I had argued for a policy of early crisis support for children affected by serious conflict and separation as far back as 2003. Although our research-based book *Divorcing children* was well received, after it was published there was

---

[684] See, for example, ibid Chapters 3 and 4, which explore the economic and social benefits of early intervention.

[685] E Munro (2011) *The Munro Review of Child Protection: Final Report: A Child-centred System* www.gov.uk

no discernible effect on subsequent policy or practice.[686] This may well have been because my co-authors and I were naive in understanding the barriers to policy and practice change in the so-called 'good times'. So as the economic crisis of 2007/08 unfolded and the extent of the new policies of austerity became apparent, I took the view that I had to make another effort to bring the needs of these children to public attention, and to do so in a way that took account of social, legal and educational policy and practice in times of austerity.

---

[686] I Butler, L Scanlan, M Robinson, G Douglas and M Murch (2003) *Divorcing Children: Children's Experience of Their Parents' Divorce* Jessica Kingsley, London.

TWELVE

Barriers obstructing a preventive mental health approach

Introduction: austerity and the shrinking state

In the early days of the Coalition government's deficit reduction measures many thought that these would be merely temporary and that once government had succeeded in getting the nation's finances into surplus (initially intended by former Chancellor Osborne to have been achieved by 2015) and after much needed efficiencies had been achieved, hard-pressed public services would once again receive the financial support needed to at least sustain their most socially important elements, such as family legal aid, child and adolescent mental health services and so on. But gradually, as the extent of the cuts in public welfare provision began to take effect, it began to the realised that, as Farnsworth and Irving point out:

> Austerity is taking the capacity out of the welfare state and changing the direction, role and function of social policies in a way that is difficult to reverse.[687]

For example, because the Ministry of Justice had to reduce its budget by 25% or more, many family court officials whose courts were closed or merged lost their jobs or were transferred. So the capital of their professional experience was lost. Likewise, many family solicitors forced out of the field by cuts in civil legal aid and by market forces took with them knowledge and experience which may be lost to public service forever. It is true that some solicitors retrained as mediators or in some other way found outlets for their skills in the private sector.[688] But a

---

[687] K Farnsworth and Z Irving (2015) *Social Policy in Times of Austerity: Global Economic Crisis and the New Politics of Welfare* Policy Press, Bristol at p175.

[688] M Maclean and J Eekelaar (2016) *Lawyers and Mediators: The Brave New World of Services for Separating Families* Hart Publishing, Oxford. These two Oxford-based scholars have produced an extremely well-documented account of the policy process resulting from cuts in legal aid.

public service system which had taken years to build up was suddenly structurally damaged. In its place, as Michael Gove, a former Minister of Justice in the Cameron Conservative government, recognised on taking office, a two-tier system of justice has emerged: one for high net worth families and the other for the rest of society.[689] Salvaging the valuable remnants of the previous system may take years to reconstruct in a new and effective way, for example, in respect to ideas about the secondary prevention support role of Cafcass in a restructured family justice system (which I outlined in Chapter Eleven).

So the questions arise: how permanent are recent austerity measures likely to be? Will they, as many suspect, lead to a major reconfiguration of public services? I am among those who consider that behind the overt intention to reduce the deficit in public finances lie deeper political values. These are based on ideas concerning the competitive value of private markets as offering to individuals and families more choice coupled with a desire to shrink the size of the state to the extent that public 'welfarism' becomes a minimum safety net for those lacking the means to enter the private market place. If I am right, then in addition to a return to a two-tiered family justice system, there are also serious implications for the future of our public education system and its role in providing first responder crisis support for children grappling with the emotional stresses and complexities of intense parental conflict and separation. Of course the same applies to whatever backup support services could be provided to these children by the family justice system, both by mediators and Cafcass officers. In both situations the gap in quality of service between private and public provision is likely to increase, based on growing inequalities in wealth and power, to take advantage of the market. At the same time tax payers will increasingly be given the message that public welfare is 'a residual burden rather than a collective good'. Mayo et al neatly summarise this political philosophy thus:

> Welfare provision was to be determined on the basis of rational consumer choice rather than being determined by paternalistic professionals and public sector bureaucrats deciding what is best for people – 'the nanny state'.[690]

---

[689] M Gove (23 June 2015) 'What does a one nation justice policy look like?' Lecture to the Legatum Institute www.gov.uk/government/organisations/ministry-of-justice

[690] M Mayo, G Koessel, M Scott and I Slater (2015) *Access to Justice for Disadvantaged Communities* Policy Press, Bristol at pp15–16.

Quoting Julian Le Grand and colleagues:

> Monopolistic state providers were to be replaced with competitive independent ones – welfare provision was to be transformed ... marketisation works by commodifying services and labour, increasing the scope for competition, creating opportunities for markets to develop and restructuring accountability mechanisms in public services.[691]

I will give below a brief indication of how these processes have been applied to schools and more particularly in the family justice system, as that is my main area of experience. But first a word about marketisation as it applies to children's access to services.

Marketisation: does the process serve children's interests?

In his book *What money can't buy: The moral limits of markets* Michael Sandel, a philosopher and professor of government at Harvard University, charts the expansion of the market philosophy into ever increasing areas of modern Western life: medicine, education, government, law, art, sports, even family life and personal relations.[692] He argues that 'Market choices are not free choices if some people are desperately poor or lack the ability to bargain on fair terms.'[693] He further argues that even in a society without inequalities of wealth and power, 'market values crowd out norms worth caring about',[694] in the sense that they tend to reduce public-spirited civil values and social morality. This crowding-out effect of marketisation in Sandel's views has big implications for economics:

> It calls into question the use of market mechanisms and market reasoning in many aspects of social life, including financial incentives to motivate performance in education, health care, the workplace, voluntary associations, civic life

---

[691] J Le Grand and W Bartlett (1993) *Quasi-markets and Social Policy* Macmillan, Basingstoke.

[692] M Sandel (2012) *What Money Can't Buy: The Moral Limits of Markets* Allen Lane, London at pp94–129.

[693] Ibid at p112.

[694] Ibid at p113.

and other settings in which intrinsic motivations and moral commitments matter.[695]

Sandel's purpose is to alert us to the way that markets and commerce change the character of the goods and social practices they 'touch'. As he says, 'we have to ask where markets belong – and where they don't.'[696]

My answer to that question should be apparent from the preceding chapters of this book. Simply put, I do not believe that it is in the community's interest to attempt to apply market principles where the emotional and social wellbeing of our children is at stake. I do not see how the commercialisation profit motive can comprehensively be applied to the preventive community mental health practice of crisis intervention either in schools, in the health service or in the family justice system. To attempt to do so risks a two-tier structure to these services with private provision for those who can afford to pay for good-quality legal advice and assistance, psychotherapeutic help for their children and of course private education where 'extra' support in the form of counsellors and well-trained teachers will be found. But for the majority of those of more limited financial means, the choice will be either doing without or possibly relying on haphazard charitable supplementary provision. I will show below that there is already abundant evidence that these trends are increasingly apparent in the education services, child and adolescent mental health services, and the family justice system. These corrosive social trends need to be rigorously challenged.

Do children have a voice in the commercial marketplace?

We have seen how in the second half of the twentieth century, under, for example, Article 12 of the United Nations Convention on the Rights of the Child 1989, ratified by the United Kingdom in 1992, and of the Human Rights Act 1989, there has been growing recognition of the idea of children's rights and of the need to listen to the voice of the child in administrative and legal proceedings concerning them. As Nigel Lowe and I pointed out in 2001, there has been a significant cultural shift 'in which children are no longer simply seen as passive victims of family breakdown but increasingly as participants and

---

[695] Ibid at p122.
[696] Ibid at p202.

actors in the family justice process'.[697] Much the same could be said of modern approaches to education where school teachers are less paternalistically authoritarian and more inclined to listen to and take account of the views of children themselves. Even so, when it comes to the political process and legislating for policy that impacts directly on children's rights and futures, there is still a reluctance on the part of government to consult children or give them a voice in the political process (an exception might be allowing children of 16 to vote in the Scottish Referendum 2014 – but note that they were not entitled to vote in the EU Referendum of 23 June 2016 or the General Election of 8 June 2017).

In this respect, the growing influence of commercial markets and privatisation in what used to be public services has slowed if not reversed the concept of children's rights. This is because children themselves lack purchasing power. As long ago as 1991 this was recognised in an influential report by the Calouste Gulbenkian Foundation.

As that report stated:

> Our democracy is based on the premise that groups of people will stand up for their own interests and rights, but generally speaking children and young people are not in a position to do this. Children are a large but uniquely un-influential sector of the population. They are particularly powerless and vulnerable and are generally highly restricted in both the extent to which they can take decisions about their lives and the extent to which they can participate in society's overall decision-making process.[698]

Shortcomings in Whitehall's capacity to view the mental health needs of children and their families as a whole

I have already referred to Anthony King and Ivor Crewe's 'amusing and enraging compendium of ministerial errors',[699] their book *The blunders of our governments*, which lays bare the way that Westminster so

---

[697] N Lowe and M Murch (2001) 'Children's participation in the family justice system: translating principles into practice' *Child and Family Quarterly* 13 pp137–58; reproduced as Chapter 23 in J B Singer and J C Murphy (eds) (2008) *Resolving Family Conflict* Ashgate, Aldershot at pp427–445.

[698] M Rosenbaum and P Newell (1991) *Taking Children Seriously: A proposal for a Children's Rights Commissioner* Calouste Gulbenkian Foundation, London at p10.

[699] P Wilby (3 September 2013) *Review: 'The Blunders of Our Governments' The Guardian.*

often wastefully runs its administration and goes about policy making and implementation.[700] Shocking though many of the examples given in this splendid book are, they came as little surprise to me. Over 40 years as a socio-legal policy researcher I had close contacts with various government departments which commissioned research. I quickly realised that the wheels of government often grind exceedingly slowly. Numerous officials and ministers came and went before many of the relatively short-term two- to three-year research projects they commissioned were completed. Indeed, I came to appreciate that government often uses the commissioning of problem-related research as a delaying tactic to fend off public disquiet and pressures for reform – for example, in the fields of domestic violence, child abuse, adoption, divorce reform and so on.[701]

In these policy fields it often takes 10 or more years before policy makers and politicians seriously begin to take account of these and many similar research studies. Slow utilisation of findings risks these becoming out of date and the taxpayer's money being wasted. The notable exceptions in the field best known to me were the socio-legal researches preceding the Children Act 1989. These were driven forward by the Law Commission; the Minister of Health, Virginia Bottomly MP; and Lord Mackay of Clashfern, the Lord Chancellor. As a lawyer with a degree in mathematics, he appreciated research which showed the need for much improved judicial statistics that linked legal aid expenditure to the speed of case throughput in individual courts, but was frustrated by structural problems in the civil service at the time.

Part of the problem of slow utilisation of policy-related research and statistical information is because, as the House of Commons Public Administration Select Committee observed in 2015: 'The day to day too often crowds out preparations for the long term and unexpected'.[702] (In 2017 when this book was being prepared for publication, the

---

[700] A King and I Crewe (2013) *The Blunders of Our Governments* OneWorld, London.

[701] M Borkowski, M Murch and V Walker (1983) *Marital Violence: The Community Response* (study commissioned by the DHSS) Tavistock Publications, London. M Murch and C Thomas (1993) *The Duration of Care Proceedings* HMSO, London. N Lowe, M Murch, M Borkowski, A Weaver, V Beckford and C Thomas (1999) *Supporting Adoption: Reframing the Approach* BAAF, London. See also N Lowe, M Murch, K Bader, M Borkowski, R Copner, C Lisles and J Shearman (2002) *The Plan for the Child: Adoption or Long-term Fostering* BAAF, London. G Davis and M Murch (1988) *Grounds for Divorce* Oxford University Press.

[702] House of Commons Public Administration Select Committee (9 March 2015) *Leadership for the Long Term: Whitehall's Capacity to Address Future Challenges: Third Report of Sessions 2014–15* HC669 TSO, London p3.

government's preoccupation with forthcoming Brexit negotiations was distracting many in an already reduced civil service.)

There is much in this hard-hitting but balanced parliamentary report (influenced by the government's response to the financial crisis of 2007/08) which makes sober reading concerning the structural obstacles in the government's policy-making process. These will need to be confronted by anyone wishing to develop practice and policies to promote an early supportive intervention community mental health approach across schools, primary healthcare teams and the interdisciplinary family justice system. Here I pick out just a few key points from this important report which seem particularly relevant to the subject of this book:

- 'Most policy making is short-termist, reactive and uncoordinated.'[703]
- 'There is more reward for ministers and civil servants in "rising to the occasion" than preventing such occasions arising in the first place.'[704]
- The ability to pre-empt a crisis can save government from enormous financial and political consequences. However, many commentators see government inaction in the face of an impending problem only to be followed by feverish response that begins once the crisis hits.'[705]
- 'Most of the key problems faced by government are horizontal (i.e. affect a number of different departments) and most government responses are vertical (i.e. carried out in single departments).'[706]
- 'In many areas requiring inter-departmental collaboration there is a need to ensure that a "common language" is used and understood by politicians and civil servants.'[707]
- 'Although there is now the Development, Concept and Doctrine Centre in Whitehall, its work is ancillary rather than central to the business of government.'[708]

---

[703] Ibid at p5.

[704] Ibid at p5.

[705] Ibid at p8.

[706] Ibid at p12. The Select Committee gives the following example, taken from evidence given to the Committee by the British Heart Foundation: 'Public health should not be the sole responsibility of the Department of Health since a person's propensity to develop illness arises from interactions across government, from habits learned at school, to the way cities are designed, to employers' responsibility for workers' wellbeing.' British Heart Foundation (WFC0013) available at http://data.parliament.uk/writtenevidence/committeeevidence.svc/evidencedocument/public-administration-committee/whitehall-capacity-to-address-future-challenges/written/15670.pdf

[707] Ibid at p89.

[708] Ibid at p50.

- 'Long-term thinking and the considerations of emerging trends need to be the driving force behind financial management and far more coordinated with public investment decisions. At present horizon scanning has little impact on financial planning.'[709]
- 'A core role of the Civil Service is to look beyond single parliaments so that civil servants can provide advice to the government of the day on the long-term underlying issues which affect a national interest.'[710]
- 'The confidence to challenge orthodox thinking or established policy is of particular importance to civil servants engaged in horizon scanning, foresight and contingency planning. They must be able to challenge assumptions and conventional thinking on expected futures.'[711]

Of course, as one would expect, the select committee does give due acknowledgement to good examples of long-term horizon scanning and planning, and to positive efforts by government to remedy some of the structural problems. They identify, for example, the setting up in 2013 of a network of What Works Centres' supported by the Cabinet Office, including the Early Intervention Foundation and the What Works Centre for Wellbeing.[712] No doubt in time these will produce useful research findings. Indeed the Early Intervention Foundation has already produced a valuable research review of interparental relationships and outcomes for children for the Department for Work and Pensions, which was carried out by Professor Gordon Harold and colleagues at the University of Sussex.[713] I will refer to some of the conclusions of this valuable review in support of my proposals for future policy and practice in Chapter Thirteen. But first I need to briefly explain the relevance of several chosen points from the select committee's reports to thinking about the unmet support needs of children of separated parents.

---

[709] Ibid at p93.

[710] Ibid at p100.

[711] Ibid at p102.

[712] Cabinet Office (June 2013) 'What Works Network' www.gov.uk/guidance/what-works-network and has since been updated (August 2015).

[713] G Harold, D Acquah, R Sellers, H Chowdry and L Feinstein (2016) *What Works to Enhance Inter-parental Relationships and Improve Outcomes for Children* University of Sussex and the Department for Work and Pensions.

Short-termism in policy making

This of course ties in with government's austerity measures and financial cuts to child and adolescent mental health services, to which I have referred above, as well as relating to cuts in civil legal aid and its consequences, which were explained in Chapter Eleven. The problem is that once these measures were taken in response to the economic crisis of 2007/08, they became extremely difficult to reverse. Insofar as the pre-existing services assisted children coping with family problems – especially those whose parents cannot afford private provision – valuable practitioner experience can, as I have explained, be lost for good.

Lack of incentives for long-term planning and cross-departmental activity

The select committee's report mentions that there are few rewards for ministers or officials who take the long view. This is in part because of the problem of 'churn' (or rapid turnover), which often means that those who take on major policy initiatives do not see it through to full operation. If an initiative succeeds they are usually not in a position to take the credit, but likewise if it fails they cannot be held accountable. Moreover, where preventive child mental health is concerned the picture is even more problematic since, as we have seen, the issue cuts across a number of different departments (education, health, social services and even the Ministry of Justice).

Lack of a common language

One of the reasons why in Part II I went into some detail to explain the fundamentals of the Caplanian approach to preventive community mental health and its potential application to children coping with parental conflict and critical family change, is because I see it as a knowledge framework which is relatively easy for both policy makers and practitioners to understand, whatever setting they are in. Of course in certain circles this does not carry as much professional kudos as developing and using a specialism. It is rather like the difference between specialising on the one hand in public health (being concerned with unglamorous subjects like inoculations, drains, effective sewage treatment etc) and on the other in advanced cardiac medicine or the latest oncology, where there are much greater financial and professional rewards.

Challenging orthodox thinking

It should not be so, but I suppose much of what I have been writing about in this book is itself a challenge to orthodox thinking concerning both policy and practice. More particularly I should say that it is the voices of children and young people themselves which present the biggest challenge to prevailing modes of thought. There are signs, as I have explained, that this is slowly being recognised both in terms of education and family justice. This is so notwithstanding the countervailing trend towards private marketisation of services and the emergence of two-tier services reflecting growing, social and economic inequalities. Moreover, the forces that hitherto have marginalised children are still very strong, and in my opinion have received powerful political and economic reinforcement by many of the current austerity policies and activities of government, notwithstanding Whitehall's relatively new Development, Concepts and Doctrine Centre, which so far seems to be limited to military defence matters.[714]

Overcoming shortcomings in established professional modes of thinking: the need to shift mental furniture so as to consider preventive mental health responses to the voice of the child

It should not be thought that my only criticisms of existing service provision for children in these circumstances lie with the shortcomings of government's policy-making processes. The problems go wider and deeper than that, into the myriad of professional and voluntary charitable family support services which in a number of respects assume greater social significance as austerity cuts to public services take effect.

2015 Relate report: 'Breaking up is hard to do'

In this context I draw attention to an important report which was published by Relate, the UK's leading relationship support organisation, over the winter of 2015/16 – that is, in the first few months of David Cameron's Conservative administration.[715] It was based on a conference

---

[714] See www.gov.uk/government/groups/development-concepts-and-doctrine-centre
[715] D Marjoribanks (December 2015) *Breaking Up Is Hard to Do: Assisting Families to Navigate Family Relationship Support Before, During and After Separation* Relate available at www.relate.org.uk/sites/default/files/publication-breaking-up-is-hard-to-do-report-dec2015_0.pdf

for representatives of practitioner groups, policy-related government departments and leading academics. Relate, as an organisation, had experienced severe cuts to its government support grant – a fall from £3 million per year in 2010/11 to £642,000 in 2014/15.[716] Understandably it was anxious to persuade government to restore this grant to something like its former level. In this respect it turned to the Department for Work and Pensions for help, given that the then minister, Iain Duncan Smith MP, was known to be keen to support measures to foster stable family relationships. He had earlier founded the Centre for Social Justice and had been a collaborator and co-author with Graham Allen MP who, as we have seen, in 2011 published a major report on early intervention with all party support (see further below).[717]

The aim of the Relate report was to explore current provision of support 'before, during and after separation and the extent to which it is currently coordinated'.[718] There is a great deal in this report which I commend, even though for reasons which I will explain later, I think its purpose in trying to encourage many more couples to seek early help when their relationship is in difficulty is over-optimistic. While it considers the needs of children and young people, its primary focus is on finding better ways and means of providing remedial help and support for conflicted parents. Even so, it recognises the importance of hearing the views of children and young people when parents are in disputes. Thus in recommending 'joining-up support for families before, during, and after separation', it also includes 'a focus on how children and young people's voices are at the centre of this'.[719] (Unfortunately it does not explain how this is to be achieved.)

---

[716] See S Doughty (25 May 2016) 'One in five couples struggling in a 'distressed relationship': Three million people having home lives wrecked by rows and threats of a break-up' *Daily Mail* online available at www.dailymail.co.uk/news/article-3607813/One-five-couples-struggling-distressed-relationship-Three-million-people-having-home-lives-wrecked-rows-threats-break-up.html

[717] G Allen (January 2011) *Early Intervention: The Next Steps: An Independent Report to HM Government* Cabinet Office, London

[718] D Marjoribanks (December 2015) *Breaking Up Is Hard to Do: Assisting Families to Navigate Family Relationship Support Before, During and After Separation* Relate, available at www.relate.org.uk/sites/default/files/publication-breaking-up-is-hard-to-do-report-dec2015_0.pdf at p2.

[719] D Marjoribanks (December 2015) *Breaking Up Is Hard to Do: Assisting Families to Navigate Family Relationship Support Before, During and After Separation* Relate, available at www.relate.org.uk/sites/default/files/publication-breaking-up-is-hard-to-do-report-dec2015_0.pdf at p12.

Selected points from the 2015 Relate report

Among the many shortcomings of current provision for conflicted and separated couples which the Relate report highlights are many points which give an indication of the way many of those in the remedial relationship support business think. Understandably they are anxious to persuade many more couples running into stressful interpersonal difficulties to seek early help. But as I will explain below, for many there are formidable psychological barriers to be overcome in order for this to happen. Nevertheless, the Relate report[720] focuses on the following:

- Information for couples to find their way to appropriate support is uncoordinated and confusing. They need to identify trusted information from an authoritative source; that information needs to be tailored to meet parents' different experience. The report observes that 'however easy we make it to navigate information some people will always need someone to "hand hold" families though the system.'

- Navigating support is difficult. People may turn to friends, family or search online but there are few clear entry points. Apart from supportive friends and family, most people prefer to talk to a professional to resolve more serious problems. Research has shown that the first port of call for relationship problems is often the GP, a point confirmed by an investigation by Citizens Advice and by a survey of GPs. However, Relate further reports that health professionals are not widely supported to talk to patients about their relationships and, given increasing pressures on time as well as on the lack of profile relationships have in policy, relationships are not prioritised. This means GPs do not know where to refer people and 'simply prescribe medication'. The report continues: 'solicitors have traditionally been people's first port of call when facing family breakdown ... however, this route is now largely inaccessible for those unable to self-fund legal support'. (Moreover, in the wake of LASPO there are now additional barriers to the uptake of mediation, to which I have referred in Part III.)

- 'A confusing dispute resolution market place.' The Relate report talks about a confusing number of places with 'myriad providers and

---

[720] D Marjoribanks (December 2015) *Breaking Up Is Hard to Do: Assisting Families to Navigate Family Relationship Support Before, During and After Separation* Relate, available at www.relate.org.uk/sites/default/files/publication-breaking-up-is-hard-to-do-report-dec2015_0.pdf.

little way to tell which will be the most appropriate'. It observes that MIAMs are not working particularly well in informing attendees of the full range of the options concerning conflict resolution, and that the availability of mediation makes an informed choice difficult given that it is 'offered by a number of professionals from a variety of disciplines using a range of models across voluntary, private and statutory sectors'. 'There are currently six different membership structures for mediators, which can add to confusion and inhibit a coherent approach to promotion.'

- There is limited triage or holistic assessment. In this respect the Relate report observes that there is 'limited triage opportunities to steer people towards the most appropriate support' and that support is often 'single issue', even though those going through separation may need help and advice on a range of issues, such as benefit entitlements, debt management and housing needs. Moreover, 'support is often restricted to particular silos'.
- Demand for relationship support is predominantly experienced as an emergency response 'if families access support before separation – and many do not – this is often not before difficulties have become deep seated.'
- 'The problem of late or non-presentation at relationship support services has its roots in the significant cultural reticence around talking about relationships. Relationships are still seen as private spaces, with people expected to address many issues themselves ... There is increasing demand for online services because of the anonymity which they offer.'

I highlight this last point – the difficulty of encouraging conflicted parents to seek early help and the issue of specialist silos – as being fundamentally important. I have already explored the latter in the context of the family justice services. I need now to explain my view as to why so many parents are reluctant to seek help, because I suspect this is not properly understood by many in the remedial relationship business, or for that matter by policy makers and politicians.

Deterioration of the parental coalition: the reluctance to seek help for fear of losing face

As Abi Shumueli has put it:

> to those witnessing the painfulness of unremittingly conflictual and angry break-up ... it is all too easy to forget

that the current combatants seeking divorce were once a courting pair and lovers.[721]

As I discovered many years ago in my first studies of undefended divorce petitions heard in open court, the lawyers representing the petitioners (more often wives) usually gave the court a brief résumé of the history of the marriage up to the point when the decision was taken to commence divorce proceedings.[722] The point to note is that these brief vignettes (they generally lasted between five and 10 minutes) invariably started with reference to the fact that the couple had embarked on marriage with an expectation that they would live happy and fulfilled lives together. As in today's marriages, the couple's mutual investment, emotional and financial, was often high.[723] Indeed, as we all know, a whole commercial industry has built up around this major public status passage.[724] As we have seen, these days, couples generally live together before marriage. Sometimes newly cohabiting couples signal to their friends and relatives that they are now 'an item', marking this with a party or similar occasion. Likewise, at least in religious circles, the birth of a child is often signified culturally by similar rituals and ceremonies indicating the couple's new status as parents and emphasising their psychological investment in the child's future.

But as we have seen, when strains and tensions between a couple are felt by one or both to indicate that the relationship is not working, many, particularly men, find it difficult to seek support and help. I have quoted above the point made in the Relate report about the significance of the GP as being the first port of call, and the fact that the parties involved used to turn to solicitors when separation and possible proceedings were being contemplated. Culturally both of these

---

[721] A Shmueli (2012) 'Working therapeutically with high conflict divorce' in A Balfour, M Morgan and C Vincent (eds) *How Couple Relationships Shape Our World: Clinical Practice, Research and Policy Perspectives* Karnac Books, London at p139.

[722] E Elston, J Fuller and M Murch (1975) 'Judicial hearings of undefended divorce petitions' *Modern Law Review* 38(6) pp609–640.

[723] But note that high net worth couples may use prenuptial agreements as a form of insurance against failure. See Law Commission (2014) *Matrimonial Property, Needs and Agreements* Law Com No 343 HC1089 www.gov.uk

[724] M Murch (1980) *Justice and Welfare in Divorce* Sweet and Maxwell, London at p166. As Mervyn Murch wrote, quoting Michael King: 'A status passage occurs whenever there is movement on the part of the individual involving a loss or gain of privilege or power or changed identity or sense of self. The concept of status passage covers a wide variety of transitions from illness to promotion, from marriage to dying' – M King (1977) *Warwick Law Working Papers* No 8 at p8.

confidential services are seen as non-stigmatic. As such, they shield their clients from any public loss of face, at least until the matter comes to court, and even then restrictions limit public access and media publicity.

Fear of loss of face generally accompanies a sense of shame – the very reverse of the public confirmation and celebrations that accompany marriages, births and so on. Overcoming their potential client's fear of loss of face and sense of shame is one of the barriers that remedial services such as Relate and OnePlusOne have to deal with if they are to further develop their preventive services. As a recent OnePlusOne publication acknowledges:

> Although some parents may turn to others for help when they experience difficulty in their relationship, many may not choose to. Most couples view what happens in their relationship as private and not something that they want to share with others. Those who do turn to others for help sometimes find that the advice they receive is ineffective or that well-meaning friends and relatives sometimes make the situation worse.[725]

Moreover, one might speculate that the more public the first status passage the more deeply felt the loss of face and sense of shame when it comes to acknowledging the subsequent breakdown of the parental relationship. Some evidence for this proposition was found years ago in the reactions of many divorced petitioners when their cases were heard in open court – the worry most commonly expressed to the researchers being, 'Will it be in the papers?' That whole court process could be understood in sociological terms as some kind of public ritual which reinforced for the community at large the view that divorce was a serious business. As the socio-legal researchers observed at the time:

> By this line of thought the price to be paid for obtaining a decree is not only financial, it involves submitting to some kind of primitive public degradation, the function of which, apart from granting the decree, is to assure others who might be inclined not to enter into divorce lightly.[726]

---

[725] J Reynolds, C Houlston, L Colman and G Harold (2014) *Parental Conflict: Outcomes and Intervention for Children and Families* Policy Press, Bristol at p136.

[726] E Elston, F Fuller and M Murch (1975) 'Judicial hearings of undefended divorce petitions' *Modern Law Review* 38(6) at p639.

In this way, the former public ceremony of open court hearings of undefended divorces helped to control the exit from marriage.

Thus a key message which needs to be emphasised to those seeking to develop support for early preventive services for families experiencing parental conflict is that they need to be particularly mindful and sensitive to the potential client's fear of loss of face and sense of shame.

Of course there will be some who do not have such inhibitions and others who overcome it and turn to Relate and other agencies. But overall I suspect that these are in the minority. All the signs are that despite publicity campaigns designed to drum up business for remedial agencies, most couples endure their conflicted relationship. A visit to the GP, more often by women, may signal a deteriorating relationship in a disguised fashion, with presenting problems of sleep difficulties, headaches or other psychosomatic symptoms.[727] Then, as things get worse, separation may be followed by entry into the family justice system. Meantime, as we have seen, the children, as it were, look on from the wings while the drama unfolds.

So what alternative policy approach is there? My answer simply put is that one should first start by focusing directly on the children rather than the conflicted couple. In fact this was how much early divorce court welfare conciliation used to occur. As a former colleague, Gwynn Davis, used to say, "Focusing on the *parental coalition* is a much easier wicket than trying directly to address the difficulties in a failing marriage."

In my view the Caplanian model of crisis intervention and primary prevention offers a strategic way of doing this, even though I recognise that it will take careful preparation time and resources. But first one has to change the mindsets of policy makers and practitioners in order to overcome the barriers to new thinking which I have outlined in this chapter. So I turn now to the difficult question of how to change these prevailing mindsets to open up space for a serious, not just ritualised, acknowledgement of early intervention based on the paramount interests of the children. In particular, I need to consider how the Caplanian approach might in time become embedded in a whole school system committed to a child's wellbeing and resilient mental health. In the first part of Chapter Thirteen, in which I outline policy and practice proposals, I look further at how this approach

---

[727] The classic study of the interaction between patient and doctor is that of Michael Balint (1957) *The Doctor, His Patient and the Illness*, which has been updated by his son John A Balint in the millennium reprint of the second edition, published in 2000 by Churchill Livingstone.

to primary prevention should be applied not only in state schools but in the context of private boarding schools as well. Then, in the second part of the chapter, I consider its potential application in the context of child-related litigation in family courts. In the third part I touch on its relevance to child and adolescent mental health services, and argue for the development of a broader consultative preventive mental health approach to augment and complement their specialist therapeutic intervention.

THIRTEEN

Policy and practice proposals to support children and young people coping with interparental conflict and separation

Introduction: children's unmet need for bereavement support

By reframing children's grief reactions to parental conflict and separation within the term bereavement, my aim in this chapter is to suggest some ways by which to embed the Caplanian method of crisis intervention as part of a broader policy shift towards early preventive intervention. In this context one should remember that half of all mental illness starts before the age of 15. But first to recap some points from Part II.

In Chapter Five we have seen evidence from children themselves which showed how, in these circumstances, many felt temporarily overwhelmed, alone and marginalised. Some had witnessed traumatic domestic violence. Their reactions suggested that they were, in effect, experiencing a form of bereavement, although this may not have been recognised by adults with whom they were in daily contact.

A death in the family is a single life-changing event which during the grieving process normally evokes sympathetic support from concerned others. But as pointed out in Chapter Six, the response of outsiders to what is often defined as 'private' conflict between parents, particularly if it leads to a protracted acrimonious family breakdown or family separation, is usually altogether more complex and ambivalent. While the parents may well receive partisan support from friends, relatives and professionals, youngsters may feel overlooked while they struggle with conflicting loyalties and their own anxieties about their future. Moreover, the impact on their education and the way they manage their family and social life can be profound and have long-lasting consequences. Living through a stressful family atmosphere or strained and conflicted family relationships, they have the complex psychosocial task of coming to terms with and adapting to it. Therefore, a form of grieving for what has been lost and coping with uncertainty about what is to come lies at the heart of this critical process of family change.

We have seen how at such times children (and of course their parents) can be especially vulnerable. We know from researches reviewed in Chapter Three, and now confirmed by a more recent review for the Early Intervention Foundation, that many are at significant risk of developing longer-term behavioural, social and mental disorders. This is especially likely if, as the research review has shown, children are raised in families:

> under acute or chronic economic strain ... where there is poor parental health (including depression and aggression) and a pre-existing pattern of poor parent/child relations.[728]

Yet we also know that supportive encouragement at such times of destabilising family change can help children buffer the more damaging aspects of the crisis and indeed strengthen their resilience so that they are able to cope successfully with future life challenges.

So the key question is what can be done to bring about a situation where this kind of crisis support is available to all youngsters when they find themselves in crisis and having to face these complex forms of bereavement?

Meeting children's need for passage agent help

In Chapter Six I explained that the Caplanian method of crisis intervention requires the intervention of a 'passage agent' to guide children as they navigate their way through the uncertainties and conflicting interests of family breakdown and reconstruction. As we have seen, as far as litigating parents are concerned this sort of short-term intuitive support used to be provided on an individual partisan basis by solicitors when providing legal advice and representation – that is to say, before civil legal aid was withdrawn in 2013. In addition, general medical practitioners are often still the first port of call when stress provokes psychosomatic symptoms such as chronic headaches, sleeping difficulties and/or the onset of acute anxiety and depression. Some youngsters may likewise experience psychosomatic reactions and go to their family doctor, who will provide a listening ear and

---

[728] D Acquah, R Sellers, L Stock and G Harold (April 2017) *Inter-parental Conflict and Outcomes for Children in the Context of Poverty and Economic Pressures* Early Intervention Foundation, London at pp20–21.

may prescribe medication (which, if repeated, may become addictive). Practitioners in these non-stigmatic social and medical support systems, in their various ways, are therefore well placed to provide a guiding hand through the crisis. By encouraging the person in crisis, whether adult or child, to face up realistically to the consequences of the stress-provoking events, and in the process to express their feelings as a form of 'grief work' – the term which Caplan and others use to describe what is an essentially normal part of bereavement – the risk of longer-term maladaptive behaviours and mental disorders can be reduced.[729]

The proposals I outline in this chapter, both in respect to schools and family court support services, seek to address this very considerable large-scale unmet need for non-stigmatic passage agent support for children and young people as they go through this form of family crisis. As explained in previous chapters, the approach is based on a mix of empirical and clinical behavioural science research and the Caplanian model of crisis intervention. My proposals are part of a growing policy movement towards early preventive intervention, and a reaction to the political and economic background which since 2008 has led to serious financial cuts in family justice, child and adolescent mental health services, and more recently within the state-funded education system. These challenge us to develop more economical and effective policies and practices.

Part A: Primary prevention in schools: the need for early warnings and a network of first responders

In Chapter Six I outlined key features of the crisis intervention method. In Chapter Eight I explained its relevance to the 'whole school' approach for promoting positive mental health and wellbeing. As Sir Richard Bowlby wrote some years ago, outlined on the cover of an influential text by Heather Geddes:

---

[729] Powerful testimony about this process and the risks that can follow if grief is not dealt with at the appropriate time was provided in the spring of 2017 by His Royal Highness Prince Harry. He spoke movingly in a podcast interview about the sudden death of his mother, Princess Diana, and of the difficulties he had faced both at the time, as an 11-year-old, and later as a young adult. His experience provided the impetus for the setting up of the Heads Together Foundation (www.headstogether. org.uk) by himself and his brother and sister in law, the Duke and Duchess of Cambridge. The foundation exists to combat the stigma of mental illness and to change how it is perceived. It works in partnership with Young Minds and seven other mental health charities.

The education setting is probably the greatest opportunity we have, outside the family, to promote and maintain social well-being. This is most likely to come about when emotional well-being becomes built into the educational agenda, and into the structure of educational practice.[730]

In Chapter Eight I showed how the 'whole school' movement has gathered momentum in recent years, particularly since 2015 and the Carter Review of Initial Teacher Training.[731] This movement has recently been endorsed by the *First joint report of the House of Commons Education and Health Committees* concerning the role of education and children and young people's mental health, which was published just before the General Election of 8 June 2017.[732]

Teachers as first responders: providing mental health first aid

It is now well recognised that a teacher is generally best placed to first notice that a youngster is showing signs of being in crisis, whether it is caused by problems at home or, for example, is a result of being bullied and victimised by other children either directly in the school or, as is increasingly common, via social media. Thus the Joint House of Commons Education and Health Committees report devotes a whole chapter to the negative effects that social media and technology can have on young people's mental health.[733]

It follows that teachers should be trained to spot the consequent early signs of emotional distress and crisis. In 2016 the government made personal, social, health and economic education (PSHE) mandatory in all schools and colleges. This should help ensure that all teachers in future are alert to the warning signs of a child being in crisis. Schools

[730] H Geddes (2006) *Attachment in the Classroom: The Links Between Children's Early Experience, Emotional Wellbeing and Performance in Schools* Worth Publishing, London.

[731] Sir A Carter (January 2015) *Carter Review of Initial Teacher Training (ITT)* www.gov.uk/government/publications

[732] House of Commons Education and Health Committees (2 May 2017) *Children and Young People's Mental Health: The Role of Education: First Joint Report of the Education and Health Committees of Session 2016–17* https://publications.parliament.uk

[733] Ibid at p13. There it is reported that a survey for the Department for Education and the Department of Health of 11-, 13- and 15–year-olds found that 18% reported having experienced cyberbullying in the previous two months. Similar evidence was received from organisations like Childline and the NSPCC. So while it is recognised that 'teachers are not mental health professionals ... they are in many cases well placed to identify mental ill health and refer students to further assessment and support'.

should therefore enable children to receive proper support, sometimes referred to as 'mental health first aid'. How that is organised and delivered will depend on head teachers and the resources available. For example, in the children's primary school in the London Borough of Lewisham to which I referred in Chapter Eight, (reported in an article by Sally Weale, Education Correspondent of *The Guardian*[734]) the head teacher had enlisted the help of the charity Place2Be to provide a lunchtime service to children who want to talk privately with a qualified child psychotherapist.[735]

However, at the time that this book was going to press, I was told that this particular service will have to be discontinued because of cuts in the borough's education budget after August 2017. Although the school will still have two pastoral support workers and a community worker, the loss of the option for a distressed child to spend private time with the Place2Be psychotherapist removes a valuable backup support for the remaining support workers, teachers and administrators in the school. Overall, this school's mental health first aid team has therefore been weakened. This is not an isolated case. As the Joint House of Commons Committee reported, 'as schools see their funding cut, an increasing number are cutting back on mental health services such as in-school counsellors'.[736] The committee quoted a survey from the National Association of Head Teachers (NAHT) and Place2Be, which showed that:

> around 64 percent of primary schools do not have access to a school-based counsellor and 78 percent of those surveyed reported financial constraints as a barrier to providing mental health services for students.[737]

This all means that at the very time when a whole school approach to promoting pupils' mental health and wellbeing is being advanced in many quarters, and when the government itself had announced its

---

[734] See S Weale (27 January 2016) 'Schools trying to help children shut out by mental health services' *The Guardian*.

[735] Similar services occur occasionally elsewhere. For example, the Bridge Foundation offers counselling and psychotherapy to children and families at a number of schools in Bristol.

[736] House of Commons Education and Health Committees (2 May 2017) *Children and Young People's Mental Health: The Role of Education First Joint Report of the Education and Health Committees of Session 2016–17* HC849 at p11.

[737] National Association of Head Teachers and Place2Be (January 2017) *Children's Mental Health Matters* www.place2be.org.uk

intention to publish a Green Paper on children and young people's mental health,[738] further financial cuts were being made which will reduce the capacity of schools to provide prompt, responsive in-school mental health support. This is all the more astonishing given that Theresa May, the Prime Minister, announced in the debate on the Queen's Speech following the election of June 2017 that "all primary and secondary schools should have a member of staff trained to identify mental health problems and to know how to deal with these issues". It raises the question of whether one part of government – that is, the Treasury – knows what the other parts are doing.

The need for a longer-term development strategy

The Green Paper of December 2017 provides a fresh opportunity to consider long term how one might embed the preventive Caplanian crisis intervention method as one of the skills that could be applied by school teachers given suitable training and professional backup mental health support. What is required, therefore, is a strategy to develop this form of help within the teacher workforce. That will take time given that the Caplanian method in the UK is, as yet, very undeveloped despite having been long articulated and advocated in community mental health literature, particularly in the United States, as I explained in Chapter Six. In the UK it might be better to think about crisis intervention as a normal way of helping children through the five stages of grief which I also outlined in that chapter, thereby reducing the risk of stigma which children and parents might associate with other forms of early intervention (such as CBT) proposed in the Green Paper; a point which the Government itself acknowledged.[739]

Introducing the Caplanian approach to initial teacher training and continuing professional development

Thinking ahead, we need to consider how, with respect to initial teacher training, support and continuing professional development, the Caplanian method of crisis intervention could be incorporated into a broader understanding of child and adolescent development and

---

[738] HM Government (9 January 2017) 'Prime Minister unveils plans to transform mental health support' [press release] www.gov.uk

[739] Department of Health and Department for Education (December 2017) *Transforming Children and Young People's Mental Health Provision: a Green Paper* CM 9523 p39.

preventive mental health issues. From an educational policy perspective, despite current austerity measures there are some encouraging signs, such as the House of Commons Joint Committee's strictures on the subject.

The link between pupil stress and teacher stress

In educational circles during the last 30 years there has been growing concern about the state not only of pupils' emotional health and wellbeing, but of that of their teachers. Children reacting to difficulties at home, particularly boys, can act out their frustration by disruptive behaviour in the classroom. Skilful behaviour management by teachers is thus an important aspect of teacher training. The Carter Review of Initial Teacher Training found that the most effective behaviour management programmes:

> are practically focused and underpinned by deeper understanding of behavioural issues. A grounding in child development, including an understanding of mental health issues, is an important basis for understanding pupils' behaviour in the classroom.[740]

Writing in 2009, James Wetz, a former head teacher and a prime mover in the Consortium for Wellbeing in Schools, quoted a YouGov survey which found that 'half of all teachers have thought of quitting because of stress'.[741] Likewise, research by the Teacher Support Network found that 70% of Scottish teachers felt that the stress of the job was ruining their health.

Wetz's primary concern was for the numbers of so-called disaffected children who left school with few or no qualifications and who were disruptive in school. His own Bristol study in 2006, to which I have referred in Chapter Eight, found that:

---

[740] Sir A Carter (January 2015) *Carter Review of Initial Teacher Training (ITT)* www.gov.uk/government/publications at paras 2.3.28.

[741] James Wetz (2009) *Urban Village Schools: Putting Relationships at the Heart of Secondary School Organisation and Design* Calouste Gulbenkian Foundation, London at p23. The Consortium for Emotional Wellbeing in Schools is an ad hoc group that seeks 'to enable those who work in schools to have access to accredited training in child's emotional development and to gain a deeper understanding of the importance of attachment theory and its impact on the behaviour of children and young people'.

the 10 percent of children who left school in 2004 without a GCSE qualification were young people who had had to manage complex emotional and social changes in their lives. For example, they had:

- experienced a sense of isolation both at home and at school;
- undergone many changes in family and school settings between the ages of five and 16;
- experienced significant early loss and separation, particularly from absent fathers; and/or
- felt that the reliability, care, safety and consistency they had enjoyed in primary school was not available to them in secondary school.[742]

Wetz's study highlights several key points relevant to my argument in favour of developing the Caplanian method of early supportive crisis intervention in schools. First, his thinking, and that of similar educationalists such Heather Geddes,[743] is largely based on John Bowlby's attachment theory. Thus he draws attention not only to children's experience of loss and separation, particularly from fathers in their home life, but to the critical institutional transition from small primary schools, which often enable a child to form a compensating attachment to a school teacher, to larger secondary schools where the ability to form such attachments is generally lacking. The combined effect of broken attachments at home and at school can thus constitute a 'double whammy' crisis for which there are, as yet, no supportive passage agents. Furthermore, this change of school also coincides with puberty and adolescence. As mentioned in Chapter Eight, Wetz studied Danish urban village schools and the small school movement in the United States where children stay in the same school with continuity of attachments from age six to 16. This observation led him to the view that such a system should be adopted in England and Wales. He argues that it would be more human in scale and would accord with modern psychological understanding that successful childhoods are built upon long-term interpersonal relationships between children and a small number of significant adults. Wetz sees education as a joint enterprise linking home and school, which would be facilitated

---

[742] Ibid at p38.
[743] H Geddes (2006) *Attachment in the Classroom: The Links Between Children's Early Experience, Emotional Well-being and Performance in School* Worth Publishing, London

if small-scale urban village schools took children on an education
journey from age six to 16. I agree.

Separation and loss: the boarding school experience

In the UK most current educational policy discussion concerns state
schools. But it should not be thought that 'privileged' children in the
private sector are somehow immune from experiencing a life-changing
educational crisis that could threaten their long-term mental health
and wellbeing.

Moreover, it should be remembered that a number of these children
will come from homes where their parents' relationship is seriously
conflicted and this may well lead to separation and divorce. Sending
the children away to boarding school may be seen as a responsible way
of sheltering them from the tensions at home, even though that may
not be how the children themselves perceive it.

In 2015, Professor Joy Schaverien, a Jungian analytic psychologist,
produced a study, developed from clinical research and informed by
attachment and child development theories, which drew attention to
what she terms 'the hidden trauma of broken attachments'.[744] These
can arise when young children– boys and girls, some as young as eight
or even younger – are sent away to boarding school.

As a caveat, Schaverien acknowledges that while most of the accounts
in her book are taken from those who had suffered in their schools,
there are many who enjoyed boarding, particularly those who first
boarded when they were 13 or over. Also, she acknowledges that
standards in boarding schools have changed, particularly since the
1950s and 1960s when control via physical punishment, sometimes
administered by older boys to younger ones, was common place.

Even so, her study reveals vivid accounts obtained during
psychotherapy from ex-boarders who had suffered behavioural and
mental health problems in later life. Such painful feelings of loss
and bereavement, often dismissed at the time as 'homesickness',
were sometimes compounded by memories of physical, sexual and
psychological abuse. Many were left with a lasting legacy of emotional

---

[744] J Schaverien (2015) *Boarding School Syndrome: The Psychological Trauma of the
Privileged Child* Routledge, London at p229. This well-documented research study
has powerful educational, social and political implications as well as psychological
ones. In my view it should be read by all those who work in boarding schools
as well as by those parents contemplating a boarding school education for young
children.

vulnerability. This was sometimes covered up unconsciously by a defensive 'hardened' persona, which led to relationship problems in later family and occupational life. Schaverien concluded that even experienced psychotherapeutic and social work practitioners:

> may sometimes miss the depth of the wound inflicted by broken attachments and emotional neglect when the child is sent to boarding school. This is perhaps because it is not easy to believe that something so socially condoned and culturally ordinary as boarding school can be psychologically damaging.[745]

She also points out that we should not forget that many of our leading 'establishment' figures in the professions of law, medicine, the civil service, politics, the military and other highly formalised institutions have been prepared for their careers in boarding schools; some would argue to a dangerously disproportionate extent, since many will carry these hidden psychological wounds throughout their professional lives, unless of course they can find a mentally healthy way of coming to terms with them.

One conclusion that I draw from Joy Schaverien's work is that modern teachers in boarding schools, every bit as much as their counterparts in state day schools, need to be well trained in child and adolescent development and the impact of trauma and loss on their pupils' emotional wellbeing.

The point of separation from home when being sent to boarding school for the first time is clearly the most critical transition. Schaverien, using accounts from literature (for example, Roald Dahl and Andrew Motion) as well as her own patients, describes the initial moments of separation and the stages of bereavement and mourning. She concludes:

> Broken attachments and rupture of intimate bonds occur for many young children sent to boarding school. It seems that some children soon adjust; they appear to cope and adapt happily enough to living in two different places. Some schools are progressive and some children genuinely enjoy living in them. For others the disruption is unmanageable: they become used to school in term time and then have to leave their friends to return home. There they are rarely any longer simply children who belong in a family. For

---

[745] Ibid at p227.

those unhappy at school the holidays are blighted by the knowledge that the return to school looms ahead. For them the whole separation takes place again each term. Its repetition is a significant aspect of the process, which for some is a re-traumatisation each time.[746]

She then goes on to describe what she calls the 'anatomy of boarding school trauma', which can include a sense of abandonment and imprisonment. She writes: 'the trauma of long-term captivity on the child is rarely acknowledged but inevitably there are psychological consequences'[747] which for some who present in later life for psychotherapy display the classic symptoms of 'post traumatic stress disorder' i.e. symptoms of dissociation involving feelings of depersonalised detachment and flashbacks – periods when the person feels as if they are not participating in their own life.

Schaverien's powerful evidence points to the need for all boarding schools to take the mental health and wellbeing of their pupils very seriously. Notwithstanding that some come from high net worth families where their parents' relationship is seriously conflicted and broken down altogether, the dangers of broken attachments and separations are, as it were, institutionally built into the boarding school system, and it is inevitable that some children will arrive in the schools struggling with a massive emotional crisis of separation. This may take weeks, months or longer to resolve in a mentally healthy way. Such children will certainly need crisis intervention in the form of passage agent support provided by teachers, matrons and so on. The younger the child the more emotionally vulnerable they are likely to be, a point that boarding prep schools and cathedral choir schools should take particular note of. They should ensure that they have appointed well-trained staff with a good, empathetic understanding of these psychological matters, so as to be able to get alongside the grieving child and assist as far as possible a mentally healthy adaption to the unfamiliar communal setting of the school.

Support for first responder teachers dealing with children in crisis

As we have seen, dealing with distressed children in crisis can be emotionally taxing for a first responder and, indeed, for other specialists such as child psychotherapists and social workers as well. While

---

[746] Ibid at p135.
[747] Ibid at p139.

empathetic understanding and encouragement are essential, there is always a danger that a practitioner will over-identify or conversely erect an unconscious defence of denial. Gerald Caplan himself recognised that it would be necessary 'to support the care-giving supporters', as I pointed out in Chapter Six.[748] In two of his texts to which I have referred, he develops an approach to mental health consultation which he termed 'client-centred case consultation'. Here the focus of independent consultation (which is distinguished from line management supervision) is on the case presenting difficulties for the responder, rather than directly on the responder – although the consultant will sometimes suspect that a deeper personal psychological 'blockage' may underlie their defensive reactions. This book is not the place to go further into this aspect of crisis intervention, but it does raise the key question of how first responders in schools can best be provided with backup support from a preventive community mental health consultant support role, which I suggest should be developed by all child and adolescent mental health services (see further below).

The value of mentoring for teachers

The Carter Review on Initial Teacher Training recognised the value of 'high quality mentoring'.[749] While Carter saw mentoring essentially as a way of raising academic standards in particular subjects by providing 'strong role models for new teachers', he also saw 'effective mentors building the capacity of the school as a whole'. Thus the review states that:

> Teachers well trained in children's emotional development and the impact of trauma and loss are likely to be more confident and effective in providing a safe setting for all students, including the more vulnerable and challenging, leading to better pupil outcomes. We therefore advise that ITT programmes should give priority to this aspect of trainees' development.[750]

---

[748] G Caplan (1970) *Theory and Practice of Mental Health Consultation* Basic Books, New York. Also G Caplan and R Caplan (1993) *Mental Health Consultation and Collaboration* Jossey-Bass Publications, San Fransisco, CA.

[749] Sir A Carter (January 2015) *Carter Review of Initial Teacher Training (ITT)* www. gov.uk/government/publications at pp40–41 paras 2.4.8–2.4.11.

[750] Ibid at para 2.3.24.

The review cites the example of the Pendlebury Centre Pupil Referral Unit in Manchester. This offers a five-day accredited mental health awareness course for all trainees and newly qualified teachers – a course that has strong links with the University of Manchester and Manchester Metropolitan University.

It seems to me that mentoring and initiatives like this could utilise the Caplanian approach and provide backup consultative support for first responder school teachers and others, such as school counsellors, helping children to cope with stress and loss in their home and social care groups. The problem at present is that the Caplanian community mental health framework is as yet so undeveloped in the UK that we first need to establish growth points from which to disseminate an understanding of the practice of crisis intervention, and offer training around associated consultative backup skills for mentors, school-based child psychologists and psychotherapists.

A community consultative support role for CAMHS

Although I have not explored the feasibility of this idea, it seems to me that the child and adolescent mental health services are the obvious points from which to develop this form of training in preventive early intervention and for providing community-based consultative support to schools and other services applying crisis intervention (see further below). So I very much hope that educationists and policy makers take up this point and start thinking about a developmental strategy, possibly along the lines that I outline below.

From a policy point of view, a strong boost in this direction came in May 2017 from the House of Commons Education and Health Committees in their first joint report, to which I have already referred. I quote their summary:

> We support a whole school approach that embeds the promotion of wellbeing throughout the culture of the school and curricula, as well as staff training and continuing professional development. We recommend that the approach to mental health and wellbeing should be properly taken into account and reflected in Ofsted's inspection regimes and reporting.
>
> The government should strengthen mental health training and continuing professional development for teachers to ensure that they are properly equipped to recognise the early

signs of mental illness in their pupils and have the confidence to be able to signpost and refer to the right support.

Strong partnerships between the education sector and mental health services will improve the provision of children's mental health and wellbeing. At the moment there is significant variation in the quality of the links between schools and colleges and Child and Adolescent Mental Health Services (CAMHS) in the levels of financial support. The government should commit sufficient resource and build on the CAMHS link pilot to ensure that effective services be established in all parts of the country. We heard evidence of the adverse impact of funding pressures on mental health provisions in schools and colleges, including the ability to bring in external support.

With half of mental illness starting before the age of 15, it is a false economy to cut services for children and young people that could help and improve wellbeing, build resilience and provide early intervention.[751]

I strongly support all these recommendations and now it seems the Government does too following the Green Paper of December 2017. Again the Government Green Paper states that in line with this it plans to include 'a mental health specific strand' within the Teacher and Leadership Innovation Fund to support the delivery of 'whole school' approaches.[752] But as ever key questions remain: Can aspirations be translated into reality on the ground? Will financial resources to match the extent of need be forthcoming? Moreover, given the endemic government policy of ministerial 'churn' and the fact that one of the sponsoring Green Paper's Ministers, Justine Greening MP, left the Government a month later following Mrs May's 2018 new year cabinet reshuffle, there must be some doubt whether her successor as Secretary of State for Education, Damien Hurst MP, will have the same commitment to push on with the Green Paper's proposals.

---

[751] House of Commons Education and Health Committees (2 May 2017) *Children and Young People's Mental Health: The Role of Education: First Joint Report of the Education and Health Committees of Session 2016–17* https://publications.parliament.uk at p3.

[752] Department of Health and Department for Education (December 2017) *Transforming Children and Young People's Mental Health Provision: a Green Paper* CM 9523 p28.

Part B: Promoting secondary backup preventive mental health thinking in the family justice system

I return now to consider further the role of backup secondary prevention within family court proceedings. In doing so I do not intend to repeat the arguments which I developed in Chapter Ten, in particular concerning the role of mediators in the relatively new MIAM provisions under the CAP regime and that of Cafcass in preparing welfare reports for the family court, undertaking guardian responsibilities under r16.4 of the Family Procedure Rules 2010 and Family Assistance Orders under s16 of the Children Act 1989. In that chapter I argued for a greater use of these provisions notwithstanding the government's austerity measures to reduce the cost of Cafcass which, according to its Chief Executive's annual report of July 2016, succeeded in saving £2.6 million – a five percent cut – in one year in response to a request from the Ministry of Justice. This was particularly challenging in the context of rising demands on the service and the expectations of 'continued innovation and piloting of new practice models'.[753] These included a pilot programme whereby children over eight years old, supported by a Cafcass officer, met with the judge deciding the case, and collaboration with a Child Contact Intervention service to help parents find common ground when working out Parenting Plans in the context of the service's Separated Parents Information Programme (SPIP), which in 2015/16 was attended by 19,000 parents.

In this chapter I focus particularly on how to embed the Caplanian approach to supporting children through the crisis of parental conflict and support, specifically with reference to the role of Cafcass officers and possibly also mediators when they cross the constitutional boundary into the family court domain to carry out their statutory responsibilities to conduct MIAMs. My proposals address two aspects of this question: practice issues and broader policy issues.

Practice issues

Welfare reports for family courts and the use of triage psychometric instruments

As we have seen, Cafcass England is clearly constrained by the Ministry of Justice's requirement to reduce expenditure. In all probability this is not helped by the ministry having to give priority to its responsibilities

---

[753] Cafcass (7 July 2016) *Annual Report and Accounts 2015–16* www.gov.uk.

for the penal estate, which in 2016/17 was under severe public criticism concerning dangerously overstretched staff levels. Nevertheless, Cafcass's work within the interdisciplinary family justice system makes it the largest social work agency in England. Overall, despite the economic pressures it currently faces, its work has been assessed as 'good' by Ofsted according to the latest Cafcass Annual Report.[754] It is also showing itself open to innovation, as I have indicated above. This might be facilitated if Cafcass England, as a social work organisation, were to revert to the Department of Health (as is it is for Cafcass Cymru under the Welsh Government), particularly if the Green Paper's proposals for young people's mental health provision are implemented.

One important measure, pioneered by its counterpart in Wales Cafcass Cymru, was the use by child and welfare reporters of a psychometric instrument to provide standard assessment of children caught up in parental conflict and separation. Known as the Child and Adolescent Welfare Questionnaire (CAWQ), this was designed and tested by Professor Gordon Harold, currently Professor of Child and Adolescent Mental Health at the University of Sussex. It was a composite instrument based on a number of internationally recognised psychometric measures to assess the psychological impact on the child of interparental conflict and violence. Cafcass officers in Wales were trained by Professor Harold and a colleague in its use. I am told it is now an accepted part of Cafcass Cymru's agency practice. Furthermore, I am given to understand that the Department for Work and Pensions, now a lead Westminster government department concerning parental conflict resolution, is in the process of developing the instrument for wider use across all state-funded agencies that have frontline first responder contact with children and young people in these circumstances. It could therefore, after appropriate staff training, be used eventually in schools, primary healthcare teams, and local authority and voluntary social work agencies. The Department for Work and Pensions interest arose originally in the context of the £448 million Troubled Families programme (TFP) which has been amended in the light of a critical evaluation by the Department for Communities and Local Government.[755]

But of course psychological assessment of a youngster's mental health and wellbeing, as part of an inquiry for the family court, valuable

---

[754] Ibid.
[755] L Day, C Bryson, C White, S Purdon, H Bewley, L Kirchner Sala and J Portes (October 2016) *National Evaluation of the Troubled Families Programme: Final Synthesis Report* Department for Communities and Local Government, London.

though it is, may still leave a distressed and bereaved child feeling unsupported. This is where I suggest the Caplanian model of crisis intervention should come in.

Crisis intervention by child and family reporters

As things stand at the moment, Cafcass children and family reporters who encounter children in crisis during the course of preparing s7 welfare reports for the family court are faced with a priorities dilemma. Do they respond to the child's need for support during the crisis, which may prompt a continuation of short term-crisis intervention beyond the litigation between the parents? Or do they ration their response to the essentials of preparing the report? In short, what is the priority: meeting the child's need for support or the court's need for a report? The issue at stake is complicated because family court judges now have responsibilities for case management. Yet Cafcass as an organisation has to manage its resources and has a line management structure to do so.

In my opinion, the principle of how to resolve this dilemma was settled by a judgment of Sir Nicholas Wall, then President of the Family Division for the High Court, in the case of *A County Council v K, C and T [2011] EWHC 1672 (Fam) [2011] 2 FLR at 817*. This was a case in which the Cafcass line manager sought to overrule the work of a court-appointed guardian. True, it was a public law care case, but the essence of the judgment is applicable in all family court proceedings, since it establishes that guardians and court social work advisors are ultimately accountable to the family court judge. In that sense, as my colleague, Julie Doughty and I wrote:

> they are part of the family court interdisciplinary team, on a par with court administrators, led by the judge, and we would argue they share the constitutional independence attached to the court.[756]

Furthermore, this principle was acknowledged in an agreement reached between the President of the Family Division and the Chief Executive of Cafcass on 1 October 2010.

So in the light of that judgment, how might a children and family reporter proceed when confronted with the question of whether or

---

[756] J Doughty and M Murch (2012) Judicial independence and the restructuring of family courts and their support services' *Child and Family Law Quarterly* 26(3) at pp337–338.

not to go on offering crisis intervention support having completed and submitted their report for the court? If the Cafcass line manager seeks to prevent continuation of supportive crisis intervention on the grounds that it ties up scarce Cafcass staff resources, then in my view the correct step for the children and family reporter would be to turn to the family court judge for permission to continue short-term crisis support as being in the best interests of the child. No doubt if the disagreement between social worker and line manager cannot be resolved amicably, then the judge will have to decide.

In deciding in the children and family reporter's favour, the judge would have several options available – namely, appointing the court social worker as a guardian under r16.4 or making a Family Assistance Order under s16 of the Children Act 1989, along the lines that I explained in Chapter Ten. As I pointed out, the Department of Health guidance and regulations states that:

> A Family Assistance Order aims simply to provide short-term help to a family to overcome the problems and conflicts associated with separation and divorce.[757]

There are several other practice points that need to be made with respect to Cafcass officers employing short-term crisis intervention for a child in the course of preparing welfare reports. The first concerns *liaison with schools*. If, as I hope, in due course first responders in schools (teachers, school counsellors and child psychologists) take up the preventive Caplanian crisis intervention approach, there should be less need for Cafcass to do so, as the youngster will already have a supportive passage agent. As it is, I think it should be good Cafcass practice when preparing welfare reports to always check with the school to see whether the child is reacting adversely to family problems with respect to the child's educational performance. In preventive mental health terms this could be just as important as the mandatory checks of local authorities and the police which are currently part of the risk assessment concerning child abuse.

Second, there is a question of liaison and referral to *child and adolescent mental health services*. This is where the use of the Child and Adolescent Welfare Questionnaire (CAWQ) comes in. Properly administered it should be able to identify those youngsters who are reacting to parental conflict and separation in mentally unhealthy ways. The children and

---

[757] Department of Health (1991) *Guidance and Regulations: Vol 1 Court Orders* para 2.52.

family reporter would therefore receive a danger signal which would indicate the need for a referral to CAMHS, possibly via the young person's GP. Whether or not the family court judge should be consulted before this step is a professional practice issue which would have to be determined locally. The important point is to avoid delay in making the referral and of course to do so with the consent of the child and the resident parent. In this respect the Green Paper's proposals[758] for a new four week waiting time standard for access to specialist NHS services, if implemented and extended to referrals from Cafcass, would be a great help.

Continuing professional development and consultation for Cafcass staff with respect to crisis intervention support work

It is important to distinguish between the role of supervisor – a part of line management – and that of consultant, that is, an independent expert who can offer advice and support to the professional worker. As I have explained above, in respect of school staff, when undertaking short-term crisis intervention with distressed pupils, it is important to build in 'support for the supporters'. Again, as I have explained, Gerald Caplan pioneered a method termed 'client-centred case consultation'. This is fully explained in two of his texts to which I have already referred.[759] Because a consultant needs to be independent, he or she would need to be either a freestanding mental health professional or employed by an agency such as the child and adolescent mental health service, the Tavistock and Portman NHS Foundation Trust, or a well-established specialist voluntary organisation such as the Anna Freud National Centre for Children and Families. Universities also are potential resource centres where the necessary mental health consultants could be located.

The essential point is that consultants, like the first responders they are supporting, need to be committed to the preventive community mental health approach; that is to say, they should have a good understanding of the crisis model, bereavement and the psychosocial effects of broken or threatened attachments, which can trigger a crisis response.

---

[758] Department of Health and Department for Education (December 2017) *Transforming Children and Young People's Mental Health Provision: a Green Paper* CM 9523 p21–22.

[759] G Caplan and R Caplan (1993) *Mental Health Consultation and Collaboration* Jossey-Bass, San Francisco, CA. G Caplan (1974) *Support Systems and Community Mental Health: Lectures in Concept Development* Behavioural Publications, New York.

Although I am not closely acquainted with the work of child and adolescent mental health services, I am aware of the extreme financial pressures they face these days as a result of recent government cuts. The House of Commons Education and Health Committees, in their first joint report, following the Department of Health and NHS England 2015 report *Future in mind*, called for closer links between health and education services, and urged government to 'commit resources to establish partnerships with mental health services across all schools and services'.[760] I suggest this as a model approach which should also be followed in the case of Cafcass, so that a similar structured approach to referrals to CAMHS is developed across the country. It does, however, depend on CAMHS putting the emphasis on proactive prevention not just reactive treatment. This would require those services to develop their own community mental health services so that they can give the appropriate consultative support to first responders in schools, GPs and so on, and to backup crisis support for children and adolescents who have contact with Cafcass in the context of family litigation.

Policy issues: children and family solicitors in private law proceedings – the broader development of a community mental health approach within the family justice system

Reversing cuts to family legal aid

Throughout the 1980s and 1990s the cost of civil legal aid rose substantially. Various measures were taken by government to control the administration of the scheme, such as the transfer from the Law Society to a Legal Aid Board under the provisions of the Legal Aid Act 1988, special franchising to a limited number of law firms in 1997, and then the replacement of the Legal Aid Board by a new body, the Legal Services Commission, under the Access to Justice Act 1999. The effect was that legal aid was no longer demand-led but capped by government. Even so, annual expenditure eventually rose to £2.1 billion, most of which went on criminal legal aid (£1.2 billion). Family legal aid consumed most of the remainder.

As we have seen in Chapter Ten, when the economic crisis of 2007/08 occurred the Cameron-led Coalition government sought to make substantial cuts in the legal aid budget. The then Minister of Justice/Lord Chancellor, Kenneth Clarke MP, did so under the

---

[760] Department of Health and NHS England (March 2015) *Future in Mind: Promoting, Protecting and Improving our Children and Young People's Mental Health and Wellbeing.*

provisions of the Legal Aid, Sentencing and Punishment of Offenders Act 2012 (LASPO). The story of all these measures is clearly told in Martin Partington's latest 2017 edition of *Introduction to the English legal system*.[761]

I do not propose to go further into the continuing policy debate within legal circles about legal aid as a whole. This is well covered in Partington's text. Here instead I want to develop the argument that family legal aid should be seen primarily through the lens of community mental health and taken out of the Ministry of Justice's domain. From this viewpoint the partisan passage agent support role that solicitors have in the past provided to conflicted parents should have been viewed in mental health terms as much as through the orthodox prism of adversarial jurisprudence.

Where the separate representation of children is concerned, the special children's lawyer, working in tandem with a Cafcass guardian, should also be viewed from the perspective of preventive mental health, as well as being concerned to protect children's legal rights. As we have seen, in so-called private family proceedings this is an area where cuts to legal aid under the provisions of LASPO have severely reduced the public service provided by solicitors and have also had very unfortunate consequences for the fragile network of mediation services. So, in what follows, I make two proposals which could go some way to restoring the support service to families caught up in interparental conflict and separation which were previously provided by family lawyers and Cafcass officers. I deal with family legal aid first.

Proposal I: To transfer the funding of family legal aid from the Ministry of Justice (through the Legal Services Commission) to a new child and young person's mental health budget under the joint administration of the Department of Health and the Department for Education

This proposal follows from my basic argument that family justice has to be understood not only in orthodox jurisprudential terms but also from the perspective of promoting child and family mental health

---

[761] M Partington (2017) *Introduction to the English Legal System 2017–2018* Oxford University Press. See Chapter Ten 'Funding legal services', in which Partington points to various successful legal challenges to the government's original guidance to LASPO and to various further reforms that are being advocated, particularly by Lord Low's (2014) report *Tackling the Advice Deficit: A Strategy for Access to Advice and Legal Support Welfare Law in England and Wales* Legal Action Group, London.

and wellbeing. A family's interaction with the family justice system is inevitably concerned with the psychodynamics of family life when the homeostatic balance becomes disturbed by stresses associated with serious parental conflict, separation and divorce. As I see it, the issues of justice and fairness in family relationships are inexplicably linked with emotional reactions to broken attachments. In our culture resort to family justice can be understood in behavioural terms as a means of containing potentially dangerous emotions and helping the family to find a new emotional balance upon which to reconstruct their lives. You could say that this is a form of natural therapy. Even so, at the moment there are few lawyers or social policy makers who would understand it in these terms.

Over the last half century, as I have shown, the interdisciplinary family justice system has emerged as a distinct and specialist branch of civil justice which seeks to resolve such family matters in the best interests of the children. I now believe that the time has come to reflect this by disentangling family legal aid altogether from other parts of the legal aid system, so as to recognise fully the preventive mental health aspects of the family justice process, specifically, the system's support roles of mediators and family solicitors which, as I have shown, have been seriously damaged by the 2012 LASPO cuts to civil legal aid. But ensuring that family legal aid covers the work of specialist children's lawyers when they undertake commissions from Cafcass guardians under Rule 16.4 does not make up for the withdrawal of legal aid for parents.

Here we need to look at the need for legal advice when unrepresented parents arrive at the door of the family court. There may well be a case for some kind of filter or assessment mechanism to be provided by the court's own legal advisor, who could refer parents to a specialist publicly funded panel of family solicitors. The aim would be to sift out those relatively straightforward cases where the need for legal advice and guidance was minimal, from those where there was a clear prima facie justification for full representation because of the apparent legal and psychological complexity of the case. Such an approach would be a way of reducing pressure on family court judges, to which I have already referred in Chapter Eleven.

How might this scheme differ from the pre-existing arrangements that were in place before the LASPO cuts? Well, for a start it should recognise the community mental health aspects of a scheme designed to promote responsible parenting and the best interests of the child. But that cannot be considered unless we look more closely at the restructuring of the family court system, to which I turn next.

Proposal II: Reframing the family court process – from adversarial to participant justice

Are we making progress towards more child-friendly and child-focused family court practice?

Earlier I pointed to some ways in which the powers available to modern family courts might become more supportive for children and their families involved in private family law litigation. In this section I focus more on procedure within the family court itself. I argue that there is still some way to go if we are to be genuinely able to put the interests of children's mental health and wellbeing centre stage, so that they understand the role of the court and feel that their wishes and feelings have been taken account of. This means moving further away from what is popularly considered to be a traditional adversarial approach, that is, one in which the disputing parents are given the responsibility of presenting the case to an impartial judge and challenging their opponent to respond, a system where having heard the case, the judge 'hands down' the decision. Indeed, as we have seen, this assumed approach was one reason was why the Norgrove Family Justice Review in 2011 was required to consider it in its terms of reference. The concern was that the adversarial approach generates or aggravates a parental conflict, rather than seeking to promote settlement and strengthen family relations.

Yet, in their comprehensive empirical research-based study of family court judges in England and Wales, Eekelaar and Maclean demonstrated that this view of adversarial proceedings has always been something of a myth.[762] They showed that modern courts have developed a more inquisitorial approach, and that the role of the judge can be broken down into a number of distinct functions: first, under legal activity, performing the traditional role of adjudicator and umpire, acting as a scrutiniser to check and hold public authorities to account and an authoritative administrator to ensure that the proceedings comply with the rules of court procedure; second, that of manager in dealing with preparations, for example, under the various stages of the CAP (see Chapter Ten); third, helping the parties present their case, providing information and facilitating agreed outcomes.

---

[762] J Eekelaar and M Maclean (2013) *Family Justice: The Work of Family Judges in Uncertain Times* Hart Publishing, Oxford at pp81–123.

In their study, Eekelaar and Maclean, citing research by Joan Hunt,[763] acknowledged that for many parents in family proceedings going to court is a stressful, even terrifying, experience. Some considered that they were either 'not heard, or, worst of all, completely ignored'.[764] Other socio-legal researchers have found likewise.[765] It is not just the experience of going before a judge but the whole environment of court buildings which can be intimidating. Children too saw courts as 'scary places', even though many may not have set foot in the building. At the same time, Eekelaar and Maclean note that despite the formalities of the proceedings:

> judges (and the Legal Adviser) were unfailingly courteous and helpful to all parties, as also were the court staff ... [who] were clearly used to dealing with people under stress, and were pleasant and helpful.[766]

MIAM gatekeeping: a system that is failing?

It has to be remembered that before LASPO, in the days when civil legal aid was largely still available, anxious parents who went to court were invariably accompanied by their own solicitor who mostly did his or her best to reassure them. Technically officers of the court, solicitors in effect acted as its gatekeepers. But all that was to change in 2013 when the government introduced the MIAM procedure to be conducted by specially authorised mediators. With certain exceptions, mostly concerning domestic violence or allegations of child abuse, all applicants in private law children and financial remedy cases were now required to attend before their application could go forward to the court. The purpose of this gatekeeping procedure is to explain mediation and the benefits of non-court dispute resolution.[767] Following cuts to legal aid

---

[763] J Hunt (2010) *Parental Perspectives on the Family Justice System in England and Wales* Nuffield Foundation and the Family Justice Council www.judiciary.gov.uk

[764] J Eekelaar and M Maclean (2013) *Family Justice: The Work of Family Judges in Uncertain Times* Hart Publishing, Oxford at p121.

[765] C Smart, V May, A Wade, K Sharma and J Strelitz (2005) *Residence and Contact Disputes in Court* Department of Constitutional Affairs, London.

[766] J Eekelaar and M Maclean (2013) *Family Justice: The Work of Family Judges in Uncertain Times* Hart Publishing, Oxford at p121.

[767] The procedure is set under Rule 3 of the Family Procedure Rules 2010 with a supplementary guide for judges, magistrates and legal advisers, provided jointly by the Family Mediation Council and the Family Justice Council – see L Parkinson (2014) *Family Mediation* (3rd edition) Jordan's Family Law, Bristol.

– the combined effect of the MIAM gatekeeping procedure together with the Child Arrangements Programme (CAP), procedural steps of which I have already explained – the government's hope was clearly that most disputing parents would opt to avoid court proceedings and turn to mediators for help to resolve their difficulties in the interests of the child.

Nevertheless, data obtained in 2017 from the Ministry of Justice by National Family Mediation under a Freedom of Information request showed that the MIAM was largely failing to achieve its purpose. Of the approximately 90,000 private family law proceedings in 2015/16, six out of 10 bypassed the procedure. Of these, most continued as litigants in person with all the consequent pressure on judges and court staff which I explained in Chapter Ten.

Why the continued resort to family court justice?

So why, when there are supposed to be less stressful alternative dispute resolution services available, such as mediation and relationship therapy organisations like Relate, do so many disputing parents continue to follow the path to the family court, now even without the guiding hand of a legally aided partisan solicitor? Some may explain this conundrum by saying that it is likely to be a temporary phenomenon, a cultural hangover which will fade away as the problems facing litigants in person become more widely appreciated. I doubt this. Writing in 2017, three years after LASPO, there is little sign of it.

In my opinion, to understand the continued appeal of access to justice in the family court one has to look deeper into the psychology of family conflict; in other words, to consider not just the orthodox jurisprudential aspects of the way substantive family law regulates family rights and responsibilities and protects the vulnerable family members, but also the unresolved emotional tensions that disputing parents bring to the court. Elsewhere I have termed this particular interdisciplinary form of civil justice 'participant family justice'.[768] I explain it again here in the light of my concerns to provide more effective support for children. In this respect, my thinking has developed. This is because already a model of court practice with some of the same essential

---

[768] M Murch (1980) *Justice and Welfare in Divorce* Sweet and Maxwell, London at pp223–229 and pp251–269. M Murch (2012) 'The role of the family court system in England and Wales' in A Balfour, M Morgan and C Vincent (eds) *How Couple Relationships Shape Our World: Clinical Practice, Research and Policy Perspectives* Karnac Books, London at pp119–122.

features has emerged in London in the form of the first Family Drug and Alcohol Court (FDAC) in care proceedings, based upon some American models. These employ judge-led interdisciplinary teams and engage actively over a period of time with parents (see further below).

The participant model of family court practice: a recap

At the heart of my thesis is the observation that families undergoing parental separation and divorce interact with judicial procedures dealing with the legal consequences. In one respect, therefore, this interaction can be viewed as a collaborative encounter where all the actors within the family court – judges, solicitors, barristers, Cafcass officers and the mediators operating the MIAM gatekeeping function – as well as the family members themselves, including the children who wish to have a voice, can be viewed as being bound together in pursuit of a common objective about which all the parties are striving to reach agreement: namely, the aim of arriving at a fair and reasonable basis upon which the family can reconstitute itself following the emotional and practical upheavals of parental separation and divorce, paying due regard to the interests of children and the protection of vulnerable family members. Although this may at times seem difficult to achieve in the highly emotionally charged context of family court proceedings, where uncertainty about the outcome may well be experienced as yet another stressful crisis, in my view conflicted parents who otherwise have not been able to resolve their disputes often seem to be searching for a new and better emotional equilibrium. In this respect, the behavioural concept of homeostasis, which is central to our understanding of the Caplanian crisis model of mental health, is reflected symbolically in the scales of justice and the rule of law's notions of an impartial judicial authority. So while family justice practitioners address the presenting practical legal problems which the family brings to the door of the court, the underlying emotional dimensions have to be dealt with. In doing so it is usually helpful for those working within the court context to recognise two features of high conflict family disputes.

First, parents who dispute their children's future post-separation arrangements are very often struggling to resolve the emotional tension between, on the one hand, disengaging from an unsatisfactory relationship with their previous partner, while on the other wishing to continue to play an important parental role. This means in some ways trying to keep the parental coalition in being. I suggest that many parents find this such a difficult social and psychological task that they turn to outside authorities for help: in the past to solicitors to help them negotiate a settlement and to mediators. But when emotions overwhelm rational thought, many feel compelled to turn to the family court, which is perceived as having more powerful authority. Those with an understanding of psychoanalytical thinking might interpret this as a need to project unconsciously their ego function onto the judge, since under the stress of broken attachments it has become weakened. But it is not necessary to go into this kind of hermeneutic thinking to see how family judges interact with litigating parents.

The second factor which should be recognised is that conflicted parents grappling with these emotional tensions may still be feeling grief and bereavement at the breakdown in their relationship. As we have seen, defensive anger often features during the stages of grief, and this may be projected as resentment of the other partner who is seen as somehow to blame. Some may become so entrenched in these defensive positions that the dispute can appear to some judges as intractable. Yet in such cases one can see the role of the court as a containing and restraining force with, as a last resort, its capacity to control family violence through non-molestation orders, its use of injunctions to prevent harassment under the Protection from Harassment Act 1997, and its additional powers under the Domestic Violence, Crime and Victims Act 2004.

It is important to understand that in making these points I am not suggesting that the family courts should be seen as a psychotherapeutic institution, or therapeutic court as it is sometimes termed.[769] At the end of the day it has to be seen as a judicial institution operating the principles of the rule of law.

But just the same, it has to be recognised that, as the experienced marital therapist Christopher Clulow put it:

> the way people feel about what is happening to them has to be at the centre of the drama of family restructuring ... Attending to the emotional dimensions of change is key to unlocking the secrets of family behaviour.[770]

He is here referring to the need to recognise the underlying element of bereavement and grief. Clulow goes further by stating:

---

[769] See J Eekelaar and M Maclean (2013) *Family Justice: The Work of Family Judges in Uncertain Times* Hart Publishing, Oxford at p56.

[770] C Clulow (2012) 'Commentary' in A Balfour, M Morgan and C Vincent (eds) *How Couple Relationships Shape Our World: Clinical Practice, Research and Policy Perspectives* Karnac Books, London at p130.

accepting this premise implies that helping to regulate feelings (encouraging their expression when suppressed and containing them when they get out of hand) is an important function of the family justice system, one that has the potential to secure outcomes that are both just and protective of the welfare of vulnerable family members.[771]

My argument is that resort to the family court is most appropriate in those cases where the breakdown of the parents' relationship reaches a degree of interpersonal conflict and stress when the parents feel so estranged from each other, so wounded and threatened, that the only way conflict can be contained or resolved is to appeal to what is perceived as a powerful external, neutral, superordinate authority. Moreover, now that the restraining influence of legally aided solicitors has been removed from the scene, it is understandable that more parents feel compelled to go direct to the family court, with all the consequent pressures on judges and the welfare support staff which are now so apparent (see Chapter Ten). As I wrote many years ago, without the safety valve of resort to court, more angry parents would resort to domestic violence and the use of the bread knife.[772]

The continuing evolution of family court practice: what should be the next steps?

In this section I set out what I have in mind concerning the way family courts in England and Wales should operate when considering the needs of children and young people whose separated parents bring their child-related dispute to the door of the court. To do so I need briefly to recap a number of key factors already considered.

The basic principles

First is the principle that the court must make the child's welfare its paramount consideration.[773] In doing so, it must have regard to the welfare checklist set out in s1 of the Children Act 1989: that is to

---

[771] Ibid at p130.

[772] M Murch (1980) *Justice and Welfare in Divorce* Sweet and Maxwell, London

[773] For discussion of the Welfare Principle see N Lowe and G Douglas (2015) *Bromley's Family Law* (11th edition) Oxford University Press at pp401–432. Also J Eekelaar and M Maclean (2013) *Family Justice: The Work of Family Judges in Uncertain Times* Hart Publishing, Oxford at pp161–164.

say that the court must take account of the ascertainable wishes and feelings of the child concerned in the light of their age and level of understanding (s1(3)(a)); of their physical, emotional and educational needs (s1(3)(b)); and any harm they may have suffered or are at risk of suffering (s1(3)(c)); as well as other factors covered by the checklist set out under this section of the 1989 act. Also, family courts must be guided by the principle in s1(2) that in any proceedings concerning a child's upbringing, delay in determining the matter is likely to prejudice the child. These principles underlie the new Child Arrangements Programme (CAP) introduced by the senior judiciary, which sets out the timetable and procedural steps that have to be followed by parents seeking court orders, as I explained in Chapter Ten.

Second, I argue that court staff will need to be mindful of the conceptual Caplanian framework to assist understanding of the psychological and social processes of adapting to critical family change and reconstruction: specifically, the complex forms of bereavement that often follow conflicted parental separation, with all the associated emotions which may colour and shape their view of the court. Implicit in the court's response should be an acknowledgement of this factor.

Third, and linked to the last point, are the ideas which I have termed 'participant family justice' to indicate the inevitable interaction between, on the one hand, members of the family, and on the other the judge-led family court team including the court's welfare support services. As I have explained elsewhere, the conceptual ideas concerning this approach are drawn from the study of group dynamics.[774] In essence, they postulate that family and court are engaged in a shared task of searching for a fair and reasonable basis upon which the family can reconstruct itself, paying due regard to the interests of the children and protecting the vulnerable.

Fourth, and fundamental to my view of the participant model, is that of the constitutional role of an independent judicial authority (supported by well-trained, child-focused court welfare and administrative staff). I have suggested that culturally this has considerable symbolic and psychological significance. In this respect the notions of justice, symbolised almost universally by the Scales of Justice, can be linked to the psychological behavioural notion of balance, or

---

[774] M Murch (1980) *Justice and Welfare in Divorce* Sweet and Maxwell, London at pp218–229. Also M Murch (2012) 'The role of the family court system in England and Wales in child-related disputes' and C Clulow 'Commentary' in A Balfour, M Morgan and C Vincent (eds) *How Couple Relationships Shape Our World: Clinical Practice, Research and Policy Perspectives* Karnac Books, London at pp90–128.

homeostasis. As I have explained, this becomes temporarily upset or overwhelmed during the crisis of parental separation. To resort to justice, therefore, can be understood as an attempt to find a new and better emotional equilibrium for life after parental separation. It is the family court's task to facilitate this objective in child contact and residence disputes when other efforts by the parents themselves (or by solicitors in negotiations or mediators in settlement seeking) have failed to find a new acceptable balance.

Building on and adapting to recent developments

Any attempt to reform family court practice must take account of the factors outlined above and also, of course, the political and economic climate that followed the economic crisis of 2007/08, which led to major cuts in government expenditure. These seem likely to continue well into the 2020s following Brexit. Two other points need to be considered as likely to shape future family court practice. The first, as I have explained, is the evidence of high-volume consumer demand for resort to justice in parental separation cases and a relative failure of the MIAM procedure to divert large numbers of parents to out of court mediation services. The second is the apparent success in a related field of the experimental Family Drug and Alcohol Court (FDAC) based on some American models and pioneered by Judge Nicholas Crichton and colleagues in 2008 at the Inner London Family Proceedings Court. I have referred to this experiment because it contained many of the features of what I have termed participant family justice – that is to say, it involves working *with* the family in a shared attempt to resolve the parents' problems. Throughout the process the same judge deals with the case. In all cases there is a specialist multidisciplinary support team to help resolve the problematic circumstances. Thus, in the weeks following the initial hearing, there are regular fortnightly review meetings held between the judge, the support team and the parents. As an experiment, funded jointly by the Nuffield Foundation and the Home Office, the whole scheme was independently evaluated by researchers from Brunel University using a comparative control sample of 'ordinary care proceedings'.[775] On a number of scores the scheme

---

[775] J Harwin, M Ryan, J Tunnard with S Pokhrel, B Alrouh, C Matias and S Momenian-Schneider (2011) *The Family Drug and Alcohol Court (FDAC) Evaluation Project Final Report* Brunel University, London. See also J Harwin, B Alrouh, M Ryan and J Tunnard (2014) *Introducing the Main Findings From: Changing Lifestyles, Keeping Children Safe: An Evaluation of the First Family Drug and Alcohol*

was rated a success: all parents controlled their substance misuse, a higher rate of families were reunited with their children out of care and most parents reported positively on their engagement with the court. In my view, key to the success of the scheme were the elements of impartial judicial authority, continuity and concern, backed up by a multidisciplinary support team that engaged directly with the parents in their search for a solution to their drug and alcohol problems with the aim of reuniting the family.

There are many lessons here which could be more widely applied by family courts when dealing with parental disputes over arrangements for children. Obviously there are differences between public law and private law cases – the potential number of cases in the latter is much greater and the psychodynamics of interparental conflict may be different, though the elements of bereavement and loss may be present in both. Furthermore, in the FDAC the focus appears mainly to have been on the parents. The published report made little reference to hearing the voice of the child. Even so, the three elements of judicial continuity, the participant problem-solving facilitative (quasi-therapeutic) approach, and the specialist multidisciplinary court team to carry out assessments and engage with the parents on a family intervention plan seem to me to have real potential not only as a way of helping family courts to address the legal aspects of parental dispute but, most important, as a means to recognise the underlying emotional aspects. This would involve engaging with the parents and the children and young people if they so wish in their journey to recover and find a new equilibrium upon which to promote the youngsters' positive mental health and wellbeing and to reconstruct a less conflict-ridden family life. So, with that objective in mind, I make some practical suggestions as to how I would like to see family courts evolve.

An experimental scheme for participant family court procedure

The idea that I have in mind is to build on the current Child Arrangements Programme (CAP) framework but to modify it to incorporate the key features of the FDAC scheme. In doing so, I assume that those mediators that currently conduct MIAMs will form part of the family judge-led multidisciplinary team. The two key modifications which should be made to the current structure concern

Court (FDAC) in Care Proceedings Nuffield Foundation and Brunel University, London available at http://www.nuffieldfoundation.org/sites/default/files/files/FDAC_evaluation_summary_findings_01_05_14.pdf

first the gatekeeping MIAM mechanism, which in a modified form I term FCIAM (see below), and second, the way the First Hearing and Dispute Resolution Appointment (FHDRA) might work.

The family court intake process: the Family Court Information and Assessment Meeting

The initial contact that the family has with the court sets the tone for all subsequent interactions. Many parents and children come to what for them is a worryingly unfamiliar place. Naturally, many will be anxious, particularly if, lacking the support of a lawyer, they come on their own. So the first face-to-face encounter with court staff is critical.

For parents and children, going to court is generally an unfamiliar and stressful experience. Parents worry about how to present themselves to the judge and how to comply with the ritual demands of that encounter. The setting itself can be intimidating: the court buildings, the waiting areas and so on. Yet, as we have seen from Eekelaar and Maclean's study judges and family court officials are invariably courteous and pleasant and 'careful of their language, avoiding any possibility of being misunderstood as taking sides'.[776] They are well used to dealing with people under stress. Most family court judges and their staff do their best to help parents relax a bit so that they can express themselves clearly. These days more judges prefer to hear cases in chambers rather than in the formal traditional court rooms. Even so, invariably the encounter between a parent giving evidence and a judge is one where the presentation of self becomes of critical importance to the parent: 'Will the judge approve or disapprove of who I am and what I am saying?' These are often the unspoken questions. But as I observed, for example, years ago in my research into undefended divorce proceedings – first when they were heard in open court,[777] and later under the so-called special procedure (since repealed) concerning the welfare check, usually heard in chambers[778] – one could detect these unspoken questions by the witness's gestures and demeanour. This was confirmed when the researchers interviewed parents later about their experience. However brief the encounter, it was often accorded

---

[776] J Eekelaar and M Maclean (2013) *Family Justice: The Work of Family Judges in Uncertain Times* Hart Publishing, Oxford at p121.
[777] L Elston, J Fuller and M Murch (1975) 'Judicial Hearings of Undefended Divorce Petitions' *Modern Law Review* 38 at p609.
[778] G Davis, A Macleod and M Murch (1983) 'Undefended divorce: should s41 of the Matrimonial Causes Act 1973 be repealed?' *Modern Law Review* 46 at p121.

great significance by the parents, a number of whom interpreted the responses of the judge either favourably or unfavourably. Indeed, in these encounters some judges were experienced by parents as being very confirming of their efforts to be good parents when they explained that at home they were struggling against difficult economic conditions or poor housing. This capacity of the judges to encourage and to use their symbolic judicial authority to acknowledge the parents' efforts is a feature that lies at the heart of my ideas about participant justice and one which is exemplified by the FDAC experience.

Introducing the parents at the First Hearing and Dispute Resolution Appointment (FHDRA) to a judge and members of the multidisciplinary support team

The principle of judicial continuity was a key feature of the Inner London FDAC. It exemplifies the notion of a concerned impartial judicial authority to parents engaging in the participant justice approach. So, ideally, at the FHDRA the parents will meet the judge who if litigation proceeds will retain oversight of the process. Similarly, it is desirable for parents at the outset to meet a Cafcass officer who will carry out the s17 welfare enquiry and meet the children. Ideally he/she will also explain to the parents the need to ascertain the young person's views and the use of a psychometric instrument (such as the Child and Adolescent Welfare Questionnaire developed by Professor Harold and currently in use by Cafcass Cymru). Parents will be told of the need for the Cafcass reporter to carry out the usual safeguarding checks of the local authority and police. Since these enquiries can provoke defensive anxiety, it might more positively be good practice to obtain the parents' consent to approaching the young person's school to see whether or not the parents' separation was known to the school and whether it had any adverse impacts on the child's educational performance.

Cafcass and crisis intervention

When the Cafcass officers have met the parents and the child they should be in a position to assess whether the child needs short-term supportive crisis intervention to help them to come to terms with bereavement following parental separation. Of course this may already be being provided by the schools or some other service that the child is in contact with, such as a primary healthcare team. If the psychometric instrument indicates that the child is in need of more specialist psychiatric help then the Cafcass officer, with the agreement of the judge and the parents, should be able to make a direct referral to child and adolescent mental health services (see further below).

I appreciate that some practitioners believe that it is wrong to confuse the enquiry role with that of short-term crisis support. I am not convinced by this. If the Cafcass officer encounters a distressed child then an empathetic supportive response must be called for, particularly if the child is responsive and rapport has been achieved. The matter must be handled professionally and the court and parents informed. Of course, as happens already, children might wish to make disclosure of matters which they wish to be kept confidential or that they want only the judges to know about. On the whole, Cafcass officers have learnt how to handle this issue diplomatically. These matters have been examined elsewhere, not least by my co-authors in the book *Divorcing children*.[779] Here I only want to point out that Cafcass' terms of reference are not only to safeguard and promote the welfare of the child, to give advice to any court about any application made to it in family proceedings, and to make provision for children to be represented in such proceedings, but to provide information, advice and *support* for children and their families. Unfortunately in recent years, due to financial pressures, this last point has received less priority. By contrast, it is my view that if we are to adopt a genuinely preventive mental health service to help children manage critical family transitions and their aftermath, much greater priority must be given to the element of support for children during the litigation process.

Part C: Tertiary prevention: the role of child and adolescent mental health services

This book is primarily concerned with how to embed a preventive mental health approach in schools (primary prevention) and in the interdisciplinary family justice system (secondary backup prevention) with a view to supporting children and young people through the crisis of intense parental conflict and separation. But of course there is a very important tertiary prevention service concerning treatment for those youngsters whose behaviours are sufficiently problematic to be considered disturbed or mentally ill: namely, the child and adolescent mental health services (CAMHS). These, as I have mentioned at

---

[779] I Butler, L Scanlan, M Robinson, G Douglas and M Murch (2003) *Divorcing Children: Children's Experience of Their Parents' Divorce* Jessica Kingsley, London at pp190–200.

various points in this book, are under considerable pressure from rising demand and cuts in their funding. Also, as mentioned in the Preface, mounting public and parliamentary concerns led Theresa May, the Prime Minister, to announce the consultative Green Paper on child and adolescent services in England, now issued in December 2017.[780] Also as this text was going to press, the Welsh Government announced a similar public consultation and the Care Quality Commission produced its Phase One report from its ongoing review of children and young people's mental health services.[781]

Although it makes no specific reference to primary prevention utilising the crisis intervention approach for children and young people experiencing complex bereavement following serious parental conflict and separation, and has apparently not, as yet, considered the secondary preventive role of Cafcass and the family courts, the CQC Phase One Report does make a number of general points which confirm the overall picture of problems in respect of the current serious state of CAMHS which I have already reported at a number of points in this book.

For example, it points out that:

- The system that supports the mental health of children and young people is complex and fragmented.
- When children, young people, their families and carers try to access help for a mental health problem, many struggle to get timely and appropriate care. The availability of services provided by schools, local authorities and voluntary and community organisations varies from one part of the country to the next.
- Children and young people in vulnerable circumstances ... can find it particularly hard to access care ... for those who need more intensive specialist care there are significant challenges accessing services. There are long waiting lists for many of the services that provide specialist mental health care in the community and the imbalance between demand and capacity in inpatient care means that children and young people cannot always find an appropriate bed in an inpatient ward close to home.[782]

---

[780] Department of Health and Department for Education (December 2017) *Transforming Children and Young People's Mental Health Provision: a Green Paper* CM 9523.

[781] Care Quality Commission (October 2017) *Review of Children and Young People's Mental Health Services* www.cqc.org.uk at p4.

[782] Ibid at p4.

The CQC took evidence from children and young people as well as from professionals. These youngsters drew particular attention to their experiences of those working in schools and GP practices. They reported a number of concerns:

- They felt that some staff ... were not adequately trained to work with people of their age with mental health needs, and this had a negative effect on their experience of care.
- All too often, the Commission heard that children's experience of care suffered as a result of staffing changes, perceived gaps in staff skills or a feeling that staff are too busy.
- Some express concerns about a lack of continuity in their relationship with staff and professionals when people move to new jobs or staff responsibilities changed for other reasons ... they found these changes very frustrating and it could make it hard to build trust with staff.[783]

The CQC report stressed the importance of listening to and involving children, young people, their families and carers in the planning and design of mental health services. It also pointed to 'the lack of joined-up working between organisations, which can have an adverse effect on children's experience of care'. It stated that 'poor alignment between services can leave children and young people without the right support at the right time ... there can also be a failure to keep the child or young person and their family informed as to what is happening with their care'.[784]

With respect to school-based mental health support, the CQC emphasised 'the vital role that schools play in supporting the mental health of their pupils ... as teachers may be amongst the first to notice the signs that a child or young person's mental health is deteriorating'. The report endorsed the importance of school counselling services, noting that 'when children and young people can access high quality counselling through schools it can be an effective form of early intervention'. But it also noted that 'a lack of support in schools is one of the key concerns that children and young people have raised'.[785]

For the future, the CQC review will look more closely at the need to provide much better comprehensive education and training for school staff, facilitated by CAMHS, particularly around how to support those

---

[783] Ibid at p13.
[784] Ibid at p23–24.
[785] Ibid at p29.

youngsters with 'moderate mental health needs who do not meet the eligibility threshold for specialist CAMHS care'.[786]

So there is much in this report which confirms the approach that I have adopted in this book.

Here I only want to emphasise two points which I have already made. First, assuming that first responder services in schools take up the Caplanian idea of crisis intervention, then there will be a need to train them in the method and to provide consultative support. The same might apply to Cafcass staff in the family justice service. CAMHS seem to be one obvious growth point from which to develop such a strategic approach.

Second, CAMHS might well be best placed to take the lead to coordinate a broader-based preventive community mental health programme for children at both a local and a national level. In doing so they would no doubt draw on the services of pioneering voluntary organisations which are already working in the field, a number of which I have already mentioned in the text.

These two points indicate that what is needed is a reframed developmental strategy, to which I turn next.

Part D: Translating aspiration into realistic policy and practice

Time to develop a new strategic approach

It is clear that despite all the obstacles mentioned in Chapter Seven, there is a strong current of opinion in favour of doing much more to promote positive mental health and early preventive support for children and young people, notwithstanding current economic and political difficulties. This fundamental point lies at the heart of the Green Paper's proposals which complement my specific crisis intervention approach. So, in this context, how might one set about developing a coordinated system of local public services to offer direct support to children caught up in the crisis of parental conflict, separation and divorce? I suggest that a useful starting point is to agree a set of criteria which should be adopted by any service seeking to address the issue by introducing the Caplanian crisis interventive approach, which I have explained in Part II. These were put forward in 2003 in a report

---

[786] Ibid at p29.

by the Joseph Rowntree Foundation.[787] This recommended that any provision designed to support children through family change should consider the following aims:

- providing someone to listen to children's views and experiences, and support them and their parents in continuing to talk at difficult times of family change;
- helping children to understand the processes they are going through;
- encouraging children to seek support from extended family members and friends;
- enabling children and parents to continue links with schools and community groups after separation and divorce;
- enabling children to understand and manage conflict – and supporting parents to manage conflict;
- supporting parents so as to reduce stress, encourage warmth, and promote nurturing and mentoring of children;
- facilitating contact with non-resident parents unless there are good reasons for this not to happen.

It is probable that the findings of this 2003 Joseph Rowntree Foundation report were shelved and failed to be translated into effective policy and practice because of mounting economic pressures on public services and because it is difficult to change established professional mindsets. But times have changed. There is growing public concern, as we have seen, about the numbers of children and young people experiencing serious mental health problems, and about the difficulty in many areas of getting a timely response from CAMHS. Likewise, there is stronger recognition of the need to provide early interventions. My aim in reviving interest in the application of the Caplanian principles of crisis intervention has been to catch the tide of this growing movement in the context of primary prevention in schools and secondary backup support from Cafcass for children when their families enter the family court system. The key questions that arise are how best to set about reframing people's thinking to encourage such a development, and

---

[787] Joseph Rowntree Foundation (March 2003) *Findings: Supporting Children Through Family Change: A Review of Services* pp1–3. For full report see J Hawthorne, J Jessop, J Pryor and M Richards (March 2003) *Supporting Children Through Family Change: A Review of Interventions and Services for Children of Divorcing and Separating Parents* Joseph Rowntree Foundation, York.

how to bring about a fundamental shift of thinking to enable a new strategy to take root.

Such questions concern the challenging long-term task of setting up a coordinated local multi-service scheme of early preventive intervention and support for children facing critical family change; they are questions that need to be understood as part of an overall strategy aimed at promoting the wellbeing and emotional resilience of the children concerned. If the Government's Green Paper proposals are implemented that would be a big step forward, particularly if they could be married up with the Caplanian approach that I have explained in this book. So in concluding this chapter, before suggesting some possible first practical steps in implementing such an approach, I need to make a few cautionary points about the use of the word 'strategy'.

The definition of strategy

Like the word 'crisis', in everyday life 'strategy' is perhaps overused to mean a number of different things in a number of contexts, becoming attached to any desirable end. Yet, in his much acclaimed book on the subject, Sir Lawrence Freedman, a former diplomat, suggests that strategy:

> remains the best word we have for expressing attempts to think about actions in advance, in the light of our goals and our capacity. It captures a process for which there are no obvious alternative words, although the meaning has become diluted through promiscuous and often inappropriate use.[788]

He then explains that when used properly, strategy has a number of features relevant to the use of the word in the context of this book. He shows, for example, that a strategy is much more than a plan:

> strategy is required when others might frustrate one's plans because they have different and possibly opposing interests and concerns.[789]

And of course any new scheme such as I propose is bound to challenge some established interests and ways of doing things, particularly

---

[788] Lawrence Freedman (2013) *Strategy: A History* Oxford University Press at ppx.
[789] Ibid at pxi.

when resources are scarce. So innovators have to be aware of such considerations and proceed sensitively and carefully in their negotiations to win collaborative support.

Freedman also points out that:

> the inherent unpredictability of human affairs, due to chance events as well as the efforts of opponents and the missteps of friends, provides strategy with its challenge and drama. Strategy is often expected to start with a description of a desired end state.[790]

This of course is one of the purposes of this book. But Freedman cautions that:

> in practice there is rarely an orderly movement to goals set in advance. Instead the process evolves through a series of states, each one not quite what was anticipated or hoped for, requiring a reappraisal and modification of the original strategy, including ultimate objectives. The picture of strategy that should emerge ... is one that is fluid and flexible, governed by the starting point and not the end point.[791]

Possible first steps?

The only way I can think of to bring about such a strategic shift in thinking about the needs of children and young people experiencing stressful family change is to establish one or two experimental pilot schemes to act as research exemplars and to find out what works. Indeed the drafters of the 2017 Green Paper seem to be thinking along similar lines since it states that: 'We will therefore set up a new strategic partnership with key stakeholders focused on improving the mental health of 16–25 year olds by encouraging more coordinated action, experimentation and robust evaluation.'[792]

It also promised to: 'Commission research on how to engage vulnerable families where there is a heightened risk of parents and

---

[790] Ibid at pxi.

[791] Ibid at pxi.

[792] Department of Health and Department for Education (December 2017) *Transforming Children and Young People's Mental Health Provision: a Green Paper* CM 9523 para 133 p34.

children developing a mental health problem, seeking information from local areas when referring children and parents to both parenting and parental conflict interventions.'[793]

In what follows, therefore, I sketch out a few ideas around how this process of changing policy and practice might begin.

Setting up an initial sounding board

The first task to begin any new project is to find a few prime movers: people with sufficient interest to spend a little time thinking out ways and means to move things forward. One way of doing this could be to sound out a few people's responses to the ideas in this book, perhaps at one or two explanatory symposiums or conferences. Given that the subject concerns the promotion of good preventive mental health support for children and young people, one should look to find interested practitioners from the fields of education, child and adolescent mental health, and the family justice system. This first exploratory step will obviously raise the questions of who should organise the preliminary events, how these events should be paid for and where they should be held.

After that, assuming that the symposiums act as springboards for action, the next set of questions might look at what further steps may need to be taken to get some experimental schemes off the ground. Would it be possible to convene a small group of potential developmental prime movers to work up some plans for these schemes, including finding suitable locations, estimating the required staff and financial resources, and dealing with questions of accountability? I raise the question of the right launch machinery below, but first there is the question of location.

Choosing the locations

The work of this book has been facilitated by family lawyers in the Cardiff University School of Law and Politics. Cardiff itself is the location of the Welsh National Government, which is in close proximity to the university, with its related medical, educational, social work and law departments, all of which share established links with their respective local practitioner communities in South Wales. There is therefore a case for Cardiff being a location from which to mount this initiative. When he addressed Cardiff University staff some years

---

[793] Ibid para 123 p32.

ago, Rhodri Morgan, the original First Minister, pointed out that Wales and the Welsh Government potentially offered a really good, receptive environment for social policy, research and innovation. This is because of its compact scale.

The need for comparative evaluation

Even so, assuming that a fully resourced experimental practice initiative is set up in local schools and family courts, I think it will be important to build in from the beginning a comparative element, in order to monitor and evaluate the project through research as a 'natural experiment'. Therefore, I think this should proceed with research collaboration with an English university located near to an area with a similar potential catchment population. Here, again, the Joseph Rowntree Foundation research from 2003 provides a useful guide as to key questions that need to be addressed when evaluating future programmes offering support to children whose conflicted parents are separating.[794] These were stated as follows:

- Are the aims of the programme specified?
- Are the aims based on research?
- Does the content of the programme reflect its aims?
- How do children or parents gain access to the service?
- Are personnel involved appropriately trained?
- Is the programme age-appropriate?
- Is the programme culturally and religiously appropriate?
- How do we know the programme has reached the children or parents who need it?

Choosing the right machinery to run a project of this kind

In a book like this, it is not appropriate to detail the best form of organisation to develop and operate a comparative exemplar project of this kind. Ideas about that might emerge from the exploratory discussions that take place in the initial symposia/conferences set up to consider the issues covered in this pump-priming book. Nevertheless, in broad terms it seems there might be a number of possible options, such as turning for financial help and advice to the UK Government's Early Intervention Foundation, approaching interested national

---

[794] Joseph Rowntree Foundation (April 2003) *Findings: School-based Support Work for Children Whose Parents Have Separated* Joseph Rowntree Foundation, York.

children's charities, persuading a local child and adolescent mental health service to support and possibly lead the initiative, securing the backing of a Children's Commissioner, or involving a local authority education department and the local family court and its Cafcass support service. Of course ideally it would be more suitable for the UK Government as a whole to promote and fund a rollout of such a scheme on a cross-departmental basis.

Whether or not this proves to be the case, in the final chapter I attempt some horizon scanning to consider broader emergent social trends which seem bound to shape the context of future social and legal policy and practice in this field in the years to come.

FOURTEEN

Scanning the horizon

Introduction: finding a way forward in times of acute uncertainty

The UK's referendum vote to leave the European Union was viewed by many as a political and economic earthquake. After six years in office, David Cameron, the Prime Minister, immediately announced his intention to stand down. He did so as soon as the Conservative party chose Theresa May to replace him. The leadership of the Labour opposition was also thrown into disarray. Notwithstanding the issue of whether to leave or remain in the EU, it was clear that voting patterns were influenced by movements in the underlying social and economic tectonic plates, revealing deep divisions in the UK's social structure.[795] Mark Carney, Governor of the Bank of England, referred to the decision to leave as likely to lead to 'an economic post-traumatic stress disorder for households, businesses and markets'.[796] It may well take months, if not years, for the dust clouds of uncertainty to clear sufficiently for a proper evaluation of the political, social and economic consequences to be made. But one immediate result was that the then Chancellor of the Exchequer, George Osborne, announced that he would not be able to meet his aim of clearing the deficit by 2020. He was replaced when Mrs May announced her cabinet. Even so, economic austerity measures may well continue at a reduced rate for some years, with implications for the health service, the family justice system and the welfare state in general, particularly if there is a need for the Chancellor of the Exchequer, Philip Hammond MP, to cushion the impacts of Brexit (the British withdrawal from the European Union). In this respect it may be significant that the 33rd British Social Attitudes Survey has produced data to show that since 2010 the number of those in favour of increased taxation and more

---

[795] *British Social Attitudes 33* (June 2016) Report by Director Kirby Swales, NatCen Social Research. See also *Brexit: what will it mean for Britain? Findings from British Social Attitudes 2015*, NatCen Social Research available at http://www.bsa.natcen. ac.uk/media/39029/brexit-what-will-it-mean-for-britain-report.pdf.

[796] M Carney, Governor of the Bank of England (29 June) Statement to the press.

public spending has grown; at the same time, the number who think that current levels are about right has fallen, as has the number of those who want to reduce taxes and spend less – with almost as many people saying they want to see spending and taxation increase as those who want to see them stay the same.[797]

Although in the grand scale of things questions of social and legal policy and practice concerning the support needs of children and young people faced with critical family change may seem of relatively minor importance, there can be no doubt that the lives of thousands will be affected. If the economy declines, family incomes for many will come under increasing pressure. For those parents with strained conflicted relationships, this will add to their tensions. Moreover, if investment in public services for families is further restrained or reduced this will impact adversely on children: schools, for example, might be handicapped in their efforts to develop their own early intervention mental health services, and the current problems facing the child and adolescent mental health services (CAMHS) will continue. Similarly, resources for remedial relationship support for conflicted parents might well be more difficult to obtain from both government and charitable sources. Furthermore, the family justice system, which is already grappling to find ways of mitigating major cuts to publicly funded civil legal aid and to develop more child-friendly family courts with their own support services, may well be further handicapped. The gap between those who can pay for family justice and those who have to rely on the state might well widen further. If so, here again children will be the greatest losers. In short, the climate for innovation and improvement along the lines that I have explained in this book may well become harsher. But, as I have also pointed out, moments of social crisis can present opportunities for those willing to put on their thinking caps and search for them.

So I conclude this book with a number of challenging questions concerning the future. I have pondered on these while I have been preparing the book. They have been thrown into sharper relief by the upheavals and uncertainties following the EU Referendum and the departure of Prime Minister Cameron, and, following the General Election of June 2017, the much reduced majority of Theresa May's government while the Brexit negotiations unfold.

---

[797] *British Social Attitudes 33* (June 2016) See introduction to newsletter by Director Kirby Swales, NatCen Social Research. See Table: Attitudes to taxation and spending on health, education and social benefits 1983–2015.

As I scan the horizon to see what the future may hold and try to discern what emergent social, economic and technical factors might shape policies and practices affecting children facing critical family change, there seem to be to be five major questions:

1. Will the movement to listen to and take account of the voices of children and young people in the policy process gain more public recognition and support?
2. What will be the impact of further rapid advances in information technology on children themselves, their parents and the helping professions?
3. Will the perils of specialist expertise and the 'silo' effect be further recognised and effective policy and practice steps taken to develop a more joined up cross-disciplinary approach – strengthening horizontal links between vertically organised institutions?
4. More specifically, will principles of preventive mental health and early supportive intervention come to underlie and be integral to the work of the education services (and primary healthcare) and that of the interdisciplinary family justice system?
5. If any or all of these trends continue, what will be the implication for those in the training and research communities?

Listening and responding to the voice of the child

At various points in this book I have pointed to an ongoing cultural change, reflected in policy and practice, which accords greater recognition to the voice of the child.[798] As we have seen in Chapter Four, the principle is endorsed by both national and international law.[799] Yet the challenges of translating the principle into policy and practice remain.

The issue for practitioners was neatly summarised by Anthony Douglas, CEO of Cafcass England, who wrote that the voice of the child should be the main focus of the agency's work. As he put it:

---

[798] N Lowe and M Murch (2001) 'Children's participation in the family justice system: translating principles into practice' *Child and Family Law Quarterly* 13 pp137–158.

[799] See the Children Act 1989 S1(3)a under which the court must have regard to the ascertainable wishes and feelings of the child (considered in light of the individual's age and understanding). Article 12 of the UN Convention on the Rights of the Child. Also European Convention on the Exercise of Children's Rights Article 3 and 4. See also European Convention for the Protection of Human Rights and Fundamental Freedoms Article 6, now incorporated into UK law by the Human Rights Act 1998.

in many of the cases that we deal with the voice of the child is scarcely audible, either through the child not being properly seen or heard, or because the voices of the adults around the child are too loud for the child's voice to be heard.[800]

It may well be that more progress on this front can be made in schools than in other services. This is because teachers, by training and aptitude, have in any case better opportunities to develop their face-to-face skills in communicating with children. Moreover, as we have seen, the movement to encourage a whole school approach to foster children's wellbeing and emotional resilience, dependent on listening to the voice of the child, is also increasingly established. So in this domain I am reasonably optimistic that over time ideas about primary preventive mental health and supportive crisis intervention for children experiencing turbulent family change might strike a receptive chord. This is provided, of course, that schools allow sufficient space and time for children to safely express their worries and feelings, and provided that appropriate staff resources are developed and deployed (see further below).

The position is more complex with respect to the family justice system, particularly where so-called private proceedings involving child-related parental conflicts are concerned. Of course in public law proceedings involving allegations of child abuse and neglect, a protracted if major step forward was taken forward in 1984 by the creation of independent panels of guardians ad litem to separately represent the child. This followed the 1974 Field-Fisher inquiry into the death of Maria Colwell.[801] The provisions of s103 of the Children Act 1975 nevertheless remained largely unimplemented for a number of years. But, bit by bit, following recurrent child abuse tragedies where social services had failed to expose the need to see and listen to the child at risk, the constitutionally independent family justice system and its social work arm (now incorporated in Cafcass and Cafcass Cymru) responded by developing its safeguarding role. The level of its staff skill in ascertaining and responding to the voice of the child also improved.

Even so, use of the separate representation role of guardians in cases of parental conflict is, as we have seen, much constrained. It is still limited to 'exceptional cases of significant difficulty'. Although, as we have seen

---

[800] Cafcass (7 July 2016) *Annual Report and Accounts 2015–16* www.gov.uk p10

[801] *Report of the Committee of Inquiry into the Care and Supervision Provided in Relation to Maria Colwell* (1974) HMSO, London.

in Chapter Two, the numbers of s16(iv) applications made to Cafcass increased by 6.6% from 1,571 in 2013/14 to 1,674 in 2014/15, the numbers remain small in comparison to the numbers of cases referred by the court to Cafcass for welfare reports. These cases actually dropped by 26%, from 22,723 in 2013/14 to 16,725 in 2014/15.[802]

Where mediators are concerned, there is even more limited opportunity for them to listen to the voice of the child, both in the MIAM procedure and in the mediation process more generally. As the Relate report acknowledges, 'children and young people's voices are often absent even though the evidence is they want the opportunity to be heard'.[803]

In short, in family justice there is still quite a lot of professional ambivalence about meeting with children and listening to their views, despite the principles of the substantive law. The same problem also goes for family court judges who, as we have seen, are still divided on the matter. As I explain below, I think this is partly because family justice practitioners do not as yet properly appreciate the mental health principles which implicitly underlie their practice, and which need to be more openly acknowledged and understood. I believe this would inevitably lead to a greater recognition of the value of listening and responding to the child's point of view.

Information technology for children and young people

When in 2003 my colleagues and I conducted our survey of children in divorce proceedings, children's use of smartphones and computers was relatively unusual. No more than 10 years later it is a universal part of children's lives. The marketing people called these children 'digital natives'. As I cited in Chapter Four, in a recent book drawing on a report by Ofcom,[804] Steve Hilton, a former adviser to Prime Minister Cameron, reports data to show that:

> the average British child receives his/her mobile phone at the age of twelve; nearly one in ten receive one before the

---

[802] Cafcass (July 2015) *Annual Report and Accounts 2014–15* www.cafcass.gov.uk/media at p7.

[803] D Marjoribanks (December 2015) *Breaking Up Is Hard to Do: Assisting Families to Navigate Family Relationship Support Before, During and After Separation* Relate, available at www.relate.org.uk/sites/default/files/publication-breaking-up-is-hard-to-do-report-dec2015_0.pdf at p29 para 3.5.

[804] Ofcom (2014) *Children and Parents: Media Use and Attitudes* www.ofcom.org.uk at p29.

age of five. It is normal for young children to be inundated with technology; they are using it to go online without supervision and these trends are increasing.[805]

The Green Paper of December 2017 reports that on average five to fifteen year olds spend 15 hours a week online and that more than two in five children aged nine, and half of twelve year olds have a social media profile.[806]

Hilton is alarmed by what one might call the downside of the internet age and its impact on children: easy access to pornography and other sexualised materials, the risk of cyberbullying, and the possibility of getting involved with undesirable adults who wish to groom them for sexual exploitation. As *The Economist* critically put it, 'the internet is a free-for-all of cybercrime, malware and scams'.[807]

Yet there are positive sides to all this, especially in the way that children and young people have come to use IT as a source of mutual support among their friendship groups. My grandchildren (ages 12, 15 and 17), for example, all have smartphones, as do their school friends. Modern children's mastery of IT often far exceeds that of their parents and certainly that of their grandparents! Their generation has created a whole cyber world of social contacts available from platforms such as Facebook, FaceTime, Snapchat and Instagram. Texting their friends and families occurs regularly throughout the day. The use of passwords to access social media assumes privacy and confidentiality and the means to exclude people from an unwelcoming prying into their world. Young people are continuously creating their own electronic shorthand language, such as BTW (by the way), TBH (to be honest) and so on. I am told that to spend three or four hours a day on one's phone is quite normal. One young person I know whose family life has been blighted by stressful parental illness spends up to 12 hours a day on her smartphone and PC.

It is clear that this is an ever-growing irreversible social and technical revolution. Quite what its impact is on contemporary children and

---

[805] S Hilton (2015) *More Human: Designing a World Where People Come First* WH Allen, London at p241.

[806] Department of Health and Department for Education (December 2017) *Transforming Children and Young People's Mental Health Provision: a Green Paper* CM 9523 para 111 p29.

[807] 'WeChat's world: China's WeChat shows the way to social media's future', *The Economist* 6 August 2016 available at www.economist.com/news/business/21703428-chinas-wechat-shows-way-social-medias-future-wechats-world.

young people whose families are subject to change resulting from parental conflict and separation and divorce will not be known until further socio-legal research takes place (see below). More generally, the Green Paper reports that the Chief Medical Officer is expected to produce a report on the impact of technology on children and young people's mental health with work on the subject being undertaken by the Department for Digital, Media, Culture and Sport.[808]

Information for separating and divorcing parents

Once upon a time before legal aid became available for divorce proceedings, usually where there was domestic violence and a failure to maintain, wives who couldn't afford a solicitor would often turn to the domestic magistrates' court for advice and information about how to obtain a 'separation order'. But once legal aid became available this source of information largely disappeared. The magistrates' court, popularly known as the 'police court', carried a stigma of criminality. Instead, people preferred the privacy and confidentiality to be found in a solicitor's office. Advice and information from a solicitor became available under the so-called green form scheme. This was the situation until most legal aid was withdrawn under the Legal Aid, Sentencing and Punishment of Offenders Act 2012 (LASPO). David Cameron's Coalition government took the view not only that this would save public expenditure but that in the modern age of computers, smartphones and the like, people would be able to get their information direct from the internet. Indeed, in some respects, that is often now the case.

Yet, as the Relate report has shown, there is now such a bewildering range of information available from numerous sources that people are often confused.[809] For example, there is an online child maintenance calculator and a website to help parents put together a parenting plan,[810] a Wikivorce, a website run by Citizens Advice Bureau, and one run by the Royal Courts of Justice Advice Bureau (RCJAB) which runs in partnership with a leading firm of solicitors. One legal firm also

---

[808] Department of Health and Department for Education (December 2017) *Transforming Children and Young People's Mental Health Provision: a Green Paper* CM 9523 paras 113 and 114 p30.

[809] D Marjoribanks (December 2015) *Breaking Up Is Hard to Do: Assisting Families to Navigate Family Relationship Support Before, During and After Separation* Relate, available at www.relate.org.uk/sites/default/files/publication-breaking-up-is-hard-to-do-report-dec2015_0.pdf

[810] See www.splittingup-putkidsfirst.org.uk

provides pro bono support and has developed a tool to help people who cannot afford a solicitor to act as 'litigants in person'. Valuable though these and other sources of automated information might be, the Relate report shows that this diversity has resulted in a 'confusing mass of information but lack of a single, authoritative place to go to identify trusted information and advice tailorable to a specific family's situation'. It therefore recommends, a 'single point of access for information and support for all families before, during, and after separation, with the primary route of access via an online interactive portal'. This online provision should be supported by a 'single telephone support helpline' to help people work their way around the website.[811] Furthermore, Relate recommends that MIAMs should be reconstituted to provide more general information and advice (that is, not just about the availability of mediation services), and should explore the idea of multi-channel delivery, such as online as well as face-to-face.[812] To achieve these objectives, I have suggested in Chapter Thirteen that MIAMs could be termed Family Court Information and Assessment Meetings (FCIAM).

So there has been no shortage of innovations since LASPO. Moreover, for those who can still afford a solicitor's advice and help, some firms continue to provide face-to-face support as well as assistance for their clients via the internet. Maclean and Eekelaar, in their latest study of solicitors and mediators, give an example of a Midlands firm. This offers help to its clients in accessing online 'DIY advice plus help with documents and packages of service'.[813] This is marketed as 'solicitor managed divorce'. Where more legal help is needed, the firm steps in to provide for specific individual needs.

All these new legal services are operated by firms of solicitors offering partisan support to parents. They have had to adapt their practice following the removal of civil legal aid. But they come at a

---

[811] D Marjoribanks (December 2015) *Breaking Up Is Hard to Do: Assisting Families to Navigate Family Relationship Support Before, During and After Separation* Relate, available at www.relate.org.uk/sites/default/files/publication-breaking-up-is-hard-to-do-report-dec2015_0.pdf at p34–35 and p40.

[812] D Marjoribanks (December 2015) *Breaking Up Is Hard to Do: Assisting Families to Navigate Family Relationship Support Before, During and After Separation* Relate, available at www.relate.org.uk/sites/default/files/publication-breaking-up-is-hard-to-do-report-dec2015_0.pdf at p49 para 8 and at p50 para 12. The Relate report further suggests that 'consideration be given to establishing an expectation that SPIPs [Separated Parents Information Programmes] be combined with [MIAMs] as precursors to court applications for children issues' p50.

[813] M Maclean and J Eekelaar (2016) *Lawyers and Mediators: The Brave New World of Services for Separating Families* Hart Publishing, Oxford at p64.

price. Maclean and Eekelaar quote a firm with its own well-designed information packs and forms. In 2014 this firm charged £250 for negotiating contact, a fee of £175 for an initial consultation on financial matters plus £250 for further negotiations. For all issues mediation by a lawyer/mediator the charge was £714 and it was £570 for mediation on finance matters alone. Even so, that particular firm found that at the end of their financial year, such services were barely profitable. Maclean and Eekelaar, after years of studying the role of solicitors, conclude that since LASPO:

> greater autonomy and choice in a complex marketised legal world carries undeniable risk for vulnerable parties who lack purchasing power or the essential skills and resilience to navigate their way through the tangled market and legal complexities and pressures of family breakdown.[814]

As I proposed in Chapter Thirteen, there is an argument in favour of radically reframing our approach to family legal aid so as to view parental conflict, separation and divorce not just in orthodox legalistic adversarial terms, but primarily as a psychosocial process affecting the whole family, in which conflict resolution should also be seen from the perspective of preventive community mental health. This could change everything, not least transferring some of the costs of family legal aid and family court support services from the Ministry of Justice (these days so often taken up with penal affairs) to the health service budget, and altering the traditional adversarial approach of family courts. But before developing these ideas further, I need to consider likely long-term consequences of the IT revolution as it affects the work of family lawyers, mediators and other professionals in the family justice system. This is a subject which has been brilliantly addressed by Richard Susskind and his son, Daniel, in their well-argued, thought-provoking book *The future of the professions*.[815]

Information technology and the challenge to professional exclusivity

The Susskinds' thesis is that in the digital age, with increasingly capable automated systems, the work of the professions – doctors, teachers, accountants, lawyers and others – will be radically altered

---

[814] Ibid at p68.
[815] R Susskind and D Susskind (2015) *The Future of the Professions: How Technology Will Transform the Work of Human Experts* Oxford University Press.

and in many respects reduced, particularly in terms of their roles in providing information and advice, and in carrying out other routine administrative tasks. The nub of their argument is that:

> machines (non-thinking, high-performing systems) can already discharge many tasks that, not many years, ago we thought were beyond their capabilities; and, as machines become increasingly capable, the number of tasks that they can take on will grow and their execution will become better and quicker.[816]

To develop their thesis, the Susskinds examine the range of jobs undertaken by professionals and divide or deconstruct them into a number of constituent elements. By so doing, they identify particular tasks which humans are no longer required to perform since machines can do them quicker, better and more cheaply. They term this process 'the decomposition of professional work'. Thus clients will increasingly be able to source professional knowledge (for example, the relevant details of the substantive law and procedure) themselves from websites. As we have seen, this is already happening as a consequence of cuts to the civil legal aid and advice scheme. Likewise, diagnostic medical information is no longer the sole preserve of a monopolistic profession. One might well add that children and young people can of course also avail themselves of such online information, although whether, how and when they do so has not, as far as I know, been studied.

The importance of empathy

At the same time, while such tasks will be taken over by machines, others will continue to be performed by professionals or less well-paid paraprofessionals: individuals who are knowledgeable and skilled in their particular professional domain but who are not specialist experts.[817]

Among these tasks, which are relevant to helping children and parents undergoing critical family change, the Susskinds identify personal empathy as being particularly important. They see this as a crucial but often neglected skill of professionals and paraprofessionals: the skill to

---

[816] Ibid at p280.

[817] Ibid at p264. The authors list future roles for humans as being craft people, assistants, para-professionals, empathisers, research and development workers, knowledge engineers, process analysts, moderators, designer system providers, data scientists and system engineers.

'listen and empathise with those they help – for example, to impart bad news sensitively and to share appropriately in the good fortunes of patients and clients'.[818] This clearly tunes in with the need to listen to children and young people that I have written about in previous chapters concerning early crisis intervention within the conceptual framework of preventive mental health. Obviously empathy is a key quality for those working in schools, child health and the family justice system as well. In the future, in all these occupations, as the Susskinds acknowledge, 'there will be the need for wise empathetic, discipline-independent individuals – empathisers who can provide reassurance to recipients of their work that is often as important as the correct answer'.[819]

Technologically induced unemployment

While a capacity for empathy may well be an enduring human value for those in the helping occupations, there can be little doubt that the impact of IT will continue to transform many of our traditional professions. Thus, the Susskinds suggest that 'it will become ever more difficult, as time passes and machines become increasingly capable, to ensure that there is enough reasonably paid employment for professionals.'[820] They then go on to develop the argument that:

> as professional work shrinks once it is disaggregated into more basic tasks then it becomes apparent that a great many of these tasks are similar to those in other non-professional occupations.[821]

Over time they foresee that this will lead to technology induced unemployment in the professions.

However, although they envisage that increasingly capable machines will replace many jobs, they acknowledge that certain human tasks will remain: those involving, for example, moral deliberation, the art of judgment and the taking of moral responsibility. These aspects 'ought to be undertaken by human beings rather than machines'. But the authors do not expect the volume of such tasks to keep professionals in

---

[818] Ibid at p265.
[819] Ibid at p265.
[820] Ibid at p290.
[821] Ibid at p291.

employment on today's scale. In their view only 'the best and brightest will endure the longest'.[822]

So, what might be the implications of the Susskinds' thesis for those seeking to provide supportive help to children and their families enduring the stress of family breakup? In advancing Caplanian ideas about short-term crisis intervention, I have argued that practitioners, whether in schools, primary healthcare or the family justice system, require not only qualities of empathetic listening, but an understanding of the behavioural concepts underlying the process of crisis intervention. This will be needed so that practitioners can judge the stages in the crisis resolution process that have been reached by children and their parents, and so that they can determine, for example, whether more expert psychotherapeutic intervention is required if the young person seems not to be making a normal mentally healthy adjustment to the crisis-provoking event. But these skills are not the exclusive preserve of any one profession. They are essentially cross-disciplinary in character and can be applied in a variety of settings.

Who pays for the new services following the IT revolution?

Even so, the crucial question of costs of such services will arise. As the Susskinds write:

> the fixed costs of the initial set-up [of a service] have to be funded by someone. When we take account of these set-up costs, it might indeed appear that we have to allow those who invest to maintain some exclusivity over their product. They should then be able to charge for their service, or in some other way raise revenue to cover all their costs, and therefore be able to continue producing or distributing practical expertise.[823]

This would suggest an endorsement of the commercial principle of marketisation, which, as we have seen, raises particular difficulties for children and families on low incomes. Yet the Susskinds rightly state:

> we should be cautious here; many professionals are also driven by objectives other than profits. They do not always

---

[822] Ibid at p291.
[823] Ibid at p298.

rely on selling their practical experience to cover their costs.[824]

They cite, for example, the NHS or state education. It is of course for such reasons that I have suggested that crisis support for children and young people undergoing critical family change should be provided by the state.

As I see it, empathetic crisis intervention in the interests of children and their families is a public good, and the skills and experience of its practitioners, whatever service they are in, should be held in a 'commons'. This means that, as the Susskinds put it, 'the ownership and control of practical experience is taken out of the hands of a few large institutions (for example professional institutions, corporations and governments) and shared amongst those who participate'.[825] Whatever the case, the issue of who pays for support services for children and young people facing family breakdown is obviously crucial and unavoidable.

The Susskinds' ideas which I have sketched out above lead me to another question, namely, whether we are likely to see the growth in cross-disciplinary 'silo-busting', as Gillian Tett termed it.[826] From a different, more anthropological, perspective, this too represents a challenge to professional exclusivity and to the way that support services for children and their parents are to be provided in the future. I consider this issue next.

Silo-busting and cross-disciplinary collaboration

Gillian Tett, an anthropologist by training who became an editor for the *Financial Times*, was moved to write her book *The silo effect* by the financial crisis that erupted in 2007/08 when a number of banks took what are now considered crazy risks, by selling on sub-prime mortgages at an apparent profit. This caused an enormous global financial bubble which finally burst with the collapse, or threatened collapse, of a number of banks in the US (including Lehman Brothers) and the UK. It led to enormous bailouts by Gordon Brown's Labour government of the Royal Bank of Scotland, Northern Rock and Lloyds Bank. It created viability problems for a number of others. The

---

[824] Ibid at p299.
[825] Ibid at p296.
[826] G Tett (2015) *The Silo Effect: The Peril of Expertise and the Promise of Breaking Down Barriers* Simon and Schuster, New York.

bailouts hugely increased the government deficit and set the scene for the subsequent Cameron Coalition government's austerity cuts to public services, including those to civil legal aid and CAMHS, which I have considered in previous chapters.

Tett wanted to discover why it was that senior management in these banks apparently did not realise the enormity of the risks that were being taken by their junior staff who were setting up such complex and dodgy financial deals. In other words, why those at the top didn't know what was going in the 'silos' below them. She highlighted the:

> paradox of an interconnected world whereby despite universal communications brought about by the internet, large organisations very often are divided and then sub-divided into numerous different departments which tend to operate in isolation from one another. Such fragmentation can create information bottlenecks and stifle innovations.[827]

Referring to the work of Pierre Bourdieu, a French social anthropologist, Tett developed the idea of 'mental maps'. These develop in the minds of people in groups and organisations and, as it were, circumscribe their social organisational world and shape how they think. In government, for example, civil servants operate within hierarchical vertically managed departments with clear boundaries and relatively weak links between them. Yet stronger horizontal organisation would strengthen cooperation and coordination. So what might be needed is strong superordinate authority to ensure good liaison between departmental silos. This of course also applies to intellectual specialism, professional groups and social agencies. Tett's argument is that we have to be on our guard against the limitations of this silo effect in order to mitigate inherent dangers. So, how to do it? Tett offers five ways to do so.[828]

First, she suggests keeping boundaries between teams in big organisations flexible and fluid, for example, by rotating staff between different departments. Yet, as I have indicated, in government departments too frequent staff rotation can lead to a collective failure to get to grips with those problems, which need a considered and sustained attempt to overcome them if solutions are to be found.

---

[827] Ibid at p14.
[828] Ibid at pp247–248.

Second, she thinks ways must be found to reward collaboration between groups rather than primarily on the basis of groups' competitive performance.

Third, she advocates the sharing of information to combat the tendency for departments to 'hug information to themselves', pointing out that modern computing technology makes the sharing of data much easier. She acknowledges that 'this is not easy when there are teams of experts who use complex technical language that only they understand or when they refuse to listen to alternative ideas'. To overcome this problem she says we need 'cultural translators', that is to say, people 'who are able to cross between specialist silos and explain to those sitting in one department what is happening elsewhere'.[829] This requires people who are literate in a number of specialisms, people who can use different professional/occupational languages. In this respect she does not mention, as I think she should, the value of developing a 'common language' between specialist or occupational groups – for example, in the context of this book, the conceptual framework of preventive mental health as the common language for a number of occupational groups, as I have advanced in Part II.

Fourth, Tett suggests that people should periodically try to imagine what things look like from a different point of view. In medicine, for example, doctors could 'visualise how the patient experiences health rather than how the doctor is trained'.[830] This is why in the context of family breakdown it is so important for professionals and paraprofessionals to try to understand what it is like to be on the receiving end of their services, and why, for example, we continually need well-constructed consumer research to regularly sample the voices of children and young people in order to provide reliable feedback (see further below).

Fifth, she points out a number of potential ways in which modern technology can challenge silos. Although this does not automatically follow, as she puts it, 'the beauty of computers is that they are not born with indelible mental biases.'[831] Moreover, they can be programmed to rearrange information in different ways and to test out different ways of organising it. Somebody with imagination needs to do this. This needs people with open minds to look at the big picture. It also requires the capacity to listen carefully to what people, including children and young people of course, say about their life, and to compare it with

---

[829] Ibid at p249.
[830] Ibid at p249.
[831] Ibid at p250.

what others say. This ties in with another idea that the Susskinds use when deconstructing professions and suggesting future roles, namely, the need for what they term 'knowledge engineers, system providers, data scientists and system organisers'.

Tett concludes her book by challenging the received wisdom of the day that our whole culture exists to support specialised technical subjects. Part of the problem is that staying within a silo appears a lot easier than crossing boundaries. As she puts it, 'we live in a world where people are expected to streamline their careers and become specialists. Our schools and universities have put people into boxes at a young age and academic departments are fragmented.[832]

At various points in this book I have highlighted this issue. Thus lawyers tend to stick to the positivist approach to legal analysis, which is built largely on a study of case decisions and statutory and procedural law. As was once observed by a leading judge (it might well have been Lord Justice Ormrod, who was medically trained before becoming a lawyer), "Legal education produces sharp minds but the difficulty is that it narrows while it sharpens." Similarly, cognitive developmental psychologists largely operate within their own conceptual boundaries and have little truck with the hermeneutics of Freudian psychoanalysis or Jungian analytic psychology. Social policy academics keen to develop their particular branch of political theory and world view do likewise. All these occupations have a tendency to organise themselves into silos, as Tett puts it, 'in the name of hyper-efficiency, accountability and effectiveness in the short term'.[833] After all, within the professions this is where, up to now, most rewards have been found, and where practitioners may acquire prestige and maintain a distinct professional identity.

Over the years I have noticed that in the field of parental conflict resolution the process of creating specialisms has continued at a pace. Take mediation, for example. Here a whole variety of specialist mediators have emerged, as Maclean and Eekelaar illustrate in their book *Lawyers and mediators*. Thus they point to the developing roles of 'all-issue mediators, child related mediators, finance issue mediators, co-mediation'.[834] Some with legal training offer legal advice; others with social work backgrounds do not. Reinforcing such specialisms, particular codes of practice have developed, backed up by a range of

---

[832] Ibid at p253.
[833] Ibid at p254.
[834] M Maclean and J Eekelaar (2016) *Lawyers and Mediators: The Brave New World of Services for Separating Families* Hart Publishing, Oxford at pp122–3.

informative textbooks for use in specialist training. Similarly, a process of specialisation has developed in the last twenty or thirty years in family court social work that has its historical roots in the probation service and the early days of independent social work panels of guardians to represent the separate interests of children. These of course now operate within the more unified Children and Family Court Advisory and Support Service (Cafcass).

I must acknowledge that I have contributed to and mostly supported the development of these specialisms myself both in respect of mediation and family court welfare support services.[835] But with colleagues I have also warned against the isolating dangers of specialism, pointing to the compensatory need for a cross-disciplinary approach.[836] Moreover, as the years have gone on, I have become more aware than most that professional training reinforces the 'silo' mentality. There is an urgent need to counterbalance this in the family justice field by adapting a cross-disciplinary approach to the post-professional education of judges and other family justice practitioners, both lawyers and social workers. Fundamentally, this is because I believe that broadly based professional education is more likely to produce intellectual honesty, well-balanced minds and sound judgment than narrow specialism. After all, as I have written elsewhere:

> a practitioner with a reflective self-critical approach to learning and professional practice is a safer proposition when wielding power over other people's lives (particularly when they are caught up in some kind of personal family crisis as those who bring family troubles to the law usually are) than one who may be fixated by a single set of ideas and held in the grip of powerful beliefs or even dogma.[837]

---

[835] M Murch (1980) *Justice and Welfare in Divorce* Sweet and Maxwell, London. M Murch (2004) 'The germ and gem of an idea' in J Westcott (ed) *Family Mediation: Past, Present and Future* Jordan's Family Law, Bristol at pp21–32. M Murch and K Bader (1984) *Separate Representation for Parents and Children: An Examination of the Initial Phase* Department of health and University of Bristol.

[836] M Murch and D Hooper (1992) *The Family Justice System* Jordan's Family Law, Bristol at pp36–49 and pp110–122.

[837] M Murch and Rt Hon Lord Justice Thorpe (1997) 'The development of the family justice system in England and Wales: past, present and future' in L Salgo (ed) *The Family Justice System, Past and Future, Experiences and Prospects* Collegium Budapest, Institute for Advanced Study, Workshop Series No 3 at p34.

Of course I recognise that developing a broad understanding of social and behavioural sciences (of which the Caplanian framework is just one small element) and coupling it with ongoing legal studies requires time, opportunity, personal inclination, intellectual rigour and, as fields of knowledge develop, lifelong perseverance. I return to this matter in the final section of this chapter when considering cross-disciplinary post-professional education and continuing professional development (CPD). But first I need to consider the prospects of weaving in the Caplanian community and preventive mental health approach in the fields of children's education and family justice.

What are the prospects for developing an early preventive approach to promote children and young people's positive mental health and wellbeing?

In terms of principle, the answer to this question might seem obvious and straightforward. But the problem, as always, is translating principle into practice. Here there are many particular difficulties in reviving interest in the Caplanian model of crisis intervention. This is partly because there are so few practitioners in the UK with that particular conceptual understanding, and partly because, as we have seen, early intervention seems to take second place to emergency fire-fighting when things have gone seriously wrong.

Even so, more optimistically, there are three key factors likely to shape the future. These include an increased awareness of the need to listen to the voice of the child and the continual growth of information technology, which is opening up peer support systems for children and their families. These developments, as we have seen, are transforming the helping professions while emphasising the importance of empathy in service delivery. Then there is a growing awareness of the need to counterbalance the isolation of specialism by silo-busting and promoting a cross-disciplinary common language.

All these trends suggest that, despite the difficulties, if we are to improve children's and young people's life chances, sooner or later serious attempts must be made to develop some form of early supportive intervention for the thousands who every year face the destabilising crisis of parental conflict, separation and divorce.

Moreover, there are signs that despite serious restrictions of public expenditure, there is growing awareness of mental health issues. The *Times* newspaper, for example, continues its campaign to highlight the need for better mental health services[838] and members of the Royal family no less are lending active support. Thus Prince Harry was reported as saying that it had taken him a number of years before he felt able to talk about the death of his mother, Princess Diana. A subsequent article in the *Times* stated that:

> early diagnosis and appropriate treatment are vital. Without it a depressed child may become a school dropout. A young woman with an eating disorder may become trapped in the spiral of self-harm ... Plans to tackle mental health featured in the election manifesto of all three parties. However, access to treatment can be inadequate and subject to a postcode lottery. Last year 61% of the children referred to the Child and Adolescent Mental Health Service arm of the NHS received no treatment at all. Too many were fobbed off on school counselling services or charities. Such bodies perform exemplary work with limited resources but are no substitute for a functioning health service.[839]

But even this reflects a certain limited silo-mindset. In my view, government needs to take a wider cross-disciplinary and cross-departmental approach. In England and Wales this should involve much closer collaboration between the Department for Education and the Department of Health in respect to primary prevention, and the Ministry of Justice with respect to the work of the interdisciplinary family justice system – an approach which should ensure that funding is shaped and allocated appropriately. An important step forward in this line of thinking was taken in May 2017 by the joint report of the House of Commons Education and Health Committees. This called for stronger coordination between health and education services with respect to referrals from schools to CAMHS.[840]

As we have seen in December 2017, this was followed by the Green Paper issued jointly by the Department of Health and Department for Education. It emphasised early prevention to be based in schools supported by machinery to promote effective collaboration between

---

[838] *The Times* launched its campaign to improve access to child and adolescent mental health services on 12 March 2015.

[839] *The Times* (26 July 2016) Leading article.

[840] House of Commons Education and Health Committees (2 May 2017) *Children and Young People's Mental Health: The Role of Education: First Joint Report of the Education and Health Committees of Session 2016–17* https://publications.parliament.uk

them and specialist mental health services.[841] Yet an aspirational Green Paper issued for consultation still falls short of implementing a well financed policy on the ground. Besides, how long will the current Ministers stay in post? Will future Ministers be equally committed to tackling the problem of inter-departmental coordination and collaboration?

In the summer of 2016, Theresa May, the new Prime Minister, appointed new ministers to the Department for Education in England and the Ministry of Justice, but they were replaced after the election of June 2017 and replaced again in the reshuffles of 8 January 2018. So what are the chances of them achieving better departmental collaboration? In this respect they could do well to look again at the House of Commons Public Administration Select Committee 2015 third report *Leadership for the long term: Whitehall's capacity to address future challenges*, to see what it has to say about interdepartmental collaboration and horizontal problems confronting government while most of its responses are vertical – a critical issue which I have considered in Chapter Twelve. Might these ministers[842] be able to take a fresh and broader view of these matters?

School-based primary prevention

As we have seen in Chapter Thirteen, parliamentary pressure to develop early intervention to support pupils' emotional and social wellbeing has been sustained now for several years by parliamentarians like Graham Allen MP and Earl Francis Listowel in the House of Lords. They have been backed by organisations such as the Consortium for Emotional Wellbeing in Schools, Young Minds and Place2Be, whose patron is the Duchess of Cambridge. All have pressed for accredited teachers training in children's emotional development and attachment as an essential entitlement for all who work in schools. This bore fruit in the early days of Mrs May's administration, when the Department for Education published a framework report on core content for initial teacher training (ITT),[843] section 5 of which states that ITT providers:

---

[841] Department of Health and Department for Education (December 2017) *Transforming Children and Young People's Mental Health Provision: a Green Paper* CM 9523 p18–25.

[842] At the time of writing, Damian Hinds MP is secretary of State for Education and David Gauke MP is Lord Chancellor and Secretary of State for Justice.

[843] Department for Education (July 2016) *A framework of core content for initial teacher training (ITT)* Department for Education, London, at p17, available at www.gov.uk/government/uploads/system/uploads/attachment_data/file/536890/Framework_

> ... should emphasise the importance of emotional development such as attachment issues and mental health on pupils' performance, supporting trainees to recognise typical child and adolescent development and to respond to atypical developments.

Furthermore the Green Paper states that the Government is to add: 'A mental health specific strand within the Teacher and Leadership Fund to fund training which supports the delivery of whole school approaches.'[844]

So I am encouraged that the notion of preventive mental health is becoming integral to children's education, even if the particular Caplanian model remains as yet underdeveloped.

My worry in this respect is that since the Government is so keen to promote the Techniques of Cognitive Behavioural Therapy (CBT) and Mindfulness it will ignore the potential benefits of the crisis intervention model which I have set out in this book (Chapters Six and Seven) and which I see as complementary to these approaches. Indeed in certain respects the Caplanian approach would be preferable as a first line of school based primary intervention: First while CBT addresses symptoms (such as dealing with depression, anxiety, and so on) crisis intervention aims to support the young as soon as the crisis strikes and help them adjust realistically and come to terms with their parents' conflicted separation and divorce, thereby boosting their resilience and capacity to deal with future emotional life challenges. Secondly, CBT implicitly implies the notion of therapy which can be interpreted by young people, their parents and school staff as being stigmatically associated with mental illness. There is a paradoxical problem here which the Government itself recognised in 2011 when funding the anti-stigma campaign *Time to Change*, promising a further £31 million by 2021. By contrast, as I have pointed out in Chapter Seven, one of the reasons why I am drawn to the crisis intervention approach is that it should avoid stigmatic associations being essentially a 'normal' method of supporting young people through a grief reaction to the breakdown of their parent's relationship applied by familiar teachers in the young person's every day school context. As the Green Paper itself acknowledges: 'The school environment can also be non-stigmatising, meaning that children and their parents may be more

---

Report_11_July_2016_Final.pdf. Consortium for Emotional Wellbeing in Schools *Press Release* 18 July 2016.
[844] Ibid at para 103 p28

receptive of accepting support through these routes as compared via mental health services.'[845]

Thirdly it should be noted that while the Green Paper endorses the potential of preventive intervention such as CBT and mindfulness, it is recognised that at present according to research reviews these types of intervention 'tend to have limited long term effects'.[846]

Secondary/tertiary prevention in the family justice system

I wish I could be as optimistic about the development of preventive mental health thinking in the context of the family justice system, specifically with respect to so-called private law child-related disputes. Here, as I have already pointed out, there is a basic mindset problem which is shaped by the dominance of orthodox jurisprudential thinking. Some years ago Michael King and Christine Piper, in their thought-provoking book *How the law thinks about children* (which built on the work of the social theorists Nicholas Luhmann and Gunter Teubner), developed the observation that the legal system is essentially autopoietic. That is to say that it is a closed self-referral system, so information from other systems of thought is reinterpreted or becomes subordinate to its own dominant discourse.[847] This is a view that I have considered more fully in Chapter Eleven. While this sociological area of critical legal theory is familiar to many academics, one has to say that there are few signs that it has penetrated far into the day to day practice of law at either a national or an international level. Here the traditional jurisprudential thinking still dominates and is reinforced in the family justice system by the traditional adversarial model of justice. This conditions the mind to think largely in dyadic terms of one party versus another – notwithstanding the welfare principle of the paramount interest of the child. While the new Private Law Programme, introduced by the President of the Family Division, Sir James Munby, and his senior colleagues, is a major step forward in

---

[845] Department of Health and Department for Education (December 2017) *Transforming Children and Young People's Mental Health Provision: a Green Paper* CM 9523 at Appendix A para 4.

[846] Ibid Appendix A para 5 p38.

[847] M King and C Piper (1995) *How the Law Thinks About Children* Gower, London. M King (1997) *A Better World for Children: Explorations in Morality and Authority* Routledge, London. N Luhmann (1988) 'Closure and openness: on the reality in the world of law' in G Teubner (1993) *Law as an Autopoietic System*, Blackwell, pp25–46.

setting timetables so that the process avoids unnecessary delay, as we have seen, children's voices are still largely absent from the MIAM procedure despite the recommendations of the Family Mediation Task Force (see Chapter Six) and despite the small but significant greater use of separate representation by a guardian from the family court's own social work support service (Cafcass and Cafcass Cymru), which I have outlined in the previous chapter.

I also regret that there is still a failure to think of family proceedings in terms of participant family justice. That is to say that one should recognise that all the actors within the machinery of justice – judges, solicitors, barristers, Cafcass officers – as well as the family members themselves, including children who wish to have a voice, can be viewed as being bound together in pursuit of a common objective about which all parties are striving to reach agreement: namely, the aim of arriving at a fair and reasonable basis upon which the family can reconstitute itself following the emotional and practical upheavals of parental separation or divorce, paying due regard to the interests of the children. As outlined elsewhere, the theoretical basis for this way of thinking about the family justice process is drawn from psychodynamic group psychology.[848] Here suffice to say that although not strictly necessary, it helps to appreciate its significance to the family justice process if family justice practitioners acquaint themselves with a little psychological knowledge concerning small group psychology, as seen from a psychoanalytic perspective. But this of course depends on practitioners being willing to step across the silo boundary of conventional positivist legal thinking. It means requiring family justice practitioners, as Gillian Tett writes, to recognise how we all unthinkingly classify the world around us each day', and then how we should 'then try and imagine an alternative'.[849] At some point in the future this is an educational task for continuing professional development for family justice practitioners wishing to broaden their understanding of their interaction with families.

---

[848] M Murch (1980) *Justice and Welfare in Divorce* Sweet and Maxwell, London at pp223–227. Also M Murch (2012) 'The role of the family court system in England and Wales: towards a new concept of the family justice process' in A Balfour, M Morgan and C Vincent (eds) *How Couple Relationships Shape Our World: Clinical Practice, Research and Policy Perspectives* Karnac Books, London at pp112–122.

[849] G Tett (2015) *The Silo Effect: The Peril of Expertise and the Promise of Breaking Down Barriers* Simon and Schuster, New York at p254.

Can central government alter its approach to family justice?

Changing the traditional way of viewing family proceedings applies to central government officials even more so. I would hope to see the preventive mental health aspects of family justice fully recognised at a central government level. In particular, this will involve looking more closely at its funding so as to put it on a genuinely cross-disciplinary and cross-departmental basis. As I have explained above, the House of Commons Public Administration Select Committee has drawn attention to the problem of a lack of coordination across government departments,[850] quoting author and economist Wolfgang Michalski, who has stated that 'most of the key problems faced by governments are horizontal and most government responses are vertical'.[851] Because the family justice system and its support services are a specialist interdisciplinary branch of civil jurisdiction dealing with the problems and conflicts arising in strained close family relationships, aspects of law, social welfare, mental health and not least education are all interwoven. It seems to me obvious that this should be reflected in the way the system is funded by government. Indeed, there is already a small precedent in that direction with respect to Cafcass in Wales.

At the moment the Ministry of Justice is the main source of government finance – the exception being Cafcass Cymru, which is funded by the Welsh Government's Health Department. As I understand it, that particular arrangement reflects the fact that, before devolution, Cafcass came under the aegis of the Whitehall Department of Health and its social service inspectorate. Those in the new Welsh Government wanted it to remain in the health domain, thinking, probably rightly, that the Ministry of Justice would not have the same priorities and the same level of understanding of childcare social work issues. More broadly, the senior judiciary also had legitimate concerns that as the Ministry of Justice was to take over responsibility for penal services from the Home Office when Tony Blair's New Labour administration created the Ministry of Justice, their constitutional independence would

---

[850] House of Commons Public Administration Select Committee (9 March 2015) *Leadership for the Long Term: Whitehall's Capacity to Address Future Challenges: Third Report of Sessions 2014–15* HC669 TSO, London at para 12 p9.

[851] Sir J Elvidge (December 2012) *The Enabling State: A Discussion Paper* Carnegie UK Trust, Dunfermline at p37, available at www.carnegieuktrust.org.uk/wp/wp-content/uploads/sites/64/2016/02/pub14550116191.pdf

be eroded, and that with austerity cuts in the offing, funding priorities would go to the penal system.[852] In this they were correct.

So, given the central thrust of my argument that family justice should be seen not only in jurisprudential terms but as an important secondary preventive mental health service for children and families, I hope that the point about better interdepartmental coordination made by the Parliamentary Public Administration Select Committee will be taken on board by Prime Minister Theresa May, and that she will ask her ministers to work out a way of sharing costs so as to reflect more appropriately the interdisciplinary aspects of family justice practice. This will no doubt involve discussions with the senior judiciary in the Family Division, who I hope will support the case for such action, including the implications for judicial training, which in my opinion, requires a much strengthened understanding of *preventive* mental health, not just ways of treating mental disorders. In this respect the thinking underlying the 2017 Green Paper should, in time, be extended to include the interdisciplinary family justice system.

But there is more to it than just sharing costs between government departments. There is the vital question of ensuring adequate horizontal liaison, not only between government departments, but at a local field level between those services and agencies that should be capable of offering direct support to children and parents in these circumstances. In this respect, it may well be necessary to appoint someone with sufficient superordinate authority to ensure that the required coordination within the network of services takes place. In my view this need not be an elaborate bureaucratic task and could no doubt be facilitated by modern information technology while ensuring that

---

[852] J Doughty and M Murch (2012) 'Judicial independence and the restructuring of family courts and their support services' *Child and Family Law Quarterly* 24(3) pp333–354. My colleagues Julie Doughty and I wrote that 'the widening of ministerial responsibilities of the Lord Chancellor prompted the Constitutional Committee of the House of Lords to publish in 2006 the report *Relations between the Executive, the Judiciary and Parliament*. This Committee was concerned that there would be conflicts of interest between the traditional role of the Lord Chancellor and that of the Secretary of State for Justice. In particular the report referred to the concerns of the Lord Chief Justice that a combination of responsibilities would result in the office holder being primarily concerned with prisons and offender management. As a safeguard against this, the Committee expressed a desire for an autonomous court administration. It therefore encouraged the government and the judiciary to find an acceptable way forward. The outcome was the creation of Her Majesty's Courts and Tribunals Service (HMCTS) operating separately from the other responsibilities of the Ministry of Justice and its officials.'

consideration is given to ethical issues around respecting privacy. It is the clarity of purpose and maintenance of the aim which will be vital.

The preventive approach to community mental health within the family justice system: the need for cross-disciplinary training and research

At the end of Chapter Eleven in Part III I went into some detail about the need for interdisciplinary education within the family justice system and the problems that have arisen in this respect following financial cuts to the budget of the Ministry of Justice. On reflection, I think the aim to broaden the education of family justice practitioners (judges, magistrates, lawyers, Cafcass officers and mediators) to overcome the limitations of their respective specialist silos (or ghettos), while appropriate before the financial restrictions imposed by the Treasury under former Chancellor Osborne and Prime Minister Cameron, may be for the time being politically unrealistic. Besides, powerful social, economic and psychological forces remain, reinforcing the notion of separate specialist professional identities which offer prestige and a sense of legitimacy. This will be so notwithstanding the deconstruction of certain professions under the influence of the information technology revolution which the Susskinds have foretold, and notwithstanding the strong arguments for silo-busting advanced by Gillian Tett.

Embedding crisis intervention into the support work of Cafcass

So at a practical level, for the next decade or so it will be necessary for those committed to the interdisciplinary approach to set much more limited, research-based objectives. This is one more reason why I am drawn to the idea of reviving interest in the conceptually straightforward and practical Caplanian crisis model of mental health as a means of supporting children and families as they navigate their way through the upheavals resulting from severe parental conflict, separation and divorce. That will depend on the acceptance in principle of the idea by Cafcass and Cafcass Cymru with the support of the senior judiciary. Then it will need to begin on a relatively limited scale, backed up by suitable introductory training, monitoring and consultative support, ideally provided by CAMHS. This will depend on these services being willing to develop the Caplanian approach as part of a broader preventive community-based mental health service role, both at a primary level in schools and in support of the secondary backup preventive support work of the family justice system. Even then, the difficulties of doing so are likely to be formidable.

First of all, as far as I know, there are no current exemplars in the UK using this approach, save possibly some self-help bereavement services such as those run by Cruse. In the field of social and community psychiatry I know of only one psychiatrist still living in the UK who, as a young man worked with Gerald Caplan in the US and who for a while was enthusiastic about this model of preventive mental health practice. Yet, his subsequent career took him in another more professionally rewarding direction. The same was so for my late friend and research collaborator Douglas Hooper, clinical social psychologist, who studied for a while with Caplan in the US but later became a professor of social work and was drawn off into other fields.

Second, as far as the family justice system is concerned, without going into detail, I can envisage a possible way forward if an experimental scheme was tried, say, in South Wales. Here, if Cafcass Cymru were prepared to assist, its service already has experience of using Professor Harold's child and adolescent psychological triage tool. This might possibly provide an experimental point of entry for an expanded support role for Cafcass officers to act as short-term passage agents for children with, of course, the agreement and participation of the parents involved. They might also be able to take on the broader liaison coordination role which I have outlined above. I hasten to say that as yet I have not discussed this point with anyone.

Future research

I cannot conclude this book without a few words about the continuing need for policy and practice related socio-legal research. As the Finer Committee report stated years ago, the fundamental justification for it is that:

> the doing of justice requires knowledge of its own procedures. Legislators, judges, critics and citizens must have knowledge of the social consequences of legal actions without which a democratic society cannot keep its institutions under constant and open scrutiny.[853]

---

[853] *The Report of the Committee on One Parent Families* (The Finer Committee) (1974) Cmnd 5629 HMSO, London at p220 para 4.417.

Yet of course sometimes those institutions would rather not be so exposed to scrutiny. Some, such as government departments, have developed defensive ways to protect themselves from greater transparency: by controlling research funds, by selectively formulating research questions, by limiting access to data and, when research is permitted, through the manipulation of research findings or ignoring them altogether. Nevertheless, I have found that many of these problems can be overcome if the researchers themselves are patient and willing to develop mutual understanding with officials and practitioners, without of course sacrificing their own academic integrity and independence of thought. This is why it is vital to sustain a strong and varied academic research community that is able to attract substantial alternative sources of research funding from charitable sources, from a politically independent Economic and Social and Research Council (ESRC) and also from Europe, since international comparisons are such an important source of understanding – notwithstanding the possible advent of Brexit.

With respect to the proposals in the December 2017 Green Paper there is no specific reference to any well structured evaluative research programme apart from an indication that the Government 'intends to trial and roll out the new mental health support teams' and will pilot the first proposed reduced waiting times for access to NHS Children and Young People's Mental Health Services. Evidently these measures will be evaluated in a number of 'trailblazer' areas. What I wrote at the end of Chapter Thirteen about the need for a strategic evaluative development plan should be relevant here. Nevertheless, I regret that the Green Paper did not make a stronger case here for more detailed and costed research programmes: An opportunity missed.

In the past I have stressed the continuing evolution of family justice and that family law reform needs to be harnessed to a well-maintained, competent and interdisciplinary research infrastructure.[854] At a rhetorical level it is now commonplace for policy makers and reformers to call for robust evidence-based research upon which to make decisions. Yet funds for research, like those for sound management information, are always scarce. In times of austerity they become even more limited, both from government and the charitable foundations.

---

[854] M Murch and D Hooper (2005) *The Family Justice System* Jordan's Family Law, Bristol at pp103–109. Also M Murch and D Hooper (2005) 'Research into the family justice system: retrospect and prospect' in N Axford, V Berry, M Little and l Morpeth (eds) *Forty Years of Research and Practice in Children's Services: A Festschrift for Roger Bullock* John Wiley and Sons, Chichester at pp134–147.

Yet throughout my work on this book, I have constantly been aware of the need to update research information, given the rapidity of social, economic and technical change which shapes and frames the conditions under which children and their families live.

These complex interacting changes produce stresses and strains on family life that need to be regularly charted and evaluated if family law and social policy are to be responsive to people's lives. Moreover, there is much more that we need to know about changing family life patterns and families' use of educational, health, legal and social welfare systems. For example, as I have already indicated, we need to know much more about the way that children and young people caught up in family breakdown use the internet and social media as sources of information and peer support. What are the positives and what are the dangers of this? The child-related research which I have drawn on in this book was conducted more than 10 years ago. Since then, under the influence of the IT revolution, the child's world has changed out of all recognition. As far as separating and divorcing parents are concerned, how do they use the internet? What sources of information do they find helpful or baffling? One can think of a host of similar consumer questions with respect to the new Child Arrangements Programme, the MIAM provisions and the new local unified family courts. How is the increasing trend of marketisation of services for mediation and legal representation experienced? Do parents differentiate between those services they have to pay for, where they have the power of patronage, and those provided paternalistically free of charge by the state?

However educational, mental health and socio-legal family research is organised and paid for in the future, I hope it will consider the following:

- It should include programmes which adopt a sufficiently broad focus in order to examine issues in the round from a number of different intellectual perspectives, socio-legal and psychological. This will involve research teams comprised of staff from different disciplines.
- Since the 1980s government has increasingly sought to control the research agenda by restricting it to finding short-term answers to limited questions. The ESRC, for example, was encouraged to focus less on research that was theoretical and to fund more short-term problem-solving initiatives relevant to individual government departments – with all the endemic problems of hierarchical divisions of responsibility identified by the House of Commons Administration Select Committee, and others to which I have referred here and in Chapter Twelve. To counteract that tendency,

we need more long-term empirical studies charting the processes of family change over time and studying families' varying use of both informal social networks and formal support systems in education, health, social welfare and family justice. This is necessary in order to show up the changing use made of these systems by different social, economic and demographic sections of society, such as the differences between rich and poor.

- It should be recognised that interdisciplinary research does not just happen overnight. There needs to be a well maintained and managed research infrastructure within which cross-disciplinary research work can flourish. Researchers from different specialisms need time to learn each other's languages and occupational values. This points to the need to form more established and open research units where creative research ideas can germinate, where individuals can reflect and spark each other's imagination.

- It should be recognised that the introduction into universities of the recurrent research assessment process in the 1980s had the effect of increasing individual research competitiveness among established academics and between universities and their departments. This encouraged staff to move to better-endowed departments. It also encouraged individualism within silos at the expense of teamwork across departments, and a tendency for researchers to stick to conventional well-worn paths within safe monodisciplinary subjects, rather than going out on a limb and exploring new fields. For example, throughout the 1990s and first decades of this century, life for experienced, alert-minded contract researchers became increasingly financially hazardous if they wanted to pursue their own lines of thinking, especially since government departments and some research-funding charities abandoned the response mode of funding.

So, as I end my research career, I call on the powers that be for a major rethink on these research matters, not only in the fields of family justice, but in all those areas which illuminate our understanding of modern childhood and family life.

An afterword

Disseminating ideas is rather like sowing seeds of trees: one does not know how long they will take to germinate, or how many, if any will survive the rigours of the first winter and the ravages of pests in spring. Some will shoot up and make brittle, sappy growth, while others will eventually grow slowly into strong timber. While completing this book I was smitten with this image when I re-read Jean Giono's classic little parable of *The man who planted trees*.[855]

It is a story of a traveller roaming the barren foothills of the French Alps in 1913. Hungry and thirsty, he comes across a lonely shepherd, Elzéard Bouffier, who invites him into his shelter for the night and feeds him. In the morning the traveller notices that after tending to his small flock of sheep, the shepherd takes a bag of acorns and sets off around the hills making holes with his staff into which to plant them. After the First World War, and having survived the battle of Verdun, the traveller returns to find the hills full of vigorous young oak saplings alive with birdsong. What were once dried-up streams and abandoned villages are again running with clear spring water. Eventually Bouffier dies in the 1950s, by which time a whole landscape and community of busy little villages in the valleys has been regenerated.

So, having completed this book in my 80th year, I hope younger generations will live to see a complete transformation in our currently fragmented, patchy, piecemeal and somewhat niggardly approach to providing early non-stigmatic support to children and young people experiencing critical family change. Perhaps at least some of the ideas in this book will take root to help this process.

---

[855] Jean Giono (1989) *The Man Who Planted Trees* Peter Owen Publishers, London. I would recommend everyone to read this little book with its delightful wood engravings.

Index

Note: Page locators in *italics* refer to figures.

A

academic attainment 35–7, 56, 135
academies 138
adjusting and learning from breakup 83–8
  children continuing to experience
    difficulties 86, 87, 101–2, 103
  overall picture of adjustment 86–8
  positive adaptation 84–5, 87, 102–3
Advocate's Gateway Toolkit 232
Aikens, Lord Justice 247
alcohol abuse, parental 47–8, 61
Allen, Graham 276, 277, 291
American Psychiatric Association 27
anger, feelings of 73, 101, 107, 325
Atkinson, Maggie 48
attachment theory 129, 164–5, 166, 306
austerity measures
  damage to structure of family justice
    system 281–2
  financial crisis 2007/8 355–6
  following financial crisis 4, 242, 281
  post-Brexit 343–4
  welfare provision 282–3
Australia, study of children in mediation
  process 203
Avon Longitudinal Study of Parents and
  Children (ALSPAC) 52–3, 110

B

behavioural problems in children 40–2
  Department of Health factsheet for head
    teachers 24, 33–4
  link between family conflict, academic
    attainment and 37
  risk factors for violent and abusive 34
bereavement 101–2
  parents grappling with 325–6, 327
  studies 94–5, 106
  support, children's unmet need for
    299–300
Bishop, Paul 240
Black, Lady Justice 246–7
blaming themselves, children 37, 40, 56,
  71, 107
boarding school experience 307–9
Borkowski, M. 261
Bott, Elizabeth 93
Bowlby, John 95, 129, 164–5, 166, 306

Bowlby, Richard 301–2
Brennan, Ursula 250
Brexit 343–4
British Academy, *Social Science and Family
  Policies* 26
British Social Attitudes Survey 343–4
Butler, I. 57–8
Butler-Sloss, Elizabeth 245

C

CAADA Report 2014 56n148
Cafcass *see* Children and Family Court
  Advisory and Support Service
  (Cafcass)
Calouste Gulbenkian Foundation 285
Cameron, David 14, 343
CAMHS *see* Child and Adolescent Mental
  Health Services (CAMHS)
Cantwell, Brian 226–7
CAP *see* Child Arrangements Programme
  (CAP)
Caplan, Gerald 89, 94, 95–6, 103–4, 106,
  115, 116, 123, 160, 310
Cardiff *Divorcing Children* study 49, 53–4,
  65–6, 69–88
  children finding out about separation
    70–2
  communicating effectively with children
    69–70
  decision-making processes in families
    57–8
  friends, support from 60
  grandparents, support from 59–60
  informing school and talking to teachers
    82–3
  keeping children informed 56–8, 76–8
  participants 69
  preparing for separation 75–6
  reactions to separation event 72–5
  supporting a parent after breakup 107
  surviving and learning from breakup
    83–8, 101–2, 102–3
  telling others 78–81
Cardiff University study 1999-2001 37
Care Quality Commission Phase One
  report 333–5
Carter review of Initial Teacher Training
  131–2, 305, 310–11

Child and Adolescent Mental Health
  Services (CAMHS)
  Cafcass liaison with 316–17
  community consultative support role for
    311–12
  continued pressure on resources for 140
  cuts to budgets 42, 120–1, 130, 137,
    140, 144
  Green Paper proposals for 117, 118
  increased funding in 2014 132
  IPPR Report findings 137
  Labour government response to review
    of 133
  limited access to 134, 137, 361
  referrals to 144, 317, 318
  role in a preventative mental health
    approach 332–5
  waiting times for treatment 130, 137
Child and Adolescent Welfare
  (psychometric instrument) 41, 104–5,
    314, 316–17, 369
Child Arrangement Orders 18, 156, 157
  enforcement of 219
Child Arrangements Programme (CAP)
    190–1, 209–40, 210
  aim of 211–12
  Cafcass preventative community mental
    health thinking and family justice
    system 220–30
  children meeting judges 231–4
  children meeting magistrates 235–6
  communicating with children 234–5,
    240
  listening to voice of child in family
    court 230–6
  listening to voice of child in mediation
    236–40
  making process 'child friendly' 200, 236
  mechanisms to hear voice of child in
    disputed family court hearings 213
  Parenting Plans 212
  recommended websites 212
  role of Cafcass officers and WFPOs in
    preparing welfare reports 217–19
  safeguarding role of Cafcass and Cafcass
    Cymru 213–17
  selection of judges 236
'child friendly' practices 200, 236, 321–2
Childeric Primary School, New Cross
    141–2
Childline 61
Children Act 1948 166
Children Act 1989 18, 155, 172, 215,
    219, 228, 235, 262–3
  amendment of s41 of Matrimonial
    Causes Act 1973 168, 172–3
  Family Assistance Orders 316
  welfare checklist 326–7

welfare principle 5–6, 49
Children and Adoption Act 2006 228
Children and Families Act 2014 174–5,
    180, 186, 206
  repeal of s41 of Matrimonial Causes Act
    1973 155, 156–7, 172
  speed of legislative change 187
Children and Families Bill 2012, House
    of Commons Justice Committee pre-
    legislative scrutiny of 186–7
Children and Family Court Advisory and
    Support Service (Cafcass)
  consultation for staff 317–18
  Consultation Report 2010 54–5, 57,
    59, 61
  crisis intervention and 226–8, 331–2,
    368–9
  enforcement of Child Arrangement
    Orders 219
  guardians 20, 218–19, 223–6, 346–7
  liaison with CAMHS 316–17
  liaison with schools 316
  need for consistent practice between
    mediation services and 237–40
  preventative community mental health
    thinking and family justice system
    220–30
  proposal for parents to meet officer at
    outset of process 331
  public law proceedings taking
    precedence over private law
    proceedings 182–3
  reducing costs of 313
  safeguarding and representing children
    in court proceedings 208–9, 213–17
  short-term crisis intervention by child
    and family reporters 315–17
  statistics on private law child-related
    cases referred to 18–19
  use of Family Assistance Orders 228
  welfare reports 191, 217–19, 222
Children and Family Court Advisory and
    Support Service (Cafcass) Cymru
  funding 366–7
  psychometric instrument use by Family
    Court Advisers 41, 104–5, 314,
    316–17, 369
  role in preparing s7 reports for family
    court 217–19
  role when child proceedings are to be
    commenced 213–17
Children and Young People's Improving
    Access to Psychological Therapies
    programme (CYPIAPT) 133
Children and Young People's Mental
    Health and Wellbeing Taskforce 132,
    134–6
Children's Commissioner for England 12

children's rights 262, 284–5
  Resolution's list of 200
  right to be heard 48–51
Children's Views of Their Changing Families
  (Joseph Rowntree Foundation) 51–2
'churn'
  ministerial 151–2, 265, 289, 312
  problem of staffing 151–2, 263–6, 289
Clarke, Kenneth 249, 251, 252
Clulow, Christopher xv, 27–8, 100–1, 325
Cobb, Mr Justice 190, 230–1, 233, 234,
  235
Cobb Report 190–2, 218
cognitive behavioural therapy (CBT) 363
cohabitation
  stability of 14
  statistics 15–16
collaboration, interprofessional
  understanding and 266–74, 355–60,
  361–2, 368
communication with children, skills for
  234–5, 240
conduct disorders 31, 33, 135
confidentiality 194, 201, 239
Constitution Committee 187, 189
consultative support 116–17, 310, 317–18
  role for CAMHS in community 311–12
Contact Order applications 18
contact with parent who leaves home 53,
  54, 55, 77–8, 102
  and impact on children's adjustment to
  breakup 85, 86, 87
continuing professional development 272,
  304–5, 311–12, 317–18, 365
cost benefits of early interventions 120–1
A County Council v K, C and T [2011]
  EWHC 1672 (Fam) [2011] 2 FLR at
  817 315
Cretney, S. 159, 162, 166, 173
Crewe, Ivor 258, 265, 285–6
Crime and Courts Act 2013 189, 190,
  255
crises, simultaneous 97
crisis intervention
  adjusting approach to stages in crisis
  resolution process 105–9
  Cafcass and 226–8, 331–2, 368–9
  Coalition review of early 276–7
  experimental short-term, for fathers left
  suddenly alone 115–17
  justifying 38
  preventative community mental health
  approach 103–5
  role of passage agent 110–12
  short-term, by child and family
  reporters 315–17
  support 109–10

triage mechanism for children at risk 96,
  104, 127
  see also schools, primary preventative
  crisis intervention in
crisis intervention support, policy and
  practice proposals 299–341
  bereavement support 299–300
  family justice system, back up secondary
  prevention in 313–32
  passage agent help for children 300–1
  pilot schemes 338–41
  role of CAMHS 332–5
  schools, primary prevention in 301–12
  translating aspiration into realistic policy
  and practice 335–41
crisis model of mental health 66, 67,
  89–103
  adaptive and maladaptive reactions to
  recovery 102–3
  bereavement and other critical stresses
  94–6
  categories of crisis 96
  complementarity between
  developmental psychology and 90–1
  constructing psychological defences
  101–2
  development of conceptual building
  blocks 92–6
  families and their social networks 93
  homeostasis in family relations 92
  onset of grief 98–101
  outline of concept 91–2
  shock and disbelief 98
  simultaneous crises 97
  social psychiatry movement 93
  stages of crisis resolution 97–103, *99*
  triage mechanism for children at risk 96,
  104, 127
culture of family justice system, changing
  see family justice system, changing
  culture of
Curtis Committee 166

D

data collection 187
  and failure to invest in information
  technology 255–9
decision-making on children's futures
  48–51
  children's involvement in 57–8, 87
denial, defence of 74–5, 103, 107–8
Denning Committee on Procedure in
  Matrimonial Causes 158, 159, 162,
  164, 165

Department of Health and Department of Education Green Paper 2017 xi, 21, 43, 63–4, 117, 118, 124, 126, 143, 144–5, 312, 338–9, 348, 362–3, 363–4, 370
Department of Health factsheet for head teachers 2008 24, 33–4
depressive disorders 27–8
developmental psychology, child and family 38–42
complementarity between crisis model of mental health and 90–1
Diagnostic and Statistical Manual of Mental Disorders (DSM-5) 27
Dicks, Henry 165
divorce from child's viewpoint 69–88
on informing school and talking to teachers 82–3
keeping children informed 76–8
key stages in process 70–2
preparing for separation 75–6
reactions to separation event 72–5
surviving and learning from breakup 83–8
telling other people 78–81
divorce law reform 155–77
demise of welfare check in undefended cases 158–67, 277–8
legal aid and women's access to divorce 162–3
naming co-respondents in cases relying on adultery 176–7
renewed calls for 175–7
repeal of S41 of Matrimonial Causes Act 1973 155, 156–7, 172–3
research on 172–5
social class of divorcing couples and judges 163–4
social context of post-war 161–4
welfare check history 168–72
Divorce Reform Act 1969 13, 15, 169, 173
divorce statistics
changing marriage and 13–14
numbers of children of divorcing parents ix, 12, 15
Divorcing Children study *see* Cardiff *Divorcing Children* study
domestic violence
children witnessing 41, 72
legal aid for cases of 243
Doughty, Julie 315
Douglas, Anthony 345–6
Douglas, Gillian 155, 156, 174, 205–6, 208, 222, 228, 229, 235, 243, 244
Drake, H. 27
Duncan Smith, Iain 291

E

Early Intervention Foundation 146, 277, 288, 300
Economist 4–5, 348
educational research 22, 23–6
on impact of parental conflict on academic attainment 35–7, 56, 135
Edwards, Jenny 133–4
Eekelaar, J. 250, 273, 321, 322, 330, 350, 351, 358
Elliot, J. 35, 40
emotional
abuse of children 34–5
disputes between parents 251–4, 323, 324–5, 327–8
empathy, importance of 352–3
Etzioni, Amitai 138
European Union Referendum 343–4

F

Family Assistance Orders 227, 228, 313, 316
family behavioural studies 22, 26, 38–42
Family Business Authority (FBA) 189–90, 266
Family Court Information and Assessment Meeting (FCIAM) 330–1
family court process: from adversarial to participant justice 321–28
experimental scheme for participant family court procedure 329–32
Family Court Information and Assessment Meeting (FCIAM) 330–1
introducing parents to judge and support team at FHDRA 331
reasons for continued resorting to family court justice 323–4
reframing process from adversarial to participant justice 321–2
reversing cuts to family legal aid 318–19
family courts, unification of local 180, 186, 189, 190, 255
family crisis, parental separation as a 54–6
Family Drug and Alcohol Court (FDAC) 47, 236, 324, 328–9, 331
Family Justice Board 185, 192, 196–8, 215, 266
omission of children's voice and right to information in annual reports 200
review of information technology 256–7, 258
family justice system
altering central government approach to 366–8
basic principles 326–8
children's perceptions of proceedings of 194–5

children's right to be heard in 48–51
as distinct from criminal and other civil
  jurisdictions 194
funding 4–5, 138–40, 366–8
Gove on need to reform 150–1
importance of non-stigmatic associations
  194–5
interdisciplinary training 233
interdisciplinary working 271
length of hearings and progress of cases
  through system 245–6
likelihood of children becoming centre-
  stage participants in 195–6
ministerial churn and uncertainty over
  future reform 151–2, 289
minority of cases coming repeatedly
  before courts 251–4
move towards a more inquisitorial mode
  of trial 254–5
possible privatisation of courts 5
principle of protecting children's welfare
  5–6
return to a two-tiered 150, 282
shift away from adult-focused,
  paternalistic 195
voice of child in 47–8
family justice system, changing culture of
  241–74
adverse effect of cuts in legal aid on
  mediation 250–1
attempts to overcome obstacles to
  interprofessional understanding and
  collaboration 266–74
barriers to overcome 242
failure to invest in information
  technology 255–9
litigants in person, increase in numbers
  of 245–8
misunderstanding parental disputes
  251–4
move towards a more inquisitorial mode
  of trial 254–5
'normalisation' of divorce and problem
  of scale 259–60
political philosophy overriding realistic
  appraisal of withdrawal of legal aid
  249–50
problem of 'churn' in staffing 263–6
problem of labelling cases as 'private law'
  260–3
removal of legal aid in most 'private'
  family law cases 242–55
family justice system in time of
  uncertainty 343–60
information for separating and divorcing
  parents 349–51
information technology and challenge
  to professional exclusivity 351–4

information technology for children
  347–9
listening and responding to voice of
  child 345–7
paying for new services following IT
  revolution 354–5
silo-busting and cross-disciplinary
  collaboration 355–60
family justice system, promoting
  secondary backup preventive mental
  health thinking in 313–32, 364–5
continuing evolution 326–9
MIAM gatekeeping 322–3
policy issues 318–19
practice issues 313–18
proposal to transfer legal aid funding to a
  new mental health budget 319–20
psychometric instrument use by Family
  Court Advisers 41, 104–5, 314,
  316–17, 369
family justice system regime change
  179–209
broader context of 193–8
Coalition government vision for 180
drivers for Coalition government reform
  182
Family Justice Board 185, 192, 196–8,
  200, 215
Family Justice Young People's Board
  (FJYPB) 193, 196–7, 200
Family Mediation Task Force 192–3,
  200, 204, 205, 207
House of Commons Justice Committee
  186–7
issues of voice, information and support
  for children 198–209
measures against which to evaluate new
  regime 181–3
Munro Review of Child Protection
  187–8
Norgrove Family Justice Review
  179–80, 183–6, 196
Norgrove Family Justice Review
  approach concerning children in
  private law proceedings 198–209
Private Law Working Group 190–2
reviews and legislative development
  183–93
Ryder Review and Family Justice
  Modernisation Programme 189–90
tension between responsibilities of
  Executive and Judiciary 180–1
Voice of the Child Conferences 197–8,
  207
Family Justice Young People's Board
  (FJYPB) 193, 196–7, 200
Family Law Act 1996 172, 173, 174–5,
  215, 259

non-implementation of Part I 176
repeal of Part II 155
Family Links 142
Family Man system of data recording 257,
    258
Family Mediation Task Force 8, 192–3,
    200, 204, 205, 207, 236–7, 238
family social networks 93
family structures, diversity of 17
Farnsworth, K. 281
FHDRA *see* First Hearing and Dispute
    Resolution Appointment (FHDRA)
field theory 93
Fincham, F.D. 38–9
Finer Committee on One Parent Families
    160, 194, 369
First Hearing and Dispute Resolution
    Appointment (FHDRA) 191, 208,
    213, 214, 217
    proposal to introduce parents to judge
        and support team at 331
Five year forward view for mental health 140
Fortin, Jane 262
Freedman, Lawrence 337–8
Freud, Sigmund 95
friends
    support from 60, 110
    telling, about separation 78–9
funding family justice system 4–5,
    138–40, 366–8
future for family justice in time of
    uncertainty *see* family justice system in
    time of uncertainty
future research 369–72

G

gender
    behavioural problems by 24
    reactions to parental conflict differing
        by 40
General Household Survey 1979–2007 15
general practitioners 136, 292, 294–5,
    300–1
'ghettos,' professional 122, 267–9, 355–60,
    361–2, 368
Gibson, Colin 162–3
Glaser, B.G. 111
Goldstein, J. 214
Gove, Michael 150, 151, 282
grandparents 55–6, 59–60
Green Paper 2017 *(Transforming Children
    and Young People's Mental Health
    Provision)* xi, 21, 43, 63–4, 117, 118,
    124, 126, 143, 144–5, 312, 338–9,
    348, 362–3, 363–4, 370
grief
    crisis intervention 106–7
    delayed reactions 94–5

onset of 98–101
parents grappling with 325–6, 327
Grych, J.H. 38–9
guardians 346–7
    appointment 20, 218–19
    research on children's views on having
        223–5
    research on parental views 225–6
    role of Cafcass 223–6

H

Hall, John 168
Harold, Gordon 39, 70, 314
Hedley, Mark 233–4
Her Majesty's Courts and Tribunal
    Service (HMCTS) 189
    Case Monitoring System (CMS) 257–8
Hewison 27
Hill, Reuben 94
Hilton, Steve 46, 347–8
homeostasis in family relations 92
House of Commons Education and
    Health Joint Committee Report 2017
    143–4, 311–12, 318, 361
House of Commons Justice Committee
    186–7
House of Commons Public
    Administration Select Committee 258,
    264–5, 286–8, 362, 366
Hughes, Simon 197–8, 200, 207, 238,
    239
Hunter, Rosemary 246, 247

I

information
    from children, soliciting 261–2
    keeping children informed 56–8, 76–8
    online information hub and other
        providers of, for children 46, 199–201
    for separating and divorcing parents 212,
        349–51
    telling children in advance of separation
        75–6
information technology
    and challenge to professional exclusivity
        351–4
    for children and young people 46–7,
        347–9
    failure to invest in 255–9
    importance of empathy 352–3
    induced unemployment 353–4
    paying for new services following
        revolution in 354–5
Ingleby Committee 166–7
Initial Teacher Training (ITT)
    in Caplanian method of crisis
        intervention 304–5
    Carter review 131–2, 305, 310–11

Family Links' workshops 142
training in children's emotional
development and attachment 362–3
Institute for Public Policy Research
(IPPR) report 2016 137–8
interdisciplinary understanding and
collaboration 266–74, 355–60, 361–2,
368
internet
children's use of 29, 348–9
providing information to children
experiencing parental separation 46,
199–201
intra-familial behavioural studies 22, 26,
38–42
Irving, Z. 281

J

Joseph Rowntree Foundation
*Children's Views of Their Changing
Families* 51–2
*School based support work for children whose
parents have separated* 36–7
*Supporting Children Through Family
Change* 23, 52–3, 336, 340
judges, family court
meeting children 231–4
parent encounters with 330–1
selection of 236
skills required for communicating with
children 234–5
social class of divorcing couples and
163–4
study of 321–2
a view on mental health services for
children 134
judicial continuity 231, 331
juvenile delinquency 165, 167

K

Kids Company 139
King, Anthony 258, 265, 285–6
King, Michael 110–11, 364

L

labels, positive and negative 28–9
Lake-Carroll, Angela 205
language, importance of a common
121–2, 289
le Grand, Julian 283
legal aid, civil
adverse effect of cuts on mediation
services 250–1
cuts to 4, 5, 19, 168, 170, 277
decrease in private law cases as a result
of cuts to 191–2, 230–1
Gove on 150

and 'intractable,' emotional disputes
252–3
political philosophy overriding realistic
appraisal of 249–50
proposal to transfer funding to a new
mental health budget 319–20
removal from most 'private' family law
cases 242–55
removal of support from partisan
solicitors after cuts to 212
reversing cuts to family 318–19
unintended consequences of cuts to 182,
187, 192, 230, 244, 277
website information in lieu of 212
and women's access to divorce 162–3
Legal Aid, Sentencing and Punishment
of Offenders Act 2012 192, 243, 277,
349
role of solicitors since 350–1
legal services, new 350–1
legal system as autopoietic 268–9, 364
length of hearings 245–6
Leve, L.D. 70
Lewin, Kurt 93
Lindemann, Erich 94–5, 101
Lindner v. Rawlins 246
litigants in person 4–5, 206, 243, 244, 273
consequence of increasing numbers of
245–8
online tools for 350
local authority children's departments,
establishment of 166, 167
lone parents
prevalence of mental disorder in
children of 24
statistics 17
loneliness, feelings of 74
Longfield, Anne 12
loss of face, fear of 293–7
Lowe, N. 155, 156, 174, 195, 208, 222,
228, 229, 235, 243, 244

M

Mackay of Clashfern, Lord 271–2, 286
Maclean, M. 250, 321, 322, 350
magistrates' courts, stigma of 349
magistrates, meeting children 235–6
Manifesto for Family Law 200
marketisation 283–5, 354–5
voice of children and 284–5
marriage
statistics 13–14
tax advantages 14
Matrimonial Causes Act 1973 17
principle and assumptions behind s41
158
repeal of S41 155, 156–7, 172–3

Matrimonial Proceedings (Children) Act 1958 158
May, Theresa ix–x, 142–4, 151, 304
Mayo, M. 282
McGregor, O.R. 170
mediation
  adverse effect of cuts in legal aid on 250–1
  confidentiality 239
  distinction between child-centred and child-inclusive 201–2
  failure in 206
  MIAMs an opportunity to consider voice of child 206–8
  need for consistent practice with Cafcass in child-inclusive 237–40
  reduction in referrals to 231
  voice of child in 202–6, 236–40
Mediation, Information and Assessment Meetings (MIAMs) 156, 180, 293, 350
  failing to achieve purpose 322–3
  modified as Family Court Information and Assessment Meeting (FCIAM) 330–1
  and voice of child 156, 157, 206–8, 220–1
mental disorders in children
  Department of Health factsheet for head teachers 2008 24, 33–4
  developing long-term mental health issues 61–2, 300
  prevalence 21
  protective factors to prevent development of 35
  raising awareness in schools 25, 42–3
  stigma 28
  terminology and definitions 26–33
mental health consultation for care givers and first responders 116–7, 311–7
mental health services, children's see Child and Adolescent Mental Health Services (CAMHS)
mental maps 356
mentoring for teachers 310–11
MIAMs see Mediation, Information and Assessment Meetings (MIAMs)
ministers, 'churn' of 151–2, 265, 289, 312
Morton Commission (Report of the Royal Commission on Marriage and Divorce) 158, 159, 160, 164
mothers, adulterous 161–2
Munby, James 190, 209
Munro, Eileen 119–20, 187–8
Munro Review of Child Protection 113, 114, 119–20, 187–8, 278

N

National Association of Head Teachers (NAHT) 303
National Audit Office (NAO) report 5, 248, 250–1
National Children's Bureau (NCB) 129, 130
National Institute for Health and Clinical Excellence (NICE) 23, 128
New Zealand, study of children in mediation process 203
Norgrove, David 179, 183, 193, 241
Norgrove Family Justice Review 179–80, 183–6, 196, 241
  approach concerning children in private law proceedings 198–209
  case duration 215
  on information technology 256

O

Observer 140
O,Neill, Dennis 166
OnePlusOne 26, 295
open court hearings 295–6
  in undefended divorce cases 168–70

P

Panorama 244
Parad, Howard 104
parent who leaves home, child's relationship with 53, 54, 55, 77–8, 102
  and impact on children's adjustment to breakup 85, 86, 87
Parenting Plans 212, 313
parents
  experiences of being in family court 322, 330–1
  grappling with grief 325–6, 327
  information for separating and divorcing 212, 349–51
  Norgrove Review recommendations for 185
  proposal to introduce judge and support team at FHDRA to 331
  reluctance to seek help 293–7
Parkes, Colin Murray 95, 106
participant family justice 50, 51, 324–6, 327, 365
  Drug and Alcohol Court as an example of 328–9
  experimental scheme for 329–32
  reframing family court process from adversarial to 321–2
passage agents 110–12, 300–1
Pendlebury Centre Pupil Referral Unit 311

Pengelly, P. 269–70
'peril of expertise' 122
Piper, Christine 269, 364
Place2Be 131, 141, 142, 303
In Plain Sight: Effective Help for Children Exposed to Domestic Abuse 56n148
policy making
  disruption under Coalition government 42–4
  lack of incentives for long-term planning and cross-departmental activity 289
  short-termism in 289
  slow speed and utilisation of policy-related research 286–8
preparing for separation 75–6
preventative mental health approach 63–4, 103–5, 113–24, 166–7
  Cafcass, family justice system and 220–30
  case for 119–24
  consultative support for professional caregivers 116–17
  cost benefits of early interventions 120–1
  cross-disciplinary collaboration 361–2
  cross-disciplinary training and research 368–9
  family justice system secondary prevention 364–5
  importance of a 'common language' 121–2
  obstacles hindering 113–18
  as part of a community's normal non-stigmatic support mechanism 124
  prospects for developing early 360–9
  school-based primary prevention 362–4
  selection of crisis first responders 117–18
  short-term intensive intervention saving later lengthy interventions 123
preventative mental health approach, barriers obstructing 113–18, 281–97
  austerity measures 281–3
  challenging orthodox thinking 290
  crisis intervention model to overcome 296
  lack of a common language 289
  lack of incentives for long-term planning and cross-departmental activity 289
  marketisation 283–5
  overcoming 290–3
  Relate report 2015 290–3
  reluctance of parents to seek help 293–7
  short-termism in policy making 289
  shortcomings in Whitehall 285–90

slow speed and utilisation of policy-related research 286–8
privacy, protecting family 79–80, 124
private family law
  decrease in cases as a result of legal aid cuts 191–2, 230–1
  division between public and 166–7
  problem of labelling cases as 260–3
  public law proceedings taking precedence for Cafcass over 182–3
  removal of legal aid in most cases of 242–55
  statistics 18–20, 191–2, 230–1
Private Law Programme 19, 191, 208, 364
Private Law Working Group 190–2
probation service 165
professional exclusivity, information technology and challenge to 351–4
protective factors to prevent developing behavioural and mental disorders 32–3, 35, 38, 103, 300
Pryor, Jan 26
psychological defences, constructing 101–2, 107–9
puberty 97

R

reactions to separation event 72–5
Relate report 2015 290–3, 347, 349–50
Relations between the Executive, the Judiciary and Parliament 189
relief, feelings of 74
Report of the Royal Commission on Marriage and Divorce (the Morton Commission) 158, 159, 160, 164
Report of the Vulnerable Witnesses and Children's Working Group 231–3
research on children's views and experiences of parental divorce 51–62
  see also voice of the child on crisis of parental separation
research reviews upon which to promote social and emotional wellbeing 21–44
  child and family developmental psychology 38–42
  impact of interparental conflict on children's academic attainment 35–7
  intra-familial behavioural issues, focus on 22, 26, 38–42
  protective factors 35
  risk factors 33–5
  schools, focus on 22, 23–6
  terms and definitions 26–33
Residence Order applications 18
resilience 32–3, 35, 38, 103, 300
  surviving and learning from breakup 83–8

Resolution 175
  Manifesto for Family Law 200
  survey 2014 6–7
Reynolds, J. 34–5, 97, 108
Richards, Martin 36, 40
risk factors for developing behavioural and
  mental disorders 26, 32–3, 33–5, 132
Roberts, Marian 202–3
Robinson, M. 57–8
Rogers, Brian 26
Rutter, Michael 26, 35, 38, 108
Ryder, Lord Justice 241, 266
Ryder Review 190

S

Sandel, Michael 283–4
Scanlan, Lesley 57–8
Scarman, Leslie 168, 169
Schaverien, Joy 307–9
*School based support work for children whose
  parents have separated* (Joseph Rowntree
  Foundation) 36–7
schools
  academic attainment 35–7, 56, 135
  Cafcass liaison with 316
  Department of Health factsheet for head
    teachers 2008 24, 33–4
  Green Paper proposal to strengthen
    collaboration between CAMHS and
    117, 118
  informing, and talking to teachers 82–3,
    100
  moving from primary to secondary 97,
    101, 130–1, 306
  non-stigmatising environment of 124
  raising awareness of mental disorders in
    25, 42–3, 127
  research reviews upon which to
    promote wellbeing focusing on 22,
    23–6
  whole school approach to promote
    social and emotional wellbeing 126,
    136, 143, 146–7, 301–2, 311–12, 346
schools, primary preventative crisis
    intervention in 125–47
  academisation 138
  boarding school experience 307–9
  Carter review of Initial Teacher Training
    131–2
  caution over funding of initiatives
    138–40
  Childeric Primary School, New Cross
    141–2
  Children and Young People's Mental
    Health and Wellbeing Taskforce
    support for early intervention 134–7
  community consultative support role for
    CAMHS 311–12

continued pressure on resources for
    CAMHS 140
  CQC Phase One report on 334–5
  cuts to school budgets 144
  helping children unable to access mental
    health services 141–2, 144
  introducing Caplanian approach to ITT
    and CPD 304–5
  involvement of voluntary organisations
    141–2
  links between pupil and teacher stress
    305–6
  need for a longer-term development
    strategy 304
  need for early warnings and network of
    responders 301–12
  overview of promotion of children's
    social and emotional wellbeing 128–9
  policy for development of mental health
    provision in schools 129–42
  policy since 2017 under May 142–5
  priority dilemma 132–4
  proposed mental health support teams
    145
  prospects for developing 362–4
  reasons to focus on schools 126–7
  support for first responder teachers
    309–10
  taskforce support for early intervention
    132, 134–7
  teachers as first responders 302–4
  value of mentoring for teachers 310–11
  whole school wellbeing programme and
    146–7
self harm 21, 29
Separated Parents Information
    Programmes (SPIPs) 19, 219, 313
shame, sense of 295–6
shock and disbelief
  crisis intervention to absorb 105–6
  at parental separation 54, 73, 98
Shumueli, Abi 293–4
'silos,' professional 122, 267–9, 355–60,
    361–2, 368
smartphones 46, 47
social media 29, 302, 348
social networks, family 93
social psychiatry movement 93
Social Science and Family Policies 26
solicitors, family 212, 252, 281, 292,
    294–5, 350
  adjusting since LASPO 350–1
special procedure, operation of 168,
    170–1
staffing, problem of 'churn' in 263–6, 289
Statement of Arrangements 155, 168,
    171, 172, 173, 174
statistics 11–20

cohabitation 15–16
lone parents 17
marriage and divorce 13–14
numbers of children with divorcing parents 12, 15
observations and shortcomings 11–13
private family law involving contact and residence orders 18–20
stigma
avoidance of 124, 136, 194–5, 294–6, 363–4
of divorce 161
strategy, defining 337–8
Strauss, A.L. 111
substance misuse, parental 47–8, 61
support systems, children's use of 51–2, 59–62, 87
children seeking outsider support 60–1
friends 60, 110
grandparents 55–6, 59–60
natural caregivers 103, 109
Supporting Children Through Family Change (Joseph Rowntree Foundation) 23, 52–3, 336, 340
surviving and learning from parental breakup 83–8
children continuing to experience difficulties 86, 87, 101–2, 103
overall picture of adjustment 86–8
positive adaptation 84–5, 87, 102–3
Susskind, Richard and Daniel 351–6
Symptoms and Difficulties Questionnaire (SDQ) 41–2

T

Targeted Mental Health in Schools Project 131, 133
Tavistock Family Discussion Bureau (FDB) 165
Tavistock Institute of Human Relations 50, 94, 164, 165
teachers
as first responders 302–4
stress and links with pupil stress 305–6
support for first responder 309–10
talking to 82–3
value of mentoring for 310–11
telling children about separation
in advance 75–6
keeping children informed 56–8, 76–8
telling other people about separation 78–81
informing the school and talking to teachers 82–3
reasons for 81
Tett, Gillian 122, 355–8, 365
theme interference reduction 116–17
The Times 5, 6–7, 246

campaign to improve access to child and adolescent mental health services 133–4, 360–1
campaign to overhaul divorce and protect children 176
timetable for the child 214–17
training
in making process 'child friendly' 236
need for interdisciplinary 233, 271, 368–9
Transforming Children and Young People's Mental Health Provision (Green Paper 2017) xi, 21, 43, 63–4, 117, 118, 124, 126, 143, 144–5, 312, 338–9, 348, 362–3, 363–4, 370
triage mechanisms
for children at risk 96, 104, 127
limited availability 293
psychometric instruments 41, 104–5, 314, 316–17, 369
Trinder, Liz 175–6, 246, 247, 248
Troubled Families Programme (TFP) x–xi, 314

U

unemployment, technologically induced 353–4
United Nations Convention on the Rights of the Child (UNCRC) 49, 119, 156, 284

V

voice of the child
children's right to be heard 48–51
in commercial marketplace 284–5
in family justice 47–8
issues in family court context 230–6
judge/child communication 231–4
listening and responding in times of uncertainty 273–4, 345–7
mechanisms to hear, in disputed family court hearings 213
in mediation 202–6, 236–40
and Mediation, Information and Assessment Meetings (MIAMs) 156, 157, 206–8, 220–1
Norgrove Review on need to consider 184–5, 199
research to explore 51–62. *see also* voice of the child on crisis of parental separation
Voice of the Child Conferences 197–8, 207
Voice of the Child Dispute Resolution Advisory Group 46, 238–40
voice of the child on crisis of parental separation 69–88
finding out about separation 70–2

informing the school and talking to
teachers 82–3
keeping children informed 76–8
key stages in divorce process 70–2
preparing for separation 75–6
reactions to separation event 72–5
surviving and learning from breakup
83–8
telling others 78–81
voluntary organisations 139, 141–2

W

Walker, Janet 200, 201, 203, 204–5, 237
wardship of children 6, 161
Warwick Review 23, 24, 30
on mental disorders and wellbeing 31–3
Weare, Kathleen 23, 25, 30–1, 128–9
websites for parents 212, 349–50
welfare checklist 326–7
welfare checks
demise in undefended cases 158–67,
277–8
emerging child and family mental health
approach and 164–7
history 168–72
justification for 158–60
open court hearings in undefended
divorce cases 168–70
operation of special procedure 170–1
principle and assumptions behind s41 of
Matrimonial Causes Act 1973 158
welfare of children, state responsibility for
6, 161
welfare reports 165, 169, 172, 191, 214,
222, 314, 347
Cafcass short-term crisis intervention
while preparing 315–17
role of Cafcass and WFPOs in preparing
217–19
special procedure requests for 170–1
Wetz, James 129, 130–1, 305–6
whole school approach to promote social
and emotional wellbeing 126, 136,
143, 301–2, 311–12, 346
weaving crisis intervention model into
146–7
wishes of the child, taking account of 40,
49–50, 205, 211, 222, 235, 240, 327
Woodhouse, D. 269–70

Y

Young Minds 43, 120, 130, 140

Z

Zeldin, Theodore 122, 268